Beginning with Mr. Canby's experiences at home and abroad during the First World War, he moves from New Haven to New York, the great literary center of the western world, to become the editor of the *Saturday Review*. It takes him through the founding and amazing growth of the Book-of-the-Month Club, for which he has been from the beginning Chairman of the Selection Committee. Throughout this period he had, of course, intimate contacts with a very large number of leading English and American writers, among them H. G. Wells, John Buchan, George Bernard Shaw, Willa Cather, Sinclair Lewis, Christopher Morley, Ellen Glasgow, Stephen Benèt, Robert Frost, F.P.A., Vachel Lindsay, and Thomas Wolfe. In the book-battles of the twenties and thirties between antagonistic literary ideologies and against the censorship stranglers, Mr. Canby had always a ringside seat and was frequently inside the ropes himself. His report of old battles, some of them stillbeing fought, is illuminating and will be as useful to future historians of the period as it is fascinating to present-day readers. Throughout this time Mr. Canby was digging deeper and deeper into the history and spirit of American literature and produced his two definitive biographies of Thoreau and Whitman. It is this background which gives the book its enduring importance.

J.D'N.COSGRAVE II

American Memoir

American Memoir

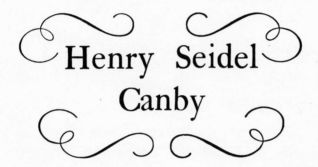

Henry Seidel
Canby

HOUGHTON MIFFLIN COMPANY BOSTON

The Riverside Press Cambridge

1947

The Riverside Press
CAMBRIDGE · MASSACHUSETTS
PRINTED IN THE U.S.A.

The first two sections of this book, *The Age of Confidence* and *Alma Mater*, were originally published in somewhat different form by Rinehart and Company, Incorporated.

Grateful acknowledgment is made to *The Atlantic Monthly* for permission to reprint 'The Diamond Age of Lecturing,' 'How the Book-of-the-Month Club Began,' and 'The Reviewing of Books,' and to *The Saturday Review of Literature* for permission to reprint 'Adventures in Starting a Literary Magazine' and 'Death of the Iron Virgin.'

Preface

THIS MEMOIR runs continuously from the latter eightee~~n~~ eighties, when I was a child, to the present; but if its ~~ob~~ servations of changing values in American living have useful ness and interest, this will be chiefly, I suppose, for the eighteen-nineties through the nineteen-thirties. I was too young to do much observing before 1890, and I have dealt lightly with the confused and tragic nineteen-forties, which are not yet in perspective in my mind, or anyone else's. This book is not autobiography, although personal throughout. It is made of memories and estimates and interpretations of the times in which I have lived. Its motto might be Virgil's ' . . . *quorum pars magna fui,*' as paraphrased in the line which Tennyson gave to his Ulysses, 'I am a part of all that I have met.'

These memoirs were not written all at one time. I doubt whether any memoirs should be. Most men and women live at least three different lives, as the frog lives two; and there should be occasional summings-up before the last phase blurs or distorts the earlier ones. I did my first summing-up in 1934, which was of my youth in a small American city. This was in a book called *The Age of Confidence.* Revised, but not changed, and minus some irrelevancies, it is Part One of this volume. I did my second summing in 1936, this time of the American college world of which I was part from my undergraduate days until after the end of the First World War. The book was called *Alma Mater: The Gothic Age of the American College.* I have heavily cut and revised, though not rewritten it, in order to free the interpreted memories from an overload of educational criticism. This is Part Two of the present volume. Part Three, which has never been published except for a few extracts in *The Saturday Review of Literature* and *The Atlantic Monthly,* deals with my third life in the brief golden age of literature and journalism in New York of the nineteen-

PREFACE

...nineteen-thirties, with some inevitable reflections
twenties nineteen-forties, since it was written in 1945 and
upon e, too, I was a part of all that I met, or, to be more
1946. it became a part of me.
accu

HENRY SEIDEL CANBY

ovember, 1946

Contents

PART ONE
The Age of Confidence

PART TWO
Alma Mater

PART THREE
Brief Golden Age

PART ONE
The Age of Confidence

Preliminary

LIFE IN AMERICA began on the farm and was continued in the small city or town. In the eighties and nineties of the last century the fathers and mothers of most families had been born in the country, but we, who are the oldest generation now, prevailingly owe our provenance to the town. It is the small town, the small city, that is our heredity; we have made twentieth-century America from it, and some account of those communities as they were in, say, the nineties, we owe to our children and grandchildren; for they will never understand the America into which they were born, and which they have (somewhat grumblingly) accepted, without the aid of something more personal than history, and more reliable than romantic or satiric fiction.

Historians will blend the discordant mixture of urban, suburban, and rural, which was the background of the nineteen-hundreds, into an intelligible, if somewhat generalized, explanation of why we are what we are today. My task in this first section of a memoir is less pretentious, but perhaps, in a modest way, quite as important. I knew one small city, and knew it with the intimacy of youth, backed by a long tradition, since my family had lived in it for seven generations. I am trying to recall and to analyze, in the chapters that follow, this rather typical community, trusting to memory, rather than documents, for in such an endeavor facts are not so important as impressions, and my own facts, such as they are, more valuable for this record than facts of others, which might easily be misinterpreted.

I prefer, in short, to contribute to history (for the most modest memoir is a contribution to history) rather than to write it. History, as I shall repeat later in this volume, deals with the present in terms of the future. The tendencies of a period, for an historian, may be more significant than the period, but that is not how those who lived then felt. For them, the present was naturally more important than posterity, and the present of one era (the late eighties, the nineties, the earliest nineteen-

3

hundreds) I have tried to recapture as a sensitive youth saw and felt it from childhood to earliest maturity. No era lives on its tendencies, though it has to live with them. It lives for itself, and can only so be rightly understood, and its own values estimated before the historian approves or discards them.

Memory — and I have trusted to memory entirely — is bound to be narrow, to be unduly selective, to be prejudiced by the accidents of experience, to be intensely personal, to be occasionally inaccurate. But documents also are equally certain to lend themselves to wrong interpretation, to get detached from the emotions or the ideas that made them significant, to be colored by the prejudices of the historian, and to become more fact than truth. And memory and documents make a bad mixture, in which both are falsified. I have, therefore, chosen to write of what I knew and saw — a scene unimportant if it had not been a significant part of America; unaware, generally speaking, of me, who was only a youth in what was still the youth of America; a small city in the East, much loved, possessing perhaps more of the faults and more of the virtues of its era than others; an authentic part of the soil from which our troublous civilization of the nineteen-hundreds sprang.

But in writing this book I have been neither a *laudator tempores acti* nor a disillusioned critic of my native town — but, so far as possible, both. I believe that there were values in that period called the nineties and scandalously misdescribed in current films and novels, which were as worthy (greatness aside) as any cultural period has ever developed, and which are now lost, perhaps irrevocably. I have tried to describe them, because nothing is really irrevocable except one's own youth. But I believe also that no one living in the distressed twentieth century, and writing of this past Age of Confidence, can fail to see in looking back the seeds of dissolution, the shams, the animated corpses of belief, the diseases of culture, which were also coexistent with this pausing time in our American history, when there was such real content and such a complacent yet enviable and sometimes splendid trust in the future; when, if I may quote from myself in a subsequent chapter, for the last time in living memory everyone knew exactly what it meant to be an American.

☞ I ☞

The Town

OUR TOWN was founded where two creeks ran together and made a channel which led to the broad stretches of the lower Delaware. The Swedish pioneers of 1638, who were timid navigators, sailed from the ocean on up the river until the creek mouth tempted them, and entering found a point of rocks on which they could land dryshod. The rocks were the last outpost of a range of hills, and up these hills our town was built.

In my youth Wilmington was still a red-brick town with streets of cobble, through which horsecars bumped and rattled. Along one creek shore railroads and factories covered the old marshes and meadows, with here and there a fine gable of a settler's house unnoticed in the dirt and smoke. As the town grew, it climbed. Walking uphill on Market Street was a progress through the history of American architecture, past dilapidated colonial houses and really lovely banks and markets of the beginning of the nineteenth century, to the Second Empire of the Grand Opera House, and the shapeless severity of the library and the one big hotel.

From the ballroom at the top of the opera house where we went for dancing school there was a view of the whole town at once; and it always surprised me to see how deeply its crisscross of streets was buried in foliage. The factory districts below were grimy and bare, but to the north and the west the roofs were hid in a forest with only a 'mansion' here and there or a church steeple projecting.

Beyond the business and shopping section, and toward the hilltops, were tight little streets, heavily shaded and walled with red-brick fronts built cheek-to-cheek, with decent chins of white marble steps, and alley archways for ears. Here the well-to-do had lived when the city was still a little town, and had been content to hide their arbored side porches and deep if narrow gardens from the street.

The industrial prosperity of the eighties had ended this Quaker restraint. In my day those who could afford it lived farther westward in houses that sprawled in ample yards, thick-set with trees and shrubbery behind iron or wooden fences. Here was a God's plenty of architecture. Brick boxes of the seventies, with cupolas or mansard roofs, and porches screened with graceful scrolls of ironwork were set in old-fashioned contrast beside new contraptions, some of green serpentine, but the latest of brick pseudo-Gothic, with turrets, pointed towers, and Egyptian ornaments of wood. And a little off line with the right-angle streets were still to be seen a few old farmhouses of weathered Brandywine granite as colorful as a slice of plum cake, so severe and pure in line that they made the neighboring mansions seem opulent and vulgar, as indeed many of them were.

The main streets were cobble, too rough for our hard-tired bicycles which had to keep to the brick sidewalks, rutty with the roots of the many trees. Side streets were bedded with yellow clay, morasses in the spring and most of the winter and impassable then except on stepping-stones. Two-wheeled carts dragged through them and sometimes stuck fast. Every house of any pretensions had its iron hitching-post and marble landing-block on which fastidious feet could step from the carriages. There were iron stags on the lawns, but our specialty was iron dogs, especially greyhounds, which crouched on either side of the steps. It was a comfortable region of homes, never quite beautiful, nor ugly, certainly not monotonous, and entirely innocent of those period houses out of magazines, with their shrubbery by the local dealer, which are the current ideal of the American home.

To the southward of the hilltops lived the 'plain people' by thousands in rows of brick houses with identical windows and doors, no more differentiation in homes than in their lives; and below them again, reaching down into the factories, were the slums, where congestion was painful, dirty water ran over broken pavements, and the yards behind were reduced to a dump heap. Here the decent order of our town broke into shrill voices, fighting, smells, and drunkenness.

Each street had its character for us, at least in those neighborhoods where we felt at home. There were subtle social distinctions which by no means ran with size or elegance of dwelling. The town indeed was divided into neighborhoods, so that the division by streets was as artificial as the division of the Union into states. Nothing of this, however, showed geographically. There was only a progression from older to newer as the prosperous American felt for elbow room. Zoning, of course, was rudimentary. Each neighborhood outside the slums was a little town in itself, with a store or two, a livery stable, wooden houses tucked in behind for the darkies, vacant lots held for speculation, solid dwellings of the quality, raw-built mansions of the new rich, and rows of little houses for the 'plain people.'

It all began to seem very ugly when the change of taste came in the early nineteen-hundreds, yet, looking back now, it has a quiet beauty of its own. There were so many trees, so much variety, such individualism manifest. Homes then did represent some quality of the inhabitant, for the architects, having no style of their own, gave the buyer what he wanted: the *nouveaux riches* got exactly the parapets and ornamental porches and zig-zag skyline they longed for; simple people had simple houses; solid folk solid brick with plate-glass windows and heavy metal roofs; and transients, who stayed a year or so and then moved on, precisely the thrown-together houses they deserved. As the Scotch or English farmer was known by the name of his farm, so when I think of many of our citizens I see their homes before I can recall their faces.

And in every neighborhood were houses of mystery — withdrawn in dense trees or shrubbery, little lighted, always shuttered, where misers, old maids, or eccentrics that did not like their fellow humans, found homes that exactly suited them. Where do such people find congenial surroundings now? For you cannot take cover in an apartment house!

On the very top of our hill was a stone house, of perhaps 1750, above a spring sheltered by an oak that certainly was old when the Swedes sailed up the Delaware. A recluse lived there in a confusion of family portraits, letters, documents from the makers of the Republic, and furniture of that excellent beauty which Philadelphia craftsmen of the seventeen-seventies and eighties had mastered. Each year or so he sold a lot from his estate, and each year a red-brick house stepped nearer to the old gray place, which shrank as the town intruded, and closed every door and shutter. It was the one property which boys respected, even though both walnuts and cherry trees grew by the house. When the first new home was built on the very edge of the noble lawn which had once stretched down in a long green curve toward the river, old Caesar Rodney shot himself. Thus, part old in dignity, part plain and simple, part new and pretentious, part dirty and vicious, our town told its story to whoever could read.

❧ 2 ❧

The People

IT WAS A BOURGEOIS TOWN, but not middle class — an important distinction. 'Bourgeois,' of course, would have been
meaningless in the Delaware of the eighties and nineties, unless
to those 'freaks' in blue uniforms who used to leave tracts on
Henry George and the single tax at our front doors. For Delaware is so small that someone is forever attempting to buy or
convert it, and never quite succeeding. But 'middle class' would
have insulted everyone but the white laborers and the darkies.

The Quakers of the early eighteenth century came nearest
to capturing the state. They poured down into the Brandywine Valley from lower Pennsylvania, quiet, shrewd people,
already conditioned to pioneer life, and with a vision of a society where all should be as friends. By 1800 their influence prevailed in the valley and in the little town of Wilmington; but
south of Christiana Creek they met another tenacity which
they never overcame. The land flattened out below the creek
into plantations, often of thousands of acres, running with only
a wrinkle from wall of woods to wall of woods. To propagate
an idea of spiritual equality amongst the hundreds of Negroes
who worked these broad acres and the poor whites squatted on
the margins was difficult. My Quaker cousins who got that far
relapsed into Southern aristocrats. Their houses had molded
doorways and decorated cornices, whereas ours relied for beauty
on proportion and the excellence of good material used with
taste. The town that I knew was austere and Northern, though
the metropolis of what remained, to the southward, an alien
state.

The Quakers were bourgeois, like all the early Americans.
They expected to earn their way by working and were bitter
enemies of privilege, yet they had their own upper class. It was

9

a society formed long before my day, but I lived in its tradition. What set this class apart was, of course, first of all wealth, and consistent industry, but neither was much talked about. Their pride of class was shown chiefly in ways of life, for they had made a compromise with worldliness which was deeply satisfying. Things, the things that money could buy, were, of course, only impediments in comparison with the Inner Light by which they professed to live, and often truly did live. Yet, even as meditation in spiritual quiet led to decorous behavior and a tranquillity which shone in their faces, so the peace of the spirit craved an environment which should be the physical counterpart of spiritual well-being. No show, no pretense, no Puritan hypocrisy either, but solid mahogany, good silver, clothing plain but of silk or broadcloth, good manners, good food, no formal gardens but great tulip poplars shading decent turf edged by hardy borders, few books but good, low voices — quality in everything. For Quakerism being a religion of perfectibility in this world, where God is in every man's bosom, the Quaker's body, once his soul is tranquil, seeks its legitimate satisfactions. I could trace a logical curve from the day when George Fox put off his leather breeches because his protest against pretense and vain show had been heard, to the terrapin suppers at my grandfather's table, where the silver was older than it looked, and the glass better, and the sherry as good as it tasted, and the conversation, though certainly not brilliant, rich in experience and friendliness and sense.

Our society in the town was thus a class society. There were the Negroes, and the working people, and the 'plain people,' and Us. As for Us, we were by no means all Quaker, even by tradition or inheritance. The professional people among us were nearly all Episcopal or Presbyterian Democrats from 'down-state' plantations. To be a Democrat in our town was rather disgraceful unless you came from down state or its affiliates, in which case it might be a social distinction. To be a Democrat was a prerogative of birth, not of class or opinion, which explains much that was curious in our politics, and indeed in American politics generally.

Democrats, of course, were inevitable, since Delaware was on the border line between North and South, but there were plenty of non-Quaker Republicans among us too. While the Quakers had been making a society, the Episcopalians and the Presbyterians had got control of its politics, and with the votes of the Methodists and the Baptists in their pockets had governed it. Some of them grew famous at it, more famous than any of our quiet Quakers. And indeed even in my generation there was a temperamental division in the society we called Us that a Quaker boy could feel. The houses of the worldly (as our great-grandfathers would have called them) were tumultuous to our ears. Doctor Traylor (come up from Sussex County) bawling up through the columns of the portico at his family from his office windows, to stop their quarreling, gave a thrill of realities unencountered. Accustomed to a decorous self-restraint, passion, even trivial passion, was salt on our tongues, uncomfortable but stimulating. These people spoke out as we never did. And their morals differed perceptibly from ours. In their houses wine came off the sideboard and whiskey out of the closet, at every thirsty look, and there was a Horrid Example in each family group. Also clever, shady people who obviously did not, like us, believe in the perfectibility of society, were tolerated, and even approved, if they were successful and had the right name. Levi Brown who drove a high dogcart with red wheels, cursed before women, and was said to get drunk and say his prayers with equal regularity every night. He was a shouting, weeping defense attorney who had freed more known criminals than any other man in the state, but was one of Us, nevertheless. That made life for a Quaker boy seem complicated and therefore interesting. It was wrong to be like him, yet right to ask him to dinner. There was something, then, beyond, if not above morality. You kept your own soul, but were tolerant in matters not of the soul, if other conditions were satisfied. A drunkard who remained a gentleman was more valuable in some respects than a mean Methodist who kept sober. We stuck by our class, which in its small-town exclusiveness put up stiffer barriers than the societies of New York or Philadelphia. We supposed those societies to be just like our own, except more promiscuous and more extravagant. Extravagance was bad taste in my town, for the Quakers had made their tradition prevail that far. Champagne at large parties was regarded as vulgar. If money was to be lavished, it must be behind lowered shades, without ostentation.

As for the 'plain people,' they were the pit from which we were dug. Most of Us had relatives among them, and their children do not know now that their parents were 'plain.' It was by no means a name for financial inferiority, nor did it even always refer to birth. Some of the Capeaus were plain and some were not, and all had for remote ancestor a Huguenot gentleman. The difference between them and Us was a subtle one of manners and tradition, chiefly tradition, for our manners were not always good. You lived according to a tradition of customs most conscious when breached; or you lived unconscious of a family past. You lived in two dimensions, the present and your breeding, or you lived in one dimension of current opinion. The families in our absurdly self-conscious upper class were often stuffy people whose intellectual life was bounded by a set of Dickens and a steel print of the 'Stag at Eve'; yet there was a security in their houses that was more than ordinary manners. They had a feeling for quality in living, which was sometimes only a memory, and often no more than decorum or the ease of geniality. A visitor could be sure of courtesy, and was safe against raw inquisitiveness. There was an expectancy that being so-and-so one had to be a gentleman which stiffened morale and gave to the most trivial social contacts vague but interesting overtones which made every occasion seem a little more than it was. A dim Platonic ideal overhung homes that, described by a satiric realist of our day, would get a laugh for their crude naïveté. Indeed, something, neither crude nor naïve, is lacking in the plays and novels about the eighties and the nineties which have been so mirth-provoking to the nineteen-hundreds. What our current writers are too ignorant to know, or too insensitive to recall or comprehend, was the felt distinction of the families I write about, more important than money or descent — their substitute for culture.

The 'plain people' in our town lived with no sense of family history. You could tell just by hearing their talk or laughter that there was no perspective in their lives or respect for a name as representing an idea of living. They were the shopkeepers, and small and often large business people, and the canny folk on the way up, and the hundreds of simple-minded who were mediocre and a little vulgar and loved being so. They weren't often stuffy, but they *were* common, and their gossiping and give-and-take of conventionalities seemed as colorless and insignificant as ours doubtless was also. They were much more realistic than Us, and saw themselves as small-town folk concerned with daily business; and it was easy for them to do so because they took life as it came without any responsibility for an inherited attitude. They heard no echoes from the past, while our ears were full of them — not clear ones, of course, but still one heard them.

In that last epoch of American stability of which I write, the plain people argued nothing either backward or forward. They were content with their place, like the peasants of Europe. They neither upset stability, nor made it. Therefore, historians and historical novelists and dramatists looking backward neglect them, because the America they represented was the end of an epoch and has survivals in small towns everywhere, yet no real issue leading toward a future. But history is not only becoming, it is also being, although few historians since Darwin's time have written it that way. It is a stream with pools. I am myself in this book trying to forget the current, or the cataract toward whose plunge the pessimists think we are flowing, for I am tired of seeing the history of these United States interpreted in terms of what the pioneers or soldiers of the Civil War did for the Chicago of 1933 or for John Smith who runs a filling station on the Northern Boulevard. There is a fallacy in this teleological view of history, which would make Lake Ontario important only because it flows into the Gulf of Saint Lawrence, and every stream that runs into the Mississippi useful only in terms of the depth of the channel at the port of New Orleans. And may I be forgiven by more tendentious writers if I try to recall the quality of one reach of the American river at a moment when in our town it ran smooth and slow, if not deep, and had a definable quality, which no one is asked to envy at this exciting moment of the machine age, but may enjoy remembering with an understanding mind. And indeed the purpose of this section of my book is only this, to recollect the last era in the United States when there was a pause, and everyone, at least in my town, knew what it meant to be an American.

The 'plain people' knew it better than the families that made up Us, for we had a consciousness of national responsibilities that vaguely but surely reached beyond the present Republic. We had been Federalists (the last of the Federalists were in Delaware and Connecticut), or Copperheads in the Civil War, or Quakers who kept even their opinions neutral in the Revolution, or Colonials content to be British subjects as long as they were let alone, and there was a memory in every family of different times and beliefs. It was a vague memory, and I cannot say that it made more than a shade of difference, but that shade was important. The 'plain people,' living entirely in the present, really believed all they heard on the Fourth of July or read in school readers. They set on one plane of time, and that the present, the Declaration of Independence, the manifest destiny of America, the new plumbing, the growth of the factory system, the morning paper, and the church sociable. It was all there at once, better than elsewhere, their own, and permanent. It never occurred to them to put the blame on the American system when a panic reduced their earnings, or they 'lost their money,' that bourgeois tragedy. They had just the country they wanted, for they had been told from childhood that it was what they wanted, and they believed it would be the same, except for more bathtubs and faster trains, forever. They were simple people who admired success, but were content themselves with a very cheap brand of it. And so were we, with the minuscule differences I have noted.

Lastly, to conclude this classification of the social strata which seemed important to us, and gave stability to our world, there were the working people and the Negroes. With the workingmen, I who write only of what I remember lived chiefly in a feudal relationship. They were the 'men' your father talked of in his iron mill, collectively troublesome, but as individuals liked and trusted. There was always a Bill or a Jim who was a human link with the slave world of laborers on which our society rested. They made the bread that we ate, but were understood to be helpless without us. Unlike the 'plain people,' they never seemed — though we did not phrase it this way — a part of the conscious head of our America: they were its arms and its legs. And no one ever went up or down between Us and them. If, like the 'plain people,' they had frequently to move West for a job, they never came back with new clothes and different manners. If they moved, it was always in their own world, and if their children escaped, it was not in our town.

We knew a few of them well. Derry Winslow, our carpenter, was a family friend, respected by my father and grandfather far more than clerks and small shopkeepers. He was independent like the farmers, and never tried to be anything but just a good carpenter. He gave me a dog named Powder, a token of friendship from one class to another. His daily wages he got promptly, but we would never have thought of paying him for the dog, nor would he have taken the money. He was a carpenter, not a dog seller.

Later circumstances made me for a while a workman myself. I was being 'kept out of nonsense' for a year while I was waiting to be old enough to go to college, some steady employment being deemed useful for a boy who was to be risked in the known irregularities of higher education. The kind of work was unimportant if I were made to stick at it, so my father got me the job of gallery boy in an electric light station. I had to turn wheels to keep the current up or down, a routine so boring that I soon learned to handle my job with one hand and half a brain, reading a book while dimness settled down over the city, and jerking our night life back to brightness at the end of every exciting paragraph. I was a curiosity to the wipers and engineers who used to spend their many lazy minutes on my platform. From them I learned what it was to be a hearty animal with no sense of the past, and also no care for the future. I learned from them that the consciousness of responsibility to society, and the belief that manners were necessary to self-respect, belonged to Us and not to them, a code in which they were not even interested. I saw in them that same reality of passion freely expressed which fascinated us in the Southern families, but it was only likeable, not fascinating, too pure to be interesting, like unblended wine. It meant no more for character than a dog's running after other dogs.

Yet I learned also to like them better than the 'plain people.'

They had a better time, for they let themselves go; and if the head engineer could not tell me why his current ran out on the red and came back on the neutral, so that I had to get my physics by clumsy thinking, he knew how it went, and how to start or stop it, and was obviously a person indispensable to our civilization, able to take orders as soon as we knew enough to give them. These, indeed, were our barbarians, and better than the old barbarians, for they were singularly gentle, and beat up each other only when they were drunk.

As for the rank and file of the unskilled, the stokers in the power plant, the Irish who dug ditches and carried bricks up the scaffoldings of new houses, the Greeks in the fruit-stands, and the Italians sweating on the embankments — they meant nothing to us, were only population. The Irish laborers would stagger home drunk on Saturday nights through our street, hugging the maple trees and talking to themselves, and that was ludicrous with a touch of horror. They were human animals, but extra-social. And they were Catholics, which put them still farther out of our world. They did not speak our language, even the servant girls who were usually Irish, although it was an English that they used. They had their own life, and it never occurred to us to think of that life as part of ours.

The Negroes were different. We all had Negro 'waiters' in our houses, who were good friends to boys. They would steal little things and lie, but in important matters they could be trusted. They sang spirituals while they polished the knives in the pantry, and only ha-ha-ed when a watermelon rind found a mark in the wool. Their wives, who did the washing, helped when we had company, filling the kitchens with chuckles when they came. They were part of Us, molded to our needs, a powerful element in that easy good-humor which ran all round the town. When they were sick or destitute, we took care of them if they were our darkies, but of course what they thought, if they thought, and what they wanted, if they wanted more than we gave them, was not significant. They lived, naturally, in slums of their own, where it always smelled 'darky,' and they were supposed to like it that way. Perhaps they did. Sometimes a 'waiter' went 'mean,' though not often, yet we were well aware that the savage in them was not entirely dead. It broke out in the young females, lanky Negro girls who walked up and down our street from the darky school. They would chase a small white boy, and, catching him, spit on his hair, claw his cheeks, and submit him to other horrid indignities. We dreaded them like fire — but a few years later they would be good-natured and useful like the rest. Down state and up state both they sold their votes, like the poor whites, but were not paid so much, for they weren't really interested in politics, and often would take their two dollars and just go home with it.

That was our town and age, socially considered, although merely to look at it this way is to give a twentieth-century view of its structure. To us it was a unity, indissoluble and unchangeable, like the Union. It was a culture with mores, it was a Life in which one quickly knew one's place, and began that difficult weaving of emotions with experience that is called growing up, in a set of circumstances which one could not and did not really wish to alter. Time moved slowly while your personality twisted and doubled on its course. The town waited for you. It was going to be there when you were ready for it. Its life seemed rich enough for any imagination, and you had only to catch up with one set of experiences in order to feel the pulse of some still mysterious reality beating behind the future. You belonged — and it was up to your own self to find out how and where. There has been no such certainty in American life since.

3

Childhood

THIS IS NOT A BOOK about children, although for reasons of chronology, and because its subject is an America seen by youth, the experiences of youth must be its groundwork. And indeed, I think that childhood in the eighties and nineties, and certainly in our town, was the cause of much in the attitude toward life of my generation which those born in the twentieth century call peculiar. Childhood then and there was in its period of *laissez-faire*.

Children then were just the same as always — some were good and some were 'stuck up' and some were mean and many were naughty and a few were vicious. It was the environment that differed. In our town we had just emerged from the age of discipline and there were reminiscences everywhere that a child soon learned to understand. It was the grandparents you had to watch out for. Every family had a Great-Aunt Lizzie or a Grandma Smith with a thimble for knuckles and a withering voice, while the grandfathers, when they were not affectionate, looked through children as if they were not there. Parents were by no means indulgent, yet they seemed usually to be secretly leagued with us to give the child a chance in the house. They let him alone unless he was outrageous. He was free to make his own world, provided it did not interfere with the decorum of adult life, particularly the decorum of the grandparents.

Moralities also came chiefly from the next generation but one; the parents talked a good deal about example, and being worthy, but were distinctly shy of the Bible and damnation. There was a tacit understanding between the two younger generations that hellfire had been overdone, though of course no open acknowledgment. It seemed to be agreed that if we stuck to character, hellfire need not be expected.

18

The truth was that our parents trusted the community. Sociologically speaking, they had confidence in their civilization, and resented a little the constant references to Old Testament threatenings from the elders. They believed that our town, and particularly our neighborhood and our circle of friends and relations, was an excellent place in which to grow up. Not that they had any foolish illusions of an ideal city. They knew the drunkards and the crooks and the libertines, but knew them as parts of a whole which was sound. There's a wrong turn on every road, otherwise how could you learn to go right! Did they put their children on the streets then? Of course, although the streets were, more accurately, back yards and vacant lots. It never occurred to them to insulate us from what was for them American life, because, unlike their successors, they believed in it, thought that it contained all the useful elements of experience, and that a child with good influences at home, who lived (wherever he strayed) in a good neighborhood, was safe there, had to be safe, because it *was* his environment. I think the Florentines must have felt much the same about their city, with its many vices, and its confidence in the values of community living. Of course, our confidences were set in a lower key, but they were strong. Indeed, the few families who kept their children on elastic bands or made a local society for them of governesses and relatives, committed a subtle offense against the mores of the town which was resented. Their children grew up suspicious or dependent or discontented. I know no other reason why.

We lived, then, in a *laissez-faire* world of childhood, where authority was always upstairs, but did not have to show itself often. And it was not unlike that other individualistic, *laissez-faire* world in the Far West where there was still plenty of room. But not mere space. We boys had a series of city states to play in, the 'squares' into which the town was divided, mere routine to us on the street side, but crisscrossed internally by high board fences with runways just below the top. The yards were deep and capacious, shaded by Norway maples easy to climb and willows for switches. Each was a little domain and play shifted from one to another, or along the fence tops, while for more freedom there were the vacant lots, a true frontier, where fires could be built to roast chestnuts and potatoes. There was no 'organized play,' either athletic or otherwise. Any yard did for ball-throwing, and one or two for crude tennis. When football swept in, we took to the lots, but even at school it was mob work. The feminine influence could be felt in the shrubbery corners where the girls had their doll houses, and on rainy days sex distinctions were dropped in games of Stop and Hearts inside. There was always something to do and somewhere to do it. Such a let-alone life may seem not to have made for introspection, but that is not true, there was always space for solitude — trees, and hidden corners; yet it was certainly bad for the arts which do not seem to flourish out-of-doors. Of study the parents took care. It was part of the chores, but there were not many other chores, since servants were cheap and abundant. Gardening, for example, was an avocation, not a drudgery, for black Isaiah did the heavy work. Adults took to it occasionally for fun as they did to fishing, shooting, or china painting, and we imitated them. Nevertheless, we came on up into the high-price-of-service era with an unspoiled zest for doing things with our hands.

It was no Utopia. Every little boy had a big boy who bullied him, a primitive sadism that I can't feel was vicious, since it gave the small ones delicious terrors and only now and then ran into cruelty. Every boy, too, had a crush on some girl, the phrase then, of course, was 'stuck on her.' Usually he just made eyes and never got so far as a kiss; indeed, I remember a two-year courtship conducted by glances which ended in the hideous embarrassment of a meeting with nothing to say on either side. Some girls were 'ornery,' a word I do not find properly defined in the dictionaries. It was a term not used before parents, and referred, I see now, to the high-spirited and over-sexed, and was applied by us with a derogatory smirk to someone with whom you could take liberties, twitch a garter, and probably go farther. I remember the 'ornery' girls in our community and have followed their careers. With one exception — and she has been sexually correct though excessively unsober — they seem to be model housewives now, whereas the primmest girl I knew became little better than a prostitute.

But Freudians would have found us unprofitable. We

weren't inhibited — yet. We knew perfectly well what was fas-
cinatingly nasty, but were seldom interested. There was too
much else to do. Our sex relations varied from familiarities of
slap and scratch and mud balls from behind fences to a vague
but shining romance that hung aureoles over pigtails — sometimes for weeks on end. Erotic play, as the modernists call it,
was ruthlessly extinguished when seen by our elders, and with
our entire approval. We never questioned the moral code of
society, so far as we understood it, which, since there were a
hundred legitimate things to do, certainly made for happiness.
Nobody rebelled that I can remember, for homes were no
longer stern and there was nothing to rebel against except an
easy life. The bad boy of our neighborhood ran away to sea
in search of adventure, but came back years later, fat and slug-
gish, to die of apoplexy. Breaking windows on Hallowe'en,
swearing, pasting a cow with rotten eggs, or lining the horse-
car tracks with percussion caps to make the spavined horses run
down grade, were protests against being 'goody-goody.' Real
offenses — stealing, lying, impudence to parents, and playing
cards on Sunday — were known to be definitely wrong, like the
rest of the sins supposed to be mentioned in the Ten Commandments. People did them, but shouldn't — we accepted
both good and bad as ingredients of an intelligible world.

In school and in Sunday School both, moralities were plentiful but held in suspense. Nothing was rubbed in, though
there was no possibility of escaping the knowledge of what the
community felt to be right or wrong. You heard, and then
went out into the hinterland on your own responsibility. And
if you sinned you knew it was sin, and if you did not sin, that
was what was expected of you. I think the grandfathers and
grandmothers had done too much switching and pinching and
tying to chairs, discharged too many second-hand threats involving Satan or Jehovah. The parents were slow even at
spanking. They were pacifists in discipline, believing in a
competent police power and much moral influence. And as
long as they believed in such a method, we did.

The same *laissez-faire* existed in our social relations. No
parent among us ever spoke of classes in society to her children — she merely let them be felt. Hence our back-yard

groups were as free as if the wind had blown them together, yet subtly differentiated. At school and on the fences the children of the 'plain people' were as good as Us, if they did not happen to be better. Weight, height, speed, pluck, or good looks and high spirits, were all that counted. It was an absolute democracy within its limits. Yet we all knew that children who belonged to Us had standards of conduct stiffer than the manners of the 'plain people,' and far more rigorous than the creed of the hated 'micks.' It was not always a pleasant knowledge, for what counted was conduct. We had to be polite under stress, and to wear clean underwear — the outer clothing made no difference. With two others, one an older boy very much of the 'plain people,' I used to go bird-egging, and was always deputed to ask permission, hat in hand, of the owner of the orchard. The competence in finding eggs was the older boy's, and I admired him immensely for it. He could sense the hummingbird's nest on a knuckle of lichen far above in the overhanging limbs, but he knew and I knew that courtesy was my job because it was my responsibility. The fighting word with us was not 'liar' or 'bastard,' but 'mick.'

A 'mick' was a tough boy from the slums or the near-slums. He went to public school, which, in our town, none of Us, and in our part of the town few of the 'plain people's' children ever did, except as a result of disaster. He was, in our day, usually Irish, hence, I suppose, the name. The Marxians, if they had observed our class wars, would have been strengthened in their prophecies, since the deep animosities, the sense of absolute difference, and inevitable conflict, which certainly did not exist between our elders and the working people, were alive and intense for us youngsters. No relations except combat were possible or thought of between our gangs and the 'micks.'

It has made me understand the vigorous joys of London in the days of warring apprentices, and the delight beyond politics which kept fires burning between Guelphs and Ghibellines in Florence. Our town was saved from the boys' Arcadia of the story books by this sharp edge of an almost daily experience.

The long walk to school each day was a replica in small of the journeys across the Plains of three decades earlier. It began in home country down a broad street doubly lined with maples, over pavements rich in 'she bricks' which would spout up water after a rain if stamped upon, and bordered by spiked fences with gates to swing upon. Just halfway down there was a trading post, the sisters Millicents' store, where the rationed two cents daily of allowance could be spent upon sourballs or licorice shoestring. Then vigilance began, for next came 'Number Five' public school, with 'micks' swarming schoolward from the lower regions of the town. Each of us, by one of those tacit agreements made between enemies, had his particular 'mick,' who either chased, or was chased (the former usually, since the 'micks' were tough) on sight. If he was not waiting, the only danger was a gang, for the 'micks' seldom fought as individuals unless they were bigger.

It was an awful joy to spot your own 'mick' hiding behind a sycamore on Eleventh Street, to get a quick start down Madison before he saw you, to shin over the Pennypacker back fence, dodge down the Howland grape arbor, double back to the Pennypacker lawn, and if no footsteps followed, to sink panting on the iron greyhound that pointed its slim muzzle down West Street, cooling a hot cheek on his lifted head.

West Street was decorous and romantic respectability, old Quaker Wilmington of red brick and white marble. There was time to loiter down its quiet shade, with a curious glance at the Chinese idol that gazed so contemptuously from Commodore Gillis's window. Then came the Catholics.

There was a school of them at Sixth Street, little fellows, but like bees, and they had to be passed before you reached safety and the gates of our school. If the hour was unlucky, they would swarm around a belated boy, screaming, 'Quaker, Quaker, quack, quack, quack!' throwing stones, and even horse dirt. The best way was to butt through them in the new football fashion they were teaching at school. Books swung on a strap helped to clear the path to the two big elms, the old red meeting house come down from another world than ours, the disordered pile of our school building, and the playground of crushed stone across which the last comers were hurrying.

It was not honorable to evade these chances of combat, although it would have been easy to choose other streets and so escape them. But to rattle through the war zone hid in a furniture van, or to be towed, in great leaps, past a threatening mob behind a smartly trotting grocer's wagon, was a triumph of tactics. Yet even when caught and battered, there was no complaining at home. These feuds were our own affair. They were intrinsic to life.

And here again we were part of a society with an instinct for what ought to be, which is so much more powerful than any rationalization and so much deeper than self-consciousness.

The 'micks' had no code. They put stones in their snowballs, which was unethical, and jumped on a small boy, or pulled a girl's hair at chance meetings, not waiting for an invasion of territory or other cause for fighting. They spat in faces and kicked below the belt. I think that for us, with ideals reflected from our elders, they represented the anarchy and lawlessness that ever since the Civil War the country had been trying to subdue. (That this lawlessness, this anarchy, was even worse in high finance and industry was true enough, but that was covert, the other open.) They were the evil, the disorganizing principle, which roused the opposite in us, and made us believe that there was something real in the precepts of our elders which usually droned above our heads. Occasionally, moved by something not expressed, and without planning, we would assemble the fighting strength of the neighborhood and drive the 'micks' into their school yard until the nine o'clock bell stopped the shower of mudballs and reduced the captives we had taken to weeping entreaty; or we would burst like a storm upon the massed Catholics and send them scurrying behind fluttered sisters who came to rescue. It was not a pogrom. They were still the alien, and had to be shown their place. But this was America; if they would adopt our manners (such was our arrogance), we would tolerate them.

And this was all *laissez-faire*. The houses of those days were big enough for the children's affairs to bubble out from repression, finding their own space. There were sheds and shed roofs, stables, grape arbors with high, shaky seats in the sun. There was plenty of room for our own life, and we took it, so that customs, codes, ideals, and prejudices were absorbed from our elders as by one free nation from another. Even the school was disciplinarian only in working hours. That planned day, which is the school régime for boys and girls of our kind now, was scarcely thought of, and was certainly unnecessary. School spirit had not yet been substituted for the vague but powerful influence of the spirit of a community. 'Self-government' had not yet been invented, since we were in active contact with community government of which the school was part. We dodged the 'cops,' knew the penalty for stolen gates, saw drunkards arrested, took our own punishment in the principal's office, learned that Jimmie had been expelled for stealing pencils, and our neighbor Jenkins arrested for embezzling a bank, all on the same plane, with only an age difference. No one organized our athletics, except in football, where the standardization for efficiency of American life was just beginning, and we did not take football very seriously. It was still play.

Much was missed, of course. The perfunctory gymnastics and cold school lunches did not make those beautiful bodies, as standardized as the clothes cut for them, of the modern 'prep school' boy. Nor, except in intellectual discipline and in ethics, did the school rise above the standards of the community. Art and music were as foreign to us as to our parents. The creative faculties (except in mechanical invention) were merely tolerated, not encouraged. Girls played the piano, but stopped with marriage. Drawing was obscurely useful, but not painting. The school was not concerned with self-expression; knew it only as a form of naughtiness. Of this more later. Here *laissez-faire* was bound to produce a race of Philistines, and did so.

And yet, do the fine arts ever guarantee happiness? In the art of adjustment to actual life we had every freedom, and our experience as a caste amidst slightly differentiated barbarians was more like the community training in Plato's Republic than is a modern boys' school.

We emerged more knowing in affairs of the family, and hence far more adjustable to family life, wiser in typical American experience than are college graduates today, yet narrowly educated, imperfectly developed physically, and intensely local. We had been, I think, very happy as children because we had been let alone in a good environment. As youth, when the life of the community, seen nearer, began to lose complexity and glamour, we had rushed after the nearest new experience and acquired before twenty that insufferable complacency of the small-town 'sport,' or been bored and restless at the very moment when modern education tries to drive back the horizons of still unformed minds. With an Athens, or Florence, to live in, we might have done well, needing no theory in order to get what progressive education plans for living, but finds nowhere outside the imagination. Our old town was not Athens, or Paris, or even Stratford-atte-Bowe. Yet so far as it went, a child's life there was rich and varied and deep. He had by fourteen what anthropologists call *a* culture, which is quite different from *culture*. He had made himself by easy and natural experience part of a conscious, an organized, a unified society. His roots were in the ground, and whether he liked the soil or not, there was something to grow from.

ᑯ 4 ᑕ

Home

'GOD BLESS OUR HOME,' which I can just remember in worsted tapestry, framed in jigsaw walnut, and hung on a spare-room wall, never meant 'God make our home a happy one.' The blessing was asked upon virtues which were often more conducive to moral conduct and material success than happiness. And indeed it was not a superior quality of happiness that distinguished the pre-Ford, pre-radio, pre-boarding-school home from our modern perches between migrations. Those who read their social history in fiction will remember how many nineteenth-century novels deal with unhappy homes — tyrannical or stuffy homes, homes that were prisons or asylums for the suppressed and inhibited. Toward the end of the century, parents, like Jehovah as the churches preached him, began to soften. Homes were happier then, I believe, than in the previous generation, for the gradual democratizing of life had worked itself indoors and was subtly changing the atmosphere of both sitting room and kitchen. There was more give-and-take between parents and children, more liberty, and more cheerfulness.

It was confidence, however, not happiness, that made the great difference between then and now, a confidence that reached down below comfort or pleasure into stability itself. My cousins, who tiptoed around the chair of an old-fashioned, self-willed father, never knew from day to day what his authority might require of them. Their manners and their careers were both whipped into them. Yet they had this same confidence, and would be sure as I, with a memory of a happy and easy-going home, that something solid and valuable has been lost by our children.

In our town, and I think in the American nineties generally,

27

home was the most impressive experience in life. Our most sensitive and our most relaxed hours were spent in it. We left home or its immediate environment chiefly to work, and neither radio nor phonograph brought the outer world into its precincts. Time moved more slowly there, as it always does when there is a familiar routine with a deep background of memory. Evening seemed spacious then, with hour upon hour in which innumerable intimate details of picture, carpet, wallpaper, or well-known pointing shadow were printed upon consciousness. When bicycles came in and flocks of young people wheeled through twilight streets past and past again the porches where the elders were sitting, it was the first breakaway from home, a warning of the new age, but then more like a flight of May flies round and round their hatching place.

The home came first in our consciousness and thus in our culture; clubs, civic life, business, schools, society being secondary, and success there, except in money-making, a work of supererogatory virtue. The woman who could not make a home, like the man who could not support one, was condemned, and not tacitly. Not size, nor luxury, nor cheerfulness, nor hospitality made a home. The ideal was subtler. It must be a house where the family wished to live even when they disliked each other; it must take on a kind of corporate life and become a suitable environment for its diverse inhabitants. Hence a common tragedy in our town, often noted, though seldom traced to its causes, was the slow crushing of a family by its home. The sprawling house, such as they built in the early seventies, grew and grew until parents, aunts, grandparents, children, all had their districts and retiring places in its wings and stories. Though the family might quarrel and nag, the home held them all, protecting them against the outside world and each other. Deaths came, children migrated, taxes went up, repairs became numerous, yet still the shrinking remnant of the family held on from use and wont, or deep affection, until, in a final scene of depleted capital or broken health, the hollow shell of the home collapsed on a ruined estate and fiercely quarreling heirs.

So often tragedy at the end, the home of the nineties was quite as often idyllic, if not ideal, in its best years. It had a

quality which we have lost. We complain today of the routine
of mechanical processes, yet routine in itself is very persuasive
to the spirit, and has attributes of both a tonic and a drug.
There was a rhythm in the pre-automobile home that is entirely broken now, and whose loss is perhaps the exactest index of the decline of confidence in our environment. Life
seems to be sustained by rhythm, upset by its changes, weakened by its loss. An apartment house with a car at the door,
though comfort summarized, has no rhythm, except for a
broken, excited syncopation, or the spondaic movement of
boredom.

Our houses moved with felt rhythms, not set, nor identical,
yet so sensible that what one felt first in a strange home was
the tempo of life there. We were away for brief intervals only,
at home long enough to be harmonized, and even the heads of
families, whose working hours were incredible in their length,
seemed never to lose their conditioning by the home. If business and the home lived by different ethical standards, as was
commonly said, it may be because the worker was a different
man outside the rhythm of the house. And women stayed most
of the time within.

It was this familiar movement, this routine with a certainty
of repetition, that inspired a confidence in a patterned universe
missing today. (Our love of nature helped too — more of this
in a later chapter.) The European peasant got it from the
cycles of the soil, and this also made him a different creature
from the artifacts of industrialism. There was a slur upon
boarders in our town and upon the strays who lived in hotel
suites or the transients who moved from rent to rent. They
were not quite like Us, even though sometimes more cheerful;
they had no home. We could have said, with equal truth, that
they lacked something of that confidence in tomorrow and in
circumstance, which, in spite of the common incidence of misfortune or disaster, we held with a tenacity not easily explained
by religion or philosophy.

Most of Us in the late eighties and the nineties still lived in
squarish houses of red or painted brick, heavily corniced with
wood at the top, or mansarded, with porches at front and back,
and painted iron fences between the lawns and the brick side-

walks bordered by rows of buttonwoods or Norway maples. There were a few old houses of lovelier lines, and many bizarrities of Italian, Greek, Queen Anne, and Egyptian inspiration, or of bastard Gothic pointed with gray slate. All, except the very oldest, had spacious, high-ceilinged rooms, hung with chandeliers recently converted to electricity, and trimmed with dark, polished walnut which also spiraled up giant stairways. These rooms were upholstered wherever possible. Golden oak in the very latest houses relieved the gloom by substituting the frivolous for the dignified.

It is possible to describe what that generation would have called, say about eighteen-ninety, an ideal home. The hall was broad and deep, a waiting place hung with steel prints and furnished with benches, stiff chairs, and a hat rack. It was Main Street, meant for traffic. On the right the parlor, on the left the sitting room. The parlor was for decorum. It was the largest room in the house, and the least used, with the most massive tables, the biggest pictures, and the showiest chairs. Mirrors at each end gave it an illusion of still greater spaciousness, and between them was the piano, which, when used for practicing, admitted the only disorder allowed in that room. On the center table were the more pretentious gift books, for show, not reading. Indeed, there is a whole literature of gift books, all illustrated and bound in stamped leather, the only reason for whose existence was the parlor table. They came in and went out with it, and many a childish knuckle has been rapped for opening them with smutty fingers. It was a sign of change in the times when in thousands of homes parlors were made over into 'living rooms.' The date, which was the late nineties, is more significant than many better remembered.

Across the hall was the sitting room, smaller, cozier, with easier chairs, bookcases, a tall brass lamp, a gas stove in the corner (fireplaces had not yet come back except as tiled ornaments for the hall, where, of course, no one ever used them), and an air of comfort and usability. Here the family sat and friends were entertained (company went into the parlor). Here were the magazines, the books to be read, the cat, the dog, and the children studying after supper. This was the heart of the home.

The dining room, again, was formal, family portraits on the wall, a china cupboard out of which glinted what never was used even on the grandest occasion. Morning sun in the dining room was one of the specifications, as important as the sideboard and the serving table. The pantry was built up to the high ceiling in tiers of shelves and closets on and in which were kept that incredible clutter of household china and glass which every family seemed to accumulate. There was a drawer labeled 'Cake,' another 'Bread,' and a lead-lined sink with cockroach poison on the edges. The kitchens sprawled — coal stoves, laundry tubs, tables for baskets, tables for rolling dough, hooks and closets for a forest of tinware, and so on out into the shed with its tables and bins and closets. And in the cellar more bins, more shelves, a cold room, and a bricked-in furnace as big as a funeral vault.

The main stairs followed a curving serpent of black walnut to a long upstairs hall off which opened vast bedrooms. The bathroom was here (often the only one) with doors in at least two directions, accessible to all. The parents' room would be an upstairs sitting room also, with a desk somewhere spilling with small change and account books, and at the farther end a vast walnut bed whose back rose to the ceiling, a cliff of polished veneer topped by a meaningless escutcheon. Other monumental pieces of black walnut flanked it at either side, and at the foot was a crib for the smallest child, or a green plush sofa for naps.

Across the hall would be the spare rooms, usually 'blue' and 'red,' as in the White House, very bleak and usually shrouded in sheets. On their walls the outmoded pictures collected: 'Old Swedes' Church,' by Robert C., 'Scene on the Brandywine,' 'Pauline' on glass. Guests in those days usually went home at night.

The stair banister to the third floor was scratched by children's slidings. This was where freedom began. There was the boy's room and the girl's room, indistinguishable in furnishing (cast-offs mostly), but differing in the kind of disorder, and an alcove at the end of the hall for doll houses, and mineral or birds'-eggs collections. On the other side of the hall, last relic of the self-contained age of our grandparents, a 'lumber room,' with its bench, tools, oddments for repairs and plumbing, the rest of the floor space carrying a *massif* of family trunks piled up on each other in buttes and mesas. Last of all a cubicle where the visiting semptress slept and some drawers for her scanty clothes. (She came of the *good* 'plain people,' and kept up her tiny remnant of gentry by gifts of big red apples to the children.) Here freedom ended, since the next door led to the servants' quarters (white only, the black slept outside), and no one, not even a parent, was supposed to trespass there except on monthly inspections of the sanitation.

Such was the house, which lived by a rhythm in which all these familiar backgrounds had their part. Morning was early, in the winter dark and cold, with faint gurglings from the radiators and faint breaths of warmth from the registers, too late for comfortable dressing. Earlier, in bed, one heard the slender rattle of chains on the heavy storm door, the distant whisk-whisk as Isaac, the waiter, swept the front porch — or, if it were an old-fashioned Quaker house, the soft slop-slush of wet cloths over the marble steps which had to be polished each morning. The faint joyous barks of the dog released, the first streetcars banging down the hill — then, through the open window, sunlight pale on the faraway river, then bright on the carpet — the double gong ringing stridently — seven struck high and clear on the old clock far below — and a rush downstairs for breakfast.

A meal that, no snack. No fruit then — until strawberries, cantaloupes, or peaches were ripe, then in vast platters — but oatmeal and milk that was still foamy from the milkman's crook-necked cans, hot rolls or beaten biscuit, chops or scrapple or sausages with hashed potatoes, eggs as a side dish, waffles three times a week. A Quaker blessing first, heads down, but no word spoken. A full meal to all, then a scurry of children for coats and hats, the buggy at the door for father, hard-tired bicycles bumping down the pavement, green bags of schoolbooks swung against the trees.

Quiet in the home after the mother left with her basket to join the housewives of all the first families shopping down the long row of wagon tilts backed against the curb of the street market and spilling with greens, vegetables, ducks, chickens,

and bunches of wild flowers. When she had gone, the child left
behind heard the faint moaning spirituals of Isaac in the pantry
polishing the silver, 'O Lo—ad, O my Lo—ad,' more distant and
fainter the creak of the cook's laughter. The house was a personality, inscrutable, like God. It was the other half of ego,
without which the ego was only a sense of existence, it was external reality familiarly incarnate. It was something so embracing yet so intimate that a word could name it only by in-
direction and overtones. It was home.

And while the slow synthetic beat of the house pulsed in a
tempo so well known that the senses responded subconsciously,
knowing the hours of the day or night, the dawn hours being
different appreciably from those near midnight or in the sleepi-
est afternoon, many subsidiary rhythms joined or separated
with quicker or slower motions. In the yard at afternoon the
children had their moments of idle wandering or dreamy meditation, or sudden impulses to frenzied play, or hours of quiet
industry in the sand pile or on the bending branches of the
cherry trees. Sounds from within sank to the squeak of a clean-
ing cloth or the polite laugh of a guest in the parlor, then rose,
crescendo, until by supper at six the whole house was again
alive with activity. As night deepened, the tempo gently slackened. Children's feet dragged upward to bed, the street noises
sank to quiet, murmurs abovestairs drowsed down until the
clocks rang the hour through a silent house, and the head of
the household, bolting the shutters, chaining the storm door,
locking the front door, side door, back door, climbed the stairs,
and set the silver-basket on its shelf with the revolver and the
watchman's rattle, a ritual act (since burglaries were most rare)
celebrating the inviolability of the home.

I once rose at dawn and, tiptoeing out into the silent street,
saw those familiar houses relaxed and off their guard. There
was no human life about, no dogs even were stirring; it was
still dusky but clear. The slant light from the brightening east
shone on the brick façades and overhanging cornices as upon
faces, glinting with windows like eyes. And each one of those
houses became the individual it was, an organism, hunched
and humorous, or with open arms and serene forehead, a personality which recalled the family it sheltered and yet seemed

to have i̇ꞏꞏꞏ ꞏꞏꞏs. I was seeing, with that irrational ꞏꞏꞏ ꞏculiar to youth, an environment incarnate i̇ꞏ ꞏ ꞏck and mortar, feeling in those crouching house people a grudging security offered to inmates who shaped their spirits accordingly. And in that moment the insipid smile of the Judge's mansard across the way, the reticent severity of the doctor's wooden mansion behind its trees, the brutal simplicity of the brick cube that housed the ironmaster and his brother, the coquettish insincerity of the minister's turrets of *fin de siècle,* and the toothy grin of the talkative widow's cornice, seemed more real than the sleeping inmates, so real that they mocked those that they sheltered, and were indeed grotesque symbols of the power of Things protecting and coercing the impressionable spirit of Life. Then the sun rose, and looking up at our own house, bland, familiar, welcoming, surcharged with secret comforts, I shrugged away philosophy.

That feeling of a daily rhythm, in which each hour had its characteristic part, in a house where change came slowly and which was always home, nourished, if it did not create, the expectancy of our generation that the norm of life was repetition and therefore security. Our house, with the tall two-hundred-year-old clock ticking at its heart, sank into the subconsciousness and became a sense of stability and permanence. It was a proof of a friendly universe, to which memory could always return. When a home was closed on our street, its shutters flapping, its blinds pulled awry to show empty floors and bare walls, we pitied the family that had lost their external self. The homeless, like the landless men of the Middle Ages, seemed to have no country.

The family made the home, yet the home, when it was made, had its own laws. Thus the relaxing of family ties in the present era, and the auto, the radio, commuting, boarding school, and apartment life have struck direct at both the home and the laws of the home and on through to the family. Confidence is a habit which must be acquired young and from an environment that is constant and rhythmically continuous. The kaleidoscope patterns of life today are more exciting and probably liberate the intelligence when there is an intelligence to be liberated; but the pattern they make is seldom realized by youth which turns and twists and darts in an environment which to its seeing never once makes a whole. Home life in the nineties could be very sweet, and often profoundly dull, and sometimes an oppressive weight of routine inescapable; security was often bought at a ruinous price; yet what conditioned reflexes it set up! The peace movement of the early nineteen-hundreds, naïvely confident amidst a world in arms, was an attempt to make that world our home, our American home. Nor was heaven exempt from the home-making activities of the American family. We sang lustily in church —

> There we shall rest,
> There we shall rest,
> In Our Father's House,
> In Our Father's House.

The Age of Confidence got the habit of security in its homes.

5

Parents

PARENTHOOD in our town was a limited monarchy. After the child was too old to spank, physical punishment of any kind was not countenanced, and even locking in a room and such strong-arm methods were not approved by the community. A boy who was regularly strapped by his father, or a girl shut in her bedroom on bread and water, was rather expected to run away or be protected by the relatives, and this was a code so well understood that such scandals seldom occurred among good families. Sadistic fathers and hysterical mothers deferred to neighborhood opinion and chose other means of self-expression at the expense of their young. It was a kindly easy-going community almost free from the rigid prides and mean penny-pinchings which had made so many parents cruel in the past.

Yet authority maintained itself. If it were possible to explain the secret bond of respect which made the children defer to their parents in the nineties, the psychological change which has come over the country since could be more accurately described. It was certainly not respect for the opinion of the elders. If change in external circumstance is more rapid now, there was then a greater difference between the ideas and convictions of fathers and sons and mothers and daughters than in this age. I know that this statement is against all current belief, but I am sure that it is true. We did not respect our parents' opinions unless they happened to be ours, we did not share some of their most important convictions, especially as to manners and religion — and yet we deferred to them as persons.

There was a tacit agreement that parental opinion had the right of way. If you differed, it was by mental reservation, so that the calm of family relations might be broken by anger or obstinacy, but seldom by impudence or youthful dogmatism.

There was less honesty and more unity in family life. There was more expressed affection between parents and children than now, and much less companionship. Democracy had after all touched the home only superficially, which, a monarchy in form, in spirit was a republic with the elders in office.

Does this seem a slight difference from the democratic homes of today where all try so hard to be 'pals'? It was a monumental difference. Statisticians have yet to reckon the nerve strain in American life which comes from precocious attempts at maturity and painful struggles to retard middle age. Fathers and mothers today have to be big brothers and big sisters, while sixteen-year-old children are humored in their attempts to make knowledge prevail without experience behind it. The worst service done to youth by the revolution in thought of the early nineteen-hundreds and the disillusion of war was the necessity put upon them to disagree with everything said by their elders! We in the nineties might doubt parental infallibility, but we felt no sacred duty to assert our unbeliefs. Parental opinions were assumed to be based upon experience and therefore to be treated like axioms in geometry until we had a chance to test them. The middle-aged got credit for their age, and did not have to pretend sympathy with ideas they knew were wrong; the young could take shelter in their youth, and were not asked to prove what it was well known they believed. There was less argument and more useful information passed about the home.

Convictions were different. The youth of the nineties who had been reading Darwin or Herbert Spencer knew that his Methodist father was wrong in his conception of creation, violently wrong, yet respected, by habit, his judgment in more immediate matters. The fabric of life in which he lived had been made by his elders, and he liked it. The pattern he expected to change when his time came, but he had no desire to tear the weave apart because a few threads had rotted.

All this, however, is much too analytical for a true picture. One analyzes equals, but not superiors, so long as they are superiors. And if our parents were felt to be our superiors in the Age of Confidence, it was not for their opinions, or even their judgment, but because they unhesitatingly accepted the responsibility for the family, and we knew it. I do not mean that they were less selfish than parents today, and certainly they were far more dogmatic. Yet that curious atmosphere of home, compacted of rigidities and confidences, was their chief care, and we knew that also. Self-expression for youth is supposed to have brought about the great change in family life which came with the new generation. It was a cause, but an equally powerful one was self-expression for parents, who determined to stay young and live their own lives, while the boys and girls were sent off to camps and schools. Fathers and mothers in the earlier time put fatherhood and motherhood first. To fail in that, letting the children run wild or be sent off to convenient institutions, or to spend the family income on display while the home and the children's education suffered, set all the gossips talking. When children came, young men and women gave up the right to be young and assumed the responsibility for a home with no reservations, physical or mental. They did it well, or badly, but with no more protest than a tadpole makes in becoming a frog. Or if they did protest, no one listened to them. And the children felt this — it would be too much to say that they knew it.

How many brilliant personalities became housewives or mere bread-winners in the process cannot be reckoned. I think myself that the law of compensation operated, and if society suffered the family gained. Middle age came earlier and the thirties were a difficult time, but parenthood, being taken seriously, became a rich experience.

Elizabeth A. Allen's 'make me a child again just for tonight,' would never have been written so poignantly in the nineteenthirties. For all our sophistication we keep the boy and girl alive in us so much longer today that we do not have to yearn backward into the past. We insist on staying young, insist on coddling our egos, long after the age when our parents had given up youth as incompatible with running a family. Why do we try so hard to make companions of our children if not to get them to share our responsibility for their upbringing? We tell them all we know, hoping that they will learn to stand on their own feet quickly, so that our slackening race for self-expression may not be further handicapped by too much con-

cern for them. We call our sons 'pals' for much the same subconscious reason that led England to make her colonies semi-
independent. She wanted to be helped as well as to help, she
wanted to attend to her own business, and so do we.

Hence parents in those earlier days were expected to be
strict because they were responsible for the morals of youth.
They were expected to be severe because they had earned the
right to authority. They were expected to grant favors slowly
because a spoiled child was charged to their account. They
were supposed to be kind, even when they seemed the opposite,
because the home had been their willing creation. We knew all
this, and knew also from our own impulsive desires that the
father and mother denied themselves every day, if not every
hour, something for the sake of the family. If we did not
know, it was not for the lack of telling — also every day and
hour! Nor were the blunt reminders of the parents ever without some show of truth. It is tempting to trace back to these
services rendered the slushy sentiments of the cycle of mother
and 'mammy' songs that certainly began to be popular in this
age. I would not go that far, yet I am certain that the increasing vogue of sentimental memories of home and mother in
recent years is due to a consciousness that something has un-
accountably changed in the relations of parents and children,
and that what was once realism is now only romance.

But respect this parental responsibility did breed in us, and
that willing deference even to a bad parent which seems almost
incredible to modern youth. It was quite different from the
religious awe which a Clarissa Harlowe felt for her parents.
That was superstition, perpetuating the memory of the Roman
right to treat children as property. Our deference was freer
because it did not imply subservience in opinion, yet it was
genuine since it recognized tacitly that the parents, in another
sense, had deferred to us.

Parents of all kinds there were in our town, even among the
limited circle that I knew. There were parents that even today would be called modern, who shrugged off the family
while they went their own way. Yet then, far from being admired for their independence, the gossips compared them with
the Negroes, who, though affectionate by nature, never let a

child stand in the way of their kind of self-expression. Parents selfish and self-centered, in whose presence all free conversation ceased, and even the neighbors' children kept their eyes on the tablecloth. Sadistic parents, mean parents, jealous parents, and also parents so easy-going and so humorous that the family lived in a gale of laughter and took punishments like spring showers. Yet in neither the comfortable nor the uncomfortable households did I ever hear impudence lightly phrased or revolt openly expressed. We children knew well enough which kind of parent we preferred, but most were playing the game, most had given up the privileges of youth, taken on the responsibilities of a home, and deserved either affection or obedience or both. We respected a self-denial which was none the less real for being a convention.

And here the formula of *laissez-faire* breaks down. That principle by which our society so generally lived seems to have lagged in family relationships. We have it now, fully, freely, irresponsibly applied. If there ever was a pure *laissez-faire* organism, it is the typical American family today. But the Age of Confidence very definitely had no confidence in such go-as-you-must-or-please arrangements as ours. Their family code was a hold-over, like the code of a gentleman, from the doctrine of an earlier generation. It was no longer rigid, no longer sanctioned by religion, 'Honor thy father and thy mother' were only words out of a book, whereas 'Give honor where honor is due,' which was our paraphrase, squared with observation and common sense. The parents sacrificed their youth for us. We respected them for that, even when (say, after age sixteen) their idea of life and what to do with it began to seem almost ludicrously wrong.

It was Bernard Shaw, I believe, who first cracked the complacent shell of this confidence in parents. His dangerous fascination for the more intellectual youth of the early nineteen-hundreds was not due to his wit, or to his mild Fabianism, which, to us individualist Americans, living in a pretty successful economic structure, meant next to nothing. His seductive power came first, in America, from his insidious attacks upon the institution of parenthood and the family in such plays as *Man and Superman* and *Candida*. For of course the self-denial and the sacrifice of our parents were not pure, nor the respect they exacted and received all deserved. Closely studied, there were few families in which the children's deference was not exploited. Sometimes it was the vanity of a mother that required flattery; sometimes suppressed sadism given an escape; sometimes an unhappy marriage revenged upon its helpless fruits; sometimes the incurable egoism that insists upon honor at home if it cannot be procured abroad.

I suppose that as we entered the age of psychology these things had to be understood; and that some of them were true in most of our families is unquestionable. But Shaw, who never knew family life, and never until his sixties seems to have felt an emotion, was a tricky teacher. Like so many pseudo-scientific literary men he was more interested in sensation than in fact, and more able to shock than to advise. The abnormal interested him more than the typical, and our credulous intellects, misled by his emphasis, saw with such shocking clarity the sham in the family as we had known it that we were quite blinded to the realities which had been much the larger part of our experience. Just because parents, under inspection, proved to be very human, we began in that decade to distrust the confidence which had made our childhood secure. Because under the strong impulsions of the new twentieth century we clamored to break through with our little egos all the inhibitions of which we had suddenly become aware, we began to lose respect for an older generation that had been so strangely content to give up self-expression for the sake of a family, and even to suspect them of pathological motives. And thus on the flowing tide of the new realism, the family, which had been bound together (so I think) by deference as much as by economics, began to loosen its bonds, lose its close relationships between deference and responsibility, and to float out toward freedom and away from confidence.

What the end result will be who can tell? There is between children and parents now an equality in knowledge, if not in experience and in the zest for living, which should certainly be some compensation for confidences lost. Nevertheless, the home as we knew it in the nineties is gone. One more of those stabilities which in early youth arm the child against the inev-

itable maladjustments and disillusions of later life is no longer
stable. Nervousness begins earlier, goes farther. That quiet
area of memory where the mind lived in a geography that, however monotonous, was fixed, known, believed in, has shrunk
to the little island of babyhood. Psychiatrists' offices are crowded with boys and girls in their teens. It begins to be evident
that when the authoritarian home went out of fashion, not the
children so much as the parents were emancipated. They have
got back their youth, while youth has aged prematurely. We
have all got more freedom — and paid for it.

When both parents and children began to seek self-expression, children grew ruder and parents more irritable. Since
both in their different ways desired the same thing, they crossed
wills oftener and more openly. Instead of spanking there was
argument. But I am not concerned with nursery manners. In
emotional understanding of each other the generations came
closer together. This may seem a paradox in a present when
the younger generation has got itself talked about as never before, yet it is the simple truth. We are shocked by the youngsters because they do crudely what we in our new desire for
self-expression would do more subtly if we could escape from
the inhibitions of our past. We are distressed by their rowdy
frankness and their disregard of convention and precedent because we see only too clearly where self-expression would lead
us if we were entirely free of responsibility. In wish, we are
often too much like our children to control, or even to influence them. If the family I write of is now only a memory, it is
partly because children who have become parents still try to
keep their youth.

The breach between generations is not wide now; it was very
wide, I think, in the days which I am recording. The peace of
the home in the Age of Confidence has hidden this important
fact. Our town had two societies, the old and the young, a difference which ran true all the way from the darkies to Us, and
was most marked at the top. Deference concealed this chasm,
and the reticence of the young in the presence of their elders
clouded it over; but will anyone now growing old, after searching memory, deny the fact?

A youth of twenty in, let us say 1898, was already part of a new world of ideas of which his parents, except in our most advanced households, had only the vaguest perception. Our town was not behind greater cities in its admiration for the results of applied science visible on every street and in every mill, yet the older people were not aware in any penetrating way of causes. The new belief that for every phenomenon there was a physical explanation, and for every problem a scientific solution, had not really touched their minds. They wondered at science as do the raw masses today, but did not think about it, except of what it did. The children were already different. Directly and indirectly they had been educated in this faith, which was not yet called materialism, until its basic ideas were as familiar emotionally to them as Bible stories to their elders. Middle-aged reading of this and that in newspapers or magazines never goes as deep as childhood teaching. Our parents had been shaken out of their religious and moral dogmatisms by the scientific thinking of the mid-century without any real convictions resulting. The new ideas were not instinctive with them; they lay like a light snow on their faiths and prejudices, melting at the first emotional warmth. Men like my grandfather, who, reading geology with excitement, revised his opinions at seventy, were rare.

We children thought crudely, but thanks to the routine of our education in which science was the novelty, we thought materialistically. And as if that had not been enough to sever us intellectually from our parents, the realistic mood of the early nineteen-hundreds, with its ironical attack upon the complacent conventions and the sentiment of the romantic *fin de siècle,* caught us just as we passed out of adolescence. I can think of no intelligent family in our town where parents and children saw the same world or talked the same language when ideas were in question. The immigrants and their Americanized children were hardly farther apart.

If we guessed what had happened, we certainly never stressed it, indeed seldom talked about it. Our minds went one way, the parents' another, but kept within calling distance. Those terrible family quarrels when religious dogmatism was undergoing its first attacks from science, such as one reads of in Edmond Gosse's *Father and Son,* were so violent because there was no liberty to disagree. We headed away from stormy waters probably because no one was so sure of absolute truth as the orthodox had been in 1850, or the scientists became by 1920. If there was to be a row over ideas, let it be outside the home. We let sleeping dogs lie, and so did the parents. Theology and morals (in the abstract) were not discussed in the family, though each side guessed what the other thought.

And these peaceful homes, where there was more care to spare feelings than to air unpleasant truths, were possible only because children were deferential and parents liberal. Perhaps they were possible only because the intellectual differences were so great. Protestants struggle to convert Catholics and *vice versa,* when both will leave the Jews to their own religion. And yet there was one resemblance between the generations that must have helped. Both sides were confident of progress. The parents, like us, expected the new world to be different and better, and of this new world we young ones were the visible beginning.

Family conversation was, therefore, if more harmonious, certainly less honest than today. And yet I believe that the state of the home then was very good for character. That it made better characters I do not say, yet certainly it bred tolerance, self-respect, and respect for honest opinions not shared. The explosions in the homes of the Democrats and the down-state folk were emotional not intellectual, leaving no more after-effects than a thundershower, nor did they result in bitterness. We Quakers had to learn to do our thinking while keeping the peace. I shall not be surprised if the psychologists of 1950 discover that the growing intolerance of the earlier nineteen-hundreds was due to an abbreviated experience of family life, since the family is a microcosm of a world where different faiths have to try to live together. Nor does an easy companionship between the generations, such as we see today and which has such inestimable advantages of another kind, prepare the youth to endure contradiction. The modern child lives in a family just long enough to acquire a clan's suspicion of outsiders.

In my own family, an Episcopalian father, a Quaker grandfather, a harshly Presbyterian grandmother, and youngsters educated in scientific materialism, all sat down to eat together.

If there were acrid comments they were upon housekeeping and table manners, not religion, yet I could charge no one with insincerity or of lightly held beliefs. We simply had too much respect or deference for each other, as personalities belonging to the home, to fling taunts or reproaches. And if my grandmother did occasionally brandish hell or a wrathful Jehovah, the other adults quite obviously felt her to be in bad taste. We lived our family life on the surface, keeping religion for our privacy, but at least it was kept a family life, something so confident that storms and disorder were discouraged before they could enter, and that surely furthered psychological health.

Neither argument nor analysis can quite reach to the heart of the family relationship. The parents of that generation came no closer to their children's minds as both aged together. The alterations of the nineteen-hundreds were so rapid that the minds formed in the seventies dropped farther and farther behind the youths now pointing toward middle age, and one would have expected that as our parents became old there would have been a divergence which would have destroyed sympathy and mutual interest. Emphatically that did not happen. The parents and children of the nineties have kept closer together in the family bond than have the next two generations. There is a piquancy in a relationship of affection and deference between opposites. The child's doings are continually novel; the parents' opinions increasingly acquire the interest of history. The homes I knew in the nineties are too many of them disrupted by death and moving, yet where the members remain the spirit remains. There was a bond more indissoluble than the search for self-expression.

ᑲ 6 ᑲ

Society

I WISH that the religious and sex impulses of this community of the nineties had been as simple as the Society into which our parents in due course introduced us. I am not ready to extract their mingled qualities yet. But our Society was as definite as the angles of a crystal. The newspapers recognized its boundaries without difficulty and put always a bar ————.———— after the last item that belonged to Us before the doings of the 'plain people' began to be set down. Our Society was simple, and yet rather ominous, for it held in a seemingly permanent solution two elements that ought to have been separate and certainly had been separate, and would be again. Our tradition of decorum, responsibility, and friendliness blended with a stuffy respectability to make Society.

Its baptism and confirmation services were to be seen at the Assemblies, to which only the winnowed elect were invited, and after which, if invited, you became automatically one of Us. Yet even more ritualistic was the Thanksgiving Dance, for which the right people still received invitations even if they had not lived for thirty years in Wilmington, and what was judged the wrong kind of wealth or manners was not invited, also after thirty years.

The Assemblies were first held in the tawdry Second Empire of the Grand Opera House (now a movie theater). In the early nineties they were translated to the pseudo-Colonial of the New Century Club, so called in anticipation of a new century, not yet arrived, which it was confidently expected would establish forever the ideals of the progressive women of the town, who believed with the rest of the country that only a little was needed to put over the American millennium.

The Assemblies began with a quadrille, led by my cousin

Fanny (who thought she looked like Dolly Madison, and probably did) dancing with that courtly hand-kisser of the old school, Colonel Billy Demond, or one of the tall Seaburys from down state. Our chief grand dames, who could endure nothing more rapid, and the self-conscious débutantes of the year with their beaus, stood up for the quadrille.

This was the earliest nineties. In the mid-decade came a lancers for the 'younger set,' a little noisier and more rapid; then, with a jar to decorum, we dropped into the *fin de siècle* and its slow waltzes and romping two-steps, of which the *Stars and Stripes* by Sousa with its minor passages (said to represent the lost hopes of the South) was a perfect expression of the mingled boisterousness and sentiment that was to be the note of the era.

The stage and the movies are delightedly reproducing the costumes and background of social life in those days, so that I need not elaborate except to say that they falsify, as history and scene-painting always do. The most sincere actor puts a touch of burlesque into costume which makes it unreal to those who remember. How can I prove that balloon sleeves and billowing skirts were beautiful, when the girl was beautiful! Or that piccadilly collars that pricked beneath the chin were as dignified as they were uncomfortable! Graceful the women's clothes were not, and yet the beauties of that time had a conquering sweep of line, a curve of shoulders emphasized, a carriage as of a swan's neck rising from waves of tulle, an imperious lift of the head like the portrait busts of the eighteenth century which slinky gowns can never equal. Woman chooses in each period a feature which to her seems noblest or most seductive, and like a modernist painter gives that its double due. I can just remember the days of waspish waists which glorified the hips. Today it is backs and breasts. Yesterday it was the ankle and the leg. In our so-limited nineties it was the neck and the face. Does this explain why among the women I have known it is the figure I remember of later beauties, but in my youth always faces? And which is the lovelier feature, a calf or the curve that rises above the shoulder?

They could romp, those creatures of innumerable skirts, corseted, puffed as to sleeve and hair, gloved to the shoulder, unpainted, with never more than an ankle showing in the wildest of 'Yales' down the length of the floor. Of course, it was a romping which the sophisticated today would call childish, nor did the crowding males, gloved too and bound in their high collars, ask more than a smile and a round of a dance. There was drinking, but always off the ballroom floor, and never by girls. There was fighting among the inevitable red-headed gamecocks, but it never but once to my memory broke the decorum of the ceremony, and that was because the two smallest men in the room collided in pursuit of the tallest girl and revenged upon each other her patronizing laugh.

We respected tradition and tradition dictated an immense respect for the women of our own class. A girl at a ball was still a woman on show, a custodian of honor and the home. Wiles were allowed her, but only to advertise her charms. She could flirt and be gay and tease and be teased, but one hint of the sexual made her 'common,' which was only one word above 'vulgar.' She was still in the tradition and so were we all of us. Few remembered the legend of that Delaware beauty of the turn of an earlier century, Miss Vining, who, with the subtlety of genius, hid always with fan or floating silk some part of her features, as if there was no man worthy of absolute view of so much beauty at once. Yet we believed that every girl should for a moment at least of apotheosis, in the midst of a ball that had become hers, at the first utter opening of her petals, be not a lovely creature of seductive flesh but a goddess manifest. Even the old libertines and young blasé rounders believed that, and came to the Assembly to see it happen and to stir the muddy romance in their hearts.

We professed to believe that these balls in the New Century Club differed only in degree, not in kind, from Society on display in New York or London, or in historical novels, but the intelligent must have only half-believed it. For between the boisterous two-steps and the dreamy waltzes there was a fatal numbness that crept through the nerves of the party. The formality of our Society was inherited, and already a little beyond the powers of a genial community, half pleasant Quaker, half easy Southerner, whose everyday manners were hard to strain into etiquette. The pretense of being an aristocracy was

difficult to keep up when after all we were only one or two re-
moves from the commonplaceness of the 'plain people.' Such
art of conversation as we had could not be keyed up to the level
of formal intercourse. We might dramatize ourselves as Vanity
Fair, but we could not speak the parts. Wit among the young
seldom rose above calling a ladyfinger a bread, and with the
middle-aged a chronic matrimony kept gallantry to conventional platitudes which soon broke down into patter about
what happened yesterday. The electric wave of sex found no
ether to move in. Youth frolicked, but beyond the twenties
Society, which requires individuals, consisted only of husbands
and wives.

As a Society, our culture was dying. The Assembly had become no more than a county fair where housewives, plump
and complacent vegetables themselves, showed the best new
blooms. As for the men, except a few surviving gallants of a
more aristocratic era, they had too obviously taken a night off
for the show, which was not their business, since in a community still too idealistic to regard marriage as a trade, it was not
business at all, and so not their real life. Nor would it have occurred to any of them to cultivate social intercourse as an art.
Our Society had many points in common with our religion.
Both were institutions from which the blood was running out.

And hence the true medium for this Society was to be found
in other regions where it had made for itself, as Societies always
will, other institutions in exacter accord with its temperament,
which with us was the temperament of a genial fellowship
quite sure of itself, proud but rather negligent of its traditions,
and capable of friendship to a degree possible only in communities where life is easy, suspicion reduced to the minimum,
habitation fixed, and all relations pervaded by that illusion of
permanence which the twentieth century was to see fly twittering down the gale of war and innovation.

I wish I could re-create in words one of the terrapin suppers
at my mother's house. All day the kitchens and the pantry
would be tense with bustle and expectancy, strange black faces
at the doorways, delightful smells from the stove. Toward evening Isaac would put on a fresh starched jacket and the maids
their new caps, or, on greater occasions, Robert himself would

bow his way into the kitchen, the family caterer with his rim
of snow-white wool and his gravity as of a Thibetan saint. Isaac
would shoo the children from their pilferings of terrapin eggs
or chocolate mints, since Robert for him represented the nobility whose presence made a feast a ritual. The guestrooms would
shed their drapings, revealing unsuspected grandeurs, steps and
porch were swept thrice, and the double outer door thrown
open wide. Robert and my mother, colleagues respectful of
each other's skill, gave the last touches to the long table, shining with linen and noble with silver and glass, and when the
clock struck seven would take reverently from the china cupboard my grandfather's terrapin bowl of Chelsea china to be
borne into the steaming kitchen.

Father and mother received in the living room before the
fireplace, she in her corals, he in his jeweled studs. The house
was warm and rich and softly lit, for candles had come back to
temper the harshness of unshaded electric lights. Symbol of
continuity and permanence assured, the old mahogany glis-
tened dully. It had come down only the year before from
attics and storerooms to replace the stale novelty of fretted
black walnut.

Entrance to supper was still formal, couple by couple, but
with the sherry after the oysters familiarity began, a teasing
badinage of charge and counter-charge, friendly, mirthful,
neither noisy nor distinguished, but pleasant to hear. It was
chatter really, as homely as Isaac's capers as he waited, and,
limited to the humorous everydays of our town, had neither
edge nor bite.

There was nevertheless decorum. The table, the wine, the
food, the succession of china, the exact correspondence of each
course to its containers and accompaniments, was a ritual controlled by a flick of the eye between my mother and Robert the
impeccable, and watched with devout attention by the women,
who never, in the utmost geniality of conversation, forgot that
this supper was a ritual, nor failed in their words of praise, not
too much, which was vulgar, nor too little, for that would be
unknowing. The men, except Uncle Billy, were grosser. Leaving consecration to their wives, they paid tribute only by a
shade of careful manners to an Occasion.

And yet they, too, were conscious of the presence of tradition. In a community growing year by year more commercialized, more cut-throat in competition, where speculation was beginning to dominate industry, and they themselves in daily intercourse put business first, such evenings as this were (and perhaps they knew it) the last stand of the old order where a man was a gentleman first and a lawyer or banker afterward, or he did not entirely belong. Certainly by tacit agreement business came to the surface only in its humors, while the realism of money-making was as firmly shut out as the night behind the curtains. It was a created world, like a novelist's, of selected realities, but these happily still vital in a group that had always been, and rather pathetically expected always to be, good friends. As their ancestors had eaten terrapin so, they believed, would their children, and even as the turtle left its mud to become a rite so they at its sacrifice would forget the hard and vulgar mood of competition outside. They had their code still, which was no more than geniality and decorum in the ceremony of eating and drinking, but still a code.

Our Society was dying, or rather it was rapidly changing from one consciousness to another. Tradition was fading with dignity; soon our little world was to become more promiscuous, more amusing and less friendly, much more expensive. The shade of a shade that still gave it a ritual was already distinguishable only in the etiquette of entertaining. Soon the Assembly would be only a dance duller than the others, only a duplicate of the social displays of Oshkosh, Keokuk, or Tallahassee. No wonder that after the war the flask came in where only decanters had been permitted. Something had to be done to make a stuffy and meaningless ceremony possible for the young. An ideal flickered out, the ideal of a polished Society in which respect and courtesy reminded us on stated occasions of their innate worth. It was a heritage of the eighteenth century which in our day was seldom more than an illusion. We could play up to tradition for only the length of a quadrille; afterward its stale conventions merely smothered new desires. Our Society was pseudo-Colonial, like the hall of its rites.

But the cult of confident friendliness where we were much more at home was real. When it declined, an epoch ended in

|6|2|

America. We cannot go back to it now, for we are not so naïve or so provincial. Our talk is better talk (when it is not too noisy to be talk at all), our liberty of opinion is greater, our tolerance far greater, the diversity of possible experience intoxicating, and the individual, when he has not been vulgarized or standardized, if he has less personality has more interesting thoughts. But that sense of permanence, so important for character, which comes from confidence in one's environment, is certainly gone.

The New Englander, I think, never had it in my time. The New Englander trusted morals and industry more than he did his neighbors. He believed in his culture, but doubted his community. We were closer in spirit to the South, to those South Carolinian planters who made for themselves a life they loved so heartily that they clung to the soil upon which it had been created long after there was any possibility of renewing experience. We were more typical than either of America at large, which in those decades could be both progressive and complacent because, except on the frontier, it was still a country of neighborhoods where like-minded people lived long together out of choice, not necessity. Though progress had brought restlessness even in those neighborhoods, and Henry Ford was just over the horizon, there were still abundant pastures for content. And if only a few ate terrapin (a great loss) and went to Assemblies (a small one), such society did give to man's universal longing for friendly intercourse an expression that in its minor way was perfect, and it deserves to be remembered for that blessing with a nostalgia which only a cynic would call sentimental.

7

Education

THE STATE OF BEING EDUCATED in our town was respectable but not well understood. Old Judge Bronson, for example, as I knew him in my youth, was a ripe intellect with that elasticity of mind which revealed true education even more than the constant allusiveness of his talk. Our people respected the competence of his judgment, and liked to hear him relate politics to literature, or the habits of the Delawareans to the mores of ancient Rome. Yet it never occurred to them that the quality of his imagination was a better criterion of his intellectual training than the shrewdness of his decisions.

They believed in schooling superstitiously as in some way not altogether clear a preliminary to success in life, yet kept a healthy skepticism as to whether it really made one man better than another. I share their skepticism, though for different reasons. The educated mind is a miracle, but that blend of humbleness and curiosity, of logic and imagination, was certainly not the chief aim of schooling with us, or for that matter anywhere else in America just then. It was said by the educators that certain kinds of work would discipline minds; that certain assemblages of facts would give us power; that certain readings and recitings would endow us with culture. We believed what we were told, taking our education like our meals, finding with some relief that the town expected from us the three R's and a little general knowledge, but neither discipline, power, nor culture in any difficult sense.

If only the faith of our educators in book knowledge and discipline had been justified! For then there would have been no tabloid newspapers now, no Republican and Democratic parties, no fifteen years of Prohibition, no gangsters, no lynchings, no conflict between production and consumption, no prostitution of the radio, no vulgarizing of the movies. Or at least not so much of any of these mental diseases. We got discipline of the kind that teaches to do it now and don't ask foolish questions; we got reading and reciting; and for the rest of the time were inflated with the rapidly multiplying volume of things to know which was to leave most of us with cluttered minds and weakened judgment. Even before the nineties what to know had been made to seem more important than how and why to know it.

It is for this reason perhaps that I seem to have encountered, either in my youth or afterward, so few educated men and women. Many learned men I knew later in the universities, but even there only a few, who, according to my lights, were really well educated. And in our town certainly the best educated were outside of the schools.

Specialism was hatching then and in its excesses has been the nurse of 'progress' and the curse of real education ever since. It glimmered so rosily in the nineties with its promise of incredible discoveries that we can scarcely be chided for not forecasting a day when there would be a hundred first-rate physicists for one far-sighted leader of men. The Age of Confidence believed that by acquiring information under discipline one could learn how to think and how to live, in which respect we are still, generally speaking, in the Age of Confidence.

School in the nineties was certainly not *laissez-faire*. Parents and teachers alike believed confidently that what we were about to receive would change our natures, and backed up their faith with command and punishment five days in the week, topped off by moralizing on Sunday.

There were no frills and little nonsense in our school, or any school that I knew, in those days. We heard much of integrity and hard work, very little of school spirit and the 'ideals of youth,' nothing of self-expression. We went to school to work, our playing was done elsewhere. Athletics in the afternoons and the gymnasiums on rainy mornings were still on the margin of education, and so matter-of-fact that the captain of our very informal football team, who had glimmerings of how a football captain was to dramatize himself in the heroic age ahead, seemed faintly ridiculous when he shouted with grim fervor, 'Hold 'em, boys, for old Friends School, *hold* 'em!'

We went to school for facts and got them. Facts about Latin, facts about history, facts about algebra, which gave us a valuable experience in taking intellectual punishment without a quaver. But of education there was very little because, with one exception, none of the teachers was really educated. They had knowledge, but, not knowing what to do with it, passed it on to us in its raw condition of fact. They knew facts, but could neither relate nor co-ordinate them. They believed in their subjects with the absolute conviction of the baker that his bread is the staff of life, but there was no passion in their belief, and, to tell truth, not much reason. If you learned history, you knew history — whether you became thus historically minded I never heard anyone either in school (or college) inquire. My grandfather's college journal shows that subjects meant just that to him in the eighteen-thirties, and probably his grandfather felt likewise. Indeed, since the passionate belief of the Renaissance that the new learning would make new men (as it did), the same confidence has endured, but ever colder and dryer as the subject matter of what was taught less and less stirred men's imaginations. In my day it had become utilitarian, with this qualification, that its utilitarianism beyond the three R's had to be taken for granted, since no one really knew why we studied Latin and advanced mathematics, and even chemistry and physics; or, if they knew, they never explained. It is true that we never asked for an explanation, but were content to believe that declensions, formulas, and new facts in general were the food on which brains grew. Miraculously when one learned them, one became educated.

We were content but never enthusiastic, which was the cause, I believe, of the romantic age of American education whose beginnings must have been not much before the days of which I write. The school as I knew it, and the university also, was growing intolerable to active youth. With no emotional outlets, our intellects were being cramped into a routine which we were asked to take on faith. I can remember how little Miss Brown, with her watery voice, reduced the campaigns of Caesar to a pulp of grammar; how mathematics in the university was made a drill so divorced from thinking that it never dawned upon us that it was a language of thought; how all art was compressed into drawing the outlines of a dirty bust. Only in literature, and faintly in the new courses in science, were there gleams of human relationships and a power over the spirit beyond the efforts of memorization. It was not surprising (but most surprising that so little has been said of it in histories of education) that the school or college as an institution, the team, the social life, should have been romanticized when there was so little flesh on the bones of our curriculum. And so to the boredom of the still realistic school, for us who were very young in the nineties, succeeded the romance of a college that had transformed itself into a glamour of beer, songs, cheers, and gaudy nights, mild in actuality beside contemporary possibilities of dissipation, but infinitely more powerful on the imagination. Although the curriculum was even duller and more utilitarian than what we had left in school, life took on a passion which if only a stucco by comparison with a zeal for intellectual power or esthetic development, was still a passion and particularly viable for youth. And the schools soon followed the colleges into the era of loyalty, strenuosity, and sentiment.

None of this, however, or very little, in our school, which was co-educational and, therefore, since girls had their own ideas of romance, not easy to awake to the glamour of an abstract loyalty. But indeed in our town we did not want it, for we in school were not yet a community apart, like modern schools and colleges. We were in organic relation to the town and reflected it in everything except the pliability of youth.

We reflected the community in our complete disregard of art as a factor in living. The creative faculty was never mentioned in our school except as an attribute of the Deity; the idea that painting, sculpture, music, and the art of living were possible subjects for serious education would never have occurred to our principal, who, like the immense majority of his compatriots, knew nothing of any of them. Our esthetics were the mild and quite unnoted influence of the old meeting-house under whose shadow we worked, pure of line and perfect in proportion; or the faint emanations from the literature we

studied. Our self-expression was in stiff debate and perfunctory writing. Our art was drawing — a meaningless routine of
imitation. Our music was nil. My total musical education from
babyhood to a bachelor's degree was the singing of 'Good
Morning, Merry Sunshine' in kindergarten, and scales in a
year of unhappiness at the piano. Our school was modern —
hence the laboratory and the one hour a week for drawing —
but its modernism never conceived of an outlet for the emotions as a part of training, nor dreamed that the arts were essential to the well-rounded life. Our drawing master was a weak
but kindly artist who had touched up half the family portraits
in town and painted all the bank presidents. His duty was to
teach us how to make curved lines look like the picture we
were copying, yet once he forgot himself in color, and I still
remember the faint stir of the creative spirit as under his stimulus the green of lily leaves on my pad began to pulsate with
light. This was accident. In drawing, in oratory, in writing,
we were held to sober utility. Someone once lectured to us
upon 'classic music,' but we were not impressed. Beethoven
was the name of a discolored bust.

And if our town was emotionally thin and trivial in everything but business and family life, and dull even to itself out
of working hours, one cause was that the children had been
taught to reason a little, had been crammed with facts, but
gone out insensitive to every form of beauty except nature,
which they got on their own, and the human face. We were
like the Franks in Constantinople who, looking at the statues
of bronze, could see only metal for coins. If a symphony orchestra had played for us, we would have giggled or shut our
ears — which were shut already, and our eyes also to imagination in anything but words.

The ugliness of the industrial city which was yet to reach its
peak, the tawdriness of democratic life when the old decorum
lost its meaning, the smug gentility of magazine literature
through this period, the banality of most middle-class experience in America, and probably our spiritual dryness, were
largely due to the schools and colleges, for there were not
enough homes where the arts were realities to counteract an
education so linguistic and factual as was ours. The com-

munity made us in its own likeness and we were exactly fitted to its narrow philistinism. The Age of Confidence was blind and dumb esthetically, and rather proud of it.

Our school building was symbolic of the town and the age and of pretty much everything of which I write. Across West Street was the meeting-house under its elms, solid, decorous, proportioned, meaningful. That decorum may have been outgrown, that proportion of living become impossible, yet beauty was realized there, and with beauty life. But our school was piled up, wall on wall, and roof on roof, tinned, pebbled, slated according to age, finished off with mansards in the style of the seventies and tipped by an irreverent peak or two in the taste of the nineties. It was haphazard, makeshift, ill-ordered, yet regimented internally into a fairly efficient factory where pupils could march from study room to assembly hall without much lost motion. The floors were bare, the desks uncomfortable, the walls strips of blackboard or plaster adorned with an occasional 'classic' picture which no one ever thought to explain. Everything was sensible, practical, and efficient except the purpose of it all, which was supposed to be education, but was actually cramming under discipline. Bells rang, tickets were sold for a hygienic lunch (cream puff and cocoa), classes proceeded so effectively that no one who wished to enter college ever failed to do so, order was kept, the principal sat like a spider in his office or tiptoed like a daddy longlegs peering through doors, all of which were glass-topped for his convenience. The Ford production line does not function more perfectly than did that school, except in education.

Outside were more anomalies of the age. Our 'yard' was large and paved with crushed granite which scraped off some hundreds of yards of skin per year from recess players. It was meticulously clean, and bad language or fighting was never tolerated (when heard or seen); yet its lower limit was the upper wall of the back yards of a filthy slum into which we looked wonderingly, seeing a life for which nothing had prepared us.

Inside everything was departmentalized. There was science — which had nothing to do with religion, and religion (on Fifth Day meeting and for five minutes each morning) which

had nothing to do with school, and literature which was concerned with Shakespeare and the Lake Poets, and Latin which
had nothing to do with anything except syntax. There were
no values (with one exception) except the values of discipline
and knowledge, and a sense (which I do not underestimate) of
the past. As in all American institutions of that day, foreign
languages were taught for reading only, it being incredible that
anyone should have to speak German or French. But the relation between science and our mores, or between the mecha-
nism of physics and the mysticism of Fifth Day meeting, or between history and the very bad politics in action at the City
Hall only five squares away, or between literature and the
emotional content of our rather pallid lives — nothing.

Some enterprising teacher sent me, a freckled-faced, rather
homely boy, to the Court House to gather material for a composition. I came back as ignorant as I went, except for puzzle-
ment as to why the seat of justice should be drenched in tobacco juice and crowded with objectionable people. The local
newspaper next morning carried a story of a golden-haired
youth with an angel face who asked how government was run
and justice administered. If anyone could have persuaded me
that I was angel-faced, I should have died of shame, but the invention was too palpable. I did learn that something had
dropped out between education and reality.

There was no philosophy of education visible in our school,
and it was one of the best. No one had ever thought through
the problem of what education should be in the nineties in
which we were living, and therefore we were dosed with the
same prescriptions as our fathers, or with new medicines (like
science) applied by the same system. It was the Age of Confidence in dosing.

I noted one exception to the absence of values not disciplinary or factual. If our school was a hodge-podge of architectures
and knowledges, it was unified ethically. Ethics breathed
through every brick of it except the boys' (and perhaps the
girls') latrines, though they did not reach the slum below the
playground wall. We had the Bible every morning and twice
on Fifth Day. Once a month we met for literary exercises in
which the most moral poets, such as Longfellow, Whittier, and

Tennyson, were most often heard from. We were lectured by visitors, who never lacked a moral. Our classes in literature always ended with a precept, and the militarism of Caesar was never lifted from its wrappings of grammar. Even physics and chemistry were made to demonstrate the perfectibility of the world.

Strange as it may seem to a new generation, we did not resent this ethical barrage. As I look back, it seems the most valuable part of my early education and perhaps the most valuable education that was offered. The glimpses of scientific method were, of course, powerful in their influences, preparing for the age of automobiles, airplanes, and radio. Yet after all, only a half-century has passed, and already we are shivering before the incapacity of man to adapt himself to the age of science and the machine.

Not that more of our school ethics would help in this emergency. They were agrarian ethics, and we town dwellers already felt their frequent inapplicability and, without realizing the cause, wearied of similes drawn entirely from agriculture. But at least they were ethics — a definite code of motives, actions, character which long experience had shown to result in more happiness and less misery than did error or reckless experiment.

Whether their precepts were one hundred per cent or fifty per cent true, we were, at least, made conscious of the necessity for an ethos. Much of the stability with its resulting content of these slow-changing years in the psychological development of America was due, I fancy, to the trial balance between wrong and right shown daily to every child. He knew that it left out realities, and that was what caused the moral revolution of the early nineteen-hundreds. He felt that it was too rigid and would have to be refigured. But he had something to start with, a frame of reference, which made it easier to grow up in an incalculable world without too much psychological distress.

These ethics, administered to us in almost hourly doses, had an impressive past. The Bible, and the Latin and Greek classics, and, unrecognized, the Hindu and Egyptian sacred books, and all Puritanism, and a good deal more Catholicism than our teachers and parents guessed, and the democratic experience of

America, all were distilled for us, and presented either dilute or in the original packages. As our confidence in the older generation was still strong, some of the distillate was absorbed into our life blood. And much of it was carried in solution in the sonorous prose of the English Bible which leaves no one who hears it esthetically or emotionally forlorn. If later generations have been deprived of this backing of the ages, it is their misfortune, not our fault. The unprecedented circumstances of scientific advance have destroyed the formulas in which we placed our confidence, by inserting new elements whose relation to the moral scheme is not yet clear, thus leaving these generations embarked upon the exciting but dangerous sea of pure experiment.

So much in general; in particular our school had its own peculiar ethics. We were a remnant of the great Quaker movement which spread from Pennsylvania north, south, west, until its shallowing waters became only an undercurrent of the communities where they still flowed. Our ethics were infused always with the central Quaker principle that men and women being essentially good, evil was due to some obfuscation of the Inner Light through accident, or evil influence, or worldly pride. We youngsters were gathered for education from all the local sects, but whatever our home environment we could not escape the insidious Quaker idea that the world was by nature friendly, and the universe also; that there was good will in every man; that reforms did not come through laws and restrictions, but by appeal to the innate goodness in every human heart. Contradictions lay all about us in a town that drank, cheated, fornicated, tyrannized, and was mean, and we had, of course, some realization of this before actual experience. It was saddening as one grew older to encounter unmistakable depravity; it was puzzling to see good men conniving in dead religions or greedy commercialism, because our ethical education (like all our education) had ignored the relationships between theory and practice, or, for that matter, between theory and theory; it stunned us to discover whole ranges of emotion that the Quakers overlooked because they were not interested, or because they knew that bricks to build ideal societies crumbled if the kiln fires were too hot.

Nevertheless, one was better prepared than seemed possible. The Quakers were well aware of the forces of worldliness. Under their gentle but powerful influence we acquired an instinct which subtly pervaded our later thinking. We found it difficult not to believe in the permanent possibility of good in any man. The naïve (and yet not so naïve either) faith in the possibilities of human nature, which was and is characteristic of many American communities, has been usually credited to our national experience in the unlimited richness of an unexploited country. A realistic study of the frontier makes this explanation often doubtful, and sometimes ridiculous. The mild but pervasive influence of the Quakers is a more probable cause, although that influence was so widespread when America was in the making that by its very dilution and absorption it lost the name of Quaker. Certainly we felt it strongly in our school and our town, and to it must be charged some of our confidence in the world.

We got confidence from our education but not unity. Quaker-reared or not, many youths of the nineties seem to have split their personalities somewhere en route to the nineteen-twenties, and for this cleft their early education must have been partly responsible.

I can testify from my own experience. Our school and our town (or at least what we knew as our town) were in excellent accord. The town was naturally more realistic, the school more idealistic; the school had begun, just begun, to think in terms of science, while the town was still assuming that science was only a means of making more money. But in general the order and discipline of our education, the way we soaked up information, the absence of subjects with disturbing emotional contents like evolution or psychology, or studies obviously not utilitarian like music or art, and the strong moral atmosphere in which we worked, were all just right for boys and girls getting ready for life in a community where kind people, honest people, industrious people with no nonsense in them, were sure to be liked. The town was descending rapidly from its old aristocratic system to the level of the 'plain people,' was becoming, like all the East and South and the nearer West, *petit bourgeois* in its mentality. If it were not mean, grasping, and utterly self-centered like a French town of the same size, or split by differences of code and culture like an English provincial city, much credit was due to an education like ours.

It was not the town that changed its character, not, at least, until a whole generation later. Those spiritual and intellectual conflicts which are so much written about seldom involve whole communities or even whole classes. It is not only peasants that have no history, but also the masses of the middle class or the proletariat, except as the type to which they belong flows with the trend of circumstance. Ten years after the upper limits of these chapters, when there was an art school and a visiting symphony orchestra in our town, what I have written above was still generally applicable, though no longer so significant, for bourgeois philistinism by then was clearly on the defensive. In the meantime the boys and girls I knew had either sunk into the mass or themselves had changed and become special cases of escape from environment.

These escapists, and I among them, whose stories have been written by a hundred American novelists, had encountered the twentieth century. Technological advance had led to commercial expansion which, in turn, had ended the isolation and self-sufficiency of the United States. Science had finally made thinking mechanistic. Wealth and easy transportation had strung easy wires to world culture. The rise of the workers in education and economic power made us question our privilege. The break-up of the old codes left us without stabilities. It began to be clear that we could not be both progressive and static without violent inconsistency, and the pausing time, which only seemed to pause because we had been so sure that its verities would last, came to an end for us in the first of the nineteen-hundreds.

And those of us who then escaped from the illusion of a stable environment into the new currents of thought and emotion found ourselves with a cleft in the mind which our generation in America has never been able to heal. We had been trained to fit into certainties, educated to suppose that Mr. Carnegie's steel mills, Sunday observance, the banking system, the Republican Party, the benefits of Latin, algebra, and a good handwriting, and the difference between the 'micks' and Us, were parts of one quite comprehensible plan. We had no more attempted to relate industrial concentration with politics, or our distrust of art with the profit-making motive, than we had tried or been taught to discover a possible connection between Caesar and chemistry, or the Golden Rule and American history.

Hence when acceleration began again, for most of us about 1910, we were cleft. Each new idea, each new emotion such as music when Wagner became comprehensible or painting when we went abroad, each discovery of a subtle relationship, such as that of the law of the conservation of energy with our reluctance to memorize the catechism, was an axe-stroke upon what had been a united consciousness. Our minds breaking up began to reflect lights from every direction, life, which always threatened dullness in our town except among the darkies and the Democrats, became more exciting, and we began to acquire what was our real education. Yet whispering at the back of the new liberal mind was always a question which became more insistent as the years went on. The community in which we had been brought up and the education ground into us were ordered, self-contained, comprehensible, while this new society was incoherent, without fixed aim, and without even a pretense of homogeneity. We were like pond fish who had been flooded into a river.

And if this confusion persists among later generations and tends toward an anarchy of opinion, is it not because the education of youth is still by unrelated units as in our school, while lacking the confidence with which we at least began? That, however, is a question on which, thank Heavens, I am not required to write here!

I have somewhat departed from my plan in this chapter, turning what was intended to be a reminiscence into an essay on the future which has now become the present. I had to do so, because, whatever happened to the individual, the pausing time of formal education still continues, and is just at this moment beginning to accelerate toward change. When I brood on the adventures of the American mind among educators I can stay in the past only by an effort of will. Then I recall with nostalgia the rectitude of those ascetic classrooms where every-

thing that mattered would sooner or later be written in chalk
upon the blackboard, where neither the romance of school life
nor the revolt of a discontented generation clouded our simple
thinking among familiar truths, where moralities equally simple were uttered in the immortal language of King James, and
the teachers spoke with the 'thee' and 'thy' of the Friends of a
world which was going to be friendly if only we would be both
learned and good.

It was about this time that my small sister shattered forever
her confidence in the miraculous healing power of the tiny
sugar pellets which homeopathy prescribed and we devoutly
believed in, by eating at a sitting vast quantities from every
bottle in the case, which neither killed her, as she faintly expected, nor made her feel better, as she had hoped. It was a
symbolic act. We had faith in our education as we had faith
in homeopathy, and faith served us moderately well. But the
test of experience was disastrous. As in the Garden of Eden,
the knowledge of good and evil brought enlightenment but
not peace.

8

Religion

I FIND MY TOO SIMPLE EPITHET, the Age of Confidence, beginning to cleave and fracture when I come to religion. Yes,
some of us were confident in religion, but only the least religious. The current dogmatism today, that economic change
precedes all shifts in philosophies, does not seem to account for
the state of religion in our community as I knew it. Our ideas
of business, or of the relations of labor and capital, or of private property, were hard set in all but the minds of cranks, and
faint memories of a time when principles were more important
than profits were only reminiscences that never went beyond
the duty to be honest; while our religious life was changing so
rapidly that parents and children spoke different languages of
the spirit.

I leave the Roman Catholics aside, as knowing nothing of
their problems, which seemed to us foreign and presumably reduced to the single problem of being a Catholic at all — such
was our religious provincialism. We ourselves, and by we I
mean Us, were divided among three religions, of which two
were spiritually dead, but still walked abroad powerfully, and
the third was dead in the body, but spiritually alive in the subconscious.

The fire had gone out of Episcopalianism and Presbyterianism, but they made up in respectability what they had lost in
fervor. Quakerism was dead. Its meeting-houses were hollow
shells where a few old voices murmured. Its plain clothing
aroused comment when seen on the street. Its mystic exaltation had long since sunk into quietism. Yet its soul lived on
after its discipline had become a picturesque rite. As for the
Baptists and the Methodists, they belonged to the 'plain people,' 'lesser breeds without the law' we would have said if Kipling had written the verse in time for us. Rigid in prejudice, a

little noisy, familiar and too democratic in manners even for those who honestly believed in the equality of souls, these churches were thought of by us as sects from which 'plain people' graduated when they ceased to be plain. And if that was snobbish, supercilious, and ignorant on our part, as it most certainly was, yet we had the frequent evidence of a change to seven-o'clock dinner or a move into a proper neighborhood turning Methodists into Episcopalians infallibly. Getting rich quick (I don't know why) was more likely to end in Presbyterianism.

Religion, like business, in our town had turned *laissez-faire*, although, granting that I had understood the term, nothing would have more surprised me than to be told so. Next to school, for my generation, there was nothing more obligatory, less *laissez-faire* in its root sense, than religion. For the middle-aged, going to church may have been a social rite, for the young it was duty. Ethically it meant very little, since, no matter how much one respected the preacher as a person, his platitudes slipped over the lazy mind. Emotionally, while the decorum and frequent beauty of the Episcopal service to which I was chiefly exposed, had its deep effect, that passion of the throbbing and uplifted heart which is always possible to youth found no air to breathe in so respectable an atmosphere. It stirred in many of us, I suspect, and flowered in some with the rebirth of ritualism. Yet my experience was probably typical. I can remember moments of almost rapturous self-dedication, never made articulate, and then a long chilling descent as the rationalism of week-day education slowly undermined naïve beliefs. Yet it was not science that emptied our religion of content, although how a youth of the nineties was supposed to study physics and anthropology on Monday without curdling in his unsubtle mind the milk of Sunday's doctrine, I fail to see. Such conflicts presented no apparent difficulties to our elders. I remember the somewhat contemptuous surprise of my professor of English at Yale when I asked him whether biology and Wordsworth were not uncomfortable neighbors. Only the young, he implied, were bothered by such problems. A poet himself, he died sterile, perhaps because it was science in his day that was fertile, not Wordsworth.

We went to church neither to be social nor to be good, nor, save for brief intervals, to be uplifted, but because of something much deeper than any of these motives, a taboo against staying away that had kept its power, although its inner significance was lost. I mean just that. The nineties, by and large, went to church because they were afraid. Social conformity had its part, and I should be most untrue to memory if I did not acknowledge the pleasant savor of duty on a Sunday still lifted above the grosser, more obvious manners of the week. For with clean collar and cuffs and a Sunday suit, one put on decorum, and in the calm of the quiet neighborhood the mind relaxed, and when the bells began, the slow march of so many church-goers ranged by families, and dressed for a rite, stirred in the consciousness a sense of immemorial racial custom. The rhythm of that day was different, and psychologists will argue that this was more important than anything we did or heard except in so far as our doing and our hearing were tuned to these Sunday iambs following a pattern long since set.

What we heard was often trivial. My memories of Sunday School are of Bible stories parroted by misses doing their duty, and of a catechism as meaningless in that untheological age as a treatise on alchemy, yet memorized and rememorized. Nor do I think that the Bible verses, also memorized, meant much more to us than my own improvisation at the age of five, 'Holy is the Ghost when the Lord shines on Her.' Nevertheless, I am sure that the Chinese are right in saying that moral precepts heard again and again eventually do something to the brain.

What we did seems even more insignificant. We went to church, we went to Sunday School, we read Sunday magazines expressly issued for youth in a Sunday rhythm, and whose content I forget far more completely than the catechism, and we walked decorously in the Brandywine woods, or on special occasions had spiritual experiences with Nature (which we spelled with a capital) that came nearer than the rest to true religion. Games were taboo, especially cards and ball playing, reading, except from the Sunday School Library, the Bible, and (why?) *Illustrated America*, were taboo also, but that restriction must have been half-hearted, since Dickens, Scott, and Sunday I associate with no sense of sin. Shouting and all uproar were taboo for children, and anything like a party for adults. What we did, therefore, outside of church was chiefly negative. The theory ran that the mind was not to be distracted from its solemn duties. The duties outside of church-going had become abstract, and no one of my acquaintance so much as thought about them. Nevertheless, the mind, freed from the weekly routine, and held back from active pleasure, did quietly fit meditation to the Sunday rhythm and mingle with boredom a sedate happiness, which is one of the experiences in living that I believe is now lost.

All this negatively, as a result of inhibition or prohibition. On the positive side, we observed Sunday, as I have said, because of a taboo, because we were afraid. It will be difficult to persuade those under thirty of this fact, for I do not know their analogous taboos, but only that they have them. We were afraid, not rationally, not of the jealous and vindictive God with whom my Presbyterian grandmother used to threaten me, which was not often, for my mother kept her off. As a child, thanks to her and an occasional sermon, I used to lie awake saying that hell was burning forever and ever and ever, biting upon the awful fact of eternity as upon an anguished tooth. But neither Quakers nor Episcopalians countenanced such child-baiting with the morbid horrors of divine revenge, nor encouraged, either, any sentimental ecstasies upon an eternity of heavenly bliss.

We were afraid, as youths, and after youth, of nothing either metaphysical or tangible, but rather with that most primitive of all fears, an instinctive dread of a broken habit, the sense of the unwisdom of not doing what the ancients had been sure was right. It was custom, which is a step deeper than use and wont, that sent us to church after church began to be meaningless. It was custom which kept us decorous on the Lord's Day. No one expected to burn in hell for a game of whist on Sunday, or thought of an escape from morning service as flouting the God of Israel. But uneasiness remained, something irrational below the line of thought, a strong unwillingness to act against the mores not unlike the will to be a gentleman. Three-quarters of my generation were church-goers, not because they feared God, but because they feared something much more real

to them than God, conscience, not the theological conscience of
the catechism, but a consciousness of the mandate of the tribe.
If I may use pre-psychological terms, the mind of the Sabbath-
breaker might scoff, but his body was afraid.

And this is why I assert that for all its obligatory aspects religion with us, like childhood and marriage, was *laissez-faire*.
For most certainly the rectors, the ministers, the elders of the
meeting in our town, never doubted that the church, if allowed to work upon us, was entirely competent to take care of
our religious life. They were aware of distractions, they
preached against non-attendance, they reiterated that the Word
of God in the Bible contained all necessary for man's salvation,
but they were incredibly blind to the rapid decline of our religion from faith and even passion to conformity, from conformity to indifference, from indifference to a habit backed by
an instinctive fear of change. The Quakers sat in stolid rows
along which the Inner Light was no longer transfused from
face to face, the Episcopalians perfected the technique of decorum, the Presbyterians piled moral on morality, the Methodists and the Baptists ranted of the Blood of the Lamb, while
year by year their motives, their observances, their very terms
became more meaningless to a generation that listened from
habit only. The church, we were told, was a heavenly city, of
which we had merely to become citizens in order to be saved.
Thirty years later we were to be told that the United States
was a perfect institution in which all conforming citizens
would become good Americans, its economic system such that
all who did their part were sure to be rich. The analogy is not
strained. Our godly leaders offered us the seventeenth century
— and we were living in the *fin de siècle*. They asked for a day
a week, and got it, and could do nothing with it because what
they said was not true; the church they offered would not function for our nineteenth-century minds; its once sweet influence
flowed over us, and left us a little disturbed, a little refreshed,
but the same men as before. *Laissez-faire* was to succeed a little
longer in politics and economics, in religion its date was already out.

Much of all this, I fancy, might have been written of any
town in America in the age which was confident of pretty much

everything but its religion; yes, and of any town in England or Scotland also, with local exceptions for the still austere fundamentalism of our South and perhaps parts of the British North, and the passionate attempts of the high Anglicans here and abroad to do away with *laissez-faire* in their own fashion. Our own local circumstances were, however, peculiar. Presbyterianism I really knew very little about, although more than of other aspects of the age and our town with which I did not have even imaginative contacts, and which I am skirting in a book that will have at least the merit of being first-hand testimony from memory and not from documents. I was dipped in its confident theism by a grandmother aforementioned, who seemed to me to talk very familiarly about God, not in the gentle Quaker fashion, but as a small boy talks of a cruel big brother who has licked him, and will lick you, on any provocation. I was married by its bleak ceremony. But chiefly I knew Presbyterians. They seemed in our community to be more troubled by morality than others of my acquaintance; at least they talked more about it, though otherwise they were indistinguishable from the rest except by a hard efficiency, the men being leaders in industry and commerce, the women founts of social service.

The truth was that this immensely energetic religion had become a pseudomorph, like a crystal which retains an original form while changing its composition. The Presbyterians among us were notoriously good; they were the backbone (and the teeth) of our ethics, and far more effective in preserving a high moral tone than the Methodists, who were always slipping into sentiment or hardening into fanaticism. Yet I never knew a Presbyterian who seemed to me religious, not even a minister. Their godliness had turned into moral energy, and the church had become a dynamo which kept up the moral voltage while never touching the heart. Presbyterian families were serviceable to the community, but tended to be hard within. The parents often dominated the children and were coldly used in old age. Brothers seldom liked brothers. Houses were austere and uncomfortable. Duty was the word used oftenest. They got on and were good citizens, but their moral energy was impersonal, a little chilled by having run so far from its source.

Their church in fact, while dead as a religion, was alive as a force that made for certain kinds of righteousness. It succeeded because it came nearer to the religion of business which every American town was preaching then than did any other American sect. Still, youth was a little shy of it — it was the kind of organization you joined when you had a tail coat for Sundays, were getting on in the bank, and needed a good address and a moral context. And then the old Presbyterians with their mumblings of a jealous God seemed rather terrible. They jarred on susceptibilities rendered sensitive by a suppressed skepticism, and made us conscious of a break in continuity between theology and efficiency. Christ seemed rather uncomfortable in the Presbyterian service, and so were we strays from the Quakers and the Episcopalians.

If I write that Episcopalianism was dead in our town also, I do so with hesitancy, since, with me at least, its memories are living. The community, like so many in the middle regions of the East, had once been in Quaker dominance, and when the slow petrifaction of that beautiful faith had driven out of meeting the generations just before ours, they had flocked from the decorum of simplicity to the decorum of an orderly ritual. And joined with them were the old Episcopalians, many of them from down state, who for centuries had been so easily fitted to their flexible religion that its prescriptions and its language were too much a part of their environment to admit of skepticism or change. But it was dead. We were not supposed to take it too seriously. It had become a rhythm, the best Sunday rhythm, providing, like no other, an accompaniment of excellent words to quiet meditation. Only the forms could be taken seriously; the altar cloths which my mother embroidered, the churches built in a good tradition, the observances duly arranged in an ordered and intelligible system historically justified and linking the present with the past. It was a human church too, which was aware that the 'beauty of holiness' was more than a phrase, and so recognized the need of an esthetic outlet for rich widows or retired industrialists who would have been ashamed to go to a symphony concert, but could satisfy a dumb craving for esthetic expression by a carved pulpit, or a stained-glass window which, if weak and smeary with Mr. Tiffany's early favrile glass, seemed to them both modern and religious, and a tribute to their taste and some dead one's virtues, all at comparatively small expense.

But I think that even when my pre-Raphaelitish sensibilities quivered at a sudden identification of the *Te Deum* which was being sung with the religious fervor of all the ages, the emotion came from literature, not the church. Except as beautiful decorum and a moral influence that church was dead. It had declined from religion into an apotheosis of esthetic respectability. There was something solid and guaranteed in the morning service — the scent of heavy flowers, choir boys marching ('micks' in private life and most of them Catholics), Prince Albert coats, flowered hats, children ranged stepwise by families, and Mr. Johns, our rector, with his side whiskers and faintly English accent. There was a surety of what would happen, what would be said next, who would be there and when; there were the tones of the Bishop's blessing and the amplitude of his Byzantine beard, the assurance at offertory that this was Saint Swithin's Day, the clink of silver, pat of rolled bills, one's father looking sanctified as he carried his plate up the aisle, the restful pause after the last chord of the Recessional, and then far off in the vestry the faint 'And now to God the Father, God the Son, and God the Holy Ghost . . . ' It was all right, exactly right for an Age of Confidence that still valued security in the midst of progress; it was so unchallengable because so perfect, like a movement of a Beethoven symphony. If the heart had lost meaning, the body lived on without a heart.

And still lives for many in both heart and body, especially those for whom its symbolism is more articulate, and who believe that, like Latin in the Middle Ages, its language can interpret every human need.

But not for most of us then at the turn of the century, when the rationalisms of science were just beginning to shoot sharp electric currents of skepticism through the mind. For us it was dead beauty, a little awesome, a little boring, an obligation more than a faith. And transparently, religion, or at least this church religion, was dead for our elders. They never talked of it, they never thought of it as such, they took their Sundays as they took their meals, for granted. Episcopalianism, especially, for them was above everything else a social unity. It seems to have been obscurely felt that the family destined for Society acquired naturally an Episcopal mind, so that the most flagrant climbing was condoned when outsiders joined the church. There was some reason in this, since our church, being manners apotheosized, the wrong people in it were as uncomfortable as in dress coats and low necks. It had also that quality of all good societies, tolerant listening, which took nothing too hard, neither social service like the Presbyterians, nor rites and observances like the Catholics. It was a gentleman's church, a cultivated church with a good literature in its prayer book, an easy-going but rather snobbish church, a church that, discouraging fanatics and sentimentalists, could provide for any well-mannered person except those who insisted on erecting altars in their own hearts.

And that was the trouble. Like our Society, it could not live up to its own meaningful decorums, which became more and more perfunctory as the congregation yielded to work-a-day commercialism and were revealed as business men and society women patronizing an institution. We younger ones, when our suppressed fervor released by the inherent beauty of the Anglican forms had sunk back to boredom, took it all at face value, an institution, decorous, respectable, protected by a taboo, capable of arousing a nostalgia for traditional emotions, but otherwise meaningless to us because our spiritual problems were in a different language. We remained Episcopalians, but little by little, as the taboo weakened, and our minds grew hot with the new ideas of the twentieth century, ceased going to church.

Among all the Protestant sects the doctrine of *laissez-faire* might seem to have been most justified among the Quakers, and among them all there did it succeed the least. Our town, which had once been prevailingly Quaker, was now, even among the descendants of the Friends, Quaker in manners only, not in name or in spirit. The Negroes, of course, had been untouched by Quakerism — it was an impossible religion for their rich, primitive natures; the Irish and most of the German immigrants had come too late; the Democrats from down state were as invulnerable as the Negroes. Meekness was not a quality which attracted them. Nevertheless the mass of the 'plain people' had a faculty for simple friendliness and a prejudice against display which was a direct inheritance from the Great Experiment when it was hoped that every man would call his neighbor brother.

My own friends were most of them descended like myself from outcasts or backsliders or last remnants of the Meeting. A father had married a Presbyterian, a mother had acquired a taste for purple and fine linen, or had followed business or fashion into a church. The growing rigidity of a sect that insisted on an outward as well as an inward unworldliness had repelled them. Yet they were quite unable to escape from an early training, and we from their influence. They still found God, when they found Him at all, in their breasts, and were curiously shy of speaking of Him, unless in the print of a prayerbook. Religion for them remained highly personal, which was one reason why they left Quakerism so easily. A collarless coat and 'thee' and 'thy' to strangers came to seem a display of religious preference repugnant to their Quaker instincts, whereas the ritualism of Episcopalianism, in which most of them took refuge, was performed in crowds and came only once a week. By a curious reversal, what had been simplicity for the old Quakers had become its opposite: the plain clothes a uniform, the plain language an affectation.

These parents of ours had kept the Quaker manners. Extravagance and affectation offended them equally and for the same reason. They hated above all things a row, as if their spirits had become tender (a favorite Quaker word) and could not be subjected to the brawlings of egoism or temper without shocks to the inner man. And much more strongly than the doctrine of their new churches they felt the value of an emotional integrity, that serenity of spirit which comes from a harmony between the ego and its environment. So in practice they left creeds and moralities to the Sunday School teachers, teaching us their religion by an evident faith in quiet and harmonious living. Of this, their true religion, they never spoke, and hence I think that we never realized it was a religion, and never relied upon its vital experiences as a conscious argument when creeds became unreal and moralities unfortified. They, too, practiced *laissez-faire*.

I went to meeting every Fifth Day — that is to say, Thursday — as a part of the routine of the Hicksite Friends School which I attended. It was not supposed to be a religious experience; in fact, probably at the instigation of our rector, or of my grandfather who was strongly Orthodox, I was told so. How could it be! They were the wrong kind of Quakers, the Hicksites, who did not believe in the Trinity, and somehow had stolen the meeting-house in days past from an Orthodox minority. And they were evidently a dying sect. On the raised benches of time-softened wood which faced us sat a bare dozen of elders, men and women, plain worn faces such as one sees in daguerreotypes, with the Quaker serenity that I knew in our ancestral portraits, and indeed in my grandfather's face, yet hardened here by a consciousness of defeat. And when they spoke — and especially Ezra Fell, who, by the convention of a society that did not believe in a paid ministry, was moved with some regularity by a concern to impart the Word — their voices were harsh and uncultivated, their eloquence ranting, their substance a defeatist plea for the immanence of what seemed to be a discouraged God.

And yet on the green-cushioned benches under the bare beams of that meeting-house, with tree branches fretting at the windows, where a hundred of us youngsters sat in silence for most of the hour, I had my most pervasive religious experiences. I did not think; I did not knowingly feel. My meditation was wordless and almost without content. I began with daydreams following the imagined path of a squirrel over the speaker's canopy, but soon they faded into quietness. Doors opened far within; the consciousness withdrew itself from externals; nerves, relaxed into tranquillity, were of an exquisite sensitiveness. We went in romping and turbulent. We came out far removed from each other, each in an island of calm over which the waves of routine would quickly sweep; yet it had been there, would be bared again. I can think of no other instance where a religious ceremony, not respected and in the charge of the crusted and incapable, almost meaningless in the words articulated, has had so powerful an effect upon so many who believed themselves alien. It made me in some respects a Quaker for life, although I had to join a church and leave it before I discovered what had happened to me in adolescence.

Here indeed was an area of experience in which *laissez-faire* might have been successful. But unfortunately the old Quakers were not content with what their meeting gave. They asked our generation feebly, where their fathers had asked the previous generation peremptorily, to come out of the world into what seemed, and often was, a stiff-necked obscurantism. Our world was not, as they asserted, only a market-place for greed and passion. It was vivid with intellectual excitements of which they were ignorant, and confident in discoveries which, far more than spiritual equality, so it seemed to us, promised hope for every man. They put their faith in negatives, in Quaker denial and Quaker renunciation, and that would have repelled us even if those worn plain figures on the high benches could have even for a moment tempted us to follow them. And yet they had a secret which was perhaps the only philosophy that could protect the innermost mind against the roar and rattle of the jazz age that was coming. They had access to quiet.

Perhaps this is the reason that in our town, still half Quaker in the nineties, I seem to remember a widespread content, sometimes merely crass, but often serene, and always pervasive, which I suspect was the last inheritance from the attempt to make all the world friends by virtue of an Inner Light that shone through all.

I may be falsifying history by thus extending the consciousness of a personal experience — but is not the only verifiable history personal? That I believe; and therefore add for the other side of the balance that the long ebb of Quakerism in our town had left a flatness of living and thought more frequently encountered than true simplicity or spiritual clairvoyance. It left gentle characters stranded and rather helpless on an unfriendly earth that did not treat them too kindly. Years afterward I met an ex-Quaker from our town still shaken from the heavy explosion of a German bomb dropped on our London street. 'I never knew how false pacifism was,' he said, 'until I saw the houses wrecked by that bomb.' The truth was that he had never before been really frightened. His dislike of violence had been only a habit, in which the fiery principle had long since sunk to ashes. And indeed in most of the Quaker-born little remained of the old faith but a manner of handling life, which was not religion, though certainly mores.

We in our town were indeed insulated from religion. The earnest moralist was let loose upon us, and the eager ritualist, and occasionally the ranter, and, as I have said, some of us experienced religion unconsciously among the dying Quakers. And yet I can remember only one impression of religion as an exclusive passion, and that in an old, blind Quaker, expecting death. The parents left it to the church, and the church left it to the service or to the Bible. I cannot say that the hungry sheep looked up and were not fed, for they seldom looked up, and yet, by any modern comparison, were crammed with doctrine. Christianity, like Americanism, was something that you were to acquire by doing what you were told. It was one of the certainties, whose much-advertised presence made the age comfortable, as well as confident, for people who liked to feel that safety was always near at hand. But there was no vital contact between its magnificent mysticisms and traditional discipline, and our cocky certainty that we lived in the age of progress. The two certainties dwelt together like a plus and minus that have not yet been joined. It was agreeable that way, since it is never comfortable to be either entirely religious or anti-religious. The decorum and the sweet influence of religion were ours without the ardors and obligations. Its moral sanctions protected us from untoward desire. We knew right and wrong by heart, and so could live by convention, which is a great convenience for a society that craves harmony. If only we went to church on Sunday, religion let us alone and we could let alone religion.

Modern paganism reached its peak, I believe, at the end of the last century, and it is only with the breakdown of the balance of power between Sunday and week-days that we have begun again to take soul or the lack of it seriously. The most blatant Communist mechanist is more truly concerned with religion than was that static age where everything stood still or moved slowly except the rapid conquest of nature which we call progress. It *was* progress then, and perhaps there was never a time when the human race, or at least the Americans, seemed to have so little need of more than a conventional religion.

ᶜᵔ⟩ 9 ⟨ᵔᶜ

Sex and Marriage

WHATEVER MAY BE TRUE of the birth-rate, sexual inter-course probably maintains a pretty constant ratio through the ages. However, it is not the amount of sexuality, but its influence upon youth, its part in maturity, that is really important. Therefore, I can understand the violence of the current attacks upon the sexual life of the end of the last century, since the writers who charge the eighties and nineties with puritanism, inhibitions, psychic sterility, hypocrisy, ve-neered lasciviousness, or frigidity, clearly feel that the estimate which any period places on its sex life is important, and are irritated by the novelists' and biographers' accounts of the last years of Victorianism. Yet as I remember life as it seemed to be, and probably was, in our town, there seem to be some striking fallacies in what now is said about it. Most that is said is true, but not true enough. There was more to the story.

A difference did exist. You could not purchase a humorless Art of Erotics in any bookstore, and even such a mild word as 'prostitute' was neither heard nor read in polite circles, but this gets nowhere near the heart of the matter. Again, every ob-server must note the extraordinary increase in the known vic-tims of sexual repression or sexual maladjustment today. If there were as many in the age of inhibition, they certainly gave less evidence of suffering either in body or in mind, prob-ably because they were fortunate in not knowing what was the matter with them. There seems to have been less appendicitis too! As for the *Ars Amatoria*, I suspect that we needed it badly, but in our crude way got along without. More of that later.

The true difference between now and then was that sex ex-periences, and, to a remarkable extent, sex desire, were canal-

79

ized. In youth we were ignorant of the art of love, but of very little else in amorous experience, good or bad. With Us and with the 'plain people' the ethics of the matter were almost identical, and changed very little as one followed through to the working people, except that the males were more frankly predatory and the females more willing to toy with the approaches to erotic experience. The sex morals of the working girl of 1890 were about the same as those of the society girl or college graduate of 1930. We who belonged to the most respectable families in the community knew from early childhood of whores and easy women, but there was no equivocation in that knowledge. Ben Franklin's injunction to practice venery only for health would have shocked us. We knew that there were addicts who could not keep away from women, just as we knew that even among our own class there were nymphomaniacs. We were as well aware of venery as of drunkenness, but no one thought of defending it. This was one of the things that oughtn't to be done, but was. Those who practiced it much joined with those who practiced it not at all, in knowing that it was wrong. Indeed, youth overstepped its natural chastity out of bravado more often than from desire. If we sinned it was with no illusions, and a mimimum of rationalization.

It was not our sins, however, but our supposed lack of sinning which gives to the 'Victorian' nineties its air of a lacy valentine, amorous but innocent. 'Nice people' in the nineteenth century, so the legend runs, were inhibited sexually, hence the thinness of their emotions, the genteelness of their literature.

I am not sure that in any true psychological sense we were inhibited at all, or at least not with companions of our own class and kind. It is perfectly true that sex in its more concentrated and obvious forms had little part in our relationships, perhaps because the female form from breast to ankle had never been more thoroughly wrapped and falsified than in our day, but much more probably for reasons that were psychical rather than physical. We were familiar by hearsay or experience with the sexual in every sense, yet did not think in those terms of the girls of our own class for a simple reason — we did not want to. That came after marriage. Before, in the dif-

ferent freedom of youth, it was what biologists call the secondary sex manifestations that excited us. Romance suffused the
American nineties, and romance was incompatible with our
quite realistic knowledge of sex. A thrilling imagination sometimes suggested the possibility of joining the two, but that was
to be later. The girl must be won first, and won romantically,
for according to the perhaps somewhat naïve belief held in my
town, she could not, if she were the right girl, be won by sexual
appeal alone. If she was so won, she was not the right girl.
That we all believed, and some went so far as to put it to the
test!

Of course, we grossly underestimated the sexual possibilities
of the refined female, yet, on the other hand, we did give the
complete woman a better chance. Beauty we estimated much
more highly than today, and perhaps, as some believe, the
girls were more beautiful, which is credible, since seductiveness
or any strong sex impulse is a disturbing factor in the absolute
of beauty. Comradeship we ranked high, and good spirits, and
character, though if a girl were pretty enough she could dazzle
us out of such sensible perceptions of the truth about women.
But sex, naked and unashamed, with no purpose but its own
gratification, was kept in its place, which was not friendship,
not even the state of falling in love.

The result was a free association of boys and girls in their
teens and early twenties that perhaps never has existed on the
same plane elsewhere in the history of the modern world. We
had confidence in each other, and we were confided in. All
through the Adirondack woods we climbed together in summer, sleeping in cabins, girls on one side, boys on the other,
following by couples all day lonely and difficult trails, and in
the winter skated far-off ponds or sat all night in the spring
on moonlit Delaware hills, falling in and out of love with
never a crude pang of sex, though in a continuous amorous excitement which was sublimated from the grosser elements of
love. It was unreal if it had lasted for life, it was unnatural if it
were to be all, it was juvenile in the limits of its emotions, and
yet there was a healthy tranquillity which served as the norm
for our excitement, a free play of character and personality
which still seems to me the best state for youth. Our fathers

and mothers had enjoyed no such freedom, for to them our
light-hearted irresponsibility would have seemed a vice, if not
a sin. Our children's liberty is much greater, but it is not our
freedom. It is not the orchard to play in, but the apple that
hangs there so self-consciously and has to be eaten, which fills
their imagination. They are sex-conscious; we were not, though
equally knowing in sex.

It was *laissez-faire* again, and possible of success only because we had our code, and lived by it. And I think that, as
with the children, environment had much to do with this success. One met one's girl, not in the transitoriness of a week-
end, or at the end of three hundred miles of auto road, but for
long acquaintance. She would be there and you would be
there next week, next year. She was one of a family, and that
family part of a community which was yours. She carried with
her the sanctions and the refusals of Society.

And hence I deny that our town, or at least the youth of our
town, was hypocritical, unless it be hypocritical to keep inflam-
mables cool and sweet. And I deny that we were inhibited; on
the contrary, by delegating our passions to the future, we were
compensated in the present for whatever intensities we may
have lost. We gained a happy comradeship, not deep, not rich,
but serene without dullness and varied without strain. Unknowing, we took fearful risks, for if our post-adolescence,
which was not so much innocent as artificial in its restraints,
should continue into full maturity, into marriage, there was
danger of an emotional infantilism in middle age. And that
was what often did happen, and is the justification of the taunts
of the emancipated moderns. Their volleys overshoot our
youth. There was something attained then, fragile, light-
blooded, impossible of long continuance, but in its way golden,
romantic, and delectable.

That was the ideal and frequently realized, but even in
youth and among the best-behaved in our community, sex adjustments were often difficult. The sex chase, where pursuit is
part of the game, is not satisfied by prostitution, which in a
small city was an affair of lust and alcohol, vulgarized, and
quite without veils or illusions, nor is it put off by a code, nor
always compensated for by the very best of companionship.

The boys sought elsewhere for what they did not get in friendship and the respectful amorousness of equals. They raided the amusement parks or the evening streets in search of girls that could be frankly pursued for their physical charms. 'Chippies' was the cant name, which implied something between shaded virtue and easy yielding. It was the old woman hunt restrained by a moral taboo on seduction and fear of results if one went too far — what the next generation called 'petting,' but simpler and more honest because her pretty face, her shapely limbs, were all there was to a 'chippy' — companionship, friendliness never entered to complicate a simple and exciting relationship except in surprising moments when a plaything, struggling against a last and not too determined assault, became suddenly a human being pleading to be aided against the ardors of her own blood.

It was erotic play, a spice for summer evenings, and to this naïve eroticism, which stretched the code without releasing or satisfying passion, may have been due some of the too common sex frustrations and maladjustments of the next decades. We learned to associate amorous ardors with the vulgar, or, worse, with the commonplace, and to dissociate them sharply from romance. Our sensual emotions escaped from the control of our imaginations, so that in love and marriage later we found it difficult to bring the two together again. Outright prostitution, or the cold-blooded sex experimentation of twentieth-century youth, may have been less dangerous than this sexual trifling.

The girls of our own kind who were high-sexed, and therefore amorous and desirous of the chase, were debased by this double standard in women. There was no compromise for them. Either they suppressed their amativeness, trying to become good companions like the rest, but succeeding only in being coquettish to the edge of hysteria or morbidly sentimental; or they yielded just enough for too tight embraces in the dance or permitted fondlings, and lost caste. The word 'degenerate' was not in common use then, but that, most unfairly, was what we felt about them. And I remember that the men were more ruthless in characterizing them than were the girls.

The excitement of free companionship, and even the romance which sublimated primitive sex desire into poetic emotion, began to wear thin by the middle twenties. In the mid-thirties the romance had either mellowed into the serenity of a good marriage, or become a facile geniality, oily and paper-thin. I doubt whether sex adjustments between husband and wife were more difficult in the age of real confidence in marriage than now, although the ideal of romantic companionship which we carried into matrimony certainly presented its difficulties. Much less was said and thought about these difficulties, and the percentage of reasonably successful marriages seems to have been remarkably high, which must have meant success in sexual relations also.

It is presumably better to enter upon wedlock aware that all males and females act, or wish to act, very much alike when embracing, than through that golden haze of romance in which we groped our way to realization that love and lust are bedfellows. Yet when that discovery is made, the real problems of sex in matrimony have only just begun. We did not give each other advice, as everyone seems to do now, in print and out of it, and therefore knew fewer ready-made solutions that would prove to be irrelevant. Free and frank sex information for all is splendid. I believe in it now and, with all my contemporaries of the early nineteen-hundreds, would have preferred it instead of being put off with the hums and haws and salacious winks of the family doctor. But too much is claimed for its benefits. The youth of a later generation crams up on a book, passes his first tests, and thinks he is educated. We blundered our ignorant way through the matrimonial college, and learned by misadventure the inadequacy of romance. Since the intimate relations of man and woman had not been stereotyped for us, we studied the art of love with humble minds, and so remained students in human relationships long beyond the age when modern youth thinks it has graduated. That is not the only reason why our marriages lasted better; there are others less creditable, yet it is certainly a reason. Ignorant and, after marriage, somewhat hypocritical in sex, when our neat categories of 'clean men' and libertines, or 'nice girls' and 'chippies,' slid into confusion in the privacies of wedlock, we acquired humility as well as complexes, and were less likely than our children to expect perfect compatibility in six months.

I write in retrospect. In the nineties marriage in our town put its emphasis elsewhere than on sex. Novelists of the period knew that when marriages went wrong, sex was almost the last thing to be taken into account, and it was quite as much their sense for current values as reticence which kept them off the bedward side of experience. Marriage with us, though not a parlor or dining-room affair, nor to be thought of only in the terms of the parenthood I have discussed in earlier chapters, was dramatized in our imaginations as a state in which sex was only incidental. Sex, as they say of poultry in the market, was steady and quiet. Old roosters were lively, young broilers up and down, but fowls kept their price, and their counsel.

There were fewer scandals than today among the married, although more was made scandalous. Anecdotes, nevertheless, throng to my memory, but to retell them would be to compose a feeble imitation of what a good novelist could do better. Since it is a key to a vanishing age that I seek, scandals or secret episodes are less useful than the curious tone of life recovered from the memory of quite trivial episodes. There were few exposures, especially among the Quaker families, that would excite a tabloid reporter of the nineteen-thirties, although more secret episodes than any of us would have believed at the time.

Yet when skeletons did emerge from our family closets, they were seldom called phallic. They were more usually attributed to drunkenness or dishonesty. If there was a woman behind, she certainly did not get all the credit, and perhaps the generation that made opinion then were right in refusing to talk about her. Woman or no woman, it was, so they believed, usually drink or extravagance that started the trouble.

This attitude toward sex-in-marriage was highly *laissez-faire*. It was the married couple's business to enjoy or endure — the possible social consequences were scarcely thought of. Maladjustment might break through convention into divorce, but short of that it seldom broke through reticence. If there were scandals, they had to be in the grand manner — a wronged woman appealing to the law and society only when she had encountered the intolerable: old General Brant flaunting opinion with a mistress kept openly at the Blue Board Tavern on the pike; the ardent and erratic Hopkinson who was said to have divided a million between his wife and the husband of the lady he wished to marry. But generally speaking, our town would have been mildly astonished if it had been told that the success of marriage depended upon embracing. They took what they found, and made the best of it according to their lights. And their marriages were at least as good as they themselves were, which certainly cannot be said of the wedlock of later decades.

Security is what they sought in marriage, possibly the best of all long-term objectives for a man and wife — but a sex-secure society, which our town also desired with a strength of will that amounted to passion, is a much more dubious affair. For outside of a happy marriage sex is secure only when it is satiated, dulled, or dead. Of course it never was secure, with houses of ill fame known to everyone and 'chippies' loose on the street, but if the Age of Confidence was sometimes naïve, it was not idiotic. While only the fanatics expected to abolish prostitution, public opinion everywhere united to keep it regarded (and restrained) as a sin. No more security could be hoped for in that quarter; but if the prostitute and easy woman could be branded as outcasts, then respectable society, so they thought, might be kept free from salacious desire.

I am not writing sociology or even psychological and social history except in a modest memoir fashion, hence I can and must neglect all the implications but one of the last paragraph — the effect in our town, upon Us, of this ideal of sex security.

It made, as I have said, a golden age of free companionship for youth, but for the middle-aged it drew the cork and let the wine flatten. The tone, the touch, the ingredient that was lacking in our society for those past their twenties was so subtle, so formless that I despair of getting it accurately into words; and yet it was because some salt was missing that society in maturity was hollow except in the home and amidst homely things. We were restless in our genial social life because we had tacitly agreed that except in sin or in the reticence of marriage, sexual desires did not exist.

As a youth I was puzzled by the after-dinner parties at our house because they did not follow the pattern familiar to me in fiction. At dinner the sexes were adequately mingled, the conversation playing upon the surface of easy banter. Afterward, without that separation for coffee practiced in more formal societies, the guests flowed into the living room and even in flowing separated into austral and oriental currents while the tides of talk rose and took on different notes. With an obvious relief the men gathered around the fireplace dropping facetiousness, while the women's conversation (much the better) sought human values around my mother's coffee table. I said that the two sexes lost interest in each other because these people were old; but they were not old, not even their glands were old; it was their imagination that had suffered from the restraint of something vital.

For these men and women (good friends all) had tacitly agreed to look upon each other as sexless, and that was becoming fatal to their companionship. By convention as strong as faith, they left out of their relationship precisely that which might have made it as stimulating as a meeting between man and congenial man or woman and sympathetic woman. Hence my father and the wife of his oldest friend, stranded in a corner, relapsed into silences, and the only men at ease with the women were the hee-hawers of stale gallantry, and the only women at ease with the men were the gigglers and teasers. 'Did they talk like this,' I asked in my naïveté, 'at the court of Louis XIV?' Disregarding the not inconsiderable difference in selection and cultural level, they certainly did not, and for the obvious reason that the Count of So-and-So was keenly aware that Madame the Marquise, while wife and mother, was also very much a woman. But that, in the Age of Confidence, was not the right idea of matrimony at all. Hence every man was all man in his club or business or at the saloon bar (and this is one reason for the popularity of the old saloon), but less than man in the company of any respectable woman but his mother or his wife. And every married woman was less than woman in mixed society because her sex was dormant, canalized, inhibited, because no male present (with the faint possibility of an exception for her husband) imagined her as she was.

While a new freedom, amounting often to libertinism, was to break through this convention, it would be a vulgar error to suppose that libertinism was what was lacking in the society of our town. There was plenty of that in a gross way, and a little in the grand manner, but society as such was not touched thereby, nor could be, nor should have been. No, the trouble was the Tennysonism of the sexular attitude, the Longfellowism of our morality. The only possible relationship between men and women that is as vital as the relationship between men or between women is one in which even the married and the be-childrened, and the faithful to their spouses, still feel a permanent possibility of sexual awakening. It does not have to be mutual, it is enough that the most settled should know that their nature is still tender, and inflammable by nature if not by will. We, in our early middle age, talked to middle-aged women as if they were cinders — agreeable, yes, admirable often, interesting often, yet cinders, good for home walks and garden beds, but long emptied of fire — and like cinders they responded. And hence that subtle interpretation of the special knowledge of each which can make an idea glow between a man and a woman was frozen at the source of its rays.

Women suffered most, for the male intellect in an age busy with things had plenty of satisfying fact to talk about. Women past their twenties, or married, suffered dumbly from an imagination that made them sexless, because they did not know what was wrong and would not have admitted the truth if it had been told to them. But men suffered too by a kind of vivacious dullness which was the note of the period. Leave out manganese (or is it magnesium?) from the diet of a bitch and she will cease to nurse her puppies. An element, not necessarily the most important, was excluded from the daily diet of our relationships, with the result that society grew anemic as it grew older. Unrest or boredom hovered in the corners under the potted palms of ballrooms; the friendship was real but the gaiety forced, and even with fine people had a note of the trivial and the commonplace. Only a few old tomcats who had kept the convention, if not the fact, of gallantry from an earlier generation, could talk, in our town, to a woman of thirty or forty as if she were more than a domestic variety of man.

The need turned and twisted sometimes like a wild animal tied, but seldom burst through repression. I had a cousin, not a near relative, but by custom all relatives were cousins in our family relationship. She was a vivid, eager woman, dominating, clever, high-spirited, willful, and incapable of self-knowledge. Her husband was a placid giant, driven with a light, sure hand by his wife. He was her very willing slave; she loved him devotedly, but her nature was too rich and varied to be exercised in its entirety by one man, especially a sleepy one. Physical and mental unfaithfulness would have been alike inconceivable to her; either would have shattered a pattern which she herself had made, and thus destroyed something much more vital than her zest for experience. But potential lovers she did, most unconsciously, crave, since, while her dominant was domestic content, her recessives of sexual and emotional potentiality needed stimulation. I think an instinct warned her that something was atrophying in her nature; and so she sought, instinctively again, vicarious remedies.

She had a daughter, a languorous beauty, moody, proud, and troubling to men. She was, I suppose, my cousin in her youth renewed, but without her aggressiveness. The household was liberal with an extra place always set at table, into which she slipped more and more often one of those genial bachelors of indefinite age that every society makes use of as a kind of social lubricant. He was good company for young or old, good-looking, humorous, and quite frankly fascinated by the daughter, who, however, even to my incurious eyes, held herself curiously aloof. The rest of the family, and especially the mother, sparkled when he came, for he had a faculty of making personalities shine or glow. Only the daughter was unkind, with an indifference which turned to petulance under her mother's obvious encouragement.

The truth was, of course, though I was too ignorant to realize it at the time, that my cousin was in love with him, in love with that recessive and unused part of her nature that had never had warmth enough to flower; and the further truth was that her daughter knew it and was subtly upset and offended. My cousin usually got what she wanted. This time it was vicarious experience. She lived in her daughter and offered her to a lover as a similitude of what she wanted herself to be. She longed (I can see it now) for a passion that would sweep away the girl, so that she herself could be swept away in her imagination. She wanted to be clasped in hot arms, but in her daughter's person. And so she made love unblushingly and quite unconsciously to her guest, in proxy for her daughter.

The family friend was neither a fool nor a romantic. He saw his answer in the daughter's shrug and felt the growing tension. His visits spaced, my cousin grew acrid, the daughter's languorous humor returned with a new spice of malice. He married elsewhere; my cousin had the next year what in weaker natures would have been a breakdown — and emerged a cheerful, witty, willful old lady, a delight to her friends, a terror to her enemies, and as sexless as a nut.

That was the way it happened sometimes; that was the body's revenge in the Age of Confidence upon the sexlessness of good women.

It was in 1902 or 1903 that three of us, two men and a girl, were huddled over a new play of Bernard Shaw's just published. The book was *Man and Superman,* and we were reading eagerly, the slow racing to keep up with the fast. It was doing something to us, just what we could not say, yet keys seemed to reach out from the pages to unlock secret doors in our minds. They were ready for unlocking, though neither what lay hid there nor what had locked them was clear in our consciousness.

That play, as I remember, deals very little with sex. It is a play of liberation — an impudent liberation from conventions, orthodoxies, and anything that blurs the reality of human relations. And it was reality that we in our twenties, and conscious of elaborate conventions in social intercourse for which we were not responsible, were then craving, in sex as elsewhere.

Our emotions had sped uninhibited along the friendly plane of companionship, but tradition, our elders, our own taboos self-imposed, and conventions unthinkingly accepted, warned us back whenever we tried to think for ourselves. Unexpected sensations, unguessed-at possibilities for living, an intoxicating freedom of thought, sparkled up from those pages. It would be hard to find these flashes now, since it was not so much the Shavian ideas as the Shavian mood and witty effrontery that kindled our emotions. Yet certainly we who had been bred in the golden age of confident companionship had our first vision of an escape from approaching satiety, and the flatness of stale romance, in the clever clowning of Shaw. He made us articulate.

And this all too surely indicated the end of the age of sex security which Whitman a generation earlier had not been able even to shake. For I think that we three were typical of an American mood, of a new generation's resolve to get closer to real desires. We set free in ourselves the compass needle which had been pointing too long to a false north of sexual convention and a false south of outlawed desires.

Our mores were substantially unaffected — that change was to come later. Our companionship was enriched by the discovery that both sexes were tired of halves and pretenses. Speech was not freer, nor actions, but the ferment was working. We were more sympathetic, when the time came, with the oncoming generation, and much more interesting to each other in middle age, than had been the men and women of the nineties. But the ice was only cracked. You cannot escape from a taboo merely by knowing that it is one. The Age of Confidence had believed that sex, like the immigrants, needed only to be Americanized in order to make no trouble for the right-minded. We suffered from that naïveté; gained also, for, if this was an illusion, yet youth, which is naturally chaste by comparison with middle age, was given a few lucid and happy years.

ᴄᴏ 10 ᴄᴏ

What They Read

I HAVE reiterated the phrases *laissez-faire* and the Age of Confidence rather dangerously in these chapters, and I am
aware that I risk one of those canting simplifications which pretend to be the answer of history. My defense is that memory
always seeks some explanation of what was once only experience but has become a past. We ourselves are the end-products
of a life, and inevitably, and irresistibly, try to find some coherence in the experience that has shaped us. These phrases
for me are not definitions so much as clues that seem to lead
toward glimpses of understanding. The scattered picture-
puzzle by their aid fits together here and there — I do not pretend to complete it.

Nowhere do they seem more useful than in trying to recall
and comprehend the powerful influence of the books we read.
The culture of our community, as I have sufficiently indicated,
was narrow and not often deep. The best of it was in the domestic arts of home-making and companionship. Culture in its
more esthetic sense was as scarce as the holly trees that sometimes were found in our woods. Painting, sculpture, music,
were alien or elementary, conversation was not a fine art, philosophy seldom transcended common sense. But we were not
starved intellectually, for many of us were passionate readers.
And there we were let alone within wide limits, and were ex-
traordinarily confident in our taste.

I think that the library in our house was typical of its period,
for I have encountered its titles and editions in so many homes
of the era, and in book sales from like houses, since. I can see
it now, and name the books from memory as accurately as those
on my own shelves.

At one end of the sitting room was a triple bookcase of wal-

nut with scalloped trimmings of morocco leather below each
shelf, intended to keep out the dust. There was a brick-red
Prescott — Peru, Mexico, and the others — that no one read;
and a leather-backed Scott in small, clear type, with steel en-
gravings of the languishing-in-moonlight variety. There were
two volumes of Grant's *Memoirs,* and two of Henry M. Stan-
ley; a set of Macaulay's essays; a green Tennyson, and two or
three *Lalla Rookhs*; there was Hawthorne in marbled boards;
'The Little Classics' of Rossiter Johnson (much read); Green's
Short History of the English People; the English poets in a
series from Gray to Byron; Longfellow and Whittier; some-
body's Shakespeare with notes; a grubby set of Dickens that
came with a box of soap; Cooper and Thackeray complete;
Bryce's *American Commonwealth*; Kane's *Arctic Explorations*;
Uncle Tom's Cabin; *Uncle Remus*; and on a lower shelf the
heavy volumes of *Illustrated America* and *Illustrated Europe*
for Sunday reading. Under all, like a foundation of brown-
stone, was the *Encyclopaedia Britannica* in leather, the edition
of 1875, the noblest issue of that great work.

At the other end of the room, beneath the bay windows, hidden by curtains and by chairs, were deep shelves where ephem-
erae of the period were hoarded, yellow, paper-backed novels,
not so much hidden as withdrawn from the respectability of the
room. There was *Love in Orange Blossoms*, and Rider Hag-
gard's *She,* the only book I have ever been told not to read, and
The Duchess and Ouida and Marie Corelli, and Anthony Hope,
and mixed with them (if my memory is not at fault) some
Howells and Mrs. Humphry Ward and the earliest Sherlock
Holmes, and other books which are now better read than some
of the would-be classics that stood on the morocco leather.

Upstairs in the nursery was the children's library, contain-
ing *The Browns* of Cincinnati, *The American Boy's Hand-
book,* and *Toby Tyler, Alice in Wonderland,* of course, Howard Pyle, Frank Stockton, the bound *St. Nicholases,* and the
Hentys, the Algers, the Optics, the Castlemans, and the Kirk
Munros, in series, with a dusty set of Rollo books inherited
from a previous generation. On the other side were the girls'
books: Mrs. Molesworth, the Katy Books, the Elsie Books;
and certain volumes of a neuter variety — *Sparrow the Tramp,*

Diddie, Dumps, and Tot, Little Lord Fauntleroy, the *Five
Little Peppers,* and Kingsley's *Water Babies.*

Finally, in my grandfather's room, was a great case with a
swinging glass door, seldom opened, in which were treasures of
our Quaker past, George Fox in a folio, John Woolman, Sewel's
History of the People Called Quakers, cheek by cheek with a
gentleman's library of the Federalist period: Addison, Steele,
Gray, Goldsmith, Moore, Byron, Hume's *History* in gold and
red, Chesterfield; with an incongruous salting of Americana:
books about the Indian and buffalo, Elizabeth Montgomery's
priceless history of Wilmington, and a yard of plushy annuals
of the eighteen-thirties and forties. The bottom shelf was all
Bibles, of every age and shape, kept not for their bibliograph-
ical interest, or for religious uses, but because of the family
births and deaths inscribed on the middle pages of each, between the Old and the New Testament.

I fancy that every well-found house in Wilmington had most
of these books, barring the Quaker specialties. From all except
the yellow backs an odor of respectable culture exhaled, and
the yellow backs seem so respectable now when I run over the
titles that I am forced to believe that the sense of acquired culture is purely subjective and dependent upon the reaction of
the mind to opinion rather than upon the nature of the book
read. We read avidly the paper backs whenever we had a
chance, but never supposed that they were good for us. We
read Thackeray when we began to feel a duty toward literature
(and enjoyed him), and soaked in the medley of brief masterpieces of 'The Little Classics,' especially the volumes called
Mystery and *Romance.* But what we fell upon, read besottedly,
thought about and were molded by were the stories of Dickens
richest in sentiment (not *Pickwick* but *David Copperfield*) and
the novels of Walter Scott.

The omissions in this library were significant. No Hardy,
though he was being printed in the magazines; no Whitman (naturally); no Mark Twain except *Innocents Abroad* — he was a
cheap and flippant writer; only a little Poe; no Wordsworth,
Keats, or Shelley, though quantities of Byron, Longfellow, and
Tennyson; no Melville of course; no Carlyle, no Matthew Arnold; no French authors or German, no Latin and Greek clas-

sics even in translation; no Dante; no science except in the *Encylopaedia Britannica* and a children's encyclopaedia which we read and reread from cover to cover; not much biography; no Emerson and Thoreau — it was not until my college days that I came under their pervasive influence in the original texts. Whittier, Macaulay's *Lays of Ancient Rome,* and Longfellow represented the poetry actually read; no religious books outside the Quaker collection except the Bible. No contemporary poetry, criticism, drama at all.

Nevertheless, we read rather widely and so did our parents, since the public library, just beginning to be a major institution, supplemented our home supplies, and the school did a little guiding. But is wide reading ever so important as deep reading? Our deep reading was in Scott and the other romancers.

Mark Twain thought that the Civil War was caused by the false sense of chivalry engendered by the passionate reading of Scott in the South. I am sure that Scott and the near-Scotts and the school-of-Scotts were such real determinants of inner life for readers brought up in the eighties and nineties that no one will ever understand the America of that day without reading and pondering upon not only *Ivanhoe* but also *To Have and To Hold* and *Richard Carvel* and *Monsieur Beaucaire* and *Under the Red Robe.* No one studied *Ivanhoe* or *Guy Mannering* in school in those days. *Ivanhoe* came down from the upper left-hand shelf, in the grimy two-column edition that belonged to the children, and was read all over the house and under the trees of a dozen back yards. When a doctor was called to scrape and cauterize the results of a tumble while bird-nesting, they gave me my half-finished *Rob Roy* for an anesthetic. The pain never reached my imagination racing through the Highlands. What Lamb felt for the Elizabethans we felt for the more homely, and equally verbose, Cooper. Reading *The Last of the Mohicans* in a savage hemlock forest, toward dusk in a Northern summer, sent thrills through the bones which still faintly vibrate. And from these romances so alien to our bourgeois Quaker town we drew an ethics for ideal conduct in emotional stress.

Their heroes and heroines, and also most of their minor characters, except the obvious villains and scamps, were good — and not good in the genteel, respectable fashion that we were bored with in our school and our Sunday School literature. They were good in the meaning of the French word *bienfaisant,* well-meaning, turning from their own concerns, and often dubious ways, to be good fellows at need, and to do good effectively with warm hearts and thorough enjoyment. The town (and I suppose all the long-settled East of America) was sprinkled with respectable citizens like our Mr. Brinker, who propelled his crab legs at nine o'clock every morning down Market Street to the bank, his mean little eyes swinging right and left over his scraggly beard. He was a good business man, and reasonably honest, and constitutionally incapable of a magnanimous action. A business society bred that kind of crustacean. Sir Walter Scott was his antithesis.

We yearned, too, after heartiness, and found it in these romances. Our small-town culture was drying up, and its genial friendliness was an end-product of a great gusto for eating, quarreling, worshiping, and money-making that our grandparents remembered. My two grandfathers, one the last of four generations of ironmasters, the other a farmer turned business executive, would shake their beards for hours on Sunday evenings over men, women, and experiences that seemed, and I believe were, much richer and heartier than anything or anyone in our parents' generation. They still savored the age of the frontier. The eccentrics, the temperamentals, and the powerful living people I knew were nearly all old in the nineties, and the stories they told were paralleled in what I read in Scott, even if far less romantic. Our generation grew up with a violent desire to be heartier, and to live more widely than our parents. Yet it was a well-meaning heartiness that we were after — our idea, romantic certainly, was that we were to rush great-heartedly upon experience, and be good for it as it would be good for us. This was the complete antithesis of the later revolt of our children against a moral code that restrained them. We wanted not to rebel but to lead, and we dramatized ourselves, not as emancipated and cynical sophisticates, but as Henty heroes, approving hands on our shoulders, and seen at the long last by our parents and our teachers as good and great men who had dared to live to the uttermost. We, like our period, were hot for expansion, with no more analysis than Scott's as to what the uttermost was in living or what expansion meant in its next stages. As for the moral formula, we wished to stretch it toward romance, not to change it.

Much of this somewhat scrambled emotion we would have had without reading, but the sentiment in our society was distinctly literary. It was made from Dickens blended with Scott, but sufficiently undiscriminating so that a single book, like *Lorna Doone,* could charge a whole community of readers. (When I reached the heroic rescue of Lorna, Wilmington, thanks to my duties as recorded in a previous chapter, was dimmed for a full five minutes.) It was not the sentiment of the *comédie larmoyante,* nor of hypocrisy; certainly neither of these, for we were not weepers in our town and there was very little cant, even on Sundays. Our family life also was undemonstrative, and girls and boys were never sentimental in speech — indeed, they were more direct and simple than today. Yet underneath I believe we were all simmering with sentiment, especially the business men and the rakes. It was precisely the sentiment that one could take over from Dickens or from Scott, according to temperament.

The ideal relationships with one's sister, one's mother, one's family, one's sweetheart, were all determined by sentiment. So was affection for the home. So was one's attitude toward the poor or weak. So was every loyalty which young men of the period manifested toward the *alma mater* that often educated them very badly. There was very little sentiment in what we were told to do by the preachers. That was right and wrong, sealed by punishment. The social code we really lived by was not an 'ought' code, but a code of honor — what an honorable man should feel toward his friend, his wife, his duty; — and I find that we thought and felt and proposed to do far more exactly rendered in *David Copperfield* and implied in *The Antiquary* than in the Bible or the prayer-book. We all of us knew so well from our romantic reading how we should feel about such matters that I doubt if there was a single family in upper-class Wilmington capable of analyzing themselves realistically. When Shaw and after him Hardy came to America in the early nineteen-hundreds, the stale sentiment they burnt up (Mark Twain's match had failed — he was too flippant) was the immense remains of the reading of Dickens and Scott.

The more obviously romantic results of our reading in Scott — chivalry, feudalism, adventurous conflict — seems at first thought to have frothed away from our childhood. We tilted with home-made spears, shot arrows from bows, and made serfs and squires of the younger kids, but these exercises stemmed from Howard Pyle's honest *Robin Hood* as much as from Scott. There was no servile class in our community, no great houses, no caste of owners as in the South of two generations earlier, where unquestionably Scott produced illusion and helped to lead to disaster. Our Quaker society was democratic, at least in spirit. Nobody wanted a feudal aristocracy, no matter how much they liked to read about one.

So it seemed, yet on second thoughts I come to a different conclusion. Scott and Cooper did not move us to reject the civilization of the moment, but they must have broken ground. All through the eighties and early nineties Gothic adornments clustered thicker and thicker on our red-brick houses, and every established family began then, and long before 'Colonial' furniture came down from the attics, its long and often very expensive search for a genealogy, to find usually dubious ancestors of impeccable nobility in England, and to acquire at still more expense a still more dubious coat of arms. It was an irony not widely appreciated that the Quaker families (whose records were scrupulously kept from the seventeenth century) usually found an ancestor who called himself gentleman and bore arms (and whose affectations his Quaker son had wiped out in meekness) while the aristocrats from down state were still floundering in the abyss which separated England from America in the days of the settlement. My mother's notepaper bore a *fess ermine* at the top, genuine enough, though my Quaker grandfather would have died before he would have used it, and genealogists being more plentiful than experts in heraldry, there was no one to tell her that females should use only an O, and never a shield.

This passed over our childish heads, though it seems to have been a first symptom in our parents of what some called snobbery, but was really the beginning of a new class spirit in America. The revelation came when the new American school of the historical romance rose overnight, blossomed like the desert in April, and withered at the first touch of twentieth-century realism.

I shall not here recount its history. Who is there past middle age who did not read *Janice Meredith, A Gentleman of France, Richard Carvel, Monsieur Beaucaire?* It was very thin Scott, very dilute Dumas, and if the novelists had kept to France or Ruritania would have had no more importance than other outcrops of best-sellers, even though this one was a landslide, millions of copies circulating among all classes except the proletariat (which is getting them now in the movies), so that each season it was certain that substantially every literate American had read one such book. The movies today are an equivalent, but they sweep through lower levels, and are not so influential upon culture because the cultured are ballasted with stronger appeals to the imagination.

It was not so then, and as soon as these novelists began to create a romantic Colonial America the intoxication began. It is hard to describe it. Suddenly we became aware of a past — our own — that seemed as good as Scott's, and much like it. It was an illusion, not a real past, and hence our furore was quite different from the intellectuals' excitement over frontier history today, which is a true story of what made us. Is illusion, however, ever less powerful for being essentially false? The romantic slaveholders, the scions of English nobility, the feudal gentlemen of these novels of an artificial Colonial period, when compared with their European originals in Scott or Dumas, show the handmarks of their creators who were plain Americans, usually from the Middle West. But we were not critical then, and how the heroes and heroines lived, what they did (I speak for the East), on roads and in houses still familiar to us, was explosive.

No pack of poets was unleashed — Lindsays, Masterses, Benéts — such as followed the new national sense of twenty years later. We read this coca-cola of romanticism, and began merely to froth. The town forgot its solid Quaker ancestry in a passionate attempt to find *émigré* great-grandfathers or runaway heiresses from overseas. The South, which was just then being sentimentalized by Thomas Nelson Page and others, was near enough so that any of our older families could trace back somewhere to the Eastern Shore or Tidewater Virginia, and thus, by presumption, to a plantation house. And so the down-state Democrats brought out what they had of old silver, and stood pat on conscious pride. We Quakers (this post-dated the ancestor flurry by some years) got out from garret, shed, and cellar treasures of simple, solid mahogany which, done over, gave our eighteen-seventy houses a colonial look, at least on the inside. Pots and pans and cheap dirty glass and cobblers' benches and such cottage curiosities were not yet in fashion. It was still nothing to boast of if one's worthless great-uncle had run away West and been drowned (probably drunk) in the Mississippi — that was to come; it was the late eighteenth century and the Federalist period that now glowed rosily, making our breasts expand with the consciousness that our decorous respectability was only a few generations away from a life which the novelists had made to seem so glamorous. And soon we saw the antique shop, Colonial Dames, Colonial architecture (so-called), and bronze tablets for American worthies (many of them in our region Tories) all come in together.

I am not exaggerating, I am minimizing the reverberations of this romantic sentimentalism. Yet these fopperies and snob-beries (which nevertheless helped to restore good taste in our architecture and interior decoration) were only superficial symptoms. Something was happening to us and to our town deeper, even more significant. There was, for example, the chivalrous attitude (it was more than a pose) toward girls, which reached its height just about the turn of the century and was literary in its origin. The decorous familiarity of the eighties was too stiff for us, but just when some frankness was entering into our sex relationship, suddenly we were whirled up into a romantic atmosphere which can still be seen in articulate perfection by readers of Stevenson's *Prince Otto* and with more pink clouds of sunset in *Richard Carvel*. We tried to see our girls as romantic beauties and ourselves as gentlemen who lived by honor. It did not last long. There had been too much free companionship, and too little mystery. The girls would not or could not play their parts, and we could write ours better than we could talk them. There was more sentiment and less sex in our associations than ever before or since, but not much authentic romance, still less that was articulate.

Indeed in our honest Quaker society there would have been little to sustain the fancy of the most fanciful, if it had not been for the visiting Southern girl. Poor usually, ill-educated, and often provincial in the extreme, she had been a local phenomenon until these novels of a bygone gallant aristocracy set ideals in the imagination which she hurried to realize. And the Southern girl of that day was romantic. She had always known how to respond to chivalry; no Puritan or Quaker inhibitions had kept her from flaunting her sex before men. If she was a little shallow, like the books out of which she now seemed to step, she had their quality of charm and inevitableness, as if created to satisfy the needs of an industrial society distressed by its own prosaicness and not knowing just what it wanted except that it must be gayer and more emotional. As our national mood has left puritanism farther and farther behind us, the vogue of the Southern girl has declined, and without loss of charm truer values have come out of the South, yet she was a blessing to us in the nineties when she crossed the border.

The more vital impacts of all this romantic-sentimental reading are not easy to explain. Although it raised our temperature perhaps one degree, yet one degree was enough for dizziness. The Spanish War, with its rather sordid imperialism, wrapped in guff about poor Cuba, the gallant onslaughts of the muckrakers upon the money-bags, the cult of Theodore Roosevelt, the glamorous expansiveness of the opening twentieth century, captains of industry, octopus trusts, the still young nation putting on greatness, up and on to the moral romance of our entry into the Great War — how much all this owes to the shot of romance in our veins and the virus of sentiment cannot be said definitely, but much I am sure. Certainly in our town, where the past and the future seemed to become romantic together at that turn of the century, I cannot separate in my own memory the bands and cheering of 'ninety-eight, Hobson, Dewey, and manifest destiny in an expectant world, from the extravagant romanticism of the shallow, unphilosophical, unpsychological novels we had all been reading. One carried over into the other, and the same color was infused through both. We entered the twentieth century with the feverish exuberance of an unhealthy child, because children whose minds had been conditioned by Scott were in their adolescence fed cheap and sometimes poisonous confectionery by these tuppenny imitators of the great.

Shakespeare was badly read by us; he was a subject for elderly ladies who took on study circles of young girls with the intention of making them cultured. And he was thoroughly feminized, and expurgated by careful selection. Thackeray was not well read; he was obligatory for those who thought well of their intellects, like Meredith two decades later. Jane Austen I never heard of, nor Howells either, although there were novels of his on our shelves. The eighteenth century meant Gray and Goldsmith. Everyone had the poems of Byron and Moore but nobody read them. The Lake poets were a school subject; Wordsworth and Coleridge we were taught, but not Keats and Shelley. Trollope was unknown, Hawthorne was read only by children. Hugo and Marie Corelli were consorted together as cosmic writers with a philosophy (it would take an essay to explain why). Whittier was a great name because he was a Quaker, but Longfellow was our real poet. Thoreau was a name only. Indeed, Concord was too intellectual for us. We understood the simple mysticism of the Quakers but not Transcendentalism. In the mid-century *Lalla Rookh* had been the favorite gift book: in my time it was the *Idylls of the King*.

Has it been sufficiently implied that our reading was confident? Nothing critical came our way, especially in fiction. For us, *Robert Elsmere*, which roused a faint storm in Episcopal circles, had no successors. Our reading was what so many today advocate as an antidote for cynical realism — positive, wholehearted, largely unliterary and unintellectual. We took it as we took our meals, asking nothing about the cook, and less of the quality, if its taste was right. We got from it strong emotional surges, reacting to *Little Women*, for example, precisely as the proletariat reacts to the movie today, and acquired habits of feeling (not, I should say, thinking) that became our stock reactions thereafter when any situation in life resembled what was familiar to us in books. It was these instinctive reactions which Bernard Shaw made to seem ridiculous. Science was not yet a subject for reading; religion, apart from the Bible, had ceased to be one. We had no reading lists, few books assigned in school, no selection except our own from ill-assorted shelves and word-of-mouth as to what was good to read in the public library. It was all *laissez-faire* except that our parents urged us away from the yellow backs toward what they regarded as literature, which meant usually Thackeray, Dickens, and Scott. Discipline in reading, 'reading with a purpose,' as the cant phrase goes, was almost unknown. I remember my father one rainy Sunday suddenly stirred to indignant reform, which in his mild self took us all by surprise. 'I'll read no more of this trash,' he said, and slammed a cheap novel on the table. 'I'm going to read the good books I used to read.' But unfortunately the Prescott he pulled down from the respectable end of the library was very Spanish, and in half an hour he was asleep.

Thus we pastured freely like mountain sheep, and since there were plenty of books took only what we liked, and since there were few new ones, got to love our favorites, which, running with the grain of life in our age, were hearty, wholesome, sentimental, romantic. And hence my reading memories are of absorption in a book, earless, eyeless, motionless for hours, a life between covers more real than outer experience, such an obsession in reading as I believe does not exist now; certainly I never see it. For our reading (ill chosen as it so often must have been) was neither drug nor irritant, neither a revelation nor a caustic. It was an extension without break of our own lives, and flowed back freely to become a part of our mentality. It did not emancipate (like the realism of the first decades of the next century), it did not even educate, but certainly it enlarged our narrow egos, leaving us quite as naïve, quite as unsophisticated, a little farther away from any probable reality, but enriched, happy, confident in the perpetual possibility of likeable experience for such people as we intended to be. And hence the paradox, that our community had more good readers and fewer well-read individuals than I have ever encountered in later wanderings. For books to us were what the bard's chants were to the tribe — a recalling, an enriching, an extension of memory. When ideas came in fashion, and realism and satire and debunking, the town (a few highbrows excepted) stopped reading real books and took to detective stories, *The Saturday Evening Post,* and the pulp magazines. They knew what they wanted.

II

Nature

NATURE also had her Age of Confidence, though I object to the 'her' which goes back to Longfellow's poem on Agassiz and a moral-sentimental conception of nature which had become stuffy before our time. Nature for us — but that is inaccurate — for some of us, was part religion, part education, part esthetics, and sometimes such a delight as Wordsworth recalled and Browning's thrush tried to recapture. For some of us only, since not even the Romantic Movement which was still strong in literature and the proximity to our town of the lovely Brandywine woods could make the tough-minded accessible to the sweet influences of nature. To the congenital cockney, even at the height of the Back-to-Nature era, birds were just birds, primroses, primroses, and the forest, trees, with the same satisfying exclusiveness as today, or in Doctor Johnson's taverns. Nor did the hunter and fisher fail to take his wood and water pleasures untroubled by Emersonian intuitions or the subtle interpretations of Thoreau. Yet nature, for those tender-minded in that direction, was in the last century a factor in living both important and difficult to describe, because both naïve and passionate in its influences. Just for a moment of experience sometimes, but often for months and years, our own natures, old as well as young, turned that way and opened. We shared what ecstasy is too purple a word to describe and pleasure too mild.

Nature in the crude, the trees, the flowers, the birds, swept in spring like a shallow sea through our town, lapping even at the shopping streets and the alleys of the slums. The old Quakers had built tight rows of brick houses, hiding their expansiveness (for they were not ascetics in everything) behind arched alley-doors, within which, once entered, you found gal-

leried porches hung over with tangles of vines and shaded by
pear trees and magnolias. The industrialists of the eighties preferred separate block houses of brick or serpentine or the harsh
blue granite of the region that takes a century to mellow. Yet
these were set in squares of turf where shrubbery too thickly
planted soon made little wildernesses never pruned by the lazy
darky gardeners. And there brown thrushes and catbirds sang,
and in the earliest spring cardinals flashed. Rabbits stole in
from the near-by country, bobbing across the lawn when the
carriage turned in the driveway, and if there was an oak or a
tulip tree left from the old forest and shading the house, hum-
mingbirds placed their nests, little lichened mounds, on the
broad limbs and dropped therein two tiny eggs like baroque
pearls that one could see from an upper window, but never
reach.

The country began in those days before the town stopped
and we could have both worlds for a little walking with no untidy fringe of suburb and gas stations in between. Within a
quarter of a mile of the trolleys bumping down cobbled streets
were dense coverts in a forest of trees which were old in the
eighteenth century, so dim and silent that the nervous muscles
relaxed and one felt that curious sense of protection which
must have eased the heart of the first man when he crawled into
his cave. In England or France such a retreat into the woods
had always a touch of the literary, appealing to spirits too sensitive for the crowd, or refined to a voluptuousness of sentiment. But we young Americans were still only a few generations away from frontiersmen whose home everywhere in the
East had been in the woods. We had been reared, even the
town-born, for a month or more out of every year on a farm
or a lake in the mountains. Our feet molded to the contour of
a path as readily as to the pavements; our eyes and ears and
nostrils still inherited the sharpness that caught a wing flash, a
leaf movement, a phoebe's note, the wry smell of a fox, or the
faint odor of wild white violets — or, if it was not an inheritance, then someone had taught us when we were very young.
And on one excuse or another most of us in every weather stole
out of town. Skating, birds' eggs, minerals, chestnuts, or the
frost-nipped persimmons, swimming, riding, shooting, took us

to the country, everything but walking for the sake of walking — that had not come in yet, but had to wait for organized athletics and be called 'hiking.' We never went without an objective, which was perhaps the reason that we went into the country, not merely through it, and learned to observe. Ten thousand motor miles see less than a morning of such purposeful rambling.

I know, of course, that those of us who were romantic were busily romanticizing nature, yet that was only the half of it. Something died in American youth when the specialism of science reached natural history, turning the woods and meadows into outdoor laboratories for children regimented on 'nature hikes.' For the romance we made of nature plus an intuitive apprehension of kindred life which was more than half religious, worked deep into the consciousness of the young people of my generation, and there, like some tenacious bulb, kept sending shoots of vivid interest to the surface, so that even the least poetical among those sensible at all to natural beauty were gently aprickle in a deep woods or happily serene in a water meadow blue with quaker ladies. We were, indeed, the last inheritors of that intuitive faith in nature which made Wordsworth a poet and Emerson a philosopher. Not that we read either of them while our mood was freshest, but they were in our air and our access was like theirs, though to no parked England or piney Massachusetts, but to the richest of Atlantic valleys, a country so old that its fields were velvety, so young that the woods on the shoulders of the hills were still authentic remains of wilderness, free to any wanderer.

Industrialism or science, either or both, cut off our franchise. The first threw out the macadam roads that turned to concrete, raised the woven wire fences, and created the machines that soon drained sensitiveness to leaf and limb and turf and flying bird into the grip on the wheel, the eye on the road, the ear on the horn. The age of gasoline spoiled smelling; in those earlier days the nose was a sense, not a filter for stenches. Dawn, noon, evening, the deep woods, fields at twilight, running water, each had the subtle gradation of odor which by close association could always restir the imagination. The odors are still there, but this age has lost its nose — the delicate nerves of smell have vibrated too long to steam heat, coal, chemicals, cigarette smoke, and stale gasoline. We go through nature like a blind man in a garden.

And science, with its double charge of utilitarianism and realism, finished the job. Objects in nature became exactly what they were supposed to be — aggregates of cells combined in well-known formulas. Evolution sent the bug crawling over the lily pad. Reaction to environment controlled the gossamer fly spinning in the sun. The crystal was mathematics; the bird song, sex.

I do not admit that we nature-lovers in the Age of Confidence were sentimental in such pleasures. Rather we were town dwellers moved by instinct and tradition alike to reach back toward the farm. My grandfather had gone from college to land that had Charles Lovelace's and William Penn's deeds on it. His eyes still lit at a good stand of corn, and he knew the richness of wheat by the feel of the grains. But even more vital was a craving in us that only the country seemed to satisfy. The something expanding that felt like a soul when the new grass burnt green in a clouded sunset, or a veery shook a trembling leaf of song in the hazel thicket, was our escape from brick-pavement, mansard-roof, marble-doorstep life. Since the great paroxysm of the Civil War respectability had been growing duller. The giant struggles of industrialism were fought far away from us. We could not get religion, hard drinking was neither novel nor fashionable, society was as I have described it. But incredible as it may seem to the sophisticated materialist, there was real excitement in a May orchard and intoxication in the woods. It was naïve and it was genuine, and not even the enthusiastic pages of Muir, Burroughs, and the lesser nature writers, who made passable literature of it, retain for those who were tender-minded toward nature the intensity of their emotion. It was a real passion with fiery particles of religion scattered through.

I had one friend who was really alive only in the country. He was a heavy youth, full-blooded and slow-minded. Shy in company, tardy at games, incurious and almost dull in town, when we set off behind his black mare for the upper Brandywine his color rose with each mile into the country. Once we

reached the back roads where the yellow clay was rutted between the hedges, his eyes would lighten, the lisp would drop
from his speech; he would fling himself over the wheel, race
ahead of our slow trot, climb a tree out of sheer exuberance,
speak inarticulately a dozen incoherences. Minerals were what
we were after, but he scarcely learned their names, dropped
what he found, and went searching for more. Our country was
strong ale to him and his hard head got drunk on it.

As for myself, I remember the commonplace settling down
like a soggy cloud in March, the ego weakening, living growing paler, even the voice failing until it seemed difficult to
speak loud and firmly. The town closed in, houses, houses,
people, people, all known, all expected, all obvious without
mystery. And then (it was October) the dull body hauled to
the country and the crest of the hill above Dixon farms, insensitive, half alive, when a pulse deep down, a tingle at the skin,
a sensation as of eyes opening, until, as at a stroke of a baton,
color burst out everywhere, winter wheat shouting in its field
beside the rich brown earth fresh plowed, the woods throbbing
color, bronze in the oaks and purple in the hickories, tulip
trees shelf upon shelf of guinea gold, while every flowing curve
of the valley was a rhythm in the blood. What the modern gets
from music, if he is capable of music, we got from nature for
the taking and with no technique but desire.

Our town had as much cussedness as you could find anywhere today, and more downright meanness, but it was not
hard. The competent young women, with hard lines on their
beauty-parlor faces, so familiar in every office-building elevator,
would have caused remark there. Mean faces, sordid faces were
common, but the hardness that shows something dulled or
frozen within was rare. The town, too friendly to breathe
cynicism even among the depressed and unfortunate, was humanitarian in an unintelligent, pre-sociological way. And I do
believe that the prevalent tenderness toward nature among all
but the slum-bound poor had something to do with the way we
held on to our humanity. The community was sprinkled with
'collections' — minerals, birds' eggs, fossils, pressed plants, and
stuffed birds and animals. Our prevalent taste for natural history was indicated by an open contempt for such cockney items

as stamps and cigarette pictures. There were natural-history societies, junior as well as senior, and out in the country the amateur ornithologist joined steps with the sportsman after quail, while mineral collectors kept pace on the way home with the fox-hunter's nag. Old men who looked as if their noses had never been out of a ledger were discovered to have spent all their nights on *lepidoptera*. As a boy I visited often a rich old Quaker, in the country, supposed to be a miser, but actually a passionate mineralogist, and he and I, seventy and eleven, jogged for miles over the Pennsylvania hills in excited search for the rare diaspore which had once been found in unique specimens in those unromantic fields.

This mania for collecting was not mere possessiveness, like the later millionaire's hoardings of art. The urge of a rapidly expanding science was behind it, and even the old farmers on whose land specimens were found and in whose woods rare plants grew, were acquainted with the scientific names, and were charitable to collectors who could talk the lingo. We weighed, measured, studied in books, used microscopes and test tubes, yet always stopped short of pure science, nor do I remember one of those youthful collectors who went on into professional eminence in his field. It may have been laziness, the amateur's hesitance before the labors of classification, the mathematics of crystallography, the technique of biology. But surely it was quite as often an instinct for what might not too pretentiously be called spiritual self-preservation. There was something in all this seeking that was in danger of being lost if the physical nature of what we were searching should be mastered. Thoreau, in a community far more philosophically self-conscious than ours, faced the same problem with an equal confusion of mind, and spilled some millions of words in an attempt to pin down his sensitive spirit to routine observation. For there was, as I have said, an emotion in our seeking that was extremely complex. We looked for an escape, even a conversion, quite as much as for a warbler's egg or a crystal of epidote. It was, I suppose, the poetry permitted to respectable people in a business community, who in nearly every other way were conventional. The best church I ever knew next to Quaker meeting was an oak knoll where wood thrushes sang at sunset above the Brandywine.

And thus, when the soft limestone clove before the steady taps of the hammer, and opened upon a sheaf of glittering crystals of tremolite, it was more than the joy of discovery that was felt, or the scientist's perception that carbonates under pressure could so neatly arrange themselves; it was a thrill resembling passion that for me (I ran with the mineralogists) enriched the routine of the week. And if I knew all the crystal names from andalusite to zoisite and zircon; and another, stars; and another, every migratory bird; and still another, the moss flowers and lichens; while many less competent were content to say the names of trees, it was not so much knowledge of nature's things as a power to make them yield something to the spirit that we essentially wanted and largely got.

All these collections, large and small, are swept into the dust heaps; or housed in museums, where they have been winnowed, catalogued, classified; and past the thickets of ironwood where we trailed the oven bird, and over the pitted hill where patient search could find the rare and tiny crystals of columbite, young people with hurried faces drive swift cars that never stop for anything so trivial as a bird's singing. All the facts we gathered are standardized now in any school course in nature study, and quite, quite dead.

Our natural history, *laissez-faire* natural history, was a vague nature worship with a passion in it that was certainly out of place in a sober science. When educators ousted the *laissez-faire* and herded natural history into the curriculum, they barred out the worship and made nature into just another commodity. This had to be, of course. The amateur scientists that were scurrying about everywhere in our day got in the way of professional science and stirred up more dust than information. Yet our occupation was probably as useful as a great deal of scientific research that never gets so far as human values; and it was a marvelous tonic for boys and girls who were told daily in school and home that to be busy was to be virtuous, that work meant happiness, and that he who produced wealth was the saviour of his country. It tonicked our confidence in a friendly universe, and was more appealing to the youthful imagination than the stable respectability which inspired such confidence in our elders. And I note the difference between the control over nature which so pleases us today and our confidence in nature as a resource back of and behind the disappointments and disillusionments of human contacts. Seeing a spiritual steadiness in many of my generation that seems lacking in their children, I can find no more convincing argument for our faith than such seeming trivial memories as of dawn in the country, the timbers of a planked bridge shaking above my head as a milk cart passed over, a ledge above the water and on it a phoebe's nest, green-moss covered, and in its cup four rosy eggs. Phoebes still build beneath the steel girders of our bridges, but who has time to look for them, or is moved when they are found! And if I hesitate to record the moment when I, a boy by no means unprotected against the world, but hurt and humiliated by a failure to hide my sensitiveness, ran to the woods and, creeping under the wild-grape vines, felt the serenity of the trees, saw with a stir of humor a brown creeper cock one eye around a flange of bark, and opened my heart (as I would certainly have called it) to the healing and renewing influence of all those visible ministers of the soil, I hesitate only because the memory is personal. I know this recourse was open to many, for reasons which are no longer ours.

12

Business, Politics, and All That

MY YOUTH was spent in precisely that American period of economic whirlwind when the predatory barons of industry were raiding under dust clouds largely of their own making the profits of technological advance and the incomparable resources of this continent. Those were the years when the 'shark-mouthed' Rockefeller was tightening his grip upon the 'narrows' through which the great stream of oil had to flow. It was the age of the unscrupulous *condottiere*, Jay Gould, of the 'empire-builder' and rate-raiser, Hill, of the prince of peddlers, Carnegie. Toward its close the great bankers, led by the fiery-nosed Morgan, closed down upon the warring captains as the armies of the national states closed down upon the *condottieri* of the Renaissance. It was the economic age of concentration. Individualists of unparalleled energy were killing individualism for the benefit of their private purses, reducing anarchy to order and chaos to form, in unwitting preparation for a new social order. Uneducated men, unprincipled, strong-willed, of first-rate ability, were ruling a continent while a feeble government looked on.

All of this passed far above our heads like driven clouds over a quiet valley. It passed over the heads of ten thousand communities in the Age of Confidence, who heard only the distant thunder of storms and were pelted only now and then by the hail of the conflict. There is an extraordinary late-Latin account of week-ending and country life in Gaul which upset my ideas of Roman history when I came across it. For here amidst a culture in full decay, with armies afield, officials corrupted, and barbarians breaking in, civilized men and women were enjoying sports and a holiday as if they had never been told that the empire was falling. So it was in its way with us — and

113

with a thousand other communities. We heard of these men, heard of these wars between magnates and systems, shared in our small way in the speculation, and took our losses, read with indignation of labor rebellions whose ultimate cause we did not suspect, and when the era of great consolidations began saw even in our town fantastic bubbles rise and burst. But what we saw and heard had little resemblance to the history of those times which everyone now is reading — no more resemblance than the week-ending picture of country life in Provence to Gibbon's history. Gould, Morgan, Rockefeller, Harriman, Hill, Huntington, were the lawless precursors of the planned economy of the twentieth century — for us they were only men of colossal wealth, more admired than feared. If they touched our welfare, as they did constantly, we seldom knew it. They were not our history — nor for thirty years would we know theirs. And this is one of the great differences between memoirs and history. The one records what seemed important at the moment, the other what was important for the future.

Our town had always been a business community. It had been the center of the flour industry under my own ancestors, it had gone in for shipbuilding and leather, for iron and railroad cars, and for a century was the producer of gunpowder for the nation. It had known speculation, of course, and there were many wealthy men, and at least one family of millionaires; but these were all local, family businesses. From our steady and prosperous community where wealth, thanks to its Quaker background, was still remarkably well distributed, no predatory captain went forth to conquer America. Our empire was made; and the inexorable laws which were at work, and being worked, by the captains of the age to reduce our local industrialism to a cog in the great industrial machine of America, must have been only dimly realized even by our company presidents and bankers. Our banks were sound, but they stuck to money-lending. Our industries expected to take care of themselves in any market. Our confidence in the future was never shaken, except by the occasional threats of free trade from the Democrats, which resembled the original sin one heard about in the churches, an evil lurking in the background which sensible people would always be able to defeat. Business with us was the small-time business of the *laissez-faire* period, though it seemed large to us. It was supposed to let politics alone when politics let it alone; it had no more sweep, no more relation to the development of society, than the farmer's handling of his land — which was also his own. Economics was only the name of a theoretical science, which was no substitute for practical common sense.

Hence one of the first great waves of the new economic thinking swept past our doors without leaving a trace behind. The very smallness of the state of Delaware has always tempted outsiders to use its disproportionate political power for their own advantage. The notorious Addicks, a captain of industry of the second class, not more unprincipled, but less able and rougher, than his associates, chose Delaware for his entrance into the Senate, and failed chiefly because he did not know how to buy votes like a gentleman. Moved likewise by the strategic power of a small state with as much representation in the Senate as a large one, the followers of that extraordinary thinker, Henry George, marched upon Delaware, a blue-coated army of propagandists, speaking at street corners, dropping handbills at our doors, arguing even with the peach farmer on his lonely plantation. Never was effort so completely wasted. We were so uneconomic in our thinking, and so confident of the essential rightness of our order, that not even a scratch was made upon the complacency of our comfortable society. No one listened, or at least no one was effectively moved, not even among the workmen on strike or the vegetable growers strangling under the grip of the one railroad that gave them access to market. I was very young at the time, yet I still remember the phrase idly bandied about, 'the single-taxers.' It was years later before I had the slightest idea what it meant, for my elders never bothered to tell me what they probably never troubled to understand themselves. It was irrelevant to what we regarded as business or politics.

It happened that in the age following, our town, through the fortuitous circumstances of an extraordinary development of the technique of chemistry and the urgent need for explosives in the Great War, became the home and center of one of the money groups that now are supposed by some to control industrial America. Almost overnight the ancient family business of the du Ponts became a trust of overpowering magnitude, uncountable millions poured into our town, quiet families that had lived for years with one carriage and a simple estate discovered fortunes that they did not know how to use, and the town itself began an orgy of speculation, which when it ended had swept away the whole fabric of society as I had known it. It is for that reason I can write so freely of the town I knew, as if it were a hundred years back instead of a few decades. For it is as historical now as was San Francisco of the gold rush to the writers of the eighties. With us the Age of Confidence and *laissez-faire* was snapped short, and memory is confused by no such belated remainders as hundreds of other American communities must still possess.

Business, in the nineties, which was the dominating occupation and chief subject of thought in our community, had no conscious relation to economics, no breadth to it, no excitement, no doubts except the doubts of profits, no responsibility to the community except dividends and salaries, no object but money-making. And yet it was much more than an occupation — it was a philosophy, a morality, and an atmosphere. Of this I was quite unaware at the time, for I breathed it as naturally, though with little liking, as a Londoner takes in his November fog. My own family had been in business or manufacturing of some kind — with interludes of farming — for at least eight generations, and I, as the first rebel, was too sensitive to the pressure of what seemed a world engrossed in business to view it with any detachment.

Furthermore, the town was divided into family businesses, of which some were socially inferior and some superior. Into some only members of the owning family could enter, others were like local colleges, with an entering class of youngsters from the best families every year. Youth felt not only the necessity of going into business, but also the duty of getting into the right business. As the younger son of one of the British county families must make his choice among the army, the law, and the church, so we in our more prosaic society were routed either for powder, ships, iron, or railroad cars, with banking and insurance in reserve for individualists.

There were, of course, plenty of lawyers among us, but they were collaborators of business; the doctors and ministers were dependent upon business; the school-teachers were an inferior caste, respected but not taken seriously. We had one real artist, Howard Pyle, and he, by some irony of circumstance, happened to be the first illustrator of his time in the English-speaking world, and the author of one of the few books of authentic romance published in America in his day; yet it was not for these reasons that he ranked with the local bankers, but because he belonged to a respectable Quaker family, held ultra-conservative Republican opinions, and was known to earn an income which was considered fantastic in our town, considering what he did for a living.

Business dominated all these classes, and even the artist warned young men away from writing because it was difficult then to make money by it. The saying, he is (or he isn't) a good business man, the warning, unless you do this or that you won't get on in business, the feeling, among the women, that the harsh necessities of business justified ethics quite different from the friendly code of ordinary life — all this hung heavy in our air when we were young. The Protestant gospel of work was at its highest authority, and was not yet tempered by ideals of social service. An interest in science, in reading, or in travel was well enough, wit and culture were well enough, a gentle spirit or a kind heart or a desire to be useful were commendable (and in our easy-going society often instinctive), but none of these things would count in business where daily bread was made. In the ominous future which was held like a big stick over every boy's head, only industry and obedience and accuracy and neatness and a contempt for the pleasures of idleness could give a leg up to success. Honesty was also mentioned, but not with such enthusiasm. There was no hope for you unless you should acquire all the virtues of a good clerk.

The effect upon the imagination was considerable, particularly in our comfortable well-to-do class, where the temptations of wealth were not strong. And indeed since the relatively small businesses of our town offered at the most good incomes rather than great riches, duty was the incentive we heard most talked about. Our business was no golden realm of adventurous exploitation, but a machine which broke you if you didn't succeed.

How the machine functioned was never explained to us; its routine was hidden in banks or factory offices, and was supposed to be quite different from the only business we saw in operation, retail selling in shops or on the street, which was socially impossible for Us. But the men who owned the machines, made the credit, and controlled the trade were familiar enough, and in a subtle but authentic fashion came to be business in our eyes. The type did not attract youth, even businesslike youth. Our local magnates could be seen eating pie at Jones's luncheon rooms or driving their own buggies home from work. Many of them were in our family circle, though the standard specimens were self-made and did not mix much yet in society. We knew them all at least by sight, and this is what made us uneasy, for usually they were not attractive men, and they were going to be the criteria of our success in life. There was Abner Smith with the stiff white beard who walked home every night from his factory, his eyes never turning to right or left; and Joseph Johnson who made cars and was smug and oily; and Reynolds, the hard little banker; and Du Vane of the chemical works who was so soft-spoken and looked so ruthless. They did not relax much even in our easy-going community; for they knew that they represented the real morale of the town, and I have wondered since whether they were aware of the great builders and great wreckers, the pirates and robber barons, who were even then devouring the West and preparing to swallow us, ships, iron, leather, powder, all together. They knew of them, of course, suffered by them probably, but were not like them, either in evil or in good. Theirs was a tight little Protestant world, where industry was god, and imagination was an old devil, romantic and dishonest, and happily engaged in destroying communities less moral than ours. At least we were told that our magnates were honest; and we could see that they were unromantic.

Hence the instinctive dread of the business life which was so common in the youth of our town was not due to any ideas of class struggle or the excesses of the Industrial Revolution. Our community had changed, like hundreds of others in the decades after the Civil War, from a market stand for the farm regions thereabouts to a center of manufacturing and trade. These men whom we disliked were of the new industrial type, hardened by competition and impersonal because their success came from selling the products of machines. But our *malaise* came from no conscious regret for an agrarian past or suspicion that anything was wrong in a present which we took for granted. We accepted the system as inevitable, without even thinking of it as a system, and indeed often boasted of our fifty industries and dozen banks. Our complaint was moral, and to call it even a complaint is inaccurate, since it was something deeper, the restlessness of young horses at the sight of the harness they do not know how to escape. And indeed, most of the generation of youngsters belonging to our class, when their chance came, broke away from business altogether. Those that inherited money quit when they got it, those who could get educated went off into engineering, law, and even agriculture. Those who were ineffective drifted into a mild trading of real estate or insurance or sold stocks to their friends. Those who could do so lived by speculation. Business, as defined in our town, which meant producing and then selling what was produced, lost us. Our father's businesses were run by other men, brought in from elsewhere. Our first families became absentee landlords of distant corporations instead of magnates of the industries whose gates had gaped for us, and if this brought economic evils with it, at least it ended a tyranny over the imagination of youth. In spite of all the moralizing, or because of it, only one first-rate business man came out of my youthful circle, and he broke through into Big Business at a fortunate moment when imagination was an asset.

We burst away from small-town business like a covey of quail, but no one of us escaped entirely from the moral effect of that dominance by business ideals. Our fathers were called before daylight, went to work at seven, came home at six, and slept Sunday afternoons and many a week-day evening. They did it by code. Through all those friendly houses and pleasant gardens an undercurrent of duty ran drably. Pioneer initiative, by their day, had subtly degenerated into a duty to be prompt, a duty to work, or seem to work, every week-day hour, to keep others working, to make the town grow, to get safely rich, to have children who were businesslike, or, if they were females, never stood in the way of business. There was no excitement in this duty, only a tension always felt and capable of chilling every other impulse. I remember my surprise when I found by accident my great-great-grandfather's journals (himself an excellent business man) and read there his concern with religion and ethics expressed in cramped lines between records of the weather, the price of wheat, and the status of the currency. Here was a business man who took time to argue with himself questions which had no relation to his affairs. It was new to my experience. Our business men were not too serious, there was plenty of back-slapping and teasing, but when they *were* serious, it was over business. The magnates of our day wagged their beards over the folly of a college education. College men didn't stick to business; they thought too much. No irony was intended!

Hence values in our town at the turn of the century were so distorted that many of us have preferred to cut the knots and start over again. If there had been an A, B, C marking system the awards would have gone something like this: a good parent, B; a brilliant conversationalist, C; a hearty, happy drinker, C; a lover of the arts, D; an honest man, B; a public-spirited citizen, C; a shrewd trader, A; a good lover (married or unmarried), C; a really kind man, B; a deeply religious person, C; an inventor, scientist, or journalist, C; a radical thinker, E; an expert in handling debts, that is, a banker, A; a good salesman, retail, B, wholesale, A; a successful producer who was also a good trader, A; a contented idler, D; a first-rate business man with all that implied, A + +.

Marks were invented for schools and colleges, but the evils they work there are as nothing to their effect upon life in general. Not to know our marking scale was to blunder again and again in our town — know the wrong people, say the wrong words, do the wrong things. Yet for a business culture resting upon an ever-increasing production, and exploiting shamelessly an extraordinary advance in technology, it was about what might have been expected. As pigeonholes await the circling pigeons, so jobs in this multiplying business structure awaited

the oncoming generation. There was the hole, and once in it
we had to produce a nest and an egg. It was lucky, and due to
our past, that courtesy and good humor and kindliness rated as
high as they did.

The effect, however, upon the wild pigeons was terrible, and,
as is well known, boys are born tame or wild in about equal
proportions. In our town the wild ones who, as they grew
older, sought whiskey, love, or reckless exercise, were condemned by the Methodists and the Presbyterians, but, if they
kept business hours, the magnates were tolerant, knowing that
the free livers would encourage the easy spenders. Those who
took out their wildness in dreaming were despised, for dreaming produced nothing, dreamers were thinking of unprofitable
things. Creative wildness, that longed to shape and invent, to
make life richer or better balanced, more vivid, less perfunctory, was regarded as eccentricity or weakness. A few such eccentrics were fortunate in discovering that they could create in
the production of goods or the management of men; their energy found an outlet in the expanding industrialism of the
age and flowed into it. The vitality of the others was dammed
up, diverted, or turned inward to grow sour and stagnant.

For there was every kind of talent in the youth of this town,
as in every town with good heredity and an ample life, and
most of it thwarted. There were girls with a sure, strong sense
of design, and nothing to use it upon but dressmaking, where
the provincial rigidity of style hampered them sorely. There
were boys with imaginations that rose *crescendo*, and then, in
an atmosphere that discouraged imagination not geared to business, relaxed and lost their vital energy. There was youth of
both sexes in which passion was ready to burst through the
artificialities of our pale-pink romanticism; but since passion
was bad for business and business men's wives, their passion
soon conformed to the kind of sexual relationship which made
the least trouble. A few of the nonconformists escaped and
worked out their destinies in a different environment, some to
success and some to failure. But most of them, even though
they did not submit to business, submitted to the ideals of a
business community, suppressing their own. They yielded
without much struggle, for we were too ignorant of psychology

and too unfamiliar with freer environments to dramatize ourselves as creative intellects fighting for life.

Yet it is easy to see now that something happened to us when we did give in to what economists would call later the profit-making motive. We acquired a neurosis which was to be like a familiar disease in American life for the next decades, cramping the creative instinct in everything but the production and distribution of commodities. Science escaped because it was new and might, though many doubted, be practical. Our escapists to science were lucky, for some laughed but no one jeered at them. Business might be able to use science. Not so with the arts. Literature, music, painting, philosophy, and the fine art of conversation, all need a supporting society. Nature is wasteful here as elsewhere and requires a thousand potential talents for every first-class achievement. Leaders need followers, if indeed followers do not make leaders. But those who aspired to the arts in our town, and indeed in America generally, suffered from an infantile paralysis contracted in their youth under the dominance of business, from which they are only now beginning to recover. They had lost confidence in their own desires and aspirations at that fatal moment of youth when a snub or a suppression lames for life. In the attempt which I have described to condition a whole community for business, youth was sterilized for activities of the pure intellect or the unfettered imagination.

Henceforth this generation, formed in the nineties, would be diffident in everything not in accord with the mores of a business community. They would read, but not too much, go to concerts, but not too often, support ideas, but not too passionately, be amateurs in many things, but professionals in none except money-making, and often not in that. This is what happened to the young in the Age of Confidence who soared or flapped instead of taking to the nest to lay a golden egg.

The confidence which the solid if unpleasing fabric of business inspired made politics in our community seem like an avocation when it was not also a business. Our attitude toward politics seems now incredibly naïve, but it had its points of advantage. We believed so thoroughly in the American system that we could afford to be indifferent as to just how it worked. Business went on, most people seemed to grow wealthier, America was a great country, hence the less concern as to how it was run the better. *Laissez-faire* seemed to reach its limit in American politics, and if that was a delusion, and if never were politics run more carefully for the benefit of business, no one ever told us so, not even the newspapers.

There were four kinds of politics in our town, and, so far as I can remember, we never made the slightest effort to think out the relationships among them. Delaware for over a century had been controlled politically by a handful of families, who usually had at least one member prominent somewhere in national political life. In my day there were two senators, and an ambassador and ex-secretary of state, all gentlemen, all friends of the family, all called 'statesmen.' We took for granted that our political system would always provide enough honest and able men of good family to keep the ship of state on her course, and never asked how they got, and how they stayed, aboard. We tipped our hats to a senator when we met him on Market Street, with a comfortable feeling of having seen a great man that day.

Closely allied to this sentimental phase of politics were the brief spells of patriotic exaltation at election time. It was the era of red fire, bands, floats, uniforms, and rows of small boys shouting in unison Y-O-U-N-G R-E-P-U-B-L-I-C-A-N — YOUNG REPUBLICAN. For a few days politics seemed important — trailing clouds of rather tawdry glory from the legendary era before the Civil War when in a border state like Delaware the clash of Abolitionist and Democrat, or earlier, of Federalist and Republican, engaged the best energies of the time.

The third kind of politics did touch business. I remember the grumbling and forebodings when, by some accident that seemed incredible to a boy brought up with confidence in his government, a dangerous and unprincipled free-trader named Cleveland was elected to the presidency. My grandfathers, so restrained and so eminently fair in everything that their judgments were like Holy Writ in the family, agreed in this, that

Democrats were bad for business and that unless the tariff were raised we should all go to the local poorhouse, a threat which the little girls took literally, and which was a secret worry even to the boys. That politics did matter if it got in the way of business, this much at least I learned, but it would be a mistake to suppose that it meant an introduction to the economic interpretation of history. Rather we shared a sincere emotional conviction, which even the few Democrats among us secretly concurred in, that the economic and the political were diametrically opposed. We believed, and all the town, even the politicians, believed, that there was a natural evolution of America toward a manifest destiny to be busier, richer, and therefore happier, and that, except for a failure of the crops, the one important enemy to progress was politics. Politicians preyed upon us, politics was the business of holding back, and holding up, business. And we regarded the 'statesmen' — the senators and judges and ambassadors whom we knew to be gentlemen and honest in spite of being in politics — as the agents of the respectable home world to whom honor was due because they had gone into public life to fight the politicians. This explains why in our strongly Republican town we respected and admired even the Democrats who were 'statesmen.' A single lecture on Cleveland and free trade by the iconoclast of my university days, William Graham Sumner, brought all my ideas of American economic history tumbling about my head. But the conception of politics as a parasite upon business, which was always right while the politicians were always wrong, was lodged much deeper than ideas of history.

That confidence was to last until 1929-33, a strong emotional prejudice coloring everything learned in experience or in education.

And of course politics, as the citizen of a small city in the East saw it in the nineties, *was* a bastard business, parasitical and deleterious. No one ever urged a boy to go into politics. It was the broken men, or the weak incapables, who found it easier to be genial than to work, that became politicians. We saw them about the Court House or the City Hall, a shifty-eyed lot, dribbling tobacco juice, badly dressed, never prosperous and self-respecting. They took care of the necessary but inferior functions of civilization: crime prevention, the institutions, ash-collecting, opening streets, making roads; the superior functions, business, law, social intercourse, getting rich, were out of politics. The garbage had to be collected, and order kept by policemen in the streets, but this was not what was regarded as a career. Let those who could not make a living otherwise attend to it, and to all politics. That was our attitude, and everything we saw bore us out. The politicians were a degraded caste, and the town, to our limited imagination, got along very nicely in spite of their known dishonesties and inefficiencies. There were slums, graft, epidemics, a ruinous lack of zoning, hopeless poverty, but these we accepted as natural. The majority of the citizens got about the environment they wanted, and without bothering with politics. And this was not at all as selfish as it sounds; part of it was moral. We were not so naïve as to be unaware that the state elections were swung by wholesale bribery of the Negroes and poor whites, nor ignorant of the close relations between the local political powers and the prostitutes and the saloon. We knew the local intermediaries, at least by sight, men who passed as lawyers or business men, but with a subtle depreciation in the community, often made articulate. They were, indeed, abused openly in the newspapers, and it must be remembered that in the Age of Confidence, when respectability was at a premium, publicity of any kind was not welcome, and bad publicity was damning. But more important, it was known to everyone that they were not scrupulous, not even honest, because they could *not* be. It was impossible to be honest in politics, that was our creed. Dishonesty in business was sporadic, like crime; dishonesty in politics was congenital. To turn toward politics, even to desire to be in politics, was like confessing a moral weakness. My father-in-law, as a young man, with a brilliant education, refused an attaché-ship at the legation at Berlin because afterward he might have to seek his career in politics.

I confess a sneaking affection for that confident age when it was not necessary to be always thinking about economics and politics. It is, of course, more intelligent to see the whole machine, realizing, as a school child is supposed to do today, that a balanced civilization is possible only when the conflicting interests of property and human rights are controlled by a government that is at least as strong as either. But for a while we did have a balance, most of us, and with so little diversion of energy from the pleasant occupation of living one's own life! No young sociologist will ever believe that the *laissez-faire* days before competition became a disease may have been pleasant ones, because no convinced sociologist was alive in a town and country with such ample margins and such easy escapes as was ours. I do not say that we used our leisure saved from attending to other people's business in any way which would have pleased Plato or even Francis Bacon. And of course our self-absorption left our town like a defective child on the doorstep of the machine age, incapable of decent growth, unplanned, and unformed — headed indeed toward every ugliness of congestion and discomfort. But there were amenities now lost in a culture without a social conscience that never worried about politics so long as the tariff stayed high, where if business was bad, just work a little harder, and if business was good, why should it not always stay so! Our town had some of that simplicity of existence with its perfect freedom within bonds, that is said to exist under successful dictatorships. Yet our people were their own masters, or thought they were; our confidence in progress kept us energetic, unskeptical, single-minded. We were not wise, but our simplicity gave us some of the fruits of wisdom — and among others much content. Only the very young and the very bold were restless in the nineties.

⌘ 13 ⌘

Conclusions

I AM WELL AWARE that this survey now concluding falls short of history. There is an omniscience in history which I am as little inclined to assume for the past as to accept for the present. This is a study in memory and must stand or fall on the values of memory.

Nevertheless, let me forestall criticism by admitting some obvious weaknesses in the record. This is the Age of Confidence as a boy and a young man saw it. I have not neglected the women where women counted in experience, but since I was born male, masculine these chapters had to be in their memories. I do not, for example, know how the girls felt about our golden age of romantic relationship, which so soon became merely gilded, for I was much too unphilosophical at the time (as well as too shy) to ask them, and cannot put their later answers now among my own memories. Again, a confident young bank clerk in this same confident age would presumably have seen in our town a community superficially like the one I describe, but quite devoid of the strains and stresses which made it so interesting and sometimes so distressing to a nonconformist like myself. I was happy, but never entirely at ease in this local Zion, and therefore my record must be regarded as the square peg's account of the round hole, which is not quite fair to history. I say this in all humility, but do not quite believe it, for the later history of our town and of the youth of the nineties that grew up with me seems, according to the best judgment I can muster, to be evidence that our confidence was artificial, a state of complacent content which, no matter how beneficial and fortunate for us, was at odds with the inevitable course of history. It was the square peg, not the round one, I think, that was most sensitive to what was happening. He could understand content without too confidently and complacently believing in it as an absolute.

Yet a somewhat sensitive and rather bookish youth, keener about nature than games, and more concerned with his own imagination than liquor, women, and human nature in the rough, was naturally limited in his observation. Nevertheless, if I have stressed the genial familiarity of our town, its friendliness, its sense of a passing code, its respectability, and its high estimate of character, it was not to erect a genteel city of the past where saloons, houses of ill fame, slums, poverty, debauchery, and embezzlement were conveniently left out of the record. No, my own experience was genteel, or when it was not genteel (which was often) left less impression on my imagination and hence on my memory than what little I saw of those habitually drunk, dishonest, or unchaste. There is a good deal of monotony in men and women obsessed with satisfying their primitive passions; what freer minds try to be and what amenities, real or seeming, they manage to achieve in social intercourse, are more important in a history of culture, and more interesting to remember. Nevertheless, our town as I have described it, is not the town that Huckleberry Finn or even Tom Sawyer would have seen, but a home town viewed by rather home-keeping boys, more adventurous in thinking than in rough-and-ready experience. The age I describe here is only one of the ages out of many that are coexistent in every era, and the town only one of many describable towns in the same place and time, yet I am confident enough of my own impressions to affirm its historical reality.

Its desirability is another question. I had thought at one time of calling this part of this book 'Nostalgia,' but realized before I had written a chapter that this title would be utterly false. If the opportunity were given to me to choose between youth then and youth in the era of my own sons, I think I should probably choose the present. Choose it with an almost agonized memory of the struggles in the early nineteen-hundreds to break away from that strong pattern of confident convention, to get through that friendly atmosphere into something that was a more vital reality, to escape from the dominance of a narrow code of morals and an inflexible impulsion toward a drab business life. These chapters are neither praise nor dispraise, unmixed and undefined, of the past. It is a study in values, and my own summary is a simple one. Our confidence was illusion, but like most illusions it had many of the benefits of a fact. Because of our confidence there were values in living in the nineties which are simply unpurchasable now. They are, in a true sense of the word, historical, and I have tried to describe them here because soon they will be discoverable only by research and then without the emotional margin which gave proportion and emphasis to the text. As experience, they are, I am sure, irrevocable, or at least not likely to occur again in our cycle; and youth of our day, whatever else it may enjoy and profit by, will not have them, and will live differently because of the loss. For I believe that while the Age of Mobility may be better or worse than the Age of Confidence, there have been these definite, describable losses to check against our gains. We can put our children on wheels to see the world, but we cannot give them the kind of home that any town provided in the nineties, not at any price.

Nostalgia for such a past does not imply approval and I have falsified the record if I have not been as emphatic in studying the neglect of important values in the complacency of those days, and the karma that followed and involved us all, as in the memory of our pursuit of what seems to me now the (often) true, the (reasonably) beautiful, and the (frequently) good.

Geographers, among all scientists, are the nearest to philosophers today, and a geographer could write the sum and conclusion of these chapters. That town, facing Europe across a narrowing sea, yet not near enough for ominous responsibility, drawing wealth for its rising factories from the great dynamo of the West, its streets still not too congested for pleasant shade, its countryward roads still quiet to walk upon, its populace mentally homogeneous, yet with too much racial admixture to be tame, its spirit as of young middle-age when nothing seems to stand in the way of an increasing success — a geographer could give good reasons for our Age of Confidence.

I myself have not dealt with ultimate causes but with results, since it was the effects of confidence that made our town so interesting. The evolution of civilization seems to differ

from the evolution of animals in this — that each era develops
modes and qualities of living that are not heritable, but belong
only to it, are gone when it is gone, and can be kept only in
memory, and should be kept, if they are good, so that we can
guess what to wish for if the chance comes again. We are paying grudgingly now for whatever harm was done us by this lost
American age, but we have taken our profits without gratitude.
The time has come to think of the eighteen-nineties as something more than a bad, small-town joke.

PART TWO
Alma Mater

Preliminary

THE SELF-MADE, SELF-TAUGHT MAN, greedy for power, set his mark on the nineties, and it was after his industrial triumphs that the small-town culture of the confident American age began to decay. But it was the college graduate who imposed his codes, his ideals, and his personality upon the next decades in the United States. His way of life was settled in a college experience which for power over the imagination has had few equals since the monastic period. It was made up of youthful adventure, a shallow culture, a set of ideals vague and seldom critical, and for his real thinking, often his real motives, the undergraduate waited or went elsewhere. Yet it was an intense experience. In spite of the numerous books upon American education in the nineties and nineteen-hundreds, I can find none that adequately describes it, or relates the college of that day to youth as I knew it. They deal with the facts better than I can, since they are broader in scope, but they leave out the immensely important element of emotion. The college I remember was more than an institution, it was a community with a vital life of its own, a state within the state.

I make no pretense of encyclopedic knowledge or of breadth of experience in recording my own memories of the American college in the days when both its new Gothic architecture and its college life tried to be romantic, and often succeeded. I have known many American colleges, but only one well. That does not, I truly believe, affect the justice of what I have to say. Harvard may have been old Harvard, as the song says, when Yale was but a pup, and of a different breed. The most ardent believer in standardization would not dare to assert that college life among the lakes of Wisconsin was identical with experience in a Princeton dormitory or upon a Southern campus. The differences, however, were unimportant when compared with the resemblances, and though each body of undergraduates boasted of an exclusive distinction in manners, clothes, slang, morale, outlook, and even in personality, and each faculty regarded itself as marked by an intellectual individualism in the eyes of the world, yet this outside world knew only a 'student' and a 'professor' who fitted very readily into types.

Furthermore, the younger colleges, whether they were 'state' or 'privately endowed' institutions, modeled their life and aspirations upon the older colleges, which were usually in the East, and which drew heavily from the oldest schools and the wealthiest or most cultivated classes. Fashions began there and spread, so that a new twist to a hatbrim or a new method of teaching traveled in a few years from ocean to ocean, and gave a unity to college life. I am not writing here of that larger organization of professional schools, service bureaus, and organs of scholarship, called a university. There history was differently made. But the American college for undergraduates ran true to form, if infinitely varied in secondary characteristics, all round the states. Its peculiar life was most highly developed in the men's colleges, which inherited the traditions (not all of them decorous) of monasticism, least developed in coeducational institutions, yet whatever the differentiation, the tailor who first adopted the word 'collegiate' for his wares was a shrewd fellow. In the early nineteen-hundreds both the college undergraduate and the college graduate could be easily recognized in their communities. They belonged to a class that was far more homogeneous than America at large.

I have seen in my time collegiate youth rise, strut, and decline into the comics. Nevertheless, from these campuses came many, if not most, of the two generations of Americans who have been in executive charge of the country, and the greater part of the codes, ideals, manners, and ideals of living which dominate the owning and the managing classes so-called. Here was the conditioning laboratory for the most energetic of our youth. These were the Utopias from which they emerged to tackle with extraordinary confidence, only recently shaken, a country which was becoming a social and economic problem while they were still fighting for the prizes of their little college world.

⚲ I ⚲

The College Town

I REMEMBER first the college town. Surely it is amazing that
neither history, nor sociology, nor even fiction, has given
more than passing attention to the American college town, for
it has had a character and a personality unlike other towns. And
quite as surely, its imprint of small-town respectability, convention, and common sense is deeper upon American education than has ever been guessed. With the rarest exceptions the
home of the college has been a small town, even if that town
was a suburb or a section, self-contained, of a city. There were
hundreds of such towns in the period of which I write, and all
with a family resemblance.

Cleaner, neater than other towns, with green spaces somewhere toward the center, and white spires or Gothic towers or
windowed domitories half hid by trees, they were the little
capitals of the academic states. As trading or industrial centers
their life might be indistinguishable from towns or cities of a
like size, but in their social consciousness there was always some
recognition of peculiarity. For the heart of the community was
a college. Its subtle influences were as pervasive if less noticeable, than the quite unsubtle symbols of college life — playing
fields, cafés, and collegiate clothing.

And in the early nineteen-hundreds the college town was no
luncheon stop for automobiles. It was secluded, even if it was
a town within a city, like the Yale section of New Haven; it
knew its boundaries and kept them; it was jealous of its distinctions; if it was uneasy, it was also proud. The campus and the
college buildings dominated its architecture like the temple
and citadel of a Greek city-state, a difficult relationship since
there was always some doubt in the minds of the town folk
whether the college was an asset or a parasite. The town with

its college was like a woman's club committee with a celebrity in tow, a credit to them but also an embarrassment and sometimes a nuisance; it was like a French village built upon a Roman camp to which tourists resort; it was like the mistress of an actors' boarding house, pleased by the notoriety but worried by the manners, or the morals, of her boarders; it was like almost anything but a town without a college. And many a college town was like a resentful mother who, expecting a quiet and manageable infant, had given birth to a Gargantua that swallowed whole streets and squares in its gigantic growing. I do not wish to be fantastic, yet only such similes will express how very unlike the rest of the United States was the college town.

New Haven, as I first knew it in the late nineties, was a decorous and beautiful town, set in the midst of a sprawling industrial city of slums, factories, and long, undistinguished avenues. The college town was old New Haven, with its Green, its bordering business streets, its campus and blocks of residences north-stretching into park and country beyond. The elm-shaded streets of this old town were lined by sedate houses which in various modes still kept the impress of the Greek revival of the early nineteenth century. Eight out of ten had a portico of wood with two Doric columns painted brown or gray or white. Down the length of shady streets these columns made a pleasant arcade, broken here and there by high brick mansions of the eighties, or a charming green-shuttered, white-walled reminder of the better proportions of a Colonial day.

It was a guarded town, very unlike the ample if ugly spaciousness of the mansarded avenues of my youth, where broad porches and open gates welcomed relatives and friends. There were no open doors in the New England college town. Behind the twin Doric columns, which might have been labeled Respectability and Reserve, two squint lights seemed always to be looking down their noses at the passer-by, fearful lest he should wish to enter. The college town, unlike the rest of America, was jealous of privacy, and doubtful of casual relationships.

Lights went out early in these bosky streets, often to be relit in upstairs studies. When the chapel bell rang ten, and the undergraduate navigating homeward across the Green filled the night with shouts and melody, the prim town pulled up its covers, shut its ears, or burrowed deeper in a book. Nights in the college town were consecrated to sleep or work.

Along these town streets, professors lived, students wandered, but also the social and professional leaders of the city sought residence, because, after all, it was the college that gave tone to the community. Academic society was therefore both town and gown, and had a double flavor which recalled in homely fashion the atmosphere of those small European courts where both prince and bishop had their following. It was not an exciting society, yet certainly it was not dull. New Haven had never forgotten that it was once a colony, all of itself, and might have been a state had it not sheltered republicans and regicides. There was a stiff, aristocratic quality in the old families, now entirely lost there as elsewhere in America. From their harsh stalks sprouted personalities of extraordinary independence, so that it was hard to tell sometimes whether decorum or eccentricity was the dominant note of the town's society. These families belonged to the college world, yet were not wholeheartedly of it. They arranged its finances, fought its lawsuits, supplied a president or a professor now and then, were mysteriously powerful sometimes in academic affairs, yet in general their attitude of respectful but slightly contemptuous toleration of learning, so characteristic of America, was tempered only by the belief that the college belonged to them and put them a cut above the aristocracies of Hartford or Springfield, and made them able to take rank even in New York. Hence the teacher, who in this money-making age lived on the edge or beyond of society, in the college town might have a definite place, though he was not society himself. Wealth and position did not so much stoop to him as restrain their privileges so that he could enter. By a self-denying ordinance, tacitly understood, the rich in the college set (and no other society counted) spent only a part of their incomes at home, eschewed butlers, denied themselves broughams, and later, for a while, automobiles, kept dues low in the clubs, and, if they did spend, put their money into that good wine and costly food which the scholar has always enjoyed. And he responded with an unexpected geniality which was sometimes grateful and sometimes lumbering, and sometimes only a courteous irony.

Thus the college was privileged socially, not only in the hand-picked sons of the cultivated or the well-to-do that came as students, but in the close contacts between the faculty and the aristocracy of the college town. But it was conditioned also by the life of a small-town community, which, no matter how good its traditions, how admirable its character, how genuine its culture, was, by definition, a little provincial, a little prig-gish, and very much inbred. And yet there was a raciness in this mingling of town and gown that gave its own flavor to the college society, and was some compensation for the gustier airs which blew through capitals and metropolises.

I can see now a characteristic 'reception' in a great house behind the broad sweep of the elms of Hillhouse Avenue, which was to the college town of New Haven what Fifth Ave-nue once was to New York — a terminus of social pride. Tables were laden with heavy, mind-satisfying food, champagne bub-bled on the sideboards, stiff-backed professors were trying to relax, while their wives, with the curious pursed mouth of the academic woman, showed more concern for their dignity than for the entertainment. Among them moved the grand dames of our town society, soothing vanities by a kind word, snubbing with a vacant look the strange uncouth creatures that science was bringing into the university, but not too emphatically, since one never knew nowadays who might become famous. And with them were our town eccentrics, women usually of old families, too sure of themselves to bother about social dis-tinctions. Worse dressed than the professors' wives, they had a confident distinction of ugliness which lifted them above our small-town limitations, and they spoke the language of the aca-demic world with understanding and tolerance, like mission-aries among an Indian tribe. Trailing behind them, yet al-ways heading back toward the champagne, were our faculty 'characters' — the great hearty souls that scholarship which is not pedantry creates in its happier moods, men whose broad-cloth might be shiny and spotted, their linen none too clean, yet with minds and faces of the great world, known in Europe and conscious of it, witty often, sarcastic usually, ill-mannered, inclined to lash out at this pompous bourgeois society, which nevertheless gave them their only chance to eat, drink, and be merry with their own kind. There was our famous Chaucerian scholar, Lounsbury, his sparse white beard wagging under his rapid tongue, his eyes a little bleary, an epigram worth quoting with every glass of champagne. 'Why do they want to inscribe old Whitney's name on the Court House wall? All he knew was Sanskrit. What did he ever do for New Haven?' says a banker. 'Do!' Lounsbury shoots back. 'By Gorry! It's enough that he lived here!'

There were subtle jealousies between town and gown which could not be assigned to differences in income. The town had inherited a Yankee distrust of ministers who talked about God but made no money, and now that ministers were less and professors more it transferred this distrust with increments. It was irritated by its own deference to an institution that did not make for profits. Energy that in other communities was organizing machine tools or life insurance, here in this college community leaked away in a trickle that sometimes carried sons and heirs with it into the academic world where it was transformed into the teaching of adolescents or into books that nobody but professors read. The town derived a goodly share of its income from the rapidly increasing expenditures of the college and its students, and this, too, it resented, feeling that it was committed to an approval of what the college was doing. It endured the noisy night life of the students, the untidy boarding houses that crowded its streets, the frequent arrogance of the academic mind, but it disliked the haunting sense of inferiority which came from knowing that it was celebrated because of the college. It listened to the endless shop-talk of the faculty and pretended to take the 'big men' of the undergraduate world at their face value, but it could not entirely respect, and still less understand, the creature upon which it lived and which it believed it had created. Not until the expansive twenties when alumni, enriched by the war and prosperity, upset their applecarts of gold into the college coffers, and made education, or at least the side-shows of education, a big business, was the town convinced that the college, its own college, was worthy of its birthplace. No Commencement orator was ever so persuasive as gifts in the millions and a building program that was a major industry.

And yet, as with Christians and Infidels living together in old Spain, there was more interpenetration than appeared on the surface. The college taught the town to discuss ideas; it taught also friendship and a delight in the companionship of like-minded men. The two blended in the adult life of the community, for the habit of the undergraduate fraternity persisted in dozens of little clubs of talkers which flourished throughout the town because their members had learned clubability. It was a rash hostess who gave a dinner party on Wednesday or Friday nights, their favorite meeting times. In these clubs scholar, lawyer, and business man ate, drank, and read papers explaining their jobs or their social philosophy. Ideas spread through the college town, freed from that taboo on abstractions which was the curse of the small town elsewhere in America, and many a scholar was saved from pedantry, or a paralysis of the emotions in the arid wastes of specialist theory, by his contacts with men whose daily task was the handling of men. Even the women became clubable; and indeed it was in New Haven that by happy inspiration Our Society was born, whose inestimable privilege after the meeting was to inspect every closet in their hostess's house. But it was a man's town.

Still another institution the college gave to the society of the town, the college widow. I knew two of them in their old age and profited greatly from my friendships. For the college widow had a depth and richness of emotional experience never developed in American life of that day outside of the few metropolises, and seldom there. She began at sixteen or eighteen as a ravishing beauty, the darling of freshmen; she passed on in the years of her first blooming from class to class of ardent youngsters, until, as her experience ripened, she acquired a taste, never to be satisfied by matrimony, for male admiration abstracted from its consequences; and, more subtly, for the heady stimulant of intimacy with men in their fresh and vigorous youth. By her thirties she had learned the art of eternal spring, and had become a connoisseur in the dangerous excitement of passion controlled at the breaking point, a mis-

tress of every emotion, and an adept in the difficult task of sub-
limating love into friendship. The students lived out their
brief college life and went on; she endured, and tradition with
her, an enchantress in illusion, and a specialist in the heart.
Twenty, even thirty years, might be her tether; and when suddenly on a midnight, a shock of reality, or perhaps only boredom, ended it all, she was old — but still charming and infinitely wise. To smoke a cigarette with her when cigarettes
were still taboo for women, and drink her coffee and liqueur,
was a lesson in civilization.

Yet in fostering in its midst the sprawling infant, gray-
headed but still growing, which was the college, the town sacrificed its own youth. There was childhood and maturity in a
college town, but no youth in between. Youth male was absorbed into the undergraduate community and came home
only on Sundays, youth female was usually sent off perforce to
school or woman's colleges, away from the dangerous glamour
of college streets. Hence the young folk in the college town
settled back into their home environment only in their mid
or late twenties, and then only did social life in a community
begin for them. There were no calf loves in the society of the
college town, no gawkish immaturity, no giggling, no rebellious
escapes. And since the young had reached the earning and
marrying stage in a society where the scale of living was based
upon an instructor's salary, their pleasures were necessarily
simple. Relative poverty was regarded as a virtue, doing without was a pride. One walked, not rode; went to concerts rather
than to the theater; danced to a piano and a cornet; gave books,
not jewelry; sat down four at a table, not eight; kept married
instead of toying with expensive ideas about lovers and divorce.

The results for the college town were by no means ill. The
tittle-tattle of a small town had little fuel here. It was an educated society, and since it could not afford to be frivolous, and
both puritan custom and economy held the passions in check,
every opportunity was given to vivacity and ideas in conversation. Talk was cheap, which did not prevent it from being
good. It was often stiff with convention and sometimes pedan-
tical, yet the fun was more civilized than country-club horse-
play, the wit, when any, aware of the nature of wit.

And yet it was all a little arid. The young people had come together too late. They had no sentimental memories to share, and thanks to the restrictions of what was, after all, a small town, and to the official nature of their college society, and to relative poverty, the sex in relationships was weak. Every emotion had its inhibition. Like the columns of the houses, the twin shrines in every heart were Reserve and Respectability.

The college town was thus the imperfect resultant of two worlds in a physical merger where souls and minds remained disparate. Even this understates the difficulty. The undergraduates belonged to the faction of the gown, but had themselves come in a vast majority from uncollegiate small towns, and so in ideas and attitudes toward learning were far closer to the Philistines of the streets than to the Israelites of the campus faculty. Their relations with the faculty could too often be described as passive resistance, usually with the sneaking sympathy of both parents and town. Hence there was a split in the college itself, so that in my days not a duality but a trinity — town, gown, and sweater — would have best described our community.

I have written of the college town with pleasure because I was happy there, and excited, and amused, and also cabin'd, cribb'd, confined; yet also with a very definite purpose. For it is impossible to think of the college of that day without its encircling town. This was the air the professor breathed, and which the student absorbed from his freshman year onward. For him the town often provided his first experience in adult social life. Nor in discussing the internal conflicts of the college itself which have been so decisive in shaping the type known as the college graduate, is it right to forget for a moment the influence of these nests of puritan respectability, given tone by the American aristocracy that clung to them for shelter from the make-money world outside. Here is a factor in education and in the faiths and prejudices of the educated and educator which has escaped the theorist and the statistician alike. We have forgotten that the types we analyze so readily — professors, alumni, humanists, scientists, scholars — were in their conditioning period American boys in a small college town.

2

College Life

WHEN I FIRST SAW the college town it was late September, and I, a somewhat frightened boy from home, was dragging a suitcase full of books across the exciting spaces of the Green. The books were for the final cram before entrance examinations, but that was only a cold trepidation hung somewhere near my heart, which was warmed by very different emotions. Coming from a small city that had never tried to be Athens, my naïve imagination had conceived of a college as an assemblage of Parthenons and cathedrals. What I saw before me that afternoon across the Green would have been disillusioning if I had been realistic. The rather dingy halls — boxes ornamented with pseudo-Gothic or Byzantine — were little like my dream, and the beautifully simple relics of the old college of brick Colonial were much too simple to mean anything to my taste tutored in the nineties. But I was far from being realistic, so that in a second of time, between Green and campus, I had dropped, with the easy inconsequentiality of youth, all illusions of architectural grandeur for the real thing, college life.

Viewed backward, this college life, which was to make such an imprint on the behavior and the ideals of the leaders of the oncoming generation, looms up, a cloud of influences, sometimes rich, sometimes sinister, sometimes trivial. Close at hand or described from memory, it seemed more like a haven for American youth, a little space of time where energy had its outlet, and where the young made a world to suit themselves, which, for a while at least, the adult world was to accept at surprisingly near the college estimate.

This much I had heard, although in language much less philosophical; and therefore a glamour hung over the college

143

town and the college at its heart, which was to increase its en-
chantments, on past the climax of senior year. Thousands like
myself (so I felt as I crossed the Green) had been there before
me in a life which was to become my experience. At home
most of us, and certainly I myself, had lived in one dimension,
with at most a family extension toward an American past. Overnight we were to step through an opening door into tradition,
a usable, sympathetic tradition of youth. It was to be our privilege to be born again, painlessly, and without introspection.
All this, which I felt, not spoke, was true.

Therefore, like all that confident generation, I accepted the
college as I found it, and believed in its life and its spirit with
a fanatic devotion. I saw that the boys who were strolling that
day in the latter nineties down the autumn streets were as easily
distinguishable among the town crowds as beings from another
world. The town was only their background, and I picked
them out in their turtle-neck sweaters under the briefest of
topcoats, as a dog sees only other dogs on a busy road. There
was an arrogant and enchanting irresponsibility in their behavior which was intoxicating. I longed to get rid of my suitcase with its irrelevant books, and into a sweater, which I saw
to be obligatory — to dress like them, be like them.

A few nights later I was herded with other freshmen into a
straggling parade, which marched to a space of torchlight and
confusion where champions wrestled for the honor of their
classes. And there were the Strong Silent Men I had read about
in the newspapers, the football and crew heroes, calming the
crowded field by the full-breasted dignity of the white letters
on their blue sweaters. And there were other slighter figures
in tiny topcoats with upturned collars, who seemed to exercise
an equal authority. These, I was told, were the Big Men, the
managers, the powers behind college life, more important, because brainier, than the athletes. These were the real masters
of this new state. I felt as if I were being naturalized into a
new government, more vital than any I had known, as indeed
I was.

It was 1896, at the very crisis of one of the few bitter and
doubtful political struggles of my time in America. Bryan had
nailed capitalism on his cross of gold and was touring the

enemy East in what then seemed a triumphal career. He spoke on the Green, and we students (how warmly I called myself by that name) thronged a thousand or so, milling about among the townsfolk but conscious, as always, only of ourselves. I remember with ironic emphasis how my curiosity as to the appearance of the Great Commoner was forgotten in a deeper thrill when I found myself pressed in the crowd against one of the 'Big Men' of the night before, who was actually asking me, 'What did he say? Could you hear?'

There was shouting and booing, hissing and applause. The students were heavily against Bryan. I felt that, but also that it was no active opposition, but only a reaction to what they had heard from home. He did not belong in their world. We were excited, and a little amused, by such a stirring of the dull adult population over matters that concerned us only a little.

My class was the entering one of 1899. 'Ninety-nine out of a hundred,' boomed the Great Commoner from his platform in the midst of the swirling mob, 'ninety-nine out of a hundred of the students in this university are sons of the idle rich.'

He had said the magic word, the rallying numeral. If the students had booed and whooped with the crowd before, now they shouted. 'Ninety-nine!' 'Nine-nine-ninety-nine!' a chorus took it up, seniors beginning, freshmen, recognizing their symbol, joining in. 'Nine, nine, ninety-nine!' It seemed to be a scurrilous attack of economic parasites upon a statesman of the people, and so the Democratic papers from coast to coast reported it the next morning. Actually it was nothing of the sort. We were too innocent to know what economic parasitism was, and indeed we were no more parasitical than any other youngsters in the educational period, and far from idle. Our chanted impertinence was only the automatic response of a society that knew no politics or economics but its own, to one of its passwords, uttered by accident. We were like a savage tribe who sees their totem embroidered on the flag of an explorer.

Years afterward I met Bryan, who well remembered this episode, but I could not persuade him that it was college life, not the bias of the idle rich, which drowned his speech in mirth and yelling. Yet that was the true explanation. I had entered a state within a state, and joined a faction of that state, the student body, aware really only of themselves, their own life, their own ideals. Nor did we guess how closely an umbilical cord attached us to the energy of our country.

The first sensation in this new world was of a wholly delightful irresponsibility. It was a one-way irresponsibility only, since we were deeply responsible to the mores of our college world, yet, so far as home and town and the world outside generally were concerned, it was like release from confinement, boredom, or pain. We kicked up our heels in that pleasant college town like colts in a pasture. It was a somewhat rowdy irresponsibility, so the town thought, which liked to bawl at night under respectable windows, smash lamp-post glass with beer bottles, and hock best suits for an evening's pleasure, scorning decorum. These childish tricks, which, I am told, are scorned as 'collegiate' by the present university generation, were only symptoms of our independence from home rules and school discipline. They were one sign that we had got a franchise in living, another being the egregious bad taste with which we furnished our rooms with cigar-ribbon pillows, bad chromos of girls dressed in the college color, and 'Turkish corners' bought entire at a department store. Among the more intellectual the same desire for self-assertion subscribed for de luxe sets of Maupassant, Balzac, or Thackeray, which seldom got finally paid for.

This rebellion against decorum and the customs of dull every day had its romance and its poetry. It was scurrilous but not insolent, bawdy but not obscene. I find its careless, happy irresponsibility best preserved in a Yale folk song of the nineties, author unknown, which I believe has never before been put in print. The scene is on Thursday or Saturday night, the setting a long table with steins and pretzels, the dramatis personae two companies of students, ranged on either side. The ship mentioned is the old *Richard Peck,* once of boisterous fame, that ran nightly from New Haven to New York, the time is 11 P.M., the mood neither drunken nor sober, the spirit that of 'Down with Respectability, drink her down.' Choruses answer each other across the table.

Invitation from the Right

I will tell you of a little scheme I've got,
And I hope, sirs, that you will refuse it not,

To go down upon the Richard Peck tonight,
And have fun aplenty in the moo-oonlight.

Acceptance from the Left

We accept your generous invitation,
Since having pleasure is our occupation.
We will meet you on the dock at twelve o'clock,
And to get the dough we'll put our watch and chain in hock.

Chorus, Both Sides

Oh, we will have the hell of a time, I'll tell you what,
Loving, lushing, stowing wine into our faces.
And we'll sit up till the morning and enjoy the light of dawning,
Hully Gee!, by God, we'll raise hell on the Peck!
> *Diddly Dum,*
> *Take my advice,*
> *Diddly Dum,*
> *On the Peck.*

Of course, all this was just youthful exuberance of animal high spirits, shot through, except for the grossest, with that traditional romance of student life which has come down to us unbroken from the medieval university, its vagabond students the Goliards, its arrogant unrespectability. The real irresponsibility went much deeper, was in fact both an escape and a new allegiance. It was the boy's escape from his duty to be conformist in his own family and respectable in his home town. It was an escape (though he would never have so phrased it) from dull bourgeois life, with its emphasis upon being businesslike and time-serving to relatives or employers. Or it was a breakaway from the moral platitudes and conventional discipline of boarding school. All this the freshman eluded by a bound into a community where the mirth and the energy he best understood were sanctioned by a powerful public opinion, and had their immediate rewards; where he could make his personality prevail if he had one; where his age was the right age, while on the horizon hung grandiose possibilities which, realized, would bring him home the boy that made good, carrying glamour with him.

A longing to escape from the inferiorities of childhood and to triumph over the elders who think that they are betters, is, and has been, of course, common to all youth. Therefore, the freshman changed his tie, his hat, his slang, as a manifesto of his escape from rule, but also of his new allegiance. He was no longer a boy from Rochester; he was a Princeton undergraduate, admitted to the rights and privileges of college life; and this consciousness went to the roots of his being, making him sensitive to every push and pull of his new environment, and therefore intensely aware of the public opinion of his new society, which, again like a Greek city-state, was simple, homogeneous in its unity, diverse in personnel, stratified socially, proud, vain, and supremely confident of its way of life. It is impossible to describe truly those shady streets of 'eating joints' and rooming houses, those bleak college halls, the cocky students, playing ball like boys on the campus grass, laughing, teasing, yet tense when their mood was serious, unless one remembers that under its aspect of flaunted carelessness this was a well-knit community, intensely self-conscious, in which emotions were easily stirred toward comedy or tragedy — a community that defined its own success, pursued it constantly, was arrogantly indifferent to the ideals of others, and asked its members for complete and wholehearted allegiance. That parody of an earlier parody, 'The Son of a Gambolier,' which we used to sing tramping home at midnight,

> What the hell do we care, what the people say,
> We are, we are, we are, we are the Yale Y.M.C.A.,

was not so much a scoff at Christian piety as a characteristic expression of the student mind, which pretended to be flippant in everything but college loyalty. It was the first line that was shouted loudest because it voiced the triumph of escape from the tame communities of the home towns.

It was the new loyalty that we felt most deeply, although our escape into self-expression was, of course, a joy in itself. We did cast off very thoroughly the bonds that tied us to the smug, the censorious, and the utilitarian; and so made a limited Utopia. Thoreau, in his way, did much the same when he escaped from the pressure of greed, and of responsibility to a society of which he did not approve, into the leafy solitudes of Walden. He went there to work as a poor student, with high thinking as his goal. We, comfortable and careless scholars, were racing after pleasure and social prestige. Yet I cannot think of that life now except with affection, in spite of its shams, its false values, and its isolation from most worldly realities except the need for competition. To let the whole being go in a frenzy of excitement at a Big Game; to lounge whole evenings through under the wistaria blooms that swung inward over our window seat; to talk endlessly of this and that, vague ideas and rambling argument hiding enthusiasm, trepidation, or desire; to be privileged beings always joking about experience, which we touched lightly because life was still a fascinating experiment — this was not trivial just because what we felt or said seems trivial now. What frankness we used, for we had little to conceal! What fresh perceptions, for we had seen so little! What confidence, since the difference between success and failure seemed still to be an accident which a push could avoid! And those moonlights, marching home from our mild carouses, hearts released in convivial expansiveness, singing —

And if it be a girl, sir, we'll dress her up in blue,
And send her out to Saltonstall to coach the freshman crew —

or, if the mood was sentimental —

Only a bluebell, emblem of con-stanc-y,
O'er life's wear-y ways, bringing her back to me.
A hundred fathoms, hunder-ed fathoms deep.

That was all an absolute good, a value, giving to the undergraduate of those days a sense of happiness in the simple emotions of friendship which he was not to lose.

In all this we of the early nineties and nineteen-hundreds were like the students of every fortunate age. They have always made their own world, and their own ways for it, and their own ideals which, whether worldly or unworldly, have had the short-term quality of youth. But the American experience of my generation differed in some important respects. No weight of political or religious responsibility hung over our community, as upon the reforming, revolutionary, or reactionary student bodies of other times and countries. We were naïvely yet arrogantly aware that we belonged to America's golden girls and boys, and had been sent to this pleasant place to work a little and play hard, until our time came. Yet, quite unaware, we were actually in the grip of the time-spirit and the local gods of our country. A philosophy bred of Protestantism and pioneering was pricking us hard. The conventional idea (and ours) of the college as a well-organized country club was quite erroneous. There never was a more strenuous preparation for active life anywhere than in the American college of those days. Our illusion of independence was perfect, but it was an illusion.

We were strenuous without thought to ask the reason why. For all but the congenitally lazy, the songful hours over beer steins, the country walks, and the midnights of intimate talk, were interludes (like our lessons) in a tense activity. The cry in our undergraduate world was always 'do something,' 'what does he *do?*' Freshmen hurried up and down entry stairs seeking news for the college paper; athletes, often with drawn, worried faces, struggled daily to get or hold places on the teams; boys with the rudiments of business ability were managers of magazines, orchestras, teams, or co-operative pants-pressing companies. Those who had a voice sang, not for sweet music's sake, but to 'make' the glee club. Long throats went in for social drinking, glib minds for politics; everything but scholarship was in my day an 'activity,' and called 'doing something for the college.' Fraternities read off each meeting night their record of successful achievements, where credit for study meant only that the brethren had kept out of trouble with the faculty. Brother Jones is left guard on the scrub; Brother Smith is 'heeling' (expressive term) religion in the Y.M.C.A.; Brother Brown is being urged to write jokes for the *Record*; Brother Robinson is manager of the chess team. Some voice seemed always to be saying, 'Work, for the night is coming.' The toil was supposed to be fun, but the rewards were serious. No one that I remember did anything that was regarded as doing, for its own sake. No, the goal was prestige, social preferment, a senior society which would be a springboard to Success in Life. And all gilded, made into illusion, by the theory that in such strenuosity we demonstrated loyalty to our society, which was the college; that thus the selfish man transcended his egoistic self-seekings, and 'did' something for Harvard, or Amherst, or Yale.

I think it all bore some resemblance to the frontier of a generation earlier, and perhaps college life at the turn of the twentieth century was the last survival in America of the faith-in-energy and confidence-in-the-future of the pioneer experience in America. We youngsters broke loose from the stabilities of our home towns in order to find independence in the midst of opportunity, precisely as did the pioneers from the East to the West. Like them we knew that same lift of spirit, release of energy, and inner fear which one finds recorded in many frontier diaries. Our competitions, like theirs, were chiefly in brawn and shrewdness, and, like hunting, fishing, exploring, and even tree-cutting, were essentially fun, though we, by choice, and they, by necessity, made work of them. The horizon of our ambitions, too, was distant and vague, with miles ahead in which to try something new if one failed at first.

And college, like the frontier, was a young man's world, where no one got tired, and no energies were saved for tomorrow. The quick emotions of the pioneer were ours also, and his boastfulness, and his ignorance of subtleties in human relationships, and his quite unjustified confidence in his self-sufficiency. From his grossness, his frequent degeneracy, his savagery and shiftlessness, we were saved by our economic security and civilized environment, though not from his frequent dishonesty. But we did not escape his maladjustment to the realities of a rapidly changing civilization. For even as many a pioneer became a restless vagabond seeking only change all his life, so many a student of my day has stayed mentally an undergraduate ever since.

Like the pioneers also, the undergraduates were expecting to get rich, but that was ultimate. The immediate goal was to be regarded as a success by your friends. Ordinary students might be satisfied with a release of energy, but the leaders of the college community wished to be known as the big men, the bad men, the bosses of the neighborhood. Strength, pluck, good nature, square-dealing among friends, shrewd trickiness with enemies, won prestige in both lives. Our emotional range was narrower, for while the pioneers dragged their women with them, there were no women in our society except the prostitutes, who were hearty barbarians like ourselves, giving and expecting nothing but a temporary companionship. But if we had no real hardships, we made our lives often incredibly hard, so that it used to be said that a prominent undergraduate was as busy as the President, racing from training table to field, from field to classroom, from classroom to fraternity conference.

The youngsters who 'heeled' the daily college paper, which was one of the surest roads to social success, slept never more than four hours a night, wore out a bicycle a month, and were rusticated or sent to the infirmary by dozens. They were, ostensibly, learning journalism, but very few of them ever became journalists; they were said to be training themselves for success in after life, a vague future success, like the pioneer's dream (not often realized) of rich and boundless land all his own. Yet, in that moment of college time, actually they were playing the game because it was strenuous, and successful strenuosity was certain of recognition by your fellows. It was power in themselves and credit for that power which they sought, not power over others — that desire came later. And so it was with the pioneers.

I suppose this is where our college generation in its maturity gets its confidence that ability plus hard work can always win the game. For many it has been an illusion. Probably it had become an illusion in America before we entered college. Yet the faith was there, and faith often upsets circumstance. It will take more than the economic shifts and the wars of our times to convince us that there is any probable set-up of forces that we cannot, if we will, overcome. Perhaps it will take the atomic bomb — which college graduates invented. In our background we have the fact of happiness, relative for most, absolute for some, and that is of immense psychological importance. We have the experience of successful co-operation in our own interest. We have the pioneer's training in self-dependence, his sense of room at the top, and his certainty that work can get him there. The laboring class of the United States has had no such experience; the white-collar class of the bourgeoisie that did not go to college have had no such experience, and if they have the faith, it has already been proved to be an illusion. It seemed no illusion to us in our fortunate time, which is one reason why will has been strongest among the graduates of college life. Now they are encountering a will equally strong, the product of a very different education, the will of unionized labor.

Our handicap was the lack of a real education. For we never learned what were the possible goals of strenuosity and the limitations of confidence, nor how to apply our energies to a co-operative endeavor which was not a kind of game to be won by our side. We were prepared to create a trust or organize a war, not to control the one for human uses and to stop the other before it began. Only the Sumners, and their like, told us what it was all about in terms that penetrated our busy brains. ·The rest of the adult thinking in our college community was as narrow as our own, even if deeper and truer.

I had a classmate whose father had been governor and was then chief justice of a state. He had been bred in the usual preparatory school routine and was as deep as any of us in the excitements of college life, and rather more irresponsible. But perhaps because he had lived in a home where ideas and their application to the conduct of society had been in daily discussion, he had acquired the rare quality of liking to think. At midnight, when the perennial topics of teams, senior societies, or the amorous or drunken exploits of Student A and Student B, had begun to stale like the pipe smoke, his skeptical spirit would often rise above the trivial, and he would begin to talk in a monologue addressed more to himself than to us.

There were ideas afloat, it seemed, which Professor So-and-So had evidently heard of, but bungled in his morning lecture, and these ideas were important to young fellows like us. It was possible that sociology and economics weren't taken seriously enough by the students — that a lot of the things being taught us, except physics (here we all spat), had stuff in them we ought to think about. Suppose it were true that while we were pretending to be loafers and drunkards the real thing was getting away from us! In Oxford and Cambridge and Paris and Berlin (he had read) there were plenty of dubs and bluffers, yet men like ourselves, who might be ignorant as hell but weren't exactly stupid, got as excited about ideas as over their football games when they had any. He had heard that discussion spread from the good minds on the faculty through the student body; that men came out of those universities ready to stir up a rum-pus in the world, ahead of the game, not behind it. Men were graduated there, not into law or the soap business, but into radicalism or imperialism, all hot with some new philosophy. They went home interested in thinking, which certainly never happened to a chair-warmer at Heublein's café, or a heeler of the football team, or the last man to be tapped for a senior so-ciety, provided that was all he did in college. What was the matter with us? Had we no *Weltanschauung* (or this is what he would have said if he had not been so rotten in German), no sense of responsibility for a country that was after all not just a place where you looked for a job?

We would shift uncomfortably, making feeble rejoinders, which grew more confident as we sketched the outline of yes-terday's economics recitation (which we knew we had flunked), asking what Ricardo meant in our young lives, until the breezes blew once more from our real interests, and the talk lifted into the untroubled blue of college gossip.

I did some thinking myself in those days; not much, for like most of my college generation, my moods were either intensely romantic or very practical, neither good for thinking. I got far enough with my self-scrutiny to begin to read a little on my own, but never to a clear realization of why abstract thinking was unfashionable in the college community.

It is clear enough now. We resisted the intrusion of abstract ideas because our skin was full to bursting of our own affairs and our minds hot with our own enthusiasms. Most of us (cer-tainly the most influential among us) were still schoolboys whose contacts with the outside world, if any, had been with the new expansionist United States, competitive, unscrupulous, intensely individualistic, grandiose in economic plans, yet with no vision beyond construction, production, accumulation. In my own time and class in college, one could have ticked off the new trusts by the sons of their beneficiaries — oil, steel, lumber — and the great railroads by their heirs. Of course we never thought that way, except shrewd managers of fraternities looking for new buildings. Yet it was true that our college was a cross-section of American wealth and a residuary legateé of economic leadership.

Our tendency was therefore to make the college into another and better competitive America. We did not want to think about it, we wanted to be it. In later times we have been taught to estimate that expansionist age in terms of great forces wielded by builders, wreckers, pirates, who were quite unconscious that they were working for anything but their own wealth and power. We of the college were innocent of such speculations, and thought of the magnates, when we thought of them at all, only as men who had made good. But of the fierce competitions in which they were the captains and the kings we were of course not unaware, being acutely conscious that success in our collegiate world would seat us on the great American bandwagon. Hence our interests, motives, and activities, which seem so adolescent to the realistic youth of today, were all subtly related to the competitive energies running loose in the American scene. We belonged by birth and breeding to the dominant party of action in America, not to the recessive and unheard opposition of those who still speculated upon how life ought to be lived. Therefore, in college, if we thought at all, it was upon how to get on, not upon the results of getting there, and we were graduated by thousands ready to join the builders and the wreckers of the country, but almost unaware that architects were needed. The interpenetration from science, scholarship, philosophy which operated in other educational systems seldom took place, because there was no room in our minds for ideas so foreign to our interests. Anything else for us just then would have been un-American — which is not to compliment America. And indeed later years have proved that there was more vitality in this college life we pursued so devotedly than in the curriculum which the 'grinds' admired. The graduates of college life have used a great orchestra to make cheap music; but the best the 'grinds' could do was to play second fiddle.

Certainly this college experience was a life, and hence, since we were young, a vital education. In every later period of my own experience I have lived several lives at once — in my business, in my home, in my thinking, and in my emotional experiences. But in the heyday of the turn of the college century, for most of us everything was concentrated in an intense and isolated unity. In the classroom, it is true, we could sit and sit while ideas about evolution or Shakespeare dropped upon us like the gentle rain from heaven, which seeped in or evaporated according to our mental temperatures. But there was no such lassitude in college life. The environment was too powerful. It burnt up old social distinctions and made new ones. It shriveled one set of illusions and created another much more powerful. In that rough-and-tumble of athletics, social drinking, and doing something for the old college, all the classes of America except the socially impossible and the intellectually prim were thoroughly mingled. Veils of glamour in older countries have protected rank and wealth — especially in those college aristocracies nearest to our own, Oxford and Cambridge. Not so with us. They were stripped away from our young plutocrats. After the sons and heirs who might have formed an American aristocracy of wealth and privilege had been shuffled in the college competitions with the shrewd children of parvenus and the good baseball players whose fathers were Irish policemen, cards were redealt in new social categories. Though John Brown might be the son of the president of the United Steel Corporation, in college he was known as left guard on the football team, or a hustler for the Y.M.C.A. who had made a senior society. Or if he had made it on steel only (which was not improbable) his prestige sank to plus zero before the end of senior year. We knew him too well to take him seriously as one who should rank above us because he was rich. In college we were surprisingly humble in the presence of the Big Men, the class leaders, who so often later proved to have been Stuffed Shirts, precocious adolescents with no staying power; yet at least they had made their own greatness, did not bring it with them unless from successes in preparatory school. But we were not impressed by the Great Names of plutocracy — by Vanderbilts, Astors, Rockefellers as such — since we saw them at first hand. And thus, in the qualified democracy of the colleges died the possibility of adding to the economic privileges of the very rich the respect given elsewhere to rank. It is thanks to the American college that smart-set society in America has seemed important only to the lower middle class.

Yet this fiercely competitive college life was romantic, not realistic to those that lived it. It is hard to recall to a colder age the deep inferiorities, burning frustrations, and glowing confidences of those few years that seemed to us so long. I can still shiver with humiliation over slights remembered for thirty-odd years, and warm at the memory of unforgettable mirth. Romance, to be valid, must be intensely real, and stand up through space and time against the tests of disillusionment. That was true for the college life of my college generation.

It was not a wine, that romance, which could be kept for others. There was too much *fin de siècle* in it. You had to drink it while you and the century were young. It is difficult to look with a serious eye upon the youngsters of my day as they appear in the old photographs. I see my classmates strolling to recitation, or draped in a row on a fence — chubby-faced boys dressed in knee-tight knickerbockers of black-and-white check, with natty little jockey caps, also checked, or with derbies cocked rakishly over ties which I remember to have been scarlet. Or it is the summer of 1899, and we are wearing tiny straw hats with negligible brims, and voluminous white ducks under neat little coats whose tails scarcely cover our waistbands. Yet under these comic collegiate clothes the hearts of even the careerists and the drunkards beat with romance, and could be stirred to a passion of loyalty at a hint that our college (by which was meant our college life) was not the best in the world.

We were barbarians, but we were romantic barbarians, and so adapted our rowdy manners very quickly to the new Tudor Gothic which was just beginning to step back the American campus into an imitation middle ages. In my day at Yale the active leaders of college life lived in the barnlike rooms of the Colonial Lyceum. That was the heart of the college. But already its romantic soul had found expression in Gothic dormitories in whose courtyards I walked often by moonlight to enjoy a setting that shed distinction upon our loyalties. The Gothic walls seemed to shut off our college competitions from the cruder world outside us, and fostered the illusion of an American Utopia. Others less impressionable than I, and more powerful, were infected with a like romance and poured out millions later into brick and stone antiquarianism to realize their ideal.

But in its beginnings this romanticism was certainly a phase of the *fin de siècle*. It set us youngsters who were literary to editing chapbooks, writing ballads, and constructing smart short stories where the quip was everything and the content nothing. We reacted from our strenuous materialism into pose and affectation as the college builders reacted from the utilitarianism of the eighties into sham parapet and needless arch. They went in for Gothic, and we for the *Yellow Book*. We were cured quickly by the realism of the tens and twenties, and by the Great War. Their delusion still persists.

I went to a reunion of my class some years ago in company with old friends who had been with me in senior year. Together we searched out the house in which we had lived off campus, which not being a college dormitory had survived the boom days of the twenties when most of the buildings so well remembered had been scrapped to make place for Gothic grandeur. Climbing familiar stairs we found the room in which we had spent so many happy hours. It was a grimy sordid mess of broken furniture, peeling walls, and rotting window seat, in which some old-clothes man had found a home. Remembering the golden excitements of those days, and seeing on the window sills initials carved of men long dead, the appropriate tears of sentiment should have flowed — for there had been nothing quite like those hours since, or could be for us, or would be in our unconfident times again. But I was not too much moved to note how commonplace after all was the room, the ornaments of the fireplace which we had built how trivial, how garish the figures of the wallpaper which we had thought so beautiful, the whole with its memories now actualized on the very spot so like an old stage set outmoded and decayed. When the vitality of youth had run out of that room there was nothing considerable left.

And this seems to be the truth about our college life. It was powerful for us, but the staying power of Puritanism, for example, the intellectual fabric of a church, the elements of a culture, were not in it. It was like a vigorous kick of a football, too high, too aimless, into a drift of adverse winds. Yet that kick, if it was not, like the shot at Concord Bridge, heard round the world, was felt throughout America. Behind it was the college spirit — naïve intellectually but emotionally vigorous, the still youthful soul of the last great age of romantic American individualism.

ᨆᨆ 3 ᨆᨆ

Education: Common and Preferred

WHEN WE HAD BEEN IN COLLEGE two or three years, and after the college town, the campus, the Green, the crowded pavements of the city streets, were tracked with our familiar comings and goings, the glamour still had gold in it. Indeed, to this day I pass on Fifth Avenue or Piccadilly a man of my own age whose name I do not know, yet whose face faintly stirs the memory — and realize that he is one of my college world of the turn of the century, a fellow traveler with me who must remember, as I remember, the confident self-sufficiency of that island in time. He, too, was in our fancied Arcady, and yet I knew him only by sight as we sat at near-by tables at Mory's or rubbed elbows in the campus crowd.

That Arcady was intensely American. Its only resemblance to the Greek pastoral romance was our naïve certainty that we were living in a golden age, and perhaps our absorption in our own affairs. College life for us was at least ninety per cent of our felt experience, and therefore ninety per cent of the college as we knew it. Thus it became, as I have said, our real education, for every hard-lived life is an education, and no education educates unless it is lived.

But that was not the opinion of the faculty, or even of the college town and our parents. The official idea of education differed sharply from ours and was formulated, whereas ours was instinctive. We had the personnel, but the faculty controlled the tenure of residence, so that a conflict was inevitable, and this conflict created one of those situations that make real history, the kind that until twenty or thirty years or a century later never gets into books.

The American college of those days was certainly one of the most irrational and confusing educational institutions the world has ever seen. Its façade had little relation to its interior, its back door was very much more important than its front. Raw boys were dipped into college life, to emerge, after four years of strenuous idleness, mature, self-sufficient, and confident that they were educated. This was the experience to which a father really referred, whether he realized it or not, when he would say proudly, 'Yes, our boy is going to college.'

But our college was also a *collegium,* a fellowship of scholars and of teachers with their pupils, devoted to disciplining and liberalizing the youthful mind by doses of an enforced curriculum. This was the college of the catalogue, about which essays upon education were written. With this *collegium* we students had a compulsory acquaintance, which varied from the bum's consciousness of a policeman just around the corner, to an amicable arrangement by which so much acquired knowledge should be paid back in small change into the dean's office, in return for an adequate minimum of marks.

This college seldom educated us, but it did temper the excesses and sweeten the content of our real, our preferred education, in college life, and it sowed in our inattentive minds seeds of ideas which often sprouted later. Also it gave us frames of reference which became useful in after life, and it sometimes, but not always, taught us how to read.

And there was a third aspect of this college of the catalogue to which I, as a junior, scorching on my bicycle from a class in English to a student meeting, was almost oblivious, but which must be mentioned here. Around the college had grown up in the latter nineteenth century a haphazard, ill-balanced collection of professional schools, attended by hard-working meager creatures with the fun drained out of them, who were looked upon with suspicion by the undergraduates, since few of them had been graduated from our college. These schools plus ourselves made up the university, a circus in which the college was the main ring, with law, theology, medicine, and graduate studies in science or the humanities, for side-shows.

The central current of American life, as it was then, flowed through the college, carrying with it the rich spoils of American prosperity, and also respect and affection for this unique institution, which was called, by a strange misapprehension of its strenuous temperament, *alma mater.* The university, feeding upon this life stream, eventually grew great upon its nourishment, but it was in my day a parasite sucking for its own excellent purposes the blood of the college, or, more accurately, of that college life which engendered the loyalty of gift-giving alumni. At the moment when the glamorous college life which dominated us and the college was most vigorous, while we sat at Heublein's drinking our beer and assessing the future in terms of the football team, the leaders of American education were planning to make the sprawling university into a vast system of professional training which now begins to dominate both the college and America.

Not so in 1900, when it was still the college that gave America the kind of education it wanted, and conferred the only class distinction that counted everywhere. Could an M.A. or a Ph.D. or an LL.B. or an M.D. make a youth into a Yale or a Harvard man? Never! Only the bachelor's degree with four years of college life behind it gave that almost sacred consecration. No one else had been baptized and confirmed in the college spirit, converted and changed to the type of college man supposedly bred only in the Yard or on the Campus.

Of education in research and for the comprehension and reconstruction of society I shall have something to say later. Higher education, as the nineties and the early nineteen-hundreds thought of it, was quite different — it was the education of college life, which was something so specific, so highly charged with emotion, so powerful in its influences upon behavior, that it may be said to have been one hundred per cent efficient at a time when higher education in the sense common to all the ages had touched only here and there American habits of thought. Whatever the science or the scholarship of these professional schools suburban to the campus (and it was considerable), it was the college that educated the class that was to rule the country for the next generation, so that in any discussion of education in the early twentieth century it is essential not to overlook this education by college life. There was, however, the other kind also, common and commonplace to all of us, but not preferred.

I went to college at a time when an old curriculum was still tottering like a rotted house about to fall and in parts already fallen. Before my day college education had been disciplinary. The curriculum was a beautiful unity; neat, harmonious, and inspiring confidence because so many generations had worked out the rules for extracting the maximum of mental discipline from the age-tested subjects of which it was composed. It consisted of the classics, long since emptied of the noble excitements of the Renaissance, but efficiently organized into exercises in grammar and bilinguality; of mathematics; of rhetoric; and of some philosophy, literature, and history — all taught by men who believed in hard work upon hard subjects as the first of the intellectual virtues. It was a training rather than an education, yet it had the merit of all systems carried through to a logical conclusion. The professors of that day were taskmasters and looked their part. Some of them still survived in our expansive period, bearded men, a little dusty, whose clothes and faces were as emphatically different from the world's as were the old-time clergymen's. Men sure of themselves, severe, arid, uncompromising, uninventive, uninterested in the constantly new thing which we call life, yet often unexpectedly wise and serene. Or so they seemed in the decay of the age of discipline.

For of course it had to decay, since its discipline was based upon a superstitious belief in the exclusive validity of an inherited learning. By our time not even the professors really believed in the efficacy of the old curriculum. They had faith in their own subjects still, but were patently aware that few agreed with them. How many classrooms do I remember where instruction consisted in a calling-up of one man after another to translate from a heavily cribbed text of Latin, Greek, or French! How many an English recitation where in sleepy routine the questions went round: 'What does our author say about Lucifer's ambitions? Who was Ben Jonson and what were his relations to Shakespeare?' Never in business, in law, even in religion, has there been more sham, bunk, and perfunctoriness than in the common education of the American college in that easy-going time. It seemed to me incredible that a mature and civilized person, who in private life had an impeccable character and often geniality and charm, should be

willing to earn a living (and usually a meager living) by asking trivial questions day after day of young men who had either
memorized the answers as the easiest way of getting on with
college life and their real education or constructed a system
of bluff so transparent that only a defeatist who did not believe in education would have stood for it. I understand more
now how hard it was for a scholar to get enough to live on in
those days. Even so I wonder when I think of men I knew who
persisted in this rigmarole for forty years.

The young members of the faculty were in still graver difficulties, as I soon discovered when after graduation I stayed on
in my *alma mater*. If they belonged to the college, they held
their heads much higher than teachers assigned to the tribes
without the law — to postgraduates, medical students, and such
rabble. And why? Because they were close to the throb of life
on the campus, where America was really in the making, because they were in power over youngsters who so obviously
were representative of the ruling class of the roaring industrial
world of outside, which in itself they dreaded or disliked.
Their training and their reason taught them that they must
fight the materialism spilling over into the campus from this
American energy on the loose, or be downed by it. Yet they
knew that they could never do it with the old curriculum,
which was as external to the real existence of the undergraduate
as his clothes to his body. They were on a hot spot, and the inconsistency of their conduct (admiring the undergraduate,
while hating his ideas) did not help to make effective the kind
of education they were hired to distribute. The tension was
good for their personalities, which often became memorable,
but effectually broke up what confidence still existed in the
old discipline.

That disciplinary education had been devised for a small
class, largely professional or aristocratic. It had given to the
lawyer not merely the Latin he needed, but a training in dia-
lectics, which may have been a factor in keeping his profession
twenty years behind the other departments of social service. It
gave to the non-professional man that look into a heart of
another culture which broadened him for life; and it could
do this because there were no distractions of college life or new

knowledge to interfere with the slow unwrapping of the grammatical husk from the rich meat of the classics. It had the merit of all incantations when the neophytes believe in their efficiency.

But the nineteen-hundreds of which I write was a new world in which science was already dominant; it was a prosperous world in America where the luxury of a class education was open to thousands; it was a world conscious of immense vitality, re-creating the behavior of societies, breaking up old orders of life. Mathematics and Virgil, Kant, rhetoric, and ancient history, were no longer enough. Even to undergraduates new subjects were being taught by scores, though usually by the old methods. Youth answered questions about physics and zoology instead of about grammar and the genealogies of the Bible. Evolution was being lectured upon. Sociology and economics were under way. Only government lagged, for we Americans still felt that the founding fathers had handed down from Sinai all we needed to know about government. The conventional curriculum was no longer a summary of the intellectual past of the race.

It became unhappily a digest of examinable subjects about which concrete questions could be answered after due memorizing, and to which other subjects could be added, such as psychology, as soon as they could be made examinable. Although the personality of great teachers might break through, although there were exceptions in new methods, that was the deadly daily round of formal college education which took the place of the old discipline. And that was how I was taught at the beginning of the century, and how I began to teach a little later after careful instruction in the routine of implanting, and then extracting, the facts which my classes were supposed to regurgitate from their texts and textbooks, turning literature into a selection of things said by an author, language into a set of declensions and conjugations, and writing into an exercise in spelling, grammar, and the making of a plan for composing what concerned no one, least of all the writer.

If this had been all to college education in those days, there would have been no alumni turning back to *alma mater,* and certainly no book, but only a dirge, to write about the American college. It was, of course, not the real college education at all. That was a life, a powerful, conditioning life, from which only the 'grinds' and rare sophisticates escaped without a molding of character and intellect, and a complete reshaping of behavior.

Why did they go to college, those thousands upon mounting thousands that crowded into the campuses in those decades? Entrance examinations were stiffened to hold them back (a boon to tutoring schools), subjects which, like Greek, the public schools refused to teach, were kept in the requirements in the hope of barring the gate. Yet still they came until in many an institution all obstacles were swept away and the prosperous multitude was greeted with a triumphant despair.

They came for the best of reasons. They swarmed from the drab experience of small town or commercial city, direct or via the boarding schools, because they had heard of college life, where, instead of the monotony of school discipline or the bourgeois experience which had succeeded their confident childhood, there was singing, cheering, drinking, and the keenest competition for honor and prestige, a life rich in the motives which were being stifled in the struggle for power in the adult world outside. They desired romance, they sought distinction, and were not unwilling to spend some bookish labor in order to win the opportunities of a class that called itself educated.

These were the naïves, and perhaps by far the largest number of aspirants. The shrewder and less romantic shared some of these anticipations, but mingled with them ambitions much more realistic. They had learned in the preparatory schools that the college world was a career as well as a Utopia; and furthermore, a career where the sharp and energetic might overcome handicaps of birth, poverty, or even of character. They knew that this college boasted of its democracy, which actually was no social democracy at all, since class lines (once drawn) were tighter than in the outside world. They knew well that it was a democracy of opportunity. In the home town you were either born into the right group, and, if your family kept its money, stayed there; or, with greater or less difficulty, depending upon where you lived, forced yourself into society and its privileges by the sheer power of money. Self-made riches came hard. But in college life there were other stairways that led to security. Money counted, social standing outside counted, yet the son of a shopkeeper could get as far on athletic prowess as the gilded child of privilege on his family momentum. Good looks counted also, more, I should say, in the men's than in the women's colleges; and so did good clothes if worn in the collegiate manner which required the slovenly use of expensive and well-cut garments. Wit, and the gift of being amusing, especially when tight, were very helpful; and so was political sagacity. And, as I have said, there were routes upward for boys who could write what the college magazine wanted, or make the kind of music that undergraduates liked; and a broad path, much trodden in my day, for the energetically pious who could organize religion, and sell God to the right kind of undergraduate. They were sure of a senior society. It was to be twenty years before Doctor Buchman would realize the exceeding potency of a blend of religious craving with social fastidiousness, and create the Oxford Movement out of his experience with undergraduates.

These shrewd and realistic students who went to college as careerists were well aware that this college climbing led to much more than a college success. From a commonplace family in a commonplace town, with no prospect ahead but a grind of money-making and association with other stuffy nobodies, the youngster whose parents had invested in a college education, might hope to pass by his own native abilities into the brave, trans-lunary world of great cities and the gilded corridors of their privileged sets. For if he could once place himself in the right college group, his own would take care of him, provided that he did not too egregiously disappoint them in his later career. From henceforth he would be not Jones of Columbus, but Jones of 'Bones' or some other tight-ringed fraternity. Thanks to his ability to catch a ball, or to organize, or to be friendly, or to drink like a gentleman, or even to capitalize his charm, he was tapped as of the elect at age twenty or twenty-one, and had precisely that advantage (and no more) which rank and privilege still gave in the Old World. If there was a good job in a brokerage firm, he would get it, because of his connections. If there was a right club where he was going, he could join it. And all this he himself could win, unaided by the power of money or the accident of social position, and find himself, after a few brief years of struggle, companioned with the sons of plutocrats and the aristocracy. It is no wonder that college life in these nineties and early nineteen-hundreds was for many an intoxicating dream.

This life was clearly an education. Its code was definite and hard. Study must not be taken too seriously, but only a fool would fail to pay the lip service to intellectual endeavor required by the authorities. Yet it did not have to be lip service only, since the undergraduates in the education they preferred had worked out a compromise with formal study very much like the tacit agreement to go to church without being religious which their elders had made with the church. These students were, after all, to be known as college men, and so they intended to become acquainted, if not familiar, with the best that was being thought and said, able at will to speak of the things of the mind without letting them get in the way of interested action. One could tell a college graduate in those days by his lighter touch upon the problems of making a living — he knew that man does not live by bread alone, yet proposed to get his bread and get it easily.

This code also recognized and required competition as the test of life. There was no fiercer competition in the business world than the undergraduate competition for social rewards. Besides its strenuosities the pursuit of marks or even of scholarship glowed dimly. And this competition was involved in that curious complex of juvenile idealism already described which made the unremitting labors of a crew manager or football captain seem a patriotic service, so that the man who had been most energetic and successful in athletics or college politics was invariably said to have done the most for his college, as indeed he had if by college one means the vital social organism to which he really belonged and not the intellectual institution in which he spent his spare time. Indeed, that fervor of public service which had animated the early Republic, especially in the South, and which had by now been submerged in a fever of individualistic industrialism, still persisted in the colleges in this adolescent form. And like all idealisms, however juvenile, it sweetened the self-interest of competitors who so evidently and consciously were feathering their own nests. This code of competition in, but also very definitely for, the group brought with it other virtues, such as loyalty, tenacity, generosity, courage, and a willingness to co-operate, which made the college career, so trivial in its immediate objectives, so irrelevant to the purposes of scholarship, nobler, or at least less selfish and sordid, than the power-seeking society for which it was obviously a preparation. It did not, I fear, make it more honest.

In short, college life, which was so often criticized or laughed at, did educate for adult life afterward, and specifically for American life in what was its most typical if not its most admirable aspect. It inculcated ideals that were viable in America as it was then, and these ideals were adaptations of general idealism (even of Christianity) to the needs of an industrialized, get-rich-quick country. It educated specifically for the harsh competitions of capitalism, for the successful and often unscrupulous pursuit by the individual of power for himself, for class superiority, and for a success measured by the secure possession of the fruits of prosperity. I do not see how a better education could have been contrived for a youth that wanted the wealth, the position, the individual power that was being worshiped just then in America — and wanted to get them quickly, easily, and with no public dishonesty.

This education by college life also began the shattering of that idea of dollar supremacy which had shocked Europeans from the beginnings of the American experiment. Of all the talents useful for success in the college community the gift of money-making was least esteemed. This was attributable only in part to the obvious fact that most of us had money from our parents, though never enough of it. Boys without resources, who worked their way through college, were respected for their pluck and sometimes reached social eminence, but it was not their skill in money-making that got them there. Our society was like the non-profit-making orders of the Middle Ages. It was a community in which what you did, not what you got, earned rewards that were never financial, although they might lead to financial security afterward. The boy who had gone through this college life was well aware of the value of wealth and usually determined to have his share of it, yet he also knew by intimate experience of the value of other sources of prestige. He would never judge the successful clergyman, doctor, or even professor by his income solely. He had become tolerant of any kind of success.

Of course, this shrewd blend of a romantic and a practical education was quite incompatible with the disinterested search for truth for which colleges, among other purposes, were supposed to be founded. We were not looking for truth — we were seeking either a romantic illusion, or material success, which often proved later to be also an illusion. If we were by nature idealists, and many were in that twilight of the Age of Confidence, we turned our backs on the unlovely but immensely vital America outside, took refuge in the Gothic of our imitation monastery, and extracted a brand of happiness by becoming true products of the mauve decade. And if we were not idealists, if we were parvenus on the make, or shrewd youngsters aware that college life was a Christmas tree for the *fortunati* who picked the right envelopes from the branches, why, then it was no great surprise to us to learn that the idols of college worship were much the same as the idols of the marketplace, if with a different coat of paint.

A dose of illusion is good for youth, and so is a shot of romance, and certainly no sociologist could fail to admire the perfect adaptation of our preferred education to the mores of the American life we were about to enter. The irony lay in a confusion of values and purposes. It is surely the duty of an educational institution to prepare for a change in mores, since mores are always in process of changing. But our college, with the university then gathering round it, carried too much earthy ballast ever to lift far above the society that supported it. The college could make a class set apart by special behavior, but it could not impregnate that class with superior ideas. College life was so vital in itself and so formative that ideas, the search for truth, scholarship, and the forecasts and interpretations of the intellect in general, were inevitably mere by-products of an institution whose service was to teach competition and the public-school code. Even professors and presidents believed that then, no matter what their mouths said. College life was the heart of the educational machine. Research became possible because loyal alumni of the college paid the heavy expenses of an institution in whose ample margins there was room and support for the reflective, the analytical, the creative mind, which could get little if any sustenance elsewhere in a bustling, money-making country.

Yet what shrieks rent the heavens when, at the end of the period of which I write, money that might have been had for the college proper began to flow into medical, law, and graduate schools! With what enormous satisfaction did the alumni welcome the final triumph of the Gothic scheme which at frightful expense (far greater than any costs of pure education) transformed the ugly college of the nineties into a new Oxford, equipped, not like the original for monastic students, but with every appurtenance of the life of the very rich, and housed in the ornate plush-in-stone of the late Middle Ages which gave such a striking effect of class exclusiveness. I write not entirely in sorrow, for the college was vital, it was happy, it deserved to be dressed in fine linen and set upon a throne. And the buildings, even the most pretentious, and certainly the reconstructions of colonial architecture which many a college has preferred to Tudor Gothic, are much superior to Main Street. And yet what possibilities of a neurosis lay in this strange set of compromises involving education, romance, and materialism!

For the college of my day was a combination of sporting resort, beer garden, political convention, laboratory, factory of research, and nurse of the liberal arts. And it was trying to be a public school of the English type, a college, and a university, all at the same time. I doubt whether values were ever more completely mixed, muddled, and concealed than in the battle (if you can call it that) between our perfunctory and our preferred education.

ᘓ 4 ᘒ

Teaching and Teachers

I WAS BROUGHT UP in a community where education was one of the lesser public utilities. Teaching as a profession was regarded by my friends and family as a last resort for those who could not do anything else. An obvious explanation, that teaching was poorly paid, did not tell the whole story. The ministry was poorly paid, but met with no such mild but rather deadly disrespect; while dentistry, though profitable, was socially less estimable than teaching.

There seems to have been an idea, not too clearly thought out, that the teacher, even the college teacher, did his work in a childish world from which adult men and women had escaped by taking up the really important tasks of life. The teacher lived on the margin of such vital affairs as business or running a household, and was perhaps not really an adult at all. It was always surprising to learn that a teacher had made money or fallen in love. Teachers were usually high-minded and cultivated people, yet belonged nevertheless among the servile classes, a cut above a nurse. This was what they thought.

And yet the economic explanation was true also. By the beginning of our twentieth century the philosophy of competition had got such a grip upon the American imagination that making money and (with less agreement) spending money had become a test of success. But a teacher ducked out of the competition at the beginning, which seemed a confession of inferiority. If the teacher was a 'she,' of course we were more tolerant.

My four years at college did not entirely uproot this vulgar prejudice, although I was shaken by my contacts with a few teachers so powerful that I was forced to regard them as I had been taught to regard other men. Absorbed in college life, which was such a vivid reflection of the competitive economics of the American world outside, we would listen, faintly amused, to dry old men who talked of syntactical irregularities with the high seriousness our fathers reserved for real estate and dividends; and we were often annoyed by the earnestness of lecturers who grew excited over problems that in our home towns were regarded as having no connection with practical life. To the teachers who gained our affection we gave familiar nicknames, such as 'Baldy,' 'Walrus,' 'Goat,' 'Speedy'; to those we disliked, less agreeable attributions, such as 'Stinker'; but in every case the break-through into recognition of the man behind the professor seems to have resulted from a surprised discovery that this creature who took astronomy or history so seriously was, after all, quite human.

By one of those twists of circumstance which are the tricks chance plays on opinionated man, I found myself, after graduation, confronted with an opportunity to study and teach, the alternatives being business, which I dreaded, or literature, which I felt with reason to be the thinnest of ice for my capacities. The influences of the college town, and the unworldly academic life within it, which was so much in accord with my Quaker inheritance, and also the desire for more knowledge which our somewhat casual association with learning had stirred in me, all had made me reluctant to go back to the everyday life which I still regarded as normal. I chose teaching, with no more 'call' to it than had my cousins at home to the bankers' and manufacturers' offices they entered as a matter of course. And so, uncorrupted by theories, untouched by the missionary spirit, unimpressed as yet by the nobility of an intellectual career, like a colt straying toward a new pasture where the grass looked green and the gate was open, I slipped into one of the six great professions.

This is no autobiography. I use personal experience only because it is my evidence for the value of the college experience that formed our generation. I am more concerned with truth in interpretation than with fidelity to the actual happening. Nevertheless, I think that my own history as a member of a faculty is significant because my ascent as a teacher from careless ignorance to eager interest and finally to spiritual agitation made me more sensitive to the issues involved than my more fortunate colleagues who, like the boy on the burning deck, knew precisely what they had to do, and did it. I was the first in nine known generations of a family to enter a profession, I was the first from my circle of friends and relatives to escape from the profits system. I came into the faculty from the college with a traditional respect for the bourgeois American's creed of business as the chief concern of normal man, and with something reaching out from my mind toward ideals of scholarship, and something shrinking back by habit from the practitioners thereof, whose language, manners, humor or lack of it, and ideas of success in life I was not prepared to understand. Gulliver felt somewhat as I did, when landing upon Laputa he found that factories made learning, and conversation was about mathematics instead of money and love.

Very early in my teaching career, which in its beginning was humble in the extreme — and fortunately so, since I knew just enough to keep one jump ahead of my classes — I brought my father to the club in our college town. He was to meet two of my superiors, elder statesmen in education for whom I had a profound respect. My father was the sweetest and most equable of men, deeply cultured in simple human relationships, but not accustomed to discussions where ideas were passed about wantonly and encyclopedic facts spilled as if everyone had plenty of them. The elder statesmen were bored, and my father was puzzled, although he did his best to find something in his very American experience which would provide a meeting-place. As he flushed, looking more and more to me for help, a tiny idea was born in my mind of the true nature of this profession of teaching. It was a resultant of the inevitable conflict between theory and practice; it was built upon the ultimate duty of scholarship to give what was needed, and made doubly difficult by the inability or the refusal of human nature to take what it lacked, and the failure of the teacher to measure his task. That day I saw for the first time the teacher's real problem — and for twenty years blundered on, ill-prepared and often mistaken, and sometimes successful, and more often self-deluded, yet, like all real teachers, hopeful, on its trail.

For I think that teaching as a profession is woefully misunderstood, and frequently by its professors. Perhaps I should qualify this statement to read teaching of the humanities, which I know most about, yet I do not feel inclined to qualify it. It may be that teaching a technique such as playwriting or the building of bridges is a simple matter hard to misunderstand, yet I am quite sure that the instant the subject taught is used for training and expanding the mind, the problem is much more complex than the simple formula: I know this, I tell it to you, now you know it — which seems to be what most laymen regard as teaching.

I never taught playwriting or metal work, but I have raised my temperature and strained my wits in the teaching of both English literature and English composition, with brief excursions into history and even logic. What I am surest of is, that what I tried to teach was never so important as how I taught it. I can conceive of no subject of instruction so important that a pupil cannot get along without it, except reading, writing, and arithmetic, unless it be ethics and religion, which few teach nowadays. Of course the race has to have the sciences if it is to keep up its standard of living, architects must have calculus, and classicists Latin, but I am writing of the individual. What *he* needs is not necessarily Greek, or physics, or geography, but an education.

My first discovery, when I began my career as a sallow-faced instructor in a black felt hat and very puritan clothing (the fashion for academic intellectuals in the early nineteen-hundreds), was that education is more concerned with ideals than with knowledge, a naïve discovery, but important. I never had the usual difficulties of young instructors, though I dreamed of them in tutor's nightmares, in which ink flew through the air while I escaped in my shirt-tails through a window. I was slight physically, unaccustomed to authority, unsure of my subject, uncertain in my methods. Nevertheless, no class 'roughhoused' me (a word of the period); when dogs were brought into my recitation, they promptly went to sleep; when fisticuffs started on the back row, I had only to throw a question in that direction. Yet I nerved myself for my classes as for an ordeal, and relapsed after them into limp vacuity. I quickly learned — intuitively, crudely, yet I learned — that whether it was the

history of the English language or Shakespeare I was trying to
teach, the actual conflict was not with ignorance, but with college life and all that it implied; and behind it the ideas and
ideals of an American society in which materialism for the moment dominated action and governed thought. One could
plant facts by waving a mark book, but when it came to ideas,
beliefs, ideals, the soil was stubborn.

There were five schools of the theory of teaching in my day:
the hard-boiled, the indifferent, the idealistic, the factual, and
the enthusiastic.

The hard-boiled school I respected, yet something in their
tenets made me stubbornly rebellious. There was a Cambridge
graduate on our faculty, an Englishman older than myself, with
whom I argued over many a stein of beer. We have the stuff,
he would say; let the little lambs come and get it if they wish.
If they are goats who won't eat good food, that is their affair. I
can give them good mathematics, and if they want mathematics,
I will work with them. If they don't, why should I coddle
them!

And so he saved his emotions for high struggles with figured
thinking, bred a few good students, made a reputation for his
scholarship, and got through his teaching with only the labor
required to talk clearly for fifty minutes.

I tried to feel his way. I knew that we coddled the undergraduate. I was aware that we tried to wheedle our doses of
instructions, like cod-liver oil, into his unwilling mouth between his hearty feedings on college life. I felt that if I could
stand on a pedestal, like my Cambridge friend, saying, 'I have
it, come and get it, or stay away,' I should be more respected
and so would my subject. But I believed that those I most
wanted to teach would never come because they would never
understand why they should come. My American tradition
held me back from such downrightness. After all, our job had
been, and was, to educate all of the people. And specifically,
our primary job was not to train teachers of English like ourselves. If it was not incumbent upon me to teach Anglo-Saxon
to guttersnipes, yet what right had I to keep Shakespeare and
Milton for the tiny minority of American undergraduates who
would take to them naturally, and who would read them with

a self-determined resolve to understand, and who might succeed me in the job of training other teachers of English to succeed them? That was important, but it was not enough. The specialist might be hard-boiled, and properly so. The Englishman might be exclusive, for in England education had always been regarded as a privilege, and hence a specialty. With us, education was what religion had been to our ancestors, something to be spread abroad to all who had minds that could be saved. Which meant that those who felt as I did worked harder over a weary football player, or a perfectly cynical broker's son, than with the fine minds already lit with enthusiasm for learning which we were sure to find somewhere in our classes. With the natural result that our energies were exhausted in trying to educate the almost uneducatable, while in any faculty meeting the discussion never got far from the lame ducks and the bluffers, and what to do about low marks.

The indifferent school of teachers had long since accepted the hopelessness of this endless siege of undergraduate interest. Without admitting it, least of all to themselves, they had become defeatists in education. The academic life was pleasant — long summers, short hours, easy requirements for the unambitious once they were placed, abundant opportunities for spending sensibly and agreeably a private income if you were fortunate enough to have one. Nor did a man have to teach or to write with distinction in order to get his job and hold it in that society which was so agreeable to the cultivated mind. There were innumerable committees needing executive talent, there were sports to be supervised, rules to be made, morale to be seen to. And there was the curriculum, which, like the power plant of a factory, had to be overhauled or redesigned every other year. A personable man of character could keep himself reasonably busy through an academic lifetime without doing one hour of really effective teaching, or writing one page that lifted beyond routine. He became, so to speak, a dean or president without portfolio and without real educational responsibility, and was often better known, and more quickly rewarded, than the true scholar or the born teacher, whose light shone less abroad among the alumni and in the college town.

Nor was the siege of the undergraduate mind necessarily unpleasant once the besieging became an end in itself. These indifferents imitated medieval warfare. Against a wall of resistance they threw up another wall of requirements, behind which they lived very comfortably while the conflict remained in *statu quo*. Boredom encountered routine, dullness met dullness, irresponsibility was checked by the marking system, and a technique was developed guaranteed to produce the expected number of grades which would test at passing or just above. Many a good man went down this sterile road in college teaching, was useful, respected, and did a little bit of everything about the college shop except educate or contribute to thinking. There they had accepted defeat. And if many college generations were bored to extinction in their classes, the wheels of college routine ran smoother thanks to such men. And if scholarship went forward never a millimeter by their efforts, at least they made no minor errors, pursued no lost causes, did no damage to convention, and proved to the suspicious American world outside that a professor could be as much of a good fellow, and as harmless, as a vice-president of a bank. Yet I fear they were not harmless. Their dead hand rests on many a mind yet.

As for the idealists, I wonder if I have the right name for them. Such a bull-headed generation I have never known in any other profession, for daily they went out to fight for their ideas, and daily they were defeated. And yet, stupid as some of them were, and blind as to what was going on and the source of their difficulties as were most, I cannot but feel that they were the only realists in the college of my day. Obstinately determined to make what they thought was truth prevail, they alone intuitively saw, or at least felt and dimly perceived, college education for what it essentially was — a battle with the natural cussedness, consistent shortsightedness, and obstinate resistance of the human animal to whatever uncomfortably raises him above the brute. They were much too dogmatic, much too inexperienced in life, very much too cerebral in their theories and naïve in their emotions, to be often entirely right. But they were on the right side of education even when they were absurdly wrong in their estimates of what their young animals needed. They were on the only side that really wanted a victory.

I numbered my best friends among the idealists, yet it was extraordinary how widely we differed in items of belief. Some of them, having hitched their wagons to an earlier century, were concerned only with the fallacies of our own. They had certain advantages over the rest of us who felt that the nineteen-hundreds were of considerable importance, since it was clear that we should have to do our living in them. A complete faith in the mores of, let us say, the age of Doctor Johnson, produced eventually in the teacher who felt that way a character so eccentric from our mores as to fascinate modern youth by his very difference. His arguments also had the force of resting upon a precedent of glamorous living. Instead of feeble remonstrances against the trivial and the sensational in our college life, where football practice or trying to make a fraternity engaged our best energies, these praisers of old days could throw wits, beauties, and statesmen at the student head, and show life fully lived in a manner so different as to challenge the dullest intelligence.

Other idealists of my acquaintance were soaked in romantic moralism. Literature was written, according to them, to illustrate the vices and virtues. Shakespeare proved that character made fate, and the lyrics of Tennyson were less 'significant' than his sermons in verse. Their students were not surprised; they had been taught that way in school, yet felt that they had been betrayed when spot passages from ribald scenes in Shakespeare or lyric lines that obviously contained no moral philosophy were put upon the examination papers. How the devil were you to interpret morally a jest of Falstaff, or the verses

> Courtesied when you have and kissed
> The wild waves whist.

I was cured myself of using all English literature as an exercise in Victorian morality by reading aloud to my class a line of Tennyson's that permitted, and did not fail to get, and with hysterical laughter, a bawdy interpretation. The relief was so obvious that I knew instantly I had been preaching, not teaching. I realized with a saving humor that good literature was

far too human to make sermons of, though sermons it might
often contain, far too human to be made into a diet of oughts
and ought nots. And I soon concluded that we who squeezed
ethics from our teaching of literature or history were dodging
the far more difficult task of making the culture of the past at
home in the imagination of the undergraduate.

The factual teachers were the happiest. They were competent men who knew every detail of their subjects. For them
teaching was a job in agriculture. Prepare the field of the mind
by threats of plowing its wild oats under. Plant the seeds of
honest fact —declensions, dates, formulas. Reap the crop at examination time, and woe to the boy with an empty basket. The
system would have been perfect if it had not been for the complete lack of fertilizer. The grain came back to the farmer, not
hundredfold, but one in a hundred, and that one often moldy.

Nevertheless, the factual was the school of teaching most popular among the faculty; naturally so, for it could do no harm,
and since facts in all subjects were the indispensable beginnings of wisdom, might do more good than the uncertainties of
theorizing and interpretation. Facts could stimulate also, and
there was little danger that they would stimulate too much.

What masses of facts I have heard poured out in the classroom! How many facts, more or less accurate, I myself have
dumped on my classes! What myriads of alleged facts I have
read in test papers! There is something sane and sensible about
a fact. Given the coefficients, can you or can you not plot a
curve? Do you or do you not know the relative dates of Charle-
magne and El Mansur? Why did the crustaceans fail to evolute
like man? What happened when Horatio met Hamlet after
the latter's escape from the pirates? If I were to go back to general teaching again, I should either break my forehead anew
on the old stone wall erected ages since to shut out ideas and
ideals, or happily and wholeheartedly go in for facts. The
teaching of linguists must be joyful, for it is nearly all facts.
An hour with a good list of factual questions to propose is like
a game — ends too like a game with the score 0-0, but a grand
sensation of having played hard. I have seen one of my own
professors become so fascinated with the sport of dropping
queries like depth bombs here and there, that he forgot to

mark, forgot to dismiss, his sweating class. There is an immense satisfaction in the concrete for both teacher and taught. The well-crammed youngster is like a siphon bottle. Press the handle and he fizzes in a welcome relief from pressure. And the happy professor well supplied with hard questions of fact is like the gardener who whiffs spray on a plant and sees the worm turn up his belly in a just agony.

It was facts I began to teach, and never afterward did I have more efficient recitations. There was a sporting atmosphere in the classroom life of the early nineteen-hundreds. Of the 'prof' it was expected that he would prepare shrewd questions touching upon hidden desposits of fact easily missed in preparation unless by chance the student had an old book with arrows inked in pointing to the treasure. The teacher asked: the pupil replied. He said he did not know, which was zero. He gave the right answer, which in our mystic marking system counted four. Or he entered upon a rambling disquisition which was meant, and intended to be understood, as a bluff. Could teacher corner him into making a statement of fact, which was sure to be wrong? If he could, that also was zero. If teacher could not catch him out, the sporting code required that he should get a complimentary two, which was passing, and he complained if he did not receive it. The class, expert in games, if not in the subject of instruction, watched the struggle, excited sometimes to the point of groans or applause.

I was cured of the factual method as a major sport in education, by a slender, sensitive youngster who had been educated by private tutors abroad. He was too intent upon his own thinking to answer directly my simple question as to what Prince Hal thought of Falstaff, by which, of course, I meant what he *said* he thought. Instead, as one interested mind to another, he began what was, by definition, clearly a bluff, yet soon became a query as to whether Shakespeare himself was not, like all playwrights, prone to bluff, letting speeches stand from history which he had been too lazy to rewrite. The class, which had set him down for a two, withdrew their favor when he went on with the discussion for the sake of an argument, which he seemed to take more seriously than his mark. But I, with my neat questions to test laborious reading all pat, felt

like a fool, and was one. The happy solace of asking contentedly, 'Was it?' and hearing 'It was' or 'It wasn't,' the day's duty
thus done, was never more mine. And yet I did not forget, nor
do I forget here, that it is upon fact that tradition by which
alone we safely live, rides from the past into the present.

I would gladly have been inspired to belong to another
school of teachers — the enthusiasts. The enthusiast was a peculiar product of the *fin de siècle*. One encountered him usually in the humanities, but there were scientists and even teachers of language who belonged in this category, and in my day
so cold and hard a subject as physics was then boasted of one.
I have heard that in the more skeptical present the enthusiast
has been ranked with the revivalists. Actually he was a by-
product of revivalism, which the great days of Moody and
Sankey and William Booth had made infectious to educated
men. But the educated men in our day were not often attracted to religion. Religion was either too dogmatic for them
or too emotional. Herbert Spencer had destroyed the prestige
of theology, and they were well aware that William James had
described conversion as a phenomenon of psychology. Hence
many with a fire of enthusiasm for the good, the beautiful, and
the true turned to art, to the wonders of nature, and most of
all to literature. One could be enthusiastic about Shakespeare
when it had already become a little vulgar to be enthusiastic
about being saved. Even the technique was the same, and
familiar comparisons, good stories, histrionics, were as effective
in lectures upon Shelley as in rantings upon the Blood of the
Lamb.

The students responded. In these men so fired with the excitements of their subject, so keen to show others that poetry
or evolution or philology was life abstracted but intensified,
they recognized a rebellion against the formalism they also
hated, and a sympathetic relationship with their own easy enthusiasms in college life. And yet I could never become one of
the enthusiasts, though I owed much to them. What this kind
of teaching required was a special gift which was not so much
oratory or histrionics as an uncritical faith in the miracle of
knowledge. When they spoke of what they loved, life for their
hearers seemed more vivid, more conscious than before. That

was good, but it did not come by mere telling. There had to
be transferred emotion, and the emotion, unless it was simple,
could not be easily transferred, not even by a revivalist. It required a special secretion of simple, intense minds, with a
genius for communication. The enthusiasts were born, not
made. They were our prima donnas, who triumphed even
when their voices went sharp or flat of the truth.

And when they had done their work the soil was plowed up,
but not planted. They made learning seem desirable, but left
it an emotion and a mystery. They gave their hearts, but few
ideas with them. Their converts did not relapse, like the
drunkards and prostitutes won by the revivalists; they remained
friends to culture, but stopped there unless someone took them
farther along the road. And yet in that boisterous college, with
its tacit agreement that only mirth and social success really
counted, to be a friend of culture was an achievement. As a
young teacher I could never let myself go in the kind of enthusiasm that sent classes home burning to read everything
from the *Koran* to *Dorian Gray,* because I was uncomfortably
aware of how little I knew of the realities that explained both
Mohammed and Oscar Wilde. Yet I envied those who had no
inhibitions in their passion for books — any books. I felt for
them the gratitude and reluctant admiration of Hamlet for
the actor who wept over Hecuba. That fellow got his audience,
and so did they.

I cast my lot, therefore, with the idealists, which name I now
discard, as being inaccurate, and call them the philosophic in
teaching, a sect which has always persisted in the crooked but
fascinating road of education, although many of its followers
in the past have, like my humble self, had little claim to be
called philosophers. Yet what is philosophy in practice but
wondering what it is all about, with a passion for trying to discover?

The college teacher, especially if he is young, has a curious
human experience, both intimate and remote. He sits half the
day examining minds at just the age when they have reached
full intelligence and yet cannot either entirely conceal or entirely reveal their texture. He has boys and girls of the best age
for playing upon, and they are a picked youth, if not always

picked for his especial purposes. And they are charming, more than ever before, more than ever afterward. Outside the classroom they become easily his friends, though never really intimate; inside they are deferential, even in their determination to resist knowledge, and often frank in what they say, though their inner lives are infinitely withdrawn. They bring their background with them, and not their words so much as their wills are intensely expressive. Teaching such a class is like lifting a thin and waving plank. It is never steady, always ready to bend and fall; an instant's release of the grip and it is down to earth.

In my day we sat on a raised dais with thirty or more youngsters sprawled beneath us. It was like an established church where the pastor, hired to save souls, faces a congregation that has come because it is Sunday. We seated the students alphabetically, making for our own use a penciled plan of the seats, each of which was numbered, and writing on it the names of the students in their assigned locations. Thus, when 'Townsend' was called, the six feet of shambling drowsiness needing a pinch which rose to its feet could be readily identified. Without this simple device there was always the chance that some little Russian Jew would grab himself an easy question and sell his knowledge for an A.

At first one's class was a sea of faces, pimply, vacuous, keen, sulky, and amiable, all dissolving into a blur of washed and rosy youth. But soon (and Buddhist priests and doctors of the Sorbonne must have had the same experience) the room disintegrated into familiar types. The pleasantest, I think, was the well-mannered, neatly dressed boy from the orthodox preparatory schools. He was deferential to teacher, polite to the scrawny high-school boy beside him. Yet he was still all boy and at each moment of relaxation would tickle his schoolmate on the other side, and be slyly punched in return, the two of them like puppies trying hard not to roll over and cuff and bite. Yet put those well-trained boys on the football field where serious life for them began, and they would tackle low, and slug and viciously kick when the umpire was not looking. A faint aroma of cereal and cream exuded from these preparatory-school boys. They had nice mothers and generous fathers.

Their world was already made for them, and, like blooded colts, they were expected to play because their future work was to be a fierce competition to make the family richer. They had the arrogance and the gentleness of the aristocrat, without his detachment from life. Every one of them expected to start in business or professional life at the bottom and to come to the top as easily as he rushed a ball past untrained opponents. The type was Spartan rather than Athenian; and, like the Spartans, they were quite inaccessible to new ideas, having closed their minds at sixteen or seventeen upon a code of success which left no room for speculation.

These fine boys, with their good voices, their courtesy and self-assurance, would sit out the hour in deferential boredom, then, at the word of dismissal, crowd the doorway in a sudden release of energy, leaving the young teacher in an agony of frustration. For they had everything — health, good looks, will, character, reserves of energy — everything but open minds, everything but cracks in their stiff brains into which ideas could flow! With consummate skill gained in long experience with clever teachers and the right textbooks, they gave to Caesar exactly what Caesar was supposed to get from them, the modicum of facts, the statements of the last lecture reduced to a formula, enough to get a B in freshman year when the footing was still unsteady, just enough for a C in senior year when the danger of flunking was past. You liked them as you like blooded show dogs. Like show dogs they defeated every attempt to teach their well-bred intellect new tricks.

Scattered here and there in every class were the 'grinds' called by the preparatory-school dilettantes either 'greasy grinds' or just 'grinds.' Actually the difference between the two varieties were subtle. The typical grind was a survival of the old college that trained chiefly for teaching and the ministry. He was usually the quiet and bloodless member of the family, afraid of rough sports, averse to competition, seeking refuge in books. His face was blank, his mind was a sponge which squeezed dry and filled again without cellular change. The young teacher found him trying, since he did everything he was told, believed all he heard, studied everything assigned to him, and at the end wrote papers that were correct with a

deathly perfection of the commonplace which showed how ineffective education could be unless it touched the emotions, of
which he had none.

The 'greasy grind' was a racial or social variant of the plain
grind. The greasy grind seldom changed his collar. He had a
sneaking cleverness which taught him to snap up the hard questions in easy courses, thus collecting high marks as a protection
against a world that, quite properly, wished to keep him down.
He would argue with teacher for ten minutes trying to get a B
changed into an A; but he had no intellectual curiosity. Education for him was a coin, useless unless you could buy something with it. The dilettante could sometimes be shocked into
a realization that there were other worlds than his, and so
other values in living; but the greasy grind was both unchangeable and inescapable, a fly buzzing about your weary head.

Another and very different type of industrious student in
those classes is well recognized now, but was then regarded by
the pink and well-soaped elect as just another undesirable. The
second generation from the East of Europe was beginning to
come to college — Polish Jews with anemic faces on which were
set dirty spectacles, soft-eyed Italians too alien to mix with an
Anglo-Saxon community, seam-faced Armenian boys, and now
and then a Chinese. These, except the last, were all in college
to learn how to live in America. Their mien was apologetic;
you could see them watching with envious curiosity the courteous indifference of the superior race; they took little part in
discussions, and asked for no credit. Yet often their more flexible minds could be felt playing round and round the confident Anglo-Saxons, admiring, skeptical, puzzled, and sometimes contemptuous. Occasionally there would be a revelation
of intellect or a hint of the future, when some Chinese boy,
caught off his guard, and forgetting the convention of the classroom which was to answer a question and sit down, would give
a *précis* of the entire lesson, and perhaps the previous one and
the next, which only a French intellectual could have equaled.
Or some Russian Jewish exile, asked to comment on an Ibsen
play, and losing control of his guarded intellect, would ex-
pound a social philosophy that made the class squirm as if a
blast of fire had scorched the seats of their comfortable pants.

Every class had also its 'freaks,' which in those college days was a familiar term with a definite meaning. And nothing could have better revealed the nature of our college community than the diversity of types which were all called, for convenience, and to indicate their difference from the true-blue college men, freaks. A freak was a nonconformist. He might be a preparatory-school boy of good family who had failed somehow to take the right impress from the preparatory-school mold. He might be, and often was, a son of the very rich, or of artistic bohemians, who had been educated in Europe, and was ill at ease in our Philistine Zion. He might be a potential homosexual distracted by his own unrecognized perversity. He might be, but rarely was, a little crazy. Sometimes he was merely an adult intellect in the society of adolescents, who refused to waste his time in organized athletics, although obviously competent, who declined fraternity elections, and was obsessed by a morbid interest in chemistry or philology. All such were 'freaks.'

The Spartan parallel again holds good, since the arts in this question of freakishness were especially suspect. To be musical and indulge in music privately was a sure sign of freakishness, as bad as private drinking or the reading of poetry in seclusion. The banjo, the mandolin, and the guitar were respectable, since skillful players of these instruments could 'make' the musical clubs and so gain social recognition; but proficiency on the violin was a sure sign of something wrong, as was skill on the piano not confined to 'beating the box,' and also the singing of 'classic' music. Radical ideas, a taste for the society of professors, silk pajamas, an interest in art, careful English, long hair (except on football heroes), uncollegiate clothes, and a lack of interest in sports, all designated the freak, who was a person dangerous to make friends with. Only religion, thanks to our evangelical heritage, was allowed eccentricities of self-expression, for it was a part of the code.

Hence the young teacher, himself a mild nonconformist, since otherwise he would never have gone into teaching, was often embarrassed by the sudden drop in classroom temperature when, misled or ignorant, he gave a freak the floor and his approval. The boy who looked at him with dumb, devoted eyes, the boy who compared Milton to Bach, the youth who knew the Italian primitives in the Art School, the freak who asked whether Christ was not a good socialist, and the exquisite who actually articulated his English, and quoted French in a foreign accent — call upon any one of these and all motion forward was stopped for that day. An Alexandrian Greek could have met with no more disapproval if asked to address the Conscript Fathers of the Roman Republic.

I soon grew accustomed to this so variegated class, learning to play one faction against another, soap, so to speak, against dirty fingernails, agile intellect against the solidity of a confident code. Yet what saved those of us who tried to be philosophers in our rôle of teaching, was another, and fortunately unfailing, contribution from America to our college classes. I remember well those first days of each teaching year: the confident moment when one looked down upon fresh faces in the old seats, and hoped that this time at last faith would be justified. And then the quick disillusion as the herd rounded up into the same old assortment of mavericks, mixed breeds, and stolid beef cattle. Yet, as with ranging question and hopeful reading of test papers we sifted and searched, always in some unexpected corners would be found those quiet minds, tenacious, reserved, cautious, practical, and yet ready to sight an idea and pursue it, and apply it, and keep faith with it — not speculative, not logical, but unshakeable in confidence that most problems can be solved — which are the best products of the great American experiment. Sometimes it was character, sometimes it was sanity, sometimes it was intellectual courage, which is very different from intellectual daring, that one found and relied upon to give some coherence to the struggle to civilize such discordant elements when oneself was so imperfectly civilized.

I never failed to get such minds in my classes but once. Then I was assigned to a division of 'repeaters,' boys who were being allowed to go through their deficient freshman work again in order that their invaluable services on various team or managerships, or as merry drunkards, should be retained at least until Christmas. And then the issue was so clear, David against Goliath, with only a sling when he needed a machine gun, that the class became a match conducted in high good humor, and with rules observed by both sides, according to which it was agreed that if I caught them they were out; with the result that a side wave from the strenuous competitions of college life washed through that classroom, football leviathans memorized Shakespeare and liked him, and boozers defended Falstaff. A committee waited on me at the end of the year, saying that I had been a good sport, and offering to teach me an infallible method for catching bluffers before they got to home plate.

I met one of that class once, a good-natured broker, fat and a little seedy since 1929. 'I remember your class,' he said. 'It's the only one I do remember. I got to like that guy Hamlet. I meant to read more about him some time. But you know how it is — I had to work when I quit college.'

They all intended to work when they left college. That was why teaching in those days was exciting. There was no belief in the student's mind that what you taught had any vital relation with real work, or, for that matter, with real life. You felt, and rightly, that it might be the last chance to bring them into contact with any values not purely utilitarian.

I wondered then, but do not wonder now, at the excitement which kept us, the young teachers, talking, brooding, dreaming over our job, which after all was miserably paid, little respected, and three quarters of it a routine as dull as a clerk's. With the added psychological danger of acquiring arrogance, pedantry, and dogmatism, which are the occupational diseases of those who spend their lives directing the intellects of the young.

I do not wonder now, because it is so clear that we were on the firing line. The pre-Civil War culture of the East had grown stale or genteel. The colleges were filled with the second generation of the industrial pioneers, who had been brought up in a tradition of *laissez-faire* and the devil catch the hindmost. The boys we faced were nourished on a great illusion, and so well nourished that there was room for little else in their minds. They believed, with that implicit faith which is so much more powerful than doctrine, that the rest of their lives would be spent in a Great Struggle for wealth and privilege, where the best grabbers would win, and where only freaks and dreamers would take time to speculate upon what it was all about and whether the result was happiness. The heir to a banker's million was just as much under the spell of the necessity to be strenuous as the son of a Jewish pants-presser. Indeed, if anything, it was the well-born and wealthy who were surest that making money was essential for their safety and would mean for them success.

And since the country was really behind them, and the times favored their ambitions, while the churches had lost their hold upon idealism, or, like the Y.M.C.A., praised such success as the only antidote to the vices of idleness, we young teachers were forced to play the part of Isaiahs preaching another God than Mammon. Irritated by our helplessness, we would make sermons out of poetry and tracts for the times from prose that was meant to be delightful. Or, puzzled and discouraged, we would yield to the current tendency and turn our classrooms into doctors' offices where bad children were given stiff doses that were sure to do them good. Or we would get through with the whole routine as easily as possible so that we could attend to our own affairs which often were quite as material-istic as the steel business or corporation law.

But sometimes some of us went at it differently, and, disillu-sioned, skeptical, defeated, fought for our ideals again and again with an intensity that was almost lyrical. We knew that the struggle was between two views of civilization, between two ideas of living, between two types of mind, variants of the tender and the tough. It was our feeble repetition of an age-long conflict — Plato versus John Rockefeller, Shakespeare ver-sus Benjamin Franklin, Milton against the stock exchange and the Y.M.C.A. This we felt, and that was why an instructor in English on fifteen hundred dollars a year was often a happy man.

⌒ 5 ⌒

The Academic Life

THE ACADEMIC LIFE in which these teachers moved and had
their being has never, I believe, been psychologically considered, except in a few novels. I do not wish to write of it
here in any psychoanalytic fashion, for I am far more interested in its values than in its quips, its quiddities, its lesions,
and its releases. Yet, regarded as a habit of life and a state of
mind, the campus communities were unquestionably an addi-
tional state in the bustling America of the early nineteen-hundreds. They were a society within the commonwealth, like the
Quakers of the eighteenth century, and they lived in oases of
relative peace while the rest of the country was madly building
roads for progress whose ultimate destination had never been
mapped.

Thoughtful spirits who in that confident and aggressive age
paused for reflection were aware of a tension which was more
complex than Theodore Roosevelt's cult of strenuosity. It was
a tension between ideals which had reached our college classrooms and was the cause of that struggle between teacher and
taught described in earlier chapters. There was an antagonism
between those who wished to know and those eager to do that
grew stronger and more confused as the great industrial age of
America mounted toward its peak. It was a conflict between
gods and giants, very academic gods it seems to me now, who
would have liked to turn the United States into a vast university, and very well-meaning giants, who, like Carnegie, said
they got rich only to benefit mankind. And

> . . . *friend and foe were shadows in the mist,*
> *And friend slew friend not knowing whom he slew.*

Yet a battle is a bad simile. As I look back to that cocksure
society of the turn of the century, it seems that thinkers and

doers, big and little, were, on the whole, very well satisfied with their country and themselves. The tension was there, but everyone supposed it would disappear just as soon as we had made a perfect state — which, whatever else it was going to become, would be prosperous, with bigger and better factories and bigger and better dormitories. So the gods and the godlings kept on educating the children, or trying to, according to their lights, and the giants and their office force kept on paying the bills and offering our graduates jobs which required a very different set of ideals from ours. Meanwhile, most of us, inside and out of the college, took this dual world for granted. Now and then there was a hint that some day this gentleman's agreement would be broken. I remember the vague uneasiness of my father when the first Roosevelt slid into the presidency. Roosevelt was a college graduate. His ideas might be bad for business. And, on the other side, behind the vehement anti-imperialism of the Spanish-War years and the Philippine settlement, was a suspicion that business was becoming our master. I suppose that the analogy which best describes the relation of academic life to the country at large is the medieval state, in which the monasteries, supported by the community and enriched by predatory king or baron, provided harborage for men violently opposed to the world that permitted them to exist. By that tension Christianity was shaped and from it came some of our greatest literature. Our tension was less obvious and less violent, but it also had results not easily estimated.

Academic life in America was, and is, peculiarly different from the habits of the rest of the community. The professor may have only a few set hours and often works at home, much to the annoyance of his wife. Many of his tasks are self-set, half of his labor is with milky youth and the other half with books whose authors are usually long since dead. He steers away from competition, and his most tense moments may come in the silence of his study. He may walk when he pleases under the quiet of the elms; yet he must never forget that he is a professor, giving example to youth.

These are his circumstances. The spiritual difference is much greater and is best understood by pursuing the comparison

with the medieval state. Our college was an adaptation of the
monastic system, a refuge for the contemplative and the analytical in a community devoted to the pursuit of prosperity.
But it was the monasticism of an industrial democracy, where
the modern monks had to take the democratic burden of general education, so that the scholar who retired from the world
must meet its offspring every morning in the classroom.

No wonder, then, that the academic community became a
true society, different at heart as well as in manners from the
rest of the country, and attracting minds that were different
from their neighbors', and making different men of them. Not
all of these were seekers, eager to advance the intellect. Many
were mere escapists from the strenuous life of industrial competition. Some were mild sadists who took their pleasure in
tormenting helpless youth. Others were seeking in education
the opportunities they no longer found in the weakening
churches. And some were drawn into the academic field by a
sense for the decencies of living which could be had in a community where there was leisure for those shrewd or rich enough
to take it, and wide intellectual and esthetic experience for
minds capable of a culture both broad and deep. For all such
the academic community was a life as well as a career, and that
is why its conditionings toward strength and weakness have
been so considerable that one wonders that the historians (who
themselves are academic products) have been so little concerned with this state within a state, in which some hundreds
of thousands of better-class Americans have in our time acquired qualities as recognizable as a priest's cassock or a sol-
dier's uniform.

As I think over the college town of that pre-war age which I
knew best, it seems to have offered to many types of mind the
best life, potentially, that America then possessed. Those quiet
streets still reminiscent of the early nineteenth century, the
vaulted college library redolent of old leather bindings and
peaceful as an island, days whose rhythm was steady yet so
much more varied than the routine of an office, since the excitement of teaching succeeded quiet study and was followed
by tennis or eager walking up Tutor's Lane in high-spirited
talk, then nights by the lamp or in a circle earnestly arguing.

And those long, long summers in the heart of the country, the active business of education folded away at Commencement, when time was all one's own, not to idle, for the prick of ambition was always sharp, but free hour upon hour to sink into books, to wrestle with ideas, to collate, analyze, ponder, and to write. There was no life like it for a man who wished to think and know.

There was also, even for the young and unplaced, an extraordinary independence in this academic life, limited in its scope, but deeply genuine — and particularly for young men who still were content with simple living. I will not say that our minds were free, for our academic conventions bound them, yet of these we were unaware, and within their limits we were not only free, we were urged, to independent thinking. And our daily life, even in term time, was independent, a source of great content. What a young teacher could do or could not do was strictly regulated by convention. Yet in the all-important area of authority and the control of time we had privileges which only those who have lost them can truly estimate. My teaching hours were fixed, but they were few in the day; and if what I taught was in general terms prescribed, how I taught it was my own responsibility. Each lecture, each recitation, was, if I wished and was able to make it so, a creative task, my own, and undictated. What relations I chose to have with my students, what disciplines, what intimacies, were of my own devising. I was only a cog in a machine, but my cog was free-wheeling, which was one reason why the college ran with such eccentricity.

And outside of my teaching hours and an occasional committee or faculty meeting, my time was my own to organize. Self-dependence was not only a privilege, it was a requisite. My mind, which theoretically belonged in its intellectual fruitfulness, if any, to the university, was left to my own initiative and my own discipline, to enfeeble or to develop. This was no clerk's or laborer's life. I was, in a very real sense, a man at the helm of his own voyage.

All this led to a pleasant eccentricity of living. There were professors who, like owls, were seen outside their classrooms only at night, keeping lonely vigil with their thoughts, while their reluctant muscles pumped out a mile of disciplinary exercise. There were men whose modishness expressed itself in an Oxford falsetto or the fashions of the undergraduate tailors. And others were like my own chief, now a distinguished figure in public life, who in those early days kept every angle of his Connecticut accent, and never wore a coat, waistcoat, and trousers which matched.

Most of this academic community had led protected lives, and many of them were ignorant of the most vital concerns of the present. In their morals, there was as much meanness, backbiting, subterfuge, and cowardice as in the outside world — as much, no more. There was much more jealousy — a feminine jealousy, not outspoken, but consuming — hid under masks of dignity, and speaking, when it did speak, always in high terms of ideals to be served and standards to be upheld. I have heard of a professor so insanely jealous of his colleagues that he wrote down his true opinions of them in his will; and I believe the story, for I knew a scientist once whose face would flush at the mention of a popular English professor, and whose forehead veins would swell dangerously at the mere word philosophy — philosophy that led his students away skating over thin ice which would not hold his literal intellect.

More significant was the mental range and elevation of these professors. They were men who had chosen to live and quarrel together in the academic life and so by necessity were concerned with thinking, and thinking in many categories. For them each chance encounter on the street was a contact with a different kind of knowledge. Not even the laziest minds were bound by the common male limitations of the day to money-making, because there was no profit for them except that which came from their job of study and teaching of subjects which usually had nothing to do with money. Even the laziest minds among them were perforce in contact daily with better minds than theirs — in books. If the tone of our academic society, even when in relaxation at the club, was a little arid, it was the aridity of a high sweeping plateau. And since abstractions are the object of all study, no matter how petty might be our own egos, the dullest and most pedantic among us had to busy himself constantly with the concerns of the human race. We talked

details of academic shop until our wives went to bed in boredom, for shop-talk was the irresistible vice that got us all; yet at
least when this talk rose above gossip the subject was the getting and acquiring of knowledge, which is certainly as interesting a theme as life insurance or manufacturing. You can be
just as dull over education as over advertising or sausage-mak-
ing, but the first has the broader implications.

This academic life was not really arid unless an arid mind
made it so. It was enriched and kept moist by that curious absorption between opposites which makes a nation victorious in
war take over the attributes of its enemy. We shared the light-
heartedness, the loyalty, and the sociability of the undergraduate, who was our nearest approach to an enemy. We were all
graduates of the college, and we kept much of the best of college life in our more matured society. The academic community in those days was emphatically a man's world, full of
clubs, free of its time for recreation or exercise, and organized
for sport and work, not love. (It *was* an arid world for women.)
We had, too, like the undergraduate, a sense of loyalty to our
institution which was quite unreasoning, and without relation
to the injustices and exploitations of our superiors, which were
frequent. Our college was intangibly something quite apart
from its president, deans, or heads of departments. They might
grind our faces for years on insufficient salaries, exploiting our
belief that our duty was to toil for *alma mater.* They might
encourage us to think that we would be happy nowhere but on
the home campus, then drop us with a sickening crash because
we were inbred. They might overwork us in teaching and then
break us because we had accomplished too little in scholarship.
All this we bitterly resented, without shaking our love and
loyalty for the college, which was for us a Platonic absolute.
This faith was so irrational that its breakdown later may have
been the beginning of a better career for the young scholar; yet
while it was strong it gave the academic life a touch of consecration, and bestowed upon it the self-rewarding quality of
service in the army or the church. Also, since we were confident of the worth of what we served, even when its agents
abused us, we were more easily happy, more generous toward
each other, more youthful in our pleasure, than the harder and

more skeptical business world outside. The paranoiac temperament was less encouraged in the college than elsewhere. Faith in that somewhat mystical entity, *alma mater,* was an antiseptic for the diseases of egoism.

This was the academic elysium for the contemplative and scholarly mind, the Utopian state within noisy, greedy, full-blooded America. Unfortunately it was a rather old-maidish Utopia, stiff with convention, easily frightened, and disposed always to play safe. We built our lives upon security.

The economics of security are peculiar. Indeed they have never been studied in this country, where opportunity, until recently, has seemed to wait just around the corner for the active man. But security has always been the goal of the teacher and scholar. It is curious that those who debate as to whether men and women can be induced to work without the profit-making motive take so little account of the great population in schools and colleges who even in the last century formed an extensive class that could not, and did not even wish to *make* money. They could not get rich, and so had to hope for security.

I am not writing economics, and am willing that others should do the deducing from this obvious and neglected fact. But certainly our college community was as dependent upon economic security as the peasant or workman in the Soviet Republics. For where could our ambitions lead us? Salaries were low, and going lower as the costs of living rose slowly but surely in the first decades of the twentieth century. Promotion was slow. The best the young married man with children could hope for was that his wages would keep pace with his minimum costs. They never did. Always there had to be a supplement — from a private income, from jobs at summer schools which cut into or cut out creative work, from lectures, textbooks, or an occasional piece of badly paid journalism. The scientist who could rent out his researches did better, but the teachers of the humanities were sorely pressed. And every such dollar earned was a handicap in the race for promotion. Our proper ambition, if we were ambitious, was research; research which consumed endless hours that might bring us fame, but no cash, if indeed we were fortunate enough not to have to pay for our publications. Our success, no matter how resounding, was a success of esteem unless it could be exchanged for an increase in salary. The more money we made in extracurricular activities, the less we got in increases from the college, which felt that we had been wasting its time and ours. And if we did succeed in research, or in writing or in journalism, the home authorities were the last to discover it. Only an offer from some other college would open their eyes. The best way to stay on in our beloved college was to threaten to leave it. And that bluff could be called.

Hence, deep down in this pleasant academic society was a subdued passion, like the peasant's for his home acres. Our strongest desire was to be made safe, to stay where we were on a living wage, to be secure while we worked. It was well enough to live with ideas, to devote oneself to vigorous assaults upon the Philistine, but bills had to be paid, children schooled, the future made possible for decent living. No scrimping, no outside earning, could safeguard us. We were dependent upon the college, which itself was always pressed for money, and could not be counted upon to be either judicious or just.

Profit as a motive was bred out of us. We were frankly ashamed of our petty money-makings on the side, and inclined to hide them, while we boasted of our activities in research which were often far less useful. We quite forgot the good sense of 'All service ranks the same with God,' turning up academic noses at attempts of our colleagues to succeed in the unacademic. I remember a friend of mine in the English department who, with a little gift in narrative, and a nice touch in the essay, wrote decidedly better (which was not saying much) than most of his colleagues. He breached the wall of the *Atlantic*, broke into *Harper's*, published a book that was called 'literary' by the reviewers, and so felt with some justice that since his job in college had been teaching how to write, it was to his credit that he had got himself read by the outside world in those forms of literature upon which it was his daily duty to lecture. 'It would have been better,' the head of his department was heard to remark, 'that So and So had written nothing, than what he has written. He should be doing research.' And that was that. The sin was not in the writing *per se*, but that it was writing for outsiders, and was critical, creative writing not chiefly concerned with the discovery of facts. And more subtly, that it had been paid for — not much, to be sure, but still it had been sold to the populace.

And thus both our needs and our ambition for academic recognition bound us tighter and tighter to a security that only the college could give us. Those who preached the humanities, and they were the backbone of the college of that era, had only this one resource. The outside world to them was truly a waste-land where wraiths of broken scholars wandered — no place, no pay, no security. There was fear at their hearts, even the best of them, even those with private fortunes. They felt that they lived on sufferance in the capitalist state.

When I was young it was this hidden fear that impressed me. As I grew older, it was the courage of those who had conquered it — those true scholars, true adventurers in the intellect, who had put the love of security behind them, and who throve upon insecurity. It took a war to teach me that there was no real security anywhere except in the mind — that if content and safety might be bedfellows, happiness and insecurity could be brothers in arms. Many — most I should say — of the academic community never learned this simple lesson. Their actions, their modes of thought, their lives public and private, were conditioned from beginning to end by the passionate need to be safe.

And that accounts for the timorousness of the academic mind and the persistent note of caution in academic life. Thought was free and speech was reasonably free, and bold men of first-rate capacity used their freedom. Most of us were not bold. We could say what we liked with no immediate penalty, but did not say it. We could do what we liked if our income permitted, but did not do it. Our timidity was emotional.

Radicalism as it exists today was rare in our college. I can remember no instance in which it became a real issue in my time. Why should we have been radical? We knew more of the weaknesses of the capitalist system than did the business world or the proletariat. We knew also very well that we were dependent upon the surpluses of great wealth. Why not? Was there any better way in which they could be spent? Was there any class that worked harder and more disinterestedly than we

did for a smaller share of the country's gains? Teaching and research would have to go on under any system, and the experience of those who had been in state universities taught us
that our freedom certainly, and our wages probably, would be
less if the people paid us. It was not parasitism upon the millionaire that made the historian or social scientist a restrained
and moderate critic. No, he *felt* that way. The unearned in-
crement by the time it got to him was being turned into benefits for society at large. The rich were compensating through
him for their exploitations. He was their abbot whose duty it
was to transmute thefts into philanthropy. And he was enough
of a philosopher to be distrustful of all systems, and particularly skeptical of the blessings of revolution. It was not until
the capitalist state showed signs of cracking that the professors
became radical. In such matters they were always cautious, but
sometimes, certainly, wise.

Their timidity was not so much of the intellect as of the
emotions. It was not the great donors they were afraid of, but
the conventions of the academic life. The college had become
a nest of specialists, each one of which knew only a little but
knew that so well that he objected to criticism from an outsider
in his subject. Having taught himself with infinite pains to be
cautious in handling his facts, he avoided like fire any opinion
upon the facts of his neighbor and resented any comment upon
his own. Conversation sometimes became an exchange of dogmatic statement. The humanist was interested in science, but
was careful not to go beyond questions. The scientist was interested in the humanities, but refused to commit himself upon
anything that could not be measured. Both often declared the
philosopher to be a meddler in other people's fields, and waged
such successful war upon him that he saved himself from op-
probrium by becoming a psychologist. While the curriculum
was much debated, there was a gentleman's agreement that the
raison d'être and relativity of the subjects of instruction should
not be argued. They were vested interests. Too much intellectual curiosity was regarded with suspicion.

How often have I heard a discussion in faculty meeting collapse like a house of cards when some unfortunate instructor,
building a theory upon a deduction, got over his own property

American society banal was not their defect. Still, the mixed air of intellectualism and social caution which their husbands breathed was not good for them, or for any female. They looked frigid, whether they were or not. One dares to write so rudely of them because their desiccation was typical, not general. The faculty wife who kept her personality and sublimated her emotions into gracious ways and the talk of a free spirit was one of the finest of American women. She made it possible to say that the academic life in those decades was, in spite of its faults, the most civilized existence which the country at large possessed.

Yet even the best had their trials. Our academic society was made for men and run according to their own tastes, regardless of their womenkind. A faculty dinner party was thus not quite like other dinner parties, although it takes some thinking to discover what made the difference.

The preliminaries were feminine and somewhat flurried, especially if mixed grades of the hierarchy were to be present, assistant professors with full professors, or a dean, or a president. One hostess of my acquaintance solved the problem by entertaining only one rank at a time. The practice was not popular; it was too much like a segregation by races at Ellis Island. The faculty wife had to know something about faculty quarrels, probable promotions, possible dismissals; and, as if this were not enough to distract a hostess, since our world was monastic, there was sure to be some crusty old bachelor of importance who thought children were messy. One young mother dosed hers with aspirin fifteen minutes before the guests' arrival. Or would it have been soothing syrup in 1910? And then the house! Professors worked at home, hence there were sure to be books everywhere except on the shelves where they belonged, and probably a dictionary or concordance dropped under the dining-room table. And the food and drink? Since everyone knew your salary, should it be simpler than necessary in order to suggest plain living and high thinking; or richer than one could afford, in order to flatter the powers who might think that here was a family of taste who did credit to an academic income?

We still escorted the ladies on our arms to the dining room

in the early nineteen-hundreds, with regard for precedence of rank, not age; and once seated there was none of your modern cocktail hilarity, but a weighty pause while we looked about to see who was there. The faculty dinner was not given for pleasure, though it might prove to be pleasurable. It was a duty, as the personnel of the party so clearly indicated. In a compact society such as ours, the satisfaction of choosing for companionship, wit, or beauty was an indulgence seldom permitted. We gave two kinds of dinners: informal informal where familiar acquaintances rotated from house to house seeing each other on different sides of many tables (no public notice was taken of such a dinner); and informal formal (the purely formal we left to deans and presidents) in which, alas, debts must be paid, heads of departments salaamed to, and new faculty members (who invariably had nervous dyspepsia in their first year) picked off the waiting list. Hence a table as incongruous as the guests of a dining car, and a conversation that too often slid into anecdote or was submerged by a monologue.

But by the salad, a mathematician, if he was present — and one usually was — might have noticed the faint, first rise of a curve of interest which was soon to attract wandering talk and focus it so persistently that, in spite of the feeble attempts of the hostess, the men looked through and soon forgot their partners, until with coffee there was a knot of black coats at one end of the room and a discouraged cloud of skirts at the other. I had seen the same symptoms before in small-town society, but this was different. The men's talk here was not of stocks and business; it was more impassioned, though always bound to the college and its shop. It was gossip, gossip of students, gossip of courses, gossip of the books of scholars, gossip which excluded women from their own province by denying any sex but the male, and left them between wind and water, their charm, if any — and there was often much — neglected for the more intoxicating passions of academic life.

It was a bad world for women, although in the coeducational institutions the atmosphere may have been much more favorable. But if they came through intact, they had learned all the social lessons, could listen to a seventy-year-old celebrity who addressed the ceiling, or talk to a Ph.D. with the milk of his thesis still bubbling on his lips. Alas, many did not come through. To scrimp and be dignified daily throughout the long wait for a professorship, while conscious that the especial gifts of woman were worse than useless without respectability and decorum, chilled the faculty wife, molded a prim face, and was responsible for a masochistic dowdiness. *Alma mater* was a jealous deity that tolerated no feminism except her own male variety.

Women in the academy society grew salty, eccentric, many-angled in character; or prudish, dry, fussy, and self-indulgent; or, transcending the limitations of their sex, sublimated their difficulties into an amenity of real culture. They were never passionate — at least in public. But I have misstated the academic male and the life he made for himself if I have implied that he also was cold, emotionless, far removed from the excitement of the passions. Nothing could be farther from the truth. Outwardly our academe was cautious in statement and timid in act, judicious rather than daring, reflective, not adventurous. And in the inner life the passions of sex were controlled, and sometimes atrophied. But those other passions — ambition, jealousy of power and place, most of all, the passionate hurling of thought and will against the wall of ignorance and through the fogs of obscurantism, and the endless struggle to think straight and true — provided emotions enough for any man. In exact contrast with the rest of America, it was the intensity of the inner life, the calm of the outer, which gave to the college a quality which made it a culture and an experience that was unique. For men, not women — however it may have been in the comparatively few colleges whose faculties were chiefly women.

Why, then, have the professor and his life been somewhat of a joke in America? Why has he been called a 'third sex,' a lazy dreamer, an unpractical idealist? Because in the nineteen-hundreds, when for the first time everybody that was anybody began to go to college, the academic life was an anomaly in the hustle and bustle of a prosperous country on the highroad of material progress? Because the professor did not make money, did not drink and wench, did not grab power as power was understood in those days, did not wear himself out at forty, did not (a little later) own a car until his neighbor had two? Because he seemed a nonconformist — what the undergraduates called a freak?

These explanations have truth, but leave me skeptical. They are too complimentary to the professor, and too superficial. There was another reason. Something in this pleasant academic life kept the professor as a class from pulling his weight in the community. Perhaps our American culture was too young to assimilate the contributions of professional thinkers, especially since these were more interested in thinking than in our culture. Perhaps it was essential (if you believe in a direction for social history) that these college towns should be oases where traditions of long-term thinking and of conserved energy (which some called laziness) should be kept alive while the *laissez-faire* system, which seemed to be making the country great, should run its course. Perhaps if the college professor had not persisted in being 'un-American,' there would have been no reserve of disinterested minds for a new era when the motto seems to be 'Plan or Bust.'

I believe all that, but feel no warmth of pride stirring my memories. We were not in those days holding off for some active future — or certainly most of us were not. We were puzzled idealists trying to keep our footing in two worlds at once. Like the college itself, we had a split personality, and paid for it in being muddled often and sometimes hypocritical. We envied the new-rich progressive country outside our quiet communities, without sufficiently respecting its vital energies, and so acquired the sense of inferiority of those who live in alien civilizations. And this inferiority we tried to conceal, even from ourselves, by an intellectual snobbery which resulted too often in pedantry or pose. Even the English we spoke had an accent of its own. Feeding knowledge to the animals, we were secretly doubtful as to whether it was wisdom, and hid our doubts under a mask of stiff dignity. We younger men in this difficult decade did become a third sex — masculine in our resolution to make the life of the reason keep pace with the instincts, feminine in our irritabilities, vanities, and our petty struggles to get that recognition from each other which the country, with a tolerant smile, quite emphatically denied us. In those agreeable academic Edens, scattered all the way from New England to California, the professor was Adam, as self-assured and as vain as the original, but there was the serpent also that kept crawling up from his uneasy conscience or his hurt pride. I leave the professor's wife out of the comparison. If she played Eve now and then, I was too young to be told about it, but I am sure that the monastic life she had to share was bad for her glands.

↺ 6 ↻

The Professor

I N MEMOIRS LIKE THESE there is a constant temptation to play
the interpretive philosopher who explains everything that
was in terms of what happened afterward. For this a vivid
memory is the best corrective. I am sure that the analysis of the
preceding chapter is accurate as far as it goes. Yet no sooner
do I write the last word of a mode of living that damped the
will while it gave a happy home to the contemplative mind
than I remember a group of outstanding professors, pure products of the academic environment, which transcends my definition of the academic life as a scene where caution and dignity
prevailed while only speculation went free. Indeed, these men
seem to me in retrospect to have had more character and richer,
more outspoken personalities than their equivalents among the
industrialists and the politicians of the age. I wonder if I have
been writing nonsense.

It was not nonsense. Precisely as the tensions and inconsis-
tencies of political life in this same period produced a Theodore Roosevelt, and the opportunities of the business world
such unique figures as Carnegie and the elder Morgan, so the
struggle between two ideals of living, which was naturally more
acute in the colleges than elsewhere, made its own great men.
We thought that they were great scholars, but that, for most of
them, now begins to seem doubtful. We believed them to be
great thinkers, which, with one possible exception in Sumner,
they certainly were not. But that they were great personalities
I am sure; and I believe that they dominated their academic
world as in the more efficient machine of the modern university
no great teacher does today. Our gods of the campus were local
deities not destined to establish lasting cults, yet they exerted
the lifelong influence of a divinity that shapes the emotions as

well as the mind. And both undergraduates and young instructor took a proprietary interest in their eminence. Our attitude
toward them was like the relation between the savage and his
idols. We loved them, or hated them, or even despised them,
but never escaped from their daily presence in our thoughts.
Such men were the justification of the old college. There were
never many, sometimes no more than one to a community, but
it is of them that the generation shaped by the college still talk.

I shall choose four from my own experience and without
more tiresome analysis try to describe personalities that are important for the young who wish to understand an American
society that will be history for them.

The first was a man of mingled sweetness and austerity, mellow in his wisdom, rich in knowledge, yet so thwarted in
achievement, so repressed in his life, and dimmed in his ordinary visage as to be an epitome of all that I have written of the
academic life at the turn of the last century. I have seen a
photograph of him in a class-book of the eighteen-sixties, where
he appears as a youth dressed in the negligent foppishness of
the young *littérateur* of the bohemian period. And indeed,
when he began the study and practice of literature, his voca-
tion seemed obvious. That was the afternoon of the Age of
Confidence in the literary art. Professors were still men of letters, lectures were essays (such as Emerson wrote), students
were gentlemen eager to acquire a genteel style. But Henry
Augustin Beers (there must still be many who will respond to
that name) was not content to be a rhetorician. His idea of
scholarship was to know and love all good literature, and all
of it he read. I have never mentioned a masterpiece in any
language that he had not been through, and from which he
could not quote; nor a poem or story of merit, even if obscure,
in our own American literature that was not fresh with all the
context of its times in his memory. For him Milton was as
much alive as Emerson, whom he had known. His arguments
were not of date and source (though he was accurate and far-
seeing), but of matters of blood and brain and sex, and of
neighbors, accidents, temperament, and sheer aptitude, which
explain what is both important and explicable in the background of art. Yet his mind, though so stocked, was never a

specialist's. He was an amateur in military history, a connoisseur in acting, especially women's acting, though he could
seldom afford the theater, and he knew in a Connecticut meadow where the gentian grew and on a hillside pasture where to
plant the pine.

He seemed an old man when I first knew him well, in 1900.
Bent over his desk, reading with difficulty from frayed note
sheets in a husky voice, he would pause at intervals to goggle
through thick lenses at his inattentive class while he asked a
perfunctory question, sometimes not waiting for an answer.
'Old Beers' they called him, with a surprised affection for so
musty a creature, from whose lips between the crash and jangle
of trolley cars outside a sentence now and then was audible
of such pith and beauty that lazy fingers began to scribble in
the notebooks.

After class some of us would linger until the routine was
over, then draw near his desk with questions.   Slowly the
drooped head would lift, the sensitive fingers begin to smooth
his limp mustache, the eyes behind the thick spectacles would
light and twinkle, the voice grow mellow; and then, if our
opening was fortunate, his real teaching would begin. He had
a mind that was skeptical, humorous, affectionate, an impeccable taste, a humanity so deep and so cultivated that as he
talked civilizations took color, authors became men, and poetry
was felt to be that rhythm of personal experience which Robert
Frost defines, and which Beers of all the critics I have known
most infallibly could bring back from the past.

Here was a man sure of his loves and hates, who questioned
the validity of good thought and beauty as little as love or
food. He did not preach culture but was the thing itself. He
had not acquired knowledge as a tool but because his mind desired it. Where his colleagues knew about literature, he knew
literature itself, and more about it that was relevant than the
most erudite. His mind was encyclopedic, but it was a commentary, not a reference book. Other scholars knew what idyll
of Theocritus was a source for *Lycidas,* he could tell why Milton read it and what he had done with his reading. The college knew, or thought it knew, why literature should be taught,
and what should be taught of it. Beers was himself an example

of that rebirth in literature which gives margins to the imagination. No one knowing him could doubt the efficacy of the humanities. And it was significant in that atmosphere of jealousy of science and the new technologies that there, too, his interests were keen.

Yet it would be too much to say that Henry Beers had a successful life. Burdened with many dependents upon an income whose real value had steadily shrunk, he was deprived of all those recreations which minds like his are made to enjoy. A reader of European literature, his only trip abroad was made in his youth. Society had to come to him, for he was too poor to go to society. I do not suppose that in twenty years he made as many journeys, even of a day, to New York or Boston. In his own college town he was a hermit, living in an unfashionable suburb, hidden away among his books. On our quiet campus his bent frame, his worn clothes, his shy and inward air as he shuffled from his classroom toward the library, were like a survival of a more pinched and austere age. Freshmen stopped to wonder as he passed. He was young in heart and the richness of his inner life must have been some compensation for the poverty of his experience. Yet he was a defeated man.

It was not his restricted means or his weight of personal responsibility that bore him down. They were the agents of his defeat, but the cause was the new utilitarianism of the campus. I do not mean the romantic materialism of the undergraduates which young instructors were vainly fighting. Beers was too intelligent and too familiar with the history of his own country not to have understood better than we the reasons for their Philistinism, and too true a humanist not to have stood up against it unbowed. Indeed, in spite of his defeatism, he became a legend among the students because of the evident sincerity of his culture. It was the demands of his own colleagues that put the mask on his face, and drove his vision inward. In his youth a professor of English was expected to be a maker as well as a teacher of literature. Much amateur creativeness of a genteel kind had resulted. But Beers was neither an amateur nor genteel. He was a poet of sorts, a prose writer of excellent skill. He deserved the name of man of letters. It is not surprising, therefore, that the demand for science in the study of literature caught him unprepared. He was a reader of literature, not a collector of facts about it, although in accurate information he had few rivals. Nevertheless, his methods were not the methods of natural science. It was conclusions, not data, that seemed to him important. He was, I believe, planning to write the literary history of America which has not yet been properly written, when philology as the Germans understood it came into fashion. There was a sudden cry for medievalists, phoneticians, and practitioners of exact research, with no literary nonsense about them. Those areas of literary history which were difficult because of their remoteness, and obscure because their poverty in artistic worth had repelled earlier readers, became the cynosures of scholarship. Anyone could write of Tennyson or Browning, but it took scholarship to discuss the *Andreas* or *Handlyng Synne.*

In the flurry, the comprehensive knowledge of all good English literature and a minute familiarity with American writing seemed of little price. Men were brought to teach what he was supposed not to know. His own classmates began to regard him as an old-fashioned putterer in outworn themes, who might at any moment publish the poetry he was known to write. His contributions already made to the history and criticism of American literature were compared unfavorably with research in the much harder history of Anglo-Saxon, his charming essays upon life in an earlier Yale were regarded as conclusive evidence against his aptitude for scholarship. And his inefficiency as a teacher of the massed young of an unliterary period put the last nail in the coffin of his reputation. In self-defense he published two books based upon a thorough investigation of romanticism, a subject then fashionable. They are still standard, but his heart was not in them. They were neither literature, of which he was capable, nor criticism of that American field where he was without a peer, but which in that day of excessive reverence for European scholarship was felt to be too trivial for a serious mind that should be engaged in establishing the authorship of a bad pseudo-Shakespearian play. When I first knew him he was already listed as a liability from the past

His old age knew a brief sunset. He lived long enough to

see a respect for literature as such appear again in the colleges, though not quite long enough to witness (with what an ironic smile!) droves of prospective Ph.D.'s turning from the exhausted veins of English literature to dig in the American soil, rediscovering often what he long since had known, but knowing so much less well what it meant and what to do with it! Before he died his house was a place of pilgrimage.

It was the times that destroyed him. The college was unsure of its own ends, uncertain of the value of the humanities, yet honorably unable to yield to the hearty materialism of the age. Compromising between rigid discipline and the romance of college life, it distrusted instinctively a man whose culture was homogeneous and of a kind that its halfway measures could never produce. If Beers had stiffened his backbone instead of withdrawing into the city of his mind, he might have been our leader. If he had been a more powerful teacher, a more self-assured scholar, he would have made it necessary to respect him. But he was not aggressive. Unfortunately those with access to the inner light of the humanities seldom are, nor are their minds the stuff out of which missionaries are made. It is too bad, for what we get from the missionaries of culture proves so often not to be the Gospel! Yet no lover of literature went out of college in my day untouched by his influence.

My second example was also a professor of English, but of a breed so different that I am left wondering whether the rich university of today can show such diverse egos. He was a bearded man, short, catlike on his feet, with a shifty eye and a quick tread across the campus that seemed always to conceal a limp. Professor Albert S. Cook was a finished product of the German philological mill, who had been brought to the university to introduce methodology — how he rolled the word on his tongue! — into our somewhat haphazard graduate school of language and literature. He had already made a reputation in Anglo-Saxon philology; indeed, his first-year book in that language was a model of its kind. He brought the gospel of science in literary studies.

No man in my day was more unpopular with the faculty and the few undergraduates that came under him, more worshiped by a small circle of devotees. He was, indeed, in our clubable community, the exact counterpart of the grind and freak among the undergraduates. Not that he worked harder than his colleagues or produced more. But instead of the lazy lecture, oft used if excellent, which was the fare of our advanced courses, he offered a battle, incalculable from the moment of beginning, impromptu, unfair from every college viewpoint, since it was impossible to guard one's weaknesses or listen to a conventional lecture with an easy mind. And, like the grind, he had an indifference amounting to contempt for the amenities of our academic living. Indeed, there was something sadistic about the man, a by-product of his intensities, which accounted in part for both the dislike and for the slavish devotion that he inspired, although the deeper cause of his unpopularity was by no means creditable to his enemies. I have seen him reduce a woman graduate student to tears, and seem to enjoy it. Of men he was afraid. If they yielded to his intellectual dominance, he would work for their advancement, but let them waver in their admiration and the knife in a second would sever the umbilical cord. You were either *his* student, or someone else's, and if someone else's, beware! No mercy, no help. Indeed, here was a perfect example of the feminine male, in whom a masculine intellect operated with all the vanity, jealousy, pettiness, and infinite subtlety of a woman.

A fine philologist, his mind was nevertheless too scattering and too prone to quick generalizations for sustained scholarship. Like the scientists of the day, his work was contained in brief papers recording discoveries, many of them minute, if not trivial. Unfortunately they were not steps in the study of the nature of light or the weight of the atom, but rather chips of literary history, the date of a Northumbrian cross, the classic parallels to a line in Milton. In such a strictly limited field as the teaching of elementary Anglo-Saxon he was admirable; and among all my teachers in that day he alone seemed interested in the relations between the categories of knowledge, in one terse sentence throwing more light on the proper development of a project in research than came from all the rest of the faculty.

But the college and its closely related graduate school encouraged his weakness rather than his strength. He knew little of literature as literature, though much of its history, little of esthetics except its theories, and nothing that was original of philosophy. Yet it was these that he taught us instead of his proper subject, which was philology. The top dressing of smug culture on the crude vigorous soil of American life was a stench in his nostrils. He felt a call to convert the heathen, to smite the Philistines. He hurled the Middle Ages at our head — his Middle Ages, not always the genuine article. He challenged us with masterpieces. He talked now of Beethoven, now of Aeschylus. If we mentioned Horace, he made us translate him. If we spoke of religion, he made us define our terms. No gentleman's agreement as to required knowledge stood for a moment with him. He demeaned himself so far as to nag women with general questions that it is certain he could not have answered satisfactorily himself. He aroused hate and a fierce opposition. He burned through our bourgeois *laissez-faire,* and set us searching for the principles upon which we lived and which we were willing to defend. He was a great teacher, if to be a great teacher is to set the mind afire, the greatest I have ever known.

There was more literature in Beers's little finger than in Cook's lifetime, though for the college at large it stayed in his little finger. Cook broke up our minds, sneered at us, bullied us, threw absurd generalizations at our heads, tripped us on trivialities, taught his women to talk solemn nonsense without knowing that it was nonsense, wrapped his own esthetic insensitiveness in words, and made us angry, and thus alive. If Beers was a belated humanist, he was a schoolman come from the Middle Ages, playing with science and literature instead of theology. And, indeed, it may be said of him as of many great medieval scholastics that he was a great teacher who was usually wrong.

Inevitably our college faculty, with its genteel reserves, its mingled contempt and fear of the raw competition outside, its defeatism and indifferentism, would acquire sooner or later such a crabbed spirit who struck blows for the sake of hurting, and tried to make us all into what he supposed was the image of an Athenian. Yet it did us good. In my education he was the whip with the nasty undercut.

For the third of my figures from these now so distant nineties and first nineteen-hundreds, I will turn to science as science was understood then.

I wish I could re-create in words William H. Brewer. He was a vast, shambling man, with the face of an old ram stretched on the drum of a great head, a ragged beard that never covered a spreading goiter, and a squeaky voice that seemed to come from some observer sitting inside. Indeed, his whole life had been concentrated on observation, and I do not believe that his imagination was ever actually in the lecture room, but rather on the deck of a sinking ship in the Arctic, or following the wild camels of Arizona, or noting the geography of the Sierras, which he explored, and where there is a great snow-based peak that bears his name. In his lectures, except for brief moments of irritation when he would show on his chart that the ancestry of some disturber on the rear seat ran back to the wild ass of the deserts, he was shadow-boxing. His subject, I suppose, was evolution; to this day I do not know what he was supposed to teach, so widely did his lectures range; but more and more as the year went on his discourse narrowed to a fierce controversy with an absent antagonist, the great German biologist Weismann, who had foully disposed of Brewer's pet theory of the inheritance of acquired characteristics, by experiments that our professor asserted to be inconclusive, insufficient, and probably fraudulent. Again and again, while we sat in boredom or fascination according to our sense for drama, the squeaky voice would rise, the broad face flush, the classroom fade from his consciousness, while with a lancelike pointer he stabbed at his visionary antagonist, and crumbled him at last with his other hand into broken bits of chalk.

We got evolution from him certainly, and useful tips on horse-races, for he was an expert in breeding and predicted the two-minute trotter within five years of its actual appearance. (He shocked the college town also by subscribing for all the racing papers.) We got glimpses of the passion and confidence of science in a day when it seemed that all wisdom as well as all knowledge was to be its province. Nevertheless, most of his squeaky eloquence drifted over our unruffled heads, so that now his classes remember only that he pronounced 'Injun' in the old American manner, and 'cigarettees' in his own peculiar fashion, leaving them certain of evolution but doubtful of what it was or how it came about. I am sorry that we let our thoughts wander, for we were watching a tragedy, and hearing a parable more truly significant for our generation than the soon-to-be-disproved physics and economics we were being taught in other classrooms. Here, indeed, was the parallel to the industrial profit-making life from which most of us had come. Here was science, unrelated to the rest of life (except horse-racing), yet cocksure and triumphant, announcing multitudes of observations collected with incredible energy, which were to reveal the Great Secret at last. No end to the amassing of scientific fact — tails of monkeys, customs of the anthropoids, the results of mixed marriages, statistics of venereal diseases, the lifting power of flood waters, the ancestry of the bulldog. Precisely as the new industrialists were piling up millions in their greed for power, which when gained they gave away or used to make new millions, so this robber baron of science took toll of everything that came to his attention and stored his loot upon innumerable note sheets. In contrast to the tight little disciplines of our curriculum, he offered us the world — as he saw the world. But alas, it was all uncontrolled experiment, the infinite details of which slid over our minds, leaving us as incapable of realizing the true significance of the growing complexity of civilization as were our fathers who had been trained in the classics. There was dynamite in Brewer's course, but no caps to set it off. He was content to make us wonder at the tricks nature could play. I am unjust, for doubtless many a man of our time was prepared by that prelude to natural science to respect (or fear) the scientist when later he began to attack our reckless exploitation of resources of wealth and humanity. Yet Brewer saw only an age of miracle where every rock and toad and gutter had its story, which to know was to understand.

After his death I had occasion to go into his study. It was a capacious room, its walls hidden by box upon box of notes, while from the ceiling a dozen baskets hung on pulleys, each overflowing with records and documents. A lifetime of observation! And they were all to be burnt! Nothing had been deduced from them that affected thinking; no man would undertake to go through them; their utility had been only the delight of observation, and what increase in knowledge his contemporaries had gained. I saw an equivalent sight twenty years later when a strongbox was opened in the nineteen-thirties. There were the accumulated profits of a capitalist lifetime, all paper and most of it worthless. Brewer was a man true to his time, true to a college that was not sure of what it wanted. Yet he was a personality that, as I recall him, makes me wish to write only in praise. Whatever he said and did, he himself was an education.

I shall close this chapter with one more scientist, whose science was above reproach, since, although its fundamental tenets have been upset since his day, they have been changed by such methods of thought and experiments as he himself taught. The physical theory he gave us proved much of it to be wrong, and indeed his was not the highly original mind to set it right, but he had the true scientific attitude, which is neither possessive nor dogmatic. He taught us not to wonder, but to reason.

Yet it was not his science that brings him to memory here. The best physics in the world would never have stirred my imagination in those days, unless freed from its husk of mathematics. It was his solution of a common college problem. He alone among all my teachers faced our Philistine contempt for high-brow nonsense, and faced it down. Charles S. Hastings was a man of some elegance, whose pince-nez held between finger and thumb was no more delicately balanced than his enunciation of an admirable English. He told no stories, embroidered upon his subject no references to undergraduate life, made no colloquial concessions to the unintellectual. If it was a dynamo he was explaining, or the conservation of energy, he kept to his theme, but to that theme he gave the skill in composition, the nicety of expression, and the urbanity of a great painter. Language for him was a garment whose every fold and shade was conditioned by the infinite complexity of truth. An artist in words, he used them, not as words merely, but as the only medium by which a thought world alien to us could be interpreted to minds that feebly but inevitably responded. It was a culture, yet not culture as we thought of culture, for the substance of his discourse was practical, inescapable fact (and yet not fact but hypothesis, so he told us), such fact as business men and engineers dealt with, and hence part of the experience that our home town regarded as reality. And yet this tangible reality became on his tongue so subtle, so evidently related to ends that no immediate application could satisfy, that in spite of ourselves we became aware of the nature of the search for truth in a region where neither sentiment nor platitude would avail.

The physics he taught we hated and learned badly; but the philosophy remained. For here was the sense of form, the devotion to abstract ends, which our college life repudiated, in a hard-boiled subject that could not be bluffed. Perhaps what he ultimately taught was not science, except in its methods of thinking, so much as literature, and indeed literature was his private passion. It was he who, long before the new Ph.D.'s discovered him, introduced me to Herman Melville. The plowing-in of formula and experiment he left to his subordinates. What he gave us himself was a pattern of exquisite thinking and an idea which we dimly apprehended that all truth must ultimately be beautiful. And also, on a lower level — but what a lesson for barbarians! — that cold facts could best be imparted in the courtesy of perfect English admirably spoken. Even the bums and the roughnecks were orderly in his class.

7

Scholars and Scholarship

ALTHOUGH Professor Brewer's collected works were only a million note sheets, now ashes, at least he fulfilled his intellectual destiny. He was of the race of explorers, men searching passionately for a river, a city, or a missing link that proves to be illusion, men whose maps are wrong, whose specimens are ill-assorted, yet they cross new passes and trackless deserts, opening trails for the better-disciplined minds that follow. His mountain in the Sierras is precisely the monument that he would have desired. Not so with most of the humanists among his younger contemporaries, the workers in history and particularly in literature, too many of whom were somewhat tragic figures, with divided minds. One word was always on their tongues — 'scholarship,' a term to which no two of them gave exactly the same definition. Indeed, they served a two-faced god.

The scholar's passion in the college of that day was for knowledge. His enthusiasm was well warmed, if not always well lit, by a burning desire to get the facts. When, just out of college ourselves, we first sat in something like intimacy under old teachers who now proposed to make teachers of us, what they taught us first was to despise the cultivated amateurs who in the last generation had lectured upon the amenities of history and literature. Lowell, whose critical essays were rich in opinions but short in facts, was held up to scorn. Longfellow was mentioned also, with a shrug — a professor who did translations. Accuracy in little things was the new virtue, and we were encouraged to believe that the world was more in need of correct texts, exact dates, and a knowledge of sources than of estimates, appreciations, and opinions which, however just, were not scientific because they could not be proved. Browning's grammarian had given the slogan —

This man decided not to Live but Know —

a line which was often quoted. Since an accurate text of a masterpiece was a necessary preliminary to a correct interpretation, insensibly the establishing of the text began to seem more important than an appreciation of the work; and, naturally, the more corrupt or the more difficult the text, the more merit there was in studying it. For great works of literary art belonging to a past era, where every resource of history had to be exhausted in order merely to understand, this obsession with knowledge gave great results. Chaucer and Dante came to life again in this age of scientific scholarship. Yet too often the scholar could tell you everything about a poem except why it was poetry.

The classicists, and the teachers of modern literature who were heirs to their dictatorship of culture, had dubiously and with unconcealed condescension given to pure science a minor place in the curriculum. Now the scientific approach became fashionable. Scholars in literature who called themselves scientific began to dominate the graduate schools and extend their influence into the sacred precincts of the undergraduate college. Applying the technique of scientific research to language, they revealed an evolution with laws of its own the discovery of which was a noble extension of knowledge. Then they moved from linguistics into literary history and soon were rewriting the vague and impressionistic chronicles of our literary past, substituting exact tests of dialect, allusion, and rhythm for the guesswork of earlier historians. The bastard works fathered upon Chaucer and Shakespeare were given rightful parents or put upon the town, and indebtedness to tradition or to environment was rightly indicated.

But neither our literature nor our history is explained by the facts of its origin or its background alone. A historian at best gives a personal interpretation. A scientific researcher at the most provides the essential facts. In poetry or fiction there is a new world created which is a whole that is by no means only a sum of its parts.

Nothing of him that doth fade,
But doth suffer a sea-change
Into something rich and strange.

The scientific impulse in literary scholarship was indifferent to such nice metamorphoses of subject matter. It sought facts where facts could be found and its disciples soon began to see all written records as a quarry in which the mysterious nature of a crystal could be ascertained by the same chemical analysis that demonstrated the composition of a block of limestone to be $CaCo_3$.

Envy was partly responsible for this singular warping of judgment. The humanist scholars of my youthful day were jealous of the great achievements of natural science. Science had begun to turn away resolutely from the 'wonders of nature' which had fascinated men like Brewer, and with specks of dirt microscopically considered, or drops of fluid in a test tube, or glacial scratches on a stone, was making discoveries of stupendous importance. In my own university before my day, research men in 'stinks' and other utilitarianisms had been tolerated, but kept in a social position definitely inferior to the humanists, so that when Harvard asked for representatives from Yale at her two hundred and fiftieth anniversary, no professors from the new Scientific School were included in the list drawn up by our president. Now science was having its revenge.

Scientists in the college of the nineteen-hundreds were still regarded as socially dubious by the wives of classicists and English professors, but the husbands of these social leaders of the college had, without being fully aware of it, become imitators of what they had so lately disdained. If boulders the plowman turned up in the fields and mice infected by disease held secrets valuable to man, why should not the bypaths and deserts and unexplored areas of literary history be as rewarding to researchers? And so began that race after the obscure, the difficult, and the neglected which, yielding rich spoils where science was the proper tool, led elsewhere to the vast accumulations of unimportant facts about literary history which clog the shelves of libraries and whiten the hair of the modern historian, who cannot write a page without consulting a shelf-ful of pamphlets, many of which cancel each other. The parallel with the world outside, where technological advance was accompanied by a senseless race for self-defeating power and by riches badly used, is too obvious to need pointing.

Both sets of competitors — the millionaires and the literary scholars — failed to define their ends; neither, as a rule, knew what to do with their prizes when they got them. But there was this difference, that while out in the world everyone appreciated the value of money, the undergraduates for whom the college had been made, their parents, and the alumni, were quite unable to comprehend the passion of the scholar who spent his life in clearing up a text, leaving the study of literature as such to lesser men, or to the next generation.

For the true scientist in history and literature, without whose work history, criticism, and intepretation are alike difficult, if not impossible, I have the greatest respect. But alas, few of us in those days were scientists by nature, but rather young men in love with books; and even if our minds had been scientific there would not have been room for us all in the regions of literary history still unexplored! These two obvious facts did not weigh for a moment with our superiors. They had seen the Chaucer canon made, and the border ballads rescued from oblivion. So they urged us on to tasks which inevitably were of lesser importance. Ambition and research became synonymous words. Literature, our reading, we might pick up in odd hours — our work, our future lay in literary history, in discovery, in new facts. Many a critic or poet was broken on the wheel. Many an able intellect, confronted with the job of classifying the paragraph endings in Cicero, left scholarship for the law or business where hard work could bring him at least a good income. The born investigators among us found themselves in a golden age where the dating of a miracle play might bring promotion to a youngster whose critical estimates of great prose or poetry were as unformed as an undergraduate's. The rest were driven and harried.

And so we all went in for literary history, except those favored few with a fortunate talent for linguistics, which was a true science and so yielded its secrets to the investigator. Human nature being what it is, we naturally sought for new literary history where no Taines or Saintsburys had been mightily exploring before us. It was Cynewulf, not Shakespeare, that we dug into, the romance of chivalry rather than Racine, and Goethe's borrowings from the Arabic instead of an interpretation of the second part of *Faust*. American literature, being regarded as both too modern and too easy for our purposes, we neglected entirely.

Some of this work was useful, much of it seems a little absurd now; but if anyone doubts the influence of this Alexandrianism let him read the list of thesis subjects in the humanities, even today, remembering how many tens of thousands of college youths have been taught their literature by men and women whose most active preparation was in a method of research (usually sound) expended upon a subject which was often not worth investigating. There went the laborious days. For we all knew that appointment and promotion in the humanities came as a result of research, and the shrewder were well aware that the best jobs (in English at least) came out of the eighth to the fifteenth centuries.

It was the cross-word-puzzle age of scholarship. The myriad intelligent minds among the populace who spend their hours over puzzles today are amateurs in a job which these scholars made professional. The cross-word puzzle is research reduced to an absurdity in which no end is proposed except the satisfaction of an occupied mind seeking a solution which answers nothing but the desire to find whatever was hid. Great scholars, as Chaucer reminds us, are not always the wisest men; indeed, they are much like other men in their impulses, and in those days it is certain that many of them were puzzle-minded. And many of their students came to believe that solving a puzzle was the essence of the study of literature. For research is the best of all puzzles because the most difficult. Nor is it surprising that when science, by fitting together the broken pieces of the earth's history, gave us a new history of man, the humanists should also get to work with their books and pencils, forgetting sometimes to estimate the value of what they sought in the pleasure of the seeking.

I knew a so-called fabulist in my days in the graduate school who for years had compared manuscript with manuscript of the fables of Aesop, tracing their indebtedness one to another by the use of 'wolf' for 'fox,' or a peculiarity in the ass that wore the lion's skin, until he had curves of dates and influences running clear across the European Middle Ages. It all meant nothing. The last fable was substantially the same as the first, for they were all copyist's work with not a touch of creativeness in the whole series. Indeed, he was careful to leave out the elaborate reworkings of the old stories in the so-called beast epic as corrupt versions adulterated by the egoism of a creative artist. It meant no more than counting the bricks in a hundred city blocks. Yet he was a happy man. His task extended onward indefinitely. He would never finish, and so need never draw conclusions. He had a puzzle so good that it got him a professorship. The case was extreme, yet illuminating.

And all this was going on in the midst of the ardent college life of the Gothic Age with its romantic materialism and its distrust of whatever made one stop and think. While we were busy with this puzzle-book scholarship, the need of the student for the gospel of sweetness and light went often by default. We graduate students were in truth kept so busy on Old French, phonetics, and methodology that it was left to our naïve minds to discover what literature itself really was, and how to teach it.

In moments of relaxation between research in the library and the teaching of a class of freshmen, I used to ask myself what was the study of literature. Even as a child I had been puzzled by conflicting ideas of knowledge. When I was an ardent collector of minerals, an old scientist told me, 'It isn't the beautiful crystal of quartz or of fluorite or of beryl that is important; it is the rare and ugly diaspore, the greasy pseudo-morph, the dull stone that points toward a new species.' Even to my boyish mind this seemed a hard doctrine. For it was not because the crystal was rare, but because it was beautiful that I wished to possess it. The hexagonal of quartz had attained a perfection in which the lumpish columbite had failed.

I remembered this when I began to think about the teaching and study of prose and poetry. Sufficient for some of our masters was the study of literary history which supplied them with problems enough and material for endless teaching. Milton's *Lycidas* attacked, worried, dissected, and put together again would keep them busy for a week.

Yet evidently this was only a preparation for the study of literature. One needed philosophy, since so much prose and
poetry was difficult to understand without experience in the
schools of philosophic thinking. There was psychology, which
got its best illustrations, outside the laboratory, in fiction.
There was religion, love, esthetics, all germane to literature.
There were the complex ramifications of social history that de-
termine the accent of a literary age. There was the continuity
of human experience, highly important, since the relation of a
book to this continuum seems to be the one criterion by which
we can test the greatness of a literary masterpiece. And unless
the teacher could integrate the literature of the past with the
living mind before him, the literature he taught stayed dead.

There was plenty for us to do, but no one — or only a Beers
here and there, and he inarticulately and by example — told
us how much. Rather, we were urged to specialize. Our teachers, having discovered by their own investigations how frequently their predecessors had been wrong in fact or date, were
determined that neither they nor we should overstep the line
of exact knowledge. Get the first thing first, which was the
facts. Let the rest wait — read in the summer — fill up the gaps
later — if you wish to be promoted contribute now to exact
knowledge, not of literature, which is too vague a term to mean
anything for a specialist, but of the facts about literature. And
since, unfortunately, and in sharp contrast to natural science,
the most important facts are known, wade in after the unimportant. To this, in our feeble hands, the study of literature
came down in the first decades of the twentieth century. No
wonder that we were ignorant and often contemptuous of the
writers of our own time. And since we youngsters of the period
were already beginning to take on the literary education of the
new generation of students, it is not surprising that, aiming to
make specialists like ourselves of our classes, we often failed to
persuade them to enjoy the most likeable books. Is this the
reason that the American college graduate of those days, especially the male graduate, unlike the educated class of any other
great nation, was not a reader of books, especially of books in
that field of belles-lettres which he most frequently elected to
study in his student days? He got the facts, and, like his instruc-

tors, let the culture wait for a better opportunity, which, as the sales of good books in the United States pathetically showed, had not yet come.

I do not forget the great teachers who broke through these conventions of scholarship, and the great scholars (fewer in number) who made use of their own researches to illumine the intricate nature of literature itself. And I am aware that the ideal of literary study I have described lies beyond the power of one man to achieve in a lifetime. He cannot accurately know all he should know, and if he guesses he is no longer scientific. But this is true even of mathematics. Push far enough and you are involved in the complex of life itself, in which yesterday's dinner or today's contact with an idea has implications involving the outermost star. Yet surely of all the professions the study of philosophy and the study of literature and the study of history most require a flexible, intuitive mind, aware that neither a lyric, nor a moral axiom, nor the fate of a nation can be disposed of finally without determining the business of the universe. And surely in such professions the willingness to link fact with fact, and where there are no facts to point the way of conjecture and interpretation, is infinitely important. In literature especially, which deals essentially with the concrete expression of emotion and thought, intuition, especially if it is based on a rich experience, should begin its work while the returns are still coming in from scientific research, and continue long after the last fact is run down. I fear that the specialist scholars of my time, who were not also great personalities, gave us too little of their own selves, of which indeed they often knew much less than of grammar or mythology. They left out the middle term of teaching — which is man the interpreter and the interpreted. Shelley seemed safest to them when studied as a by-product of the romantic movement, and Shakespeare's bawdry most examinable in terms of the laxities of the Renaissance. No reputable scientist (they thought) would exercise his intuitions upon the retreat of a glacier; nor would they upon a sonnet.

And so many a scholar in our college, which still relied upon the humanities for the core of education, became an intellectual spinster. Like spinsters, he had suppressed some of his vital functions, and narrowed the outlet for his energies. He was afraid of everything he had not investigated, and hence his work grew more and more remote from life. And like some spinsters he met with an incomprehension hard to bear. His students were also working tirelessly for ends that no philosopher would have approved. They specialized in athletics precisely as he specialized in the emendation of texts. But their objectives were easily comprehensible to the country at large and hence to themselves. Their rewards of college fame or social position were immediate, and popular opinion approved of them. The scholar's ideal was the perfect knowledge which precedes all wisdom. But unfortunately his achievement was to be seen only in books which represented fragments of imperfect knowledge, in whose ultimate use he himself seemed scarcely interested. Thus, the public could see in scholarship only something that was eccentric, futile, un-American, which could not be taken seriously by red-blooded men. The gulf between those who wished to know and those who wished to do was not bridged by such misapprehensions. Did the scholars wish to bridge it? Certainly in the product of the humanistic scholarship of those decades there was very little upon which a growing civilization could be nourished.

I apologize for this excursion into criticism. It is not irrelevant because it helps to explain what has so often puzzled me, the defeatism and timorousness of the college, which were so often accompanied by sporadic displays of magnificent courage and commanding personality. There was, I am sure, lurking in the professor's heart an uneasy sense that the research by which his colleagues judged him was not really important. He knew that his ordering of Shakespeare's sonnets or his analysis of the subjunctive in Anglo-Saxon was a permanent contribution, however slight, to the fund of human knowledge, more permanent, if less immediately useful, than a factory or a lawsuit. Yet he knew also that to the country, and to his students, his work seemed to be an eccentricity of a belated adolescent, who played twenty questions while life roared past outside his study window. Remembering Mary and Martha, he wondered whether his dutiful service in the kitchen of literature would be properly appreciated, even by the Deity. It was after such moments of painful introspection that he would close his books, and with a grim resolve to make himself felt in his generation, charge into his classroom, and grapple with the callow imagination of his pupils, until even their conventional minds were plowed up and planted here and there with distrust of their own smugness. Thus great teachers might be made.

The outcome was not usually so spectacular. Some men swung the broadaxe in the forest of obscurity, determined to make a clearing where light would shine. They were the Gummeres, Kittredges, Lounsburys, Furnesses, who gave our scholarship distinction. But the scholar of the Gothic Age was more often warped than exalted. He had lost the simple confidence of the monk in the efficacy of his beads and masses, without acquiring the hearty assurance of the layman. His eyes saw the steep and rocky road to truth, his ears heard public opinion whirring past on a cement highway. And he did queer things.

An able philologist spent his later years in literally hurling morsels of erudition at the outside world (which never read them), nodules so inconsiderable and yet so tough as to amaze the observers who knew his power over a wide range of scholarship. He had become a boy again, throwing stones at his indifferent enemies. A source of a source of a source of a great poem, he seemed to say, is more important than your turmoil of love, hate, and possessing. Another, who died frustrate in middle age, leaving behind him a tradition of subtle and penetrating lecturing upon literature, had his heart set upon poetry, not scholarship. In the critical academic atmosphere his slender talent withered. His lectures, shot through with melancholy, were the by-products of a defeated imagination. Still another scholar, finding that he had nothing in particular to say about what he studied, set himself to read by measure, his ambition, in which he succeeded, being to read through all extant Old French literature before he was sixty, making notes as he went on curiosities of grammar and vocabulary. He would announce with glee each month his current mileage.

But the most interesting instance by far of this college complex was Thomas Raynesford Lounsbury, whom I have mentioned before. Here was vigor of mind and vigor of personality such as it would have been hard to find more richly

blended elsewhere in America. He fought through four years
of the Civil War, emerging with an undying hatred for the intellectual deadness of the military life. He wrote in his youth
three or four novels which no one would publish, and closed
that chapter with hearty contempt for all incompetents who
dabbled in the making of literature. Then he set out on the
road to scholarship, and was brilliantly successful. He wrote a
definitive book on Chaucer, and having got a name, began, like
our own generation of youths whose minds were wounded in
the war, to satisfy his grudge against human stupidity. His
specialty was to expose the folly of scholars and critics of the
past. No pedantry of grammarians was too ancient for his
scorn. With wit and satire he stirred up the dust in the lumber rooms of scholarship, banging the heads of nonentities
against their own books. And while he had little feeling for
beauty and less for emotion, he so reverenced the fine mind
finely articulate that he made most of the greatest English literature his own by heart. I have heard him recite Dryden and
Chaucer by the hour without a book.

In earlier periods his fame would have been national. In
the English eighteenth century, as a classicist, he could not have
escaped high distinction. But the prestige of the classics had
waned, and no substitute like English literature could rival the
dominance of Latin and Greek over popular respect. Lounsbury was a great scholar, but except among his fellow scholars
and the more enlightened among the public, he was just a professor of English.

Does this explain the fury with which he fell upon the
dumber undergraduates? The lightnings of his wrath which
played about his books burnt out in a vacuum. The stupid
world was unaware of them. Only his rivals in scholarship, a
tiny band, were scorched. But the students, reveling in their
childish college life, this brood of illiteracy, these ignorant sons
of ignoramuses to whom Chaucer was scarcely a name and the
bright coruscations of liberated minds no more than meaningless words — their dull minds were there in the flesh before
him! If incapable of knowing what literature was about, they
could be made to translate what literature said into their weak
vernacular, describe Athene if they could never understand in-

tellectual love, give the meaning of a reference to the Augean
stables if they were incompetent to absorb the line that carried
it. With what ironic unction, glaring the while at us, he used
to pronounce the verses of Dryden —

> . . . *That unfeathered two-legged thing, a son,*
> *Got, while his soul did huddled notions try,*
> *And born a shapeless lump, like anarchy.*

This was pure thwarting, and warping, of a first-rate mind.
It was a scholar's ineffective revenge upon the anti-intellectu-
alism of college life in which he, and all he stood for, were
meaningless. But in discipline, at least, he got results. We
students used to marvel that a white beard could wag so re-
joicingly over slaughter.

I may seem to forget the college as a whole in writing of that
hybrid out of literature by science called literary scholarship,
which was one of its by-products. But the college as a whole
was deeply involved. We students and teachers of the modern
languages and literature had succeeded to the place in college
education which had been held for centuries by the classicists.
But we lacked the classicists' confidence and the classicists'
power. They had believed that a real knowledge of the great
literatures of Greece and Rome would make an educated man,
and, in spite of their overweening, had often been proved right,
until the spell of the Renaissance, which for three centuries
had made the Western world believe in the magical benefits
to be derived from even the grammar of Latin, was broken. We
scholars of a later age, substituting the grammar of Chaucer
and Milton, the facts of literary history, had changed the dosage
without renewing that vital insight into a culture which had
made Renaissance teaching and scholarship great. It was a new
culture we faced, a new Renaissance in which our most passive
student was soon to be flung amidst the complex forces of industrialism. And these forces we did not attempt to relate with
the literature which it was our business to teach, because our
training in specialized scholarship had made us incapable of
anything but skillful antiquarianism. We were afraid of the
complex emotionalism of literature, which inevitably relates
itself to every new manifestation of human nature or dies be-

cause it has no vital relation. We were afraid without knowing
that we were afraid, precisely as the clergymen of our day were
afraid without realizing it of religion as such, with its passionate and radical emotionalism. And so we fell back upon dates
and sources, or as teachers painfully broke through into a half-
knowledge of our desperate problem. One has only to compare
the contributions of the scientists in that age with the contributions of literary scholarship to know that something was
wrong.

I honor most in my memory, therefore, the great teachers,
the personalities who expressed the tension in their minds in
their classrooms if not in their books, making the students of
the old college uneasily aware of perceptions which science
could not give them, and emotions richer than their own college life. Fortunately in those little academic communities, still
walled in by privilege and prejudice from the industrialism
outside, all lived close together, and were curious each to know
more of the other's thoughts. They passed daily on the campus:
the candid and simple crew captain; the foxy-eyed boy in pursuit of social prestige; the manager of a team already aware of
how pockets were lined; Gibbs meditating theories that were
to transform science; Beers shuffling home with Emerson in his
heart; deans thinking of new buildings; and the research
scholar, annoyed because he must shortly explain Shakespeare
to the pink-faced freshman who tipped his hat and hurried on
to the gymnasium.

Monasteries at the end of the Age of Faith must also have
had their complexes. Many a young lay brother must have
been stirred to wonder, contempt, or a puzzled admiration at
the sight of Anselm at work upon his hundredth copy of a
Book of Hours. Some such collision between a new era and a
new barbarian with the peaceful world of literary scholarship
was responsible for the strains and stresses, the eccentricities,
and the futile attempts to exalt the letter at the expense of the
spirit, which were so characteristic of scholarship in our college. The erudition was genuine. It was essential, but it was
often stunted — too often inapplicable, incomplete, and as aimless as the passion of men who enrich themselves while they
forget the art of living for which riches are made.

8

The Alumni

A DESCRIPTION OF THE AMERICAN COLLEGE as I knew it without mention of the alumni would be like a picture of the Golden Throne which left out the heavenly hosts. Those paintings by Tintoretto of the celestial hierarchy, surrounded by circle upon circle of the innumerable elect out to the shining margin of space and time, might be regarded as mystic symbols of the collegiate world. The alumni were the saved and the blest, still testifying to the vigor and the virtue of the college; they were like the saints and martyrs of the hierarchies, translated but still powerful. To them it owed a part, and usually the most sumptuous part, of the visible body of buildings; from them came great draughts of financial nourishment; and their opinions, their prejudices, their ideals, and their romanticism were strong and sometimes determining factors in the academic atmosphere. An American college without its alumni is as hard to imagine as a man without an environment. They were its environment; a conditioning principle always at work.

Although it was not my idea originally, and I forget from whom I borrowed it, yet I give my heartiest endorsement to the theory that the alumni and alumnae bond is one of the most important in the social history of the United States. Our society from the beginning has been heterogeneous and disruptive. The class consciousness (I use the term in an old-style sense), which kept England stable, weakened here as soon as formed. Rank and its prestige, which stiffened society in monarchial Europe, has never been more than a shadow of a shadow in America. Nor have we at any time in our history formed those almost unbreakable bonds of membership in religious societies which lie so close beneath the surface of an otherwise

233

familiar Europe. Not even Catholicism has made a caste in the United States. In radicalism, too, we have been individualists, cold except for brief moments to revolutionary fraternities. But the inevitable impulse for the like-minded to foregather has operated here as elsewhere. We have the many fraternal organizations, such as the Shriners or the Odd Fellows, who obviously have borrowed many of their customs from the college class and the college fraternity. But far surpassing these welfare associations in cohesiveness, and in a powerful though more diffused influence upon American mores, is the strong bond of graduation from an American college. Of this the college fraternity is only a concentration. It was the shaping of minds and coloring of emotions that made the alumni a conscious class union, although economic status undoubtedly determined the personnel. I write particularly of the men now in their fifties and sixties who went to college when going to college was still a privilege, who went to college, not in the amorphous droves of the state university, but in selected groups attending the typical institution, half private, half public, half slave to convention, half free to be eccentric and individual, which I have described in previous pages.

I speak of alumni rather than alumnae, but not invidiously. The sorority of women graduates grows in extent as it becomes increasingly conventional for women to go to college, yet it is probably too late for them to feel a class apart. The universities which they now attend in such numbers are too large for the intimate class life of the old college. In the Gothic Age the alumnae were a tiny minority of the population. And they were differently worked upon by the college. Some of them went to college as professionally as we men to graduate or law school, and so never knew the conflict with college life, while the others had a home and husband in view, and so probably never gave themselves as wholeheartedly as their brothers to the life of the college. Here I may be wrong, but certainly women in college in my day were less adolescent, much less romantic, than the men. They were on a bypath away from the women's world, and were aware of it. The men were hotfooting down a main road that everyone knew about and approved. College life left the girls in need of adjustment, but

tumbled the boys into a waiting society for which their training exactly fitted them.

Graduating from college in the nineties and early nineteen-
hundreds was more painful than triumphant. The youth
stepped out into the world trailing clouds of memory behind
him. He took on a new identity as clerk, law student, or office
assistant, yet held desperately to his affiliation with a caste of
men whose memories were like his own. He might work as he
was told to work, but he thought, felt, and as far as possible
lived, as he had learned to do in college. A difference in the
way he handled experience, as observable as his different clothes
and different vocabulary, separated him from his old friends in
the home town who had not gone to college. He grew more
like them, but never just like them. There was always in his
mind a reference back to the college, even after many years.

Speaking for myself, I remember that I was arrogant without
reason and absurd without necessity when I first became an
alumnus. Now that the collegiate has become vulgar, it is hard
to realize how seriously the earlier graduates of the college life
undertook their obligations to be unmistakably college men.
(No one but the police called them college 'boys' then.) They
kept the badinage of college talk, the carelessness of college
dress fastidiously applied to rigorously selected garments, most
of all the comradeship among their equals in experience. And
this comradeship rapidly extended beyond the coterie lines of
college days, broadening into friendships which might include
anyone who had walked the campus in the golden days now
becoming historical.

Thus, as men and Americans the alumni might be dull,
bright, agreeable, cantankerous, radical, conservative, failures,
or successes, differing as widely as human nature permits within
the vague limits of an economic class. But as alumni, while
these differences persisted, there was a thin garment of resemblance which covered their personal peculiaries like an academic gown. The alumni retained that quick response to an
appeal for loyalty which they had learned in college. There
they had acquired faith in an institution, an intangible entity
which could not be wrong, however much its personnel might
wrong them. They kept an instinctive belief in the value of

co-operation within a group which was to be of inestimable advantage to the corporations and foundations of the next twenty years when industrial and philanthropic enterprise grew beyond the power of control by individuals. And much more important than these advantages, which other groups possessed also, they shared a common memory of a vivid and homogeneous experience intelligible to all of them, which, in the restless haphazard life of an America constantly on the move, gave a point of rest and departure. Subtly combined with this was an expectation of success acquired in an institution made up from the select. And outweighing all of these useful assets of the alumni was one result of college life which only psychologists have appreciated. For with rare exceptions the alumni had been happy in their colleges. Whatever their later disillusions, for the best part of four years they had been content and had, at the very least, learned to believe in the possibility of happiness. Other men, naturally, had been happy in youth, but I can think of no other institution which so successfully generated happiness over a long period and at a time when every youthful faculty was sensitive to impressions. With all its faults and virtues operating together, the college was bound to make a type of the alumnus, and did.

If this seems an exaggeration, contrast the American with the English college. There was the same high level of happiness in England, and a far better education for the intellect. Co-operation, and powerful co-operation, among men of like experience was also a product of those older colleges. But that loyalty which for good and ill became a convention with the American alumnus, in England never got beyond a respect for *alma mater*. The great generosity of the American for his college, and his deep affection, have no adequate parallels in England, where there was loyalty to ideals, but little sense of responsibility for the welfare of the college whence those ideals came.

When as alumni we began to come back to *alma mater* for our reunions and talk there of what the college had meant to us and was going to mean to our children, it was not hard to see what we wanted. There was a growing realization of the importance of the curriculum. We were old enough now to appreciate the framework of knowledge which the college had given us, and to know that, sketchy as it was, it had been valuable. But what we remembered best, and solicited its continuance for our own young, was the romance that had suffused our fierce competitions and strenuous enjoyments. We had been the last wave of the romantic movement, and with us it had interpenetrated middle-class materialism. Our loyalty was not to a system of teaching or a curriculum, but to a way of life. And it was characteristic of those college generations that the older they grew, the more romantic they became about their college years. Our memory was of a sacred community whose songs had not been as other songs, whose teams had been (and must continue to be) better than other teams, whose 'profs' were more eccentric than other 'profs,' whose college spirit was superior to the spirit of other colleges, and far superior to anything outside of college. The alumnus may have lived in a shabby frame house under a dripping elm tree, but his college life in memory was nevertheless touched with gold.

The first result of his romanticism was impressive and naïve. In those Eastern endowed institutions which set the fashions for college life, it was the loyal alumni who wiped out deficits and supplied the funds for new enterprises beyond the means of the college budget. They supported the university, but what they loved was the little old college within it, which had been in a true sense their fostering mother. While great endowments began to reconstruct the university teaching of medicine and law, in the college the golden shower was changed to stone and mortar. Slowly at first, but with increasing momentum through the boom years, the bare and nondescript college of my youth began to transform itself into a romantic alumnus's dream of a proper setting for college life. His imagination unfortunately was not strong. If he had seen his college as the hundred-per-cent American institution it certainly was, he would have ordered his architects to adapt to academic purposes the beautiful simplicity and clarity of the steel, glass, and concrete construction outside of the college campus. We should have had a new architecture. But his imagination was antiquarian, and somewhat sentimental. Having fought the curriculum for four years in college, he began belatedly to recognize the value of tradition, perhaps because he came to realize that it was his sense of historical continuity acquired in college that set him apart from ordinary uneducated men. And so, moved by instinct rather than reason, he chose the florid Tudor Gothic style, which I have already mentioned as characteristic of our *fin de siècle,* and remade the college according to his own fancy. It was a style as expensive as his own life was becoming, and in its blend of tradition, imitativeness, sham, and eccentricity, and its uncertain relationship to the America which it has spotted with ramparts, cathedral towers (sometimes very beautiful), gargoyles, machicolations, and light-resistant windows, is so characteristic of the college, which welcomed it rapturously, that I have used the word 'Gothic' to designate this age of American education.

The alumnus was romantic in other ways. He tried to keep his past intact. It is doubtful whether, as a student, he had ever understood just what his official educators were trying to do for him, unless he had been enrolled in engineering or other applied sciences, in which case he had been regarded as an inferior breed. But he had been vividly aware of the unity of his life, a unity which he now assigned, not to the vital relations between college life and the main currents of energy in America, but rather to other influences that as an undergraduate he had rather sniffed at. And so returning to the campus after ten or twenty years, he realized that his social and athletic strenuosities had in some subtle way been given tone by studies he had been forced to make in subjects which had nothing to do with activities of the campus or the business career that came afterward. And he felt that what otherwise might have been only four years of sports and rivalries had been dignified by such disciplines as history, literature, mathematics even, which made his adolescent experiences a part of the historical experience of memorable men as far back as the Greeks, and gave margins to life that made him different from uneducated barbarians.

Hence the alumnus became an educational conservative, how powerful an influence presidents and trustees know, if professors do not. He might insist that 'practical' courses in his own technical field (if he had one) should be introduced into his old college, because, thanks to his loyalty, he hoped to recruit his industry from recent graduates of his own *alma mater*. Yet talk to him at reunions or other visitings of the academic shades, and you would find him arguing for the old 'culture' that made gentlemen, by which he usually meant the Greek he had flunked in freshman year, or the literature he had escaped from with a C; for the old professors who left such indelible memories of unworldly personality behind them, and even for an extension of the old subjects to the exclusion of new scientific nonsense: Latin, Greek, classic history, and courses (here he searched his memory) on Shakespeare, Napoleon, Dante, Beowulf, George Washington, or the Augustan Age, which gave a man something about which he could talk. Such new subjects as government, economics, psychology, which have more than anything else brought the college of today into touch with the problems as well as the financial opportunities of modern life, did not interest him. What he wanted, what aroused his enthusiasm when he found it still existed, was (quite rightly) whatever strengthened character as he had seen it strengthened he knew not exactly how or why; and next an education that gilded the profit-making system and made it fit for gentlemen.

Nevertheless, the American alumnus is one of the really engaging figures of social history. In his function of elder brother to the college he has not always been admirable, but likeable he has always been. I saw in my own experience his romantic enthusiasm for 'our team' become a country-wide passion which came near to making athletics the chief purpose of so-called higher education. Like children wanting one more exciting story before bedtime, the alumni demanded victories until intercollegiate play was expanded into a professional entertainment which has slaughtered more than one educational ideal to make a November holiday. It was this crude confusion of the methods of business with the aims of education that drove many a college president to justify professional sports by their advertising value. Yet it was these same alumni who poured in not only their millions, but their little tens and fives, to make their college into a university, and their university into something which they themselves often neither liked nor understood.

Now loyalty is a quality which doubtless has done as much harm as good, and which certainly is the most easily misled of all the virtues. Yet, like strength of body or of mind, it must always command respect, no matter whence it flows, or what it furthers. The alumni, though they spoke of *alma mater,* acted like the loyal parents of a puzzling child. Criticism of the old college, often violent and sometimes virulent, was the staple of alumni conversation. But there was always an underlying assumption that we were attacking men and measures, not the college as it had been and might be. Realistic criticism which disputed the value of the institution itself or of the kind of education which could be got there, left us cold or angry. Unless one believed, as we believed, in college life, reform could mean only destruction.

Other loyalties, to church, to moral codes, to country, and even to family life, were being sadly shaken in the years when the alumni became so numerous as to constitute a class. Hence this one devotion which kept its intensity and its romance was of considerable social importance. If it made dreamers and sentimentalists, and sometimes foes to progress, of some college graduates, it also steadied them all and unquestionably sweetened their lives. In the rather drab small town and sordid city of the early twentieth century, this enduring college relationship was an alleviation not to be despised.

Yet this affection for *alma mater* led to one of the ironies of educational history. The rivers of money which poured in for every college purpose in the golden Gothic Age, did not always or even often come from farsighted patrons of education, but were the gifts, incredibly numerous, and sometimes incredibly large, of college graduates who loved their college, or of outsiders impressed by the glamour of college life. This stream had a sacrificial quality. Some of it, of course, went into Bowls and Stadiums, where the alumni with numerous companions who had never smelled a sheepskin revived their youth by yelling themselves into a bronchitis. These vast structures, now that, in the older universities, the undergraduates' interest in professionalized athletics diminishes, begin here and there to lift their half-empty bulks like the ruined amphitheaters of the Roman Empire. And still more flowed into memorial buildings of collegiate Gothic. But a large sum was given direct to the beloved college, for its own purposes, whatever they might be. It was thus that a Syracusan king gave vases of gold and statues of cunning bronze to the shrine at Delphi for the memorializing of a god.

Here loyalty had a strange reward. This money, uncritically and lovingly given in memory of college life, has destroyed college life as we knew it, even in the new housing plans devised to keep some of the old intimacies. It has made the college into a university, the university into a factory of research. Romance has fled and irresponsibility grows unfashionable. It has substituted for the old-fashioned professor, who touched our imaginations rather than our minds, a new professor, realist, member of a brain trust, efficient, aware that university education now must really educate, and who makes it do so at the expense of many pleasant amenities. And for the campus, a community with its own customs and its own happiness, it has substituted a congeries of schools, where even the undergraduates are in increasing numbers hard-working, hard-thinking, and able and willing to relate their studies to the actualities of American life. Such rigorous education does not come until it is needed. It may be said that in the Age of Confidence we did not indispensably need it. But now that it is needed, it is the alumni of the old college who have paid the bill. As this college was a preparatory school for the competitions of the early nineteen-hundreds, so the new university is a laboratory in which the problems of the later decades of the twentieth century are being studied by experts. Those who contributed to the rebuilding of the ancient nest find an office building waiting for them when they return. Not even the Tudor-Gothic trimmings, concessions to their romanticism, can hide that fact. The old college has gone — for better or worse. I personally should say for both.

It is probable that many of the traits which have made the twentieth-century American in business and the professions a strongly marked national type, recognizable as such throughout the world, are really traits of the alumni of the old American colleges. We Americans should have become in these decades more, not less, European, for since the Civil War a vast im-

migration has flooded in everywhere except the South, modify-
ing the physical type, especially in the city. And yet the typical
reactions of the country in morals, politics, religion, and economics have remained characteristically un-European, and better explained by the American past than by an Italian-Ameri-
can or German-American present. This stabilizing of character and temperament, and also of prejudice, is probably due to
the college graduate, for our alumni strengthened their bonds
and gained in class consciousness just when the so-called old
American was losing his grip.

This broadcasting of college traits by the unorganized but
powerful influence of the alumni, may explain some characteristics of our recent history which have puzzled Europeans. A
good example is the curious tenacity with which Americans
have held on to democratic ideals in a country where business
has been autocratic. It was in college that our alumni learned
to respect democracy while keeping it within strict limits.
There the underdog was welcomed when he fought his way up,
which, if not pure democracy, is certainly on its doorstep. A
college reunion beautifully illustrates this faith in democracy
when, and if, it works. After twenty or thirty years, privilege,
prestige, and progress have all had their chance to make or
remake the fortunes of a college class. Socially these returning
men have stratified, economically their fate is usually determined. Here are the results of the big game of half a lifetime
posted for anyone to see. Nobodies have become somebodies,
somebodies have remained just somebodies, and by a rough
justice everyone seems to have got just about what was coming
to him — what his personality and his character deserved quite
as much as what his privileges or lack of them made probable.
The initial handicap of economic inferiority had been too
much for some to overcome; early and easy success had been as
great a handicap for others. Some of the 'big men' of college
days were still outstanding, but not all; some of the unknown,
the freaks and the grinds, had come through, but some only.
There was quite enough evidence of success for the deserving to
justify the belief of the graduate that his brand of democracy
had worked, and that there should be a road to opportunity,
kept open if rocky, at least for collegiate America.

And still other traits of contemporary America may be traced back to the college. The outstanding characteristic of American policy in the last decades has been its violent inconsistency. Look at it. An extraordinary organization for the war in 1917-18; and a complete disorganization in the handling of the peace. An incomparably efficient organization of industry in the boom decade; and an almost complete anarchy of business and financial control of that boom, ending in an unparalleled smash. A magnificent extension of philanthropy and science applied to humanitarian ends, extending beyond our boundaries around the world; and a long delay in organizing a radical reform of our own social ills, although every corrupt municipal government and depressed community had been flying flags of distress. The most elaborate school system in the world; and the highest percentage of crime. Wealth so great that it had to be given away; and inexplicable poverty, less desperate but even more destructive, than the poverty of Europe.

For all this there were many causes, but one at least was the education of our alumni, the dominant college class. They had learned to compete, but not to analyze; they had learned to co-operate, but not to seek long-term ends; they had been given faith in their own membership, but, in spite of the Sumners, no real conception of society as a whole. They had been powerfully educated to make themselves successful in an aggressive, unscrupulous, competitive community, and less powerfully to gild their success with some approach toward fine living. But of the strong laws of cause and effect (except in applied science and trading), and of the great debate as to what makes a civilization, how it can be attained, and conserved, they had little knowledge, for their thoughts never turned that way. In all these respects the education of the graduates of the twenties and the thirties has been far better than in my college day; but unfortunately the problems have become far more difficult.

It is the college alumni that by character, tenacity, loyalty, and will, have held together a centrifugal America, and will hold it together certainly for a little while yet. The virtues of the old college were sound, yet not enough to raise greater expectations than this of its graduates. The small-town campus as we knew it, with its narrow class consciousness and its easy terms for success, was not an environment which could make the alumnus add hard thinking to his equipment of instinctive reactions. Longfellow's old ship of state that we used to urge to 'sail on' from schoolboy platforms begins to yaw and jibe. It is time to quit squabbling over party politics and set a course. And this requires navigation, a subject which in its broader implications we were never taught in college. And would have passed off with a night's cramming if it had been assigned to us.

ᔆ 9 ᔆ
A State Within a State

THE CAMPUS COMMUNITY I have been trying to recall has now drifted back in time beyond the complexities of the post-war age. It is clear, now, as I have said before, that it was a state within the state. In every culture there has been a state within the state, and a struggle, covert or open, between those who wish to learn before living and those who will not be deterred from the immediacy of life. Plato and the Venerable Bede and Erasmus were partisans in such a conflict, and the ambidextrous Napoleon tried to take both sides at once. The test of a good life is neither content while living it, since content may be either gross or stolid, nor success which results from it, since success is precarious and so differently measured. A more satisfactory criterion is the vividness of the experience, particularly when the memory persists afterward, and is pleasurable through good times and bad. That vividness the conflict of ideas within the college certainly gave, and students and faculty, each in their own way, shared its intensity.

A dozen different and better ways than ours might have been devised for educating the dominant class of twentieth-century America, but would any of them have worked better? I doubt it. We students were the irresistible upwash of a century of material progress; we were the seventh wave and strongest flowing from the turbulent exploiting of a continent morally exhausted by the Civil War. If we had found a society of perfect scholars, or radical realists, or inflexible conservers of tradition in the college, we, with the alumni behind us, would have washed them out. Our faculties were creatures of the age that made us. They fought us, often with a vigor as intense if less romantic than our own strenuosity; yet they were as inconsistent in their secret respect for our energy of materialism as we

245

were naïve in our faith that such perfect confidence as ours must conquer all difficulties.

But indeed, if I shift my point of view from student to professor, it begins to seem a little romantic to have been teaching the undergraduate at a time when the college life was so powerfully conditioning the next generation of characteristic Americans. By and large, even if our doctrine was uncertain, we kept the faith. Our embattled teaching was quite as American in tradition and spirit as the get-rich-quick ideas of our students. We kept hammering away in spite of discouragement and frustration at what we variously thought was education — Latin subjunctives, the binomial theorem, Plato's Republic, the second law of thermodynamics, Tennyson's morality, the sheer beauty of Keats, the meaning of God in an industrial civilization, the difference between meaning and a word.

And this all happened in a tight little community — in self-contained little communities scattered all over the country and each a self-conscious society within the larger framework of the nation. Yet we were unlike the equivalent academies of Greece or the universities of the Middle Ages, in that they were a terminal where men met to settle if possible the meaning of their lives, whereas our society was strictly preparatory. For the college was not then a center of thought like the new universities of this century, but primarily a nursery and testing ground for youth, where much that was said and most that was done looked forward not to *the* future, but to *a* future for the boy who then and there was preparing for active life. This accounts for the narrowness of our education, but made it bite deep into the emotions, quite as deep as the grip upon character and behavior of the intellectually still more limited English public schools.

There was a class of the redoubtable William Graham Sumner's which I attended every Monday morning. The old man sat, as always, slouched on a chair upon the dais. I do not remember that he ever spoke standing. He had no oratory; his eyes were always fixed on some vacancy over our heads as he lectured in a gruff voice that did not rise or fall, and which depended upon the pith and substance of what was said for its holding power.

It was the first lecture after a spring week-end. A roar of talk went round the seats, subduing as the clock struck the hour into the rustle of a hundred newspapers. As he began, looking more than ever like Cato on a monument, his voice was scarcely audible, but his first words beat down the confusion of sound. 'When I wish to speak through newspapers, I do it by correspondence,' he said grimly, pausing until the sarcasm went home. The front rows snickered, but since no further witticism followed, began to whisper again. 'I was to lecture to you young gentlemen,' he continued, 'on the danger of taxing the strong for the benefit of the weak.' He paused. I believe that the smug innocence of our sunburnt week-end faces roused some pity in his realist mind, and certainly it must have been the careless inattention of those polite but indifferent youngsters, holding their newspapers half-masted while they rested perfunctory pencils on their open notebooks, that made him personal for once. 'You pay no taxes. You are as yet neither weak nor strong, for you are dependents. Your first test will be earning a living, your next, marriage. You think you will succeed in both. I can tell you that statistically considered not four in ten of your marriages will be truly successful. They will fail (I hope my memory quotes him accurately) because you are too ignorant of the real values of living to make them succeed. Gentlemen, you will not find that statement in the newspapers you are reading.' They dropped them hastily, yet the next morning the statement *was* in the newspapers — characteristically shifted into sensationalism: 'Sumner says marriage in America a failure.'

That incident seems to sum up my conception of our college. The confident, healthy indifference of the student body, so self-absorbed in their hour, so easy to capture for an idea, so sure to escape from its implications. And also the defeatism of a first-rate mind in the face of this impregnable youth, which could be shown again and again the way and the truth, but did not want that way or any truth, but only to live. Youth impervious to the winds of doctrine, yet happily at least made aware that there are winds and that they may blow.

Thus and thus in the consulship of Plancus (as Beers called

an earlier and perhaps more truly golden age) did we live and have our being, and fail or succeed, not often knowing why. It must have been a rich experience, since in reading biographies I find records of like intensity only in the stories of the pioneers. That for student, teacher, scholar it was a deeply conditioning experience, perhaps needs no more argument. Although we who shared it were diverse in origin like the first immigrants to our shores, yet all were conscious of certain standards, all had a memory of happiness, or at least of energies fully exerted, all had a belief in that intangible entity, the college spirit, which I have tried to define in these chapters. And if turning in retrospect from some misty and I fear highly disagreeable decade of the latter twentieth century, the social historian of that day seeks to know what the nineties, the nineteen-hundreds, the nineteen-tens were like in his America, he should not forget the college town, the dormitories elm-shaded, the campus where two philosophies of living saluted in passing and sometimes stopped for a chat. As a contribution to a history which will some day be written, I, as an alumnus of *alma mater,* have here set down my own memories, which are critical, speculative, but most of all affectionate.

PART THREE
Brief Golden Age

I

The Ivory Tower Begins to Crack

I LOOK BACK WITH NOSTALGIA to the early years of the twentieth century which I have described in Part Two of this book. Yale then for me was a true *alma mater,* and I was haunted by the genius of the place. To walk home under the dim elms against the evening star after a day of absorbing work was a fervor of delight never to be equaled again in pursuits less pure in motive and design. We young scholars never forgot that we were the successors of the great monastic orders whose duty was the preservation of learning and the spread of good doctrine. Fortunately for us, outside the college cloisters were no Dark Ages to be spiritually enlightened, but an American community boiling with efficient energy and hot for material achievement. There was a failure, however, in co-ordination between us and the country.

Ours was the day of triumph for the research scientists who in their successful pursuit of absolute verity had become indifferent to the use which might be made of it by an industrialized society interested only in practical applications. They were less farsighted than Leonardo da Vinci, who complained that the Renaissance princes encouraged his investigations only because they hoped to use his discoveries in their next wars. The humanists, with whom I belonged, were not so arrogant, but they were equally naïve. We who taught English felt that Tennyson's *Idylls of the King* was the best polish for the freshman mind. It was easy to persuade yourself that the characteristic idealism of Arthur's court was a good antiseptic against American materialism. We brushed it in like toothpaste. But when it came back in examination papers, all that romantic gentility had evaporated, leaving only platitudes and a dogmatic sexual morality that seemed beside the point. Our boys

251

were the sons of Americans on their way up, whose ideal was freedom to succeed, a newer and more timely creed than Tennyson's. We professors of the humanities thought of it as a crude American instinct for money-making which we were delegated to reform or refine by examples of what we supposed to be a superior civilization. We asked them to be Victorian gentlemen instead of teaching the transferable values inherent in any good literature.

The World War which broke out in 1914 wrecked the ivory tower into which many of us retired (I include myself) whenever our sense of superiority failed to register with our students. The first reaction of many was impotence. I remember the day of Woodrow Wilson's message to Congress calling the country to war. Three of us — a philosopher, a poet, and myself — rushed down to Washington and offered our services for everything but fighting, for which we were not qualified, to everyone we knew. We stood in the corridors of the Capitol while war was being declared, and came home somewhat humiliated, having learned that no one seemed to need us. There was an uncomfortable feeling shared by all that our flare of patriotism had come late, and was just a little silly. We had got along in the university very well without too much concern for the country as such, and now the United States could get along very well without us.

My opportunity came less than a year later, and was the result of work done as assistant to Professor Wilbur L. Cross, later to be three times Governor of Connecticut, in the founding of a new kind of review. The old heavy cavalry of the magazine world, such as *The North American Review* and *The Forum*, were foundered. They read like the English quarterlies of half a century earlier. No university, although in a university the authority of erudition was supposed to have its source, had thought of sponsoring anything as extracurricular as a general magazine. Cross, in founding *The Yale Review* in 1911, had the sound idea of throwing the weight and prestige of scholarship behind a quarterly which would be open to contributions from serious thinkers anywhere, and be also a home for poetry and belles-lettres generally, at a time when journalism was driving literature from both newspapers and periodicals. *The Yale Review* was soon successful, especially in its poetry and criticism, although we had first to battle with the pomposity of many an old-line professor and the inarticulateness of the specialist. My first peeps through the ivory wall, my first professional contacts with contemporary American literature, of which we scholars in English then knew little, were as assistant editor of this magazine. I began to think that live authors could be as interesting as dead ones.

Now it happened that in the first years of the war, particularly before we were drawn in, there was a flow of British writers to our shores, like missionaries to unexploited South Sea islands. The English believed, and rightly, that the prestige of their literature when seen and heard in person would be good propaganda for their cause among our reading classes who then read more British than American books. So they sent popular novelists, philosophers, renowned poets, distinguished historians, and also good journalists who had written books on the more glamorous aspects of life in the trenches. If I remember rightly, it was then that Galsworthy first bent his distinguished head over our lecture desks, and H. G. Wells, who had published the soul-searching *Mr. Britling Sees It Through,* talked with a candor that embarrassed his hosts. We on *The Yale Review* welcomed all that came our way, told them what we thought the country was thinking, and got them to write for us. It was a warming experience, for they were desirous of pleasing and we were flattered to be sought out by the great and the near-great. And with the marvelous political instinct of the British people, they refrained from crude propaganda. The theme was not why we should enter the war, but why they had been forced into a world conflict.

The war, it would seem from all this, had, in New Haven, merely made life more interesting and more exciting. This would be violently untrue for most of my associates, no matter how contentedly they seemed to follow their old routines. For myself — and I am sure this is a true picture of the impact of the war on the American intellectual of those days — for myself, from the moment when on a Connecticut hilltop I watched a red moon rise, with the news that England had declared war on Germany fresh in my ears, my inner self was shocked to depths of which I had been hardly aware. The knowledge that violence, cruelty, and sudden death were once again immediate realities seemed to upset every formula by which I had lived. The snake of evil had come back into our industrious garden followed by rattlers, cobras, and vipers. Henceforth there would be no more confident steps. Twenty-five years later, when the new war broke, we had accepted violence, danger, and the cruel in our imaginations, though we still hated them. It was not suffering and death that upset us then (I think I speak for many of my generation) so much as the moral horror of an enemy that used the principles of anti-Christ as a policy, doing in cold blood what barbarians had done in hot, and far more efficiently. In 1914 we felt the war to be a lapse, a deplorable accident. We were naïve, but not too naïve for the realization that Europe, which had been a playground for most of us, had changed overnight. I myself felt an overpowering need to see at first hand what this new world was like, a need as strong as the passionate desire I felt to be of some use in the greatest conflict of my experience.

As a result of my contacts with visiting writers and some personal knowledge of England and more of its history, my chance came. In a kind of reverse lend-lease of intellects, I was invited by the British Ministry of Information to come abroad and do what I could in my small way to promote mutual understanding among the associated nations. Many other writers, editors, and professors were or had been invited for the same purpose. But my relative obscurity gave me a great advantage. I was offered every opportunity, but no guest expenses. I went on my own, using my salary on a leave of absence to which I was entitled, and a correspondent's status with contracts to write articles, as a means of living for myself and my family at home. Hence I was not dependent upon official tours and could make my own program and risk the results. I could speak my mind when I wished — when I knew it.

It was January of 1918, the low point, though I did not know it, for our side of the battle. Three weeks of a winter ocean on a convoy submarine-haunted brought me to a grim and exhausted London, where I felt like a pet dog lost in a traffic jam. Bombed the first night, I slowly adjusted myself to the new realities, and after a couple of months found my mission expanding into a liaison job in Ireland as well as England, and on all the western fronts, where I first experienced sharp danger to life. This, except in its results for my personality, is irrelevant to these literary memoirs. What I learned was published in 1919, in a book called *Education by Violence,* which those interested in how that war impressed some of my generation can read, if they can find it. It was a chilling plunge into currents of raging experience for one who had known more of King Arthur's wars than the clash of force and opinion behind a modern battle. Violence educated me, but the final results (and this was true of the U.S.A. also) were not by any means what I expected.

The excitement of (more or less) high affairs in that year remains only as a memory; the missions, the speeches, the earnest conversations, the storing of information for the use of authorities at home — all that has the uncertain importance of every effort whose results, if any, are lost in the confusions and reversals of history. What I wish to record is the effect on me, in this respect typical of thousands of Americans who for the first time left their homes to work with men and women born and bred under different skies and in a different tradition, and at a time of crisis. There is no substitute for such contacts if you wish to get reality into an international experience.

One of my self-appointed assignments was to visit the writers whose books I had read with admiration and who would speak to me about the war, so I thought, in terms I could readily comprehend. They did, but what I remember best is the impress of their personalities, pitched high, like mine, by the tensity of the times. I went down into Dorset to call on Thomas Hardy, an old, spare man, dim-eyed, watched over fussily by his young second wife. The war, he said, was too big for his poetic imagination. He could not put it into the scope of a tragedy, as he had done with the Napoleonic Wars. I made a round of visits to poets and novelists in the June countryside, mixing talk of literature and the war, sleeping once in a bed that had been Shelley's, and walking or bicycling through the lanes when I could not get a train. This English country had a permanence of quiet beauty which was familiar because I had always known it through the imagination. War and its visible effects seemed there to be only an interlude, and I was guided by books written by those who knew how to love it. Had we in America even begun on such a literature? Thoreau to me was then only a name, and our lesser native writers were obviously on the sentimental side of appreciation. But in spite of the English spell under which most of my academic generation had lived, I guessed that the end-results of slow centuries would not repeat themselves elsewhere. Our fields and forests would engender a different poetry. Years later I was to see Australian writers still trying to repeat the English pattern for their own vast scene, while the artists had already discovered the austere, authentic beauty of that empty brown and purple land. While my consciousness was busy with the war, my subconscious was absorbing facts and perceptions relative to our task at home.

In London I met more worldly writers, whose reactions were closer to those of the Cabinet members, labor leaders, and executives of the war I had been meeting at Cliveden, Lady (then Mrs.) Astor's great house. Some of them we in America thought of as clever journalists, and priggishly refused to give their work the name of literature. There was Arnold Bennett, an ugly man, flashily dressed, with a nasal voice that never ran out of something brilliant to say. With his zest for things and for quick change, and his obvious competence in the organization of the war, he seemed more American than English, more American than I was. We American academicians were still in the genteel age. He emphatically was not. I saw much more of H. G. Wells, with whom I was to have a long association. He was a vulgar man in the good sense of the word, who talked like a mouthpiece of civilization itself in a high-pitched cockney, and boasted that he wanted to be remembered by nothing that he had written, but only by his influence on his times. He regarded so-called literature as a rhetorical exercise lacking 'guts,' and was certainly seventy-five per cent right for his own or any other time. With invective, analysis, and shrewd statement, he took apart the English world I was viewing, named its leaders, ruthlessly defined them, and compared what they were doing with a philosophy of human welfare in which success and the imagination stepped out of a time machine and took us all for a ride. I called on George Bernard Shaw in his apartment at the Albany. He was electric in those days and I listened to him with veneration, for his prefaces had burnt away many of my conventions. Dark-bearded and restless, he tossed a long leg across his knee like a rope. I had just come from Dublin, center of wit and iconoclasm, where the Irish Renaissance was still in its glory and the war less important than Ireland's wrongs. But the poetry of Yeats and the mysticism of A. E., and Irish politics then burning over the conscription act, did not concern him. Like H. G. Wells, he was not interested in any localism, nor in literature as such, which he considered only a convenient vehicle for his own doctrines. He was a salesman of ideas (so he said) who cared little for art except as a technique for getting attention.

These men — great men all in their way — taught me one of the platitudes of history that a scholar often never learns: they made me realize that much of the wisdom of the ages of which we were supposed to be the conservators must have been equally charged with current passions when it was first uttered. To forget that so-called classic literature was once explosive and probably biased by personality was to lose touch with its only direct relation to actual life. The danger of studying it as we did in the light of eternity was that it lost relevance to our own emotions and also to our own current experience and behavior, and so became food for the intellect only. The golden bird of art could never be realized from its beak and skin and claws alone, even if they were the valuable remains. We were always forgetting the dirt it had scratched in, and the blood.

Later I spent a month in Oxford, a guest of Balliol College, where I was able to put together some of the material I had gathered. I had been to Oxford before, but this time I was at work there, a very different experience. My stay was enriched by a daily walk with the Master, A. L. Smith, a sympathetic student of American affairs who knew far more about certain aspects of my country than I did. Oxford was half-depopulated and its busy hum had sunk to a murmur. I worked all morning, lunched with the Fellows, who entertained almost every day some Balliol guest returned from the military front on the Continent or the political front in London. After lunch we walked, then had tea, and by five I could settle down to two hours or more of the best and hardest work of the day. It was a good life, well organized for intellectual accomplishment.

There were, I saw, two very different Oxfords, coexistent and surprisingly co-operative. I drank port with dons so withdrawn into an intellectual diffidence that they made only occasional remarks, and those usually rude ones. I met decrepit scholars with mousy beards whom I deeply respected because they could make the past so vivid that the present, at the moment, seemed transitory, if not irrelevant. This was the lunar Oxford, an emanation of its ancient towers in whose light students of the antique were preparing for a dim future which for them was never now and here.

But there was a sunlight Oxford with acute awareness of the present. This Oxford seemed far closer to its problems than the professors of the humanities in our universities, who were more truly cloistered by comparison. As I sat with the Fellows and their guests or walked with the Master, I noted a sense of responsibility for the community outside far keener than I had experienced at home, at least in myself. The men I talked with spoke of statesmen and military leaders and policy-makers from their own colleges, as if they were extensions of Oxford influence and Oxford teaching, for whom, indeed, Oxford was responsible. They were tests of Oxford scholarship, of Oxford thinking. The active world, now in such desperate turmoil, the arts and literature as they were being practiced, must show some impress of the work done under these towers, or the wealth and the cloisters of the university were not justified. I was aware, of course, that England still had a governing class, even though many of them belonged to the new Labor Party, and that it was far easier in Oxford than in America to keep a pipe line open to the world of action. Nevertheless, while I lived in these peaceful quadrangles even a live Tory seemed preferable to some of our apostles of culture in a Republic whose language they had not troubled to understand. Such a criticism cannot, I think, be made today.

What was this language of the thoughts and emotions of America at large? I began to wonder whether we specialists in literature knew. Certainly I, for one, could talk with more accurate information of the English than of the American tradition. And our teaching in the universities had been almost exclusively of English literature where a specifically American mold of thought was certainly not to be found. Was American literature only a variant of English belles-lettres, not shaped yet, but on its way to a merger? I found that I did not know what was being written, what had been written at home, that was ours entirely except for its base in Western culture and in the great tradition of earlier British literature. I could guess, but I did not know with any accuracy of scholarship or any penetration by thought. It was in England in 1918 that I first determined to devote myself after the war to a study of the tradition of my own country and its literature.

⌒) 2 (⌒
Brief Golden Age

IT SEEMS STRANGE to think of the ominous years which in 1918
began the Long Armistice as already settled into written
history. Only so are they recoverable to the young, but if history is more intelligent, it is less vivid than memory. When I
came back from Europe in the early autumn of 1918 to a country which, to use the phrase current then, was all dressed up
with nowhere to go, our great war effort had been only half-
developed and the armistice had caught us unprepared psychologically for real peace. Perhaps that always happens, but this
time there was a peculiar sense, which I felt as soon as I arrived, of taut energy having no complete release, and of frustration that was mixed with the joy of coming victory and the
war's ending. When I told a newspaper editor that the British
Foreign Office expected the war to end by the spring of 1919,
I was most illogically charged with being pro-German. We
were ready to go on for three years, he said. We had not yet
shown the enemy what we could do.

At the university everyone who had not been abroad or in
war activity was in a bad humor. There was never more jan-
gling of nerves among educated adults. Soon I grew bad tem-
ered myself, and then restless. The adrenal glands of artists,
teachers, and scholars are stimulated by war precisely as with
other men. If drawn into action, these oversensitive intellectuals are overstimulated by war or its accompaniments and the
critical and creative faculties are numbed. The final result is
a jangle which takes time to come to a harmony. Violent wars
and creative literary periods do not coincide. But after the
armed conflict is over, the excited glands continue to stimulate
and the result is often vigorous literary and artistic creation,
and sometimes along new lines. Male babies and powerful

books are produced abundantly after war has become peace. Apparently the imagination which has been charging itself from intense experience begins to discharge itself with unusual energy.

I had my share, more than my fair share, of charging, and my mind was overcharged. The transition back to teaching was not too difficult, for we were put to work on a strange course imposed by the army upon all undergraduates and kept going for some time after the war was over. My part of it was a stew of related subjects like history, literature, and economics. I do not know what the boys got out of the mixture, but such an overspecialized humanist as I had been learned much that was good for his thinking. Here I discovered, twenty-four hours in advance of teaching it, the Industrial Revolution, and with considerable excitement. Here was revealed to me that the westward-moving frontier was a key to American history. But when we all went back into our old stalls, I discovered, like many another, that nothing was so difficult as to repeat a pattern after a mind-shaking experience. Actually, my old patterns were broken; perhaps they had never been well and carefully formed. Nor did there seem to be others to be made by a man of my temperament and interests inside the liberal arts college as it was then.

My restless energies turned toward Washington where I had friends, later to be widely known, such as Felix Frankfurter and Walter Lippmann. There the fight was on for the League of Nations and I hoped to make myself useful in the cause, as I had in England. But I was too little experienced in politics and there were many in that last stand of political idealists who were more articulate than I and much better informed. And even while I was warming up, the battle was lost and 'practical men' took control, who proved to be dreamers, and bad dreamers at that. I turned back to my work, just beginning, on American literature, and gave in 1919-20 what I believe was the first advanced course in American literature against the background of American civilization. It was too advanced for me and my graduate students and we wound up the year by studying together. Not till some years later did I feel ready to try again. I was too restless for study. In England I had broken through the stiff wall which separates the student of literature and the makers thereof. Now my thoughts began to turn toward New York, where a renaissance in literature seemed to be beginning just as the American imagination in public affairs was becoming small, selfish, and corrupt.

Well, I was not an outlander as regards New York, at least not a mere tourist therein. I belonged to the Authors' Club, which in those days held rather stodgy meetings in the top of Carnegie Hall, where a few old celebrities wagged beards for the benefit of the more genteel among younger writers. I belonged to the Players, where I dined sometimes, tongue-tied except for eating, with a table full of leading men from the various theaters, also tongue-tied, but for a better reason. They did not dare to spill as much as a drop of their precious personalities before curtain-time. Of course, I did not really belong in the city, since I had done no work there except as a nonresident contributor to several magazines. But among my friends were some of the literary journalists, especially Franklin P. Adams (F. P. A.) who in his column, 'The Conning Tower' in the New York *World* of those days, was helping to shape a new kind of sophisticated humor, and educating a new audience for realistic, and especially satiric, books and plays. It was easy to understand, even from a distance, the magnetism which was drawing literary talent from all over the country to the center of publication and assessment. Much of the talent went, very wisely, home again, when it had breathed the electric air, overcome its inhibitions, and learned that New York editors and publishers were fallible men who would pay good money, but could not guarantee fame. This, in spite of reports to the contrary, had to be earned by sweat and toil at home. In 1920, however, with a suppressed energy bursting into literature, and a new interest in our native writing, the tide was naturally running strongly cityward.

Then out of the blue came a letter which, in effect, offered me a literary editorship in New York. That proposal went to the heart of the restlessness I shared with so many, and uncovered a complex which had been confusing and frustrating all the new impulses I had brought from abroad. In an academic career the vanity of prestige and the longing for security are strong passions. They had been obsessions with me. Two sides of my nature had been fighting. I wanted to break out of the ivory tower into what seemed a more creative and mind-stirring life; and I wanted passionately to be consecrated in security for the teaching I loved by the right kind of professorship which would also give me an authority that would command respect. With a strange perversity I had been struggling desperately to be tied for life to a useful routine where I had already made my contribution. Fortunately, I was in one of those dead-ends of the academic system in which only a plague or indispensability could get the kind of promotion I wished. When the offer came from New York, I fought like a hooked trout, using my opportunity to escape only as a means of getting into the safety of a quiet pool. I am the kind of temperament that shoots deep roots into environment and is most reluctant to cut them. When I lost my university battle and wrote accepting the offer from New York, I held the letter suspended in the slot of the postbox on the corner, knowing that if I let it drop I would break away for good from the old familiar places. Five months later I was on probation in literary and journalistic New York, happy, intensely energetic, and five years younger in spiritual age.

New York of 1920 was confusing but vibrant with intellectual excitement. Not only was the city itself astir with vigorous journalism and a new literature, but it was electric with induced currents from important books written elsewhere and sent for publication and review. Willa Cather's *My Antonia* was published in 1918; Cabell's *Jurgen* and Sherwood Anderson's *Winesburg, Ohio* in 1919. Edith Wharton's *The Age of Innocence,* Scott Fitzgerald's *This Side of Paradise,* and Sinclair Lewis's *Main Street* all appeared in 1920. Eugene O'Neill was demonstrating his power and originality; Elmer Rice was soon to show new theatrical technique in *The Adding Machine,* and the poetical renaissance, still active, was giving us a new style in American poetry.

New York had other sources of intellectual excitement that were more journalistic than literary. F. P. A. and Don Marquis, the columnists, were making a new type of book familiar to readers who had been content with best-sellers, and with both writers instruction and irony were sweetened by laughter. New York was becoming the richest, the most cosmopolitan, the greatest city in the world. It was already the liveliest. By comparison with London or Paris it had been naïve. Now these columnists, and many a writer of fiction or drama, were inviting the intelligent to take a seat at a great human comedy. With no high-brow pretentiousness, they made literature, and art in general, subjects for general conversation. In the columns, friends of the writers, with quick-moving minds, appeared under their own names and were dramatized into the similitude of a home-town circle. They broke down the anonymity of life in New York and made new types of urban personality and interests familiar to the general public. It was in this way, among others, that a new audience was prepared for a new literature. The same thing had happened before in the coffee-houses of London as described by Addison and Steele.

I am not sure whether this widespread interest in a national literature — which has never since abated — was not more important than the books which accompanied it. My European friends who were literary journalists in these same years abroad say that the importance was equal. They recall how when war-weariness and the loss of youthful energy by death were so evident in Germany, Austria, France, and England, the eager audience in America and the vigorous books widely read seemed the only vitality for literature in a dreary world. They could feel, even then, a reversal in the tide of influence between Europe and America. And this in spite of single geniuses like Proust and Joyce, more original than any of our writers. Indeed, at home here, the vitality of interest was easy to estimate. The nineteen-twenties is the only period I have known when it was possible to lecture successfully to great popular audiences on literary criticism and important new books, with no concessions to popularity except to try to be interesting. Individual geniuses can often create (like Milton in *Paradise Lost*) without a wide and sympathetic audience, but this is not true of a forward movement of a whole literature. A hen, picking up her food expertly, may lay an exceptionally fine egg; but feed the whole chicken house with vitamins, turn on the lights at night, and the good eggs drop by dozens.

Whether or not the early twenties was the best of a brief golden age before the gilt and stucco of the inflation, the broken lives of the Great Depression and the new war, it may be too soon to say. Yet certainly it was a golden moment for a still youngish editor and literary critic to come to New York. He had everything (almost) to learn, but everything fairly shouted to be learned and interpreted.

The literature that so excited us in the early nineteen-twenties was vigorous, but it was not so new as we thought. We believed (as many think today with more reason) that nothing could be the same again after a world war. But nineteenth-century culture was tough, and not much was radically changed by the war in America except our excess of confidence in progress, and that was only cracked. Many believed that the new gadgets which in the nineteen-twenties began to make living more comfortable were sure signs that civilization was again on the march. Others doubted whether gadgets made a civilization. Yet it was true that something new intellectually for America had come out of the first World War. Our emotional tension and startled awareness of great events, more startled, I think, than in the second war, had stirred hundreds of thousands of minds out of the commonplace. I am sure that the attacks on complacency and provincialism, so common in the books of these years, were closely related to the state of mind of American readers. They had been forced by events to stretch their imaginations to take in a current history that ran round the world. Now, with expanded vision, they began to look at home life and home affairs. What was Sinclair Lewis's *Main Street*, which set the country quarreling, but a satiric view of American small-town life as seen in world, or at least in Western world, perspective? It might have been written at any time after, say 1900, but would not in 1900 have found more than ten thousand readers. By 1920, the restless minds of the writers of the new books were getting a response from restless men and women who had been, figuratively or literally, grabbed out of their Main Streets, and then, after the war's expansions, dropped back like kittens with their eyes just opened.

And yet it was not really a new literature with new techniques and, what is more important, basically new values for living, which swept over the country in those years. The truth was (as I believe is generally the case) that the war had been only a stimulant and accelerant for American writing. What we were getting from the Frosts, the Robinsons, the Cathers, the Andersons, the Glasgows, the Lewises, was the ripe and vigorous end and summary of the latter nineteenth century. Twentieth-century American literature did not really get under way until the mid-twenties, when the generation that had no roots in our secure pre-war years began to take over. The writers who were doing their finest work in the earliest nineteen-twenties had been conditioned by the Age of Confidence. The older among them, like Theodore Dreiser and Ellen Glasgow, had long before the war been summing up the values developed in a half-century or more of American experience. Few, and least of all the professors, had taken them seriously. But after the war when, for a little while, our unsuspected physical, and also moral, power had dominated Europe, and when, turning home, we saw ourselves in a new perspective, these American writers and many others got an attention never before accorded. Also, and this was lucky, as a group they were not only significant, they were good; some of them, like Willa Cather and Dreiser in fiction and Robinson and Frost in poetry, were writers worthy of any literature. They were summing up America to date; they were explaining how we got to be what we were, and criticizing the results. They were skillfully depicting solid and established American types; and were assorting goods and ills in the values now seen to be native and original in the United States. And the material they had to work with was so rich and strong that they could be satiric, or devastatingly critical, or triumphant — and still be true to fact in any category. This was the real *fin de siècle* in literature for us, and not the dilettantish sophistry of the eighteen-nineties. And essentially, this was what was making literary journalism an exciting profession in New York.

ᏩᎤ 3 ᏩᎤ
An Arsenal of Literature

I BEGAN MY CAREER as a literary journalist in old downtown
New York. That was appropriate, for literature fits well
into a continuum where old and new are both visibly present.
From my window in an office building in Vesey Street, I could
look down on the ancient churchyard and across to the eighteenth-century belfry of Saint Paul's church, ringed about with
towers of steel. Broadway roared a block away, and to mingle
at noon in the sidewalk crowds of brokers, clerks, and chic
stenographers brushed off the scholars' cobwebs and gave a
useful sense of responsibility to a large, if indifferent, world.
North a little way were the offices of all the great newspapers
except *The Times,* which had already moved uptown; and
down toward the North River were narrow, dirty streets under
the viaducts of the Elevateds, with hole-in-the-wall restaurants,
incongruous slums huddled under million-dollar office buildings, and tiny shops for everything from ship models, trout flies,
and old books to typewriter ribbons and adding machines. The
ancient publishing house of Harpers' was not far off, entered
up a broad flight of iron steps leading to a great semicircle of
desks, from which cold eyes seemed to be looking down on the
nervous contributor. Near at hand was Walt Whitman's favorite eating place; and if the masts were all gone from the water-
front, the sea mist still blew in at our office windows, and the
mournful blasts of liners' whistles were overtones to the news-
boys' shouts of 'Extra!' and the clatter of Elevated trains.

I had come to New York to found a magazine, and it is to
the magazine in general that I refer in the title of this chapter.
For in the United States in particular, an extraordinary amount
of durable literature has been drawn into the relative perma-
nency of book form from the showcases of the magazines. Orig-

inally a magazine was just that, a warehouse of literary odds
and ends, lifted wherever they could be stolen, and with no
pretensions to originality. Slowly it acquired a life of its own,
and by the late nineteenth century, at the height of their
golden era, the great American literary magazines of the genteel age — especially *Harper's* and *The Century* — with their
groups of contributing writers and illustrators, dominated the
reading world here and had wide circulation through the English-speaking peoples.

I had written short stories for half a dozen magazines, until
I discovered that my stories were only narrative essays with
feeble plots. I had written essays — educational, critical, personal, descriptive — for many more magazines. It was a sad day
for many a writer of my generation when the gently literary
travel essay, stuffed with reflections upon beauty, quaintness,
humor, and the traveler's soul, went out of fashion along with
the local-color short story. We had always been able to pay for
a holiday in some out-of-the-way place like rural Normandy
or the High Sierras or the Smoky Mountains, by a pleasant and
easy use of the pen.

I was to see and, as an adviser, help *Harper's Magazine* under
the able editorship of Thomas B. Wells, face a new era in
which there was no patience for such agreeable dilettantism.
I watched *The Atlantic Monthly*, to which I had been a frequent contributor, push into a new field of somewhat neurotic
autobiography in the attempt to escape from the merely genteel. I saw *The Century,* for which I had written a string of
essays on American manners, first wither and then die because
it adjusted too rapidly and so killed off its old subscribers before it got enough new ones to survive. I saw *Scribner's* go
under because it adjusted too late. But the nineteen-twenties birthed more magazines than they killed. And among the
mass-production weeklies and co-operative news periodicals
were literary organs of a new type, one of which was my concern.

The New York *Evening Post*, dean of American newspapers,
but frequently regarded by the irreverent as a dean *emeritus,*
wished to establish a weekly literary supplement of high quality and worthy of its long tradition of intellectual leadership.

That was my new job. Alexander Hamilton had founded *The Post* to represent conservative interests in the young Republic, and his ghost still walked our corridors, though it had a curious way of looking more like Thomas Jefferson. For *The Post* had become what the English call a conservative radical. It praised the vested interests when they behaved themselves and was proud of having the best financial section in New York. It was liberal, and progressive up to the point where the existing order seemed to be threatened. In its subconsciousness was an impulse deeper than thought to oppose majorities whenever and however they came to power. Under Oswald Garrison Villard's editorship it had been anti-war up to 1917. We were still 'anti' to most of the current social and economic movements except world order and the League of Nations, where, as usual, we backed the minority opinion. *The Post* was probably the best written, certainly the most scholarly, newspaper in New York or, indeed, in the country. It was a high-minded and a deeply responsible paper, but it was about as popular as the president of the anti-saloon league. Nevertheless, there could have been no better foundation upon which to erect an independent, scholarly, and responsible review of literature and current books.

The Post gave me my only experience of newspaper journalism and taught me more about co-operative endeavor than I had learned in the university. An established newspaper with a tradition behind it is a corporate being in which a dozen trades, skills, and professions are inseparably bound together in a common enterprise. The editorial writer, whose specialties may be pure milk or municipal politics, becomes conscious of his dependence upon the hard-knuckled toughs who distribute the paper. The head of a literary section must learn a good deal about printing or be helpless when he is told by an ironic pressroom that type lice have eaten up his overset.

I found a newspaper as rich in eccentrics as a university, and stuffed with personality. We had an absorbed editorial writer who was not aware that he was to become a father until they telephoned him from the hospital. We had a temperamental typesetter who burst into tears whenever there was too much copy at the last moment, and had to be comforted by the lady assistants. There was a series of promotion men, all big-fisted, high-hearted fellows, who banged enthusiastically on the table, and then went out to spend a hundred thousand dollars with no appreciable results. The wise and humorous Simeon Strunsky was at the head of our editorial council, with Allan Nevins as one of his associates. At the darkest moments of those years of declining idealism he could make us believe in the inevitable survival of virtue.

First came the boom days, when Thomas W. Lamont, who had bought the paper, was abroad on affairs of the Peace, leaving his purse-strings behind. He was always a backer of good works and good will, never seeking his own advantage, and leaving us complete independence. I wish that before he left he had taught us a little about practical finance. Our motto for our readers was Tennyson's 'He needs must love the highest when he sees it.' But the general public simply could not see *The Post,* even though it was bristling with high standards. So there were bad times also. Then everyone from the editor, Edwin F. Gay, an honest and able man, though not newspaper-minded, down to the office boys, resolved together that *The Post* was an institution more important than private welfare and that we must save it. For a while we did.

There were boom days on *The Post* when I joined it in 1920, but I was so accustomed to the economy of a university that it never occurred to me to ask for my share of the promotion money being spent so lavishly. My concern was to make a Literary Review to be published with the Saturday paper, which would promote itself — and when we came to a first printing *The Literary Review* was what we called it. Both time and atmosphere were propitious. Before our régime, *The Nation* had been an organ of *The Post,* but it had gone on its own and declined into stodginess, relieved by occasional critical essays of great worth written by the old guard, whose erudition, however, did not always make up for their lack of contacts with the oncoming age. Also *The Nation* then believed that a good book could afford to wait for its review, an idea with which I have a sneaking sympathy. It used to be told of its editors that they reviewed the Christmas books for one year on the following December first. I doubt whether it mattered. *The Times* and *The Tribune* had together fallen into a rut. Their leading articles on important books were competent and well written, but too often were designed to show how much more the critic knew about the subject than did the author of the book. The book itself was buried by the review, and sometimes had no resurrection. The rest of their columns were written by reviewers who could be trusted not to say anything unpleasant. I hoped to kindle a new fire in these dry logs and brush-heaps of criticism; and, in addition, I had my own private desire, which was to bring to the interpretation of new books for the intelligent reader the trained thinking and real erudition of the universities.

And so I sharpened my pencil (a tool much more dear to me than pen or typewriter), organized my editorial staff, and set to work. Miss Amy Loveman, one of the ablest, certainly the kindest, assuredly one of the most useful, women in New York, was my associate. William Rose Benét, poet and critic, was my literary adviser. He was a man of mingled fire and honey whose concern was every human interest except his own. In a cubicle next door to my office, puffing pipe smoke at its hinges, was the columnist of *The Post,* Christopher Morley, a rusher in and out, bubbling ideas like a soda fountain; a wit, a wagster, an Elizabethan philosopher, with one of the few minds I have known that seemed to be perpetually enjoying its own versatility. There I settled down to the first office job I had ever held, and though I could never learn to work happily in shirt-sleeves and suspenders, and so was clearly not a congenital newspaperman, I spent engrossed and happy days.

Perhaps it is only on a small periodical in its formative years that there develops a family of minds which as the magazine comes to maturity gives it a personality of its own. Such a magazine at the start was *Time,* when, for a while, our family group lived and worked in the same quarters as theirs. Such a magazine was *The New Yorker,* which began after our first experiment. Such a magazine was *The Literary Review,* which, if conceived in my brain, owed its vitality, and also its longevity (for the present *Saturday Review of Literature* is the same child grown up under another name), to a group of diverse temperaments with like minds. And it would seem that these earliest nineteen-twenties were by some literary astrology the right time for a corporate literary personality to be born. As I have said before, the columnists were preparing an audience ready to support vitality and competence in either criticism or pure literature. The success of a magazine like *The New Yorker* (born 1925) would have been impossible in, say, 1910. Whatever the cause, an editor who wished to help the right people to read new books in the right way got plenty of support of the kind that cannot be bought.

This support came from the writers as well as from the audience. I was sure from my previous experience on *The Yale Review* that if we gave good writers a chance to do just what they wanted, we should not (as indeed we could not) have to pay more than modest sums for their work in reviews or criticism. It is a fact that literary writing done for nothing is seldom good for much. Apparently the author who does not expect to be paid for his work loses his sense of audience and becomes too self-regarding. He writes only to please himself, which is a form of dilettantism. But if a payment is established, the amount has little relation to the excellence of the product, provided it is all the editor can pay. The professional writer will not write better for twice the money, because he cannot. The editor's problem is to get him to write at all. A fat purse is useful when it comes to stealing authors from other periodicals; it helps to persuade a lazy man to write, though I do not think it is so persuasive as a tempting subject. But a fat purse comes from a large circulation behind it, which, in turn, means that the writer gets more money, but it is given a diluted audience, for whom often, though of course not always, he cannot write what most interests him in the way he likes best. This is the vicious and inevitable circle. Fortunately for *The Literary Review*, we were not seeking fiction or sensational news articles, the most expensive variety of magazine literature, and, with a few exceptions, we got what we wanted for as much as we were able to pay. But it meant hard work in finding the right man or woman for an appealing opportunity.

We believed that a literary supplement of a newspaper which, however excellent, was local to one city, should have a subscription list which was national in scope, even though small;

and, circularizing among the right people, we soon had eight to ten thousand readers strategically distributed all over the country. We also believed that a literary magazine should be as carefully composed as good literature itself. In our lay-out we began by breaking two journalistic conventions. The leading article had only a one-column head, which balanced the editorial essay on the other side and left room for a carefully chosen short poem in the center. It was an audacious shifting of emphasis from the news to opinion and to pure literature — from the timely to aspects of the eternal. By this change we gave poetry, or at least short poems, such distinction of place as had not been theirs in general magazines since the bad practice began of using them as fillers at the tail of prose articles. But otherwise the scheme by no means always worked, since the leading article frequently had as much of the eternal in it as either poem or editorial. Still, I like to look at that old front page, especially as we later perfected it in *The Saturday Review.*

We felt, too, and very strongly, that criticism should be liberal in its definition, and should include irony and humor and instances of pure beauty as well as fact-finding and theory. *The Review* was supposed to revolve in two planetary orbits which interwove in a harmony. One was books under review, for which the leading article was the *primum mobile.* The other was literature, in which comment on aspects of life and writing was interspersed with cartoons, sweetened by humor, and freshened by enlightened gossip about the authors who made the books. So doing, we hoped to relate the magazine to immediate life on the one hand, and to set it also in the long vistas of literary history.

We spent three months in recruiting, balancing what we got, and arranging a first number where everything was to swing into place like toy stars and planets in a model for a class in astronomy. The actual result was a sad lesson for perfectionists, though it pleased everyone but the editor. Our outline so interested the publishers that an astral storm of last-minute advertising swept away the further reaches of our orbits with their nice adjustments of minor constellations. Or, to change the figure, the rear of my magazine was a flock of billboards; and, to change it again, the first number of *The Review* looked to me, though fortunately not to others, like a man in a dress suit with the tails cut off and patches on the seat of his trousers.

My colleagues developed abilities which they did not know they possessed. Amy Loveman was soon more knowledgeable about contemporary books and authors than anyone else in town. She had been trained as an assistant on an encyclopedia, and heartily enjoyed escaping from the dead to the living. William Rose Benét, already a poet of distinction, proved to be a congenital columnist. His wise and witty comments on the human comedy of letters were soon widely quoted. Christopher Morley, his neighbor in the next cubicle, borrowed with him a name from the half-legendary figure of Sir Kenelm Digby, which they shifted backward and forward between them as a shield behind which to shoot at all and sundry, including each other. I was not only editor and chief editorial writer, but contact man in a large way. It was my task to herd the great in name or experience into our little clearing and there milk them of what they could be persuaded to let down of critical wisdom or useful erudition. It was surprising how many came.

A magazine, I decided, must have either a policy or an idea; or have both, in which case the emphasis would be sure to fall on one or the other. I had no objection to the policy magazine so long as the policy did not interfere with the job of making a good magazine. The old, rather pedantic *Nation* was turning leftward with a policy and new blood in its veins. That was good. *The New Masses* (called by a different name in our day), a portent of the fanatic ideologies and brutal politics in the storm clouds ahead, was all policy, so much so that in its reviewing pages you could tell in advance what would be said about any controversial book. Truth was not served. It was a useful irritant, but bitterly unfair, and often stupidly ignorant of any values not in its own ten commandments. Being a Quaker in mood, tolerant but passionately concerned for a more intelligent world, magazines with ideas pleased me better than magazines with dogmatics behind them. I liked *The New Yorker* because it was aware of the new sophisticated urban society, and made its own very real idealism articulate by good-humored irony with a cutting edge like a just emerging razor blade. I respected, though I did not always like, *Time,* because in an accelerating world it made an escape from our dangerous provincialism easier.

My own idea was not original. Indeed, it was only the Jeffersonian belief in the necessity of education for a successful democracy. I wanted to go in for adult education in the value of books — all kinds of books, foreign as well as native, but particularly the current books of our own country. I wished to make criticism first of all a teaching job, backed up by explorations and estimates of new ideas. Indeed, the ruling purpose with me, whether in college or on the Book-of-the-Month Club or on *The Review,* has been the passing-on of sound values to others, which is one reason why I have taken little part in the critical controversies of the so-called 'Little Magazines.' It took all one's energy to be sure of what was known already and to make it articulate. I recognized the value of speculation, even of dogmatic speculation, but left that to different minds and temperaments.

Teaching is a delicate affair — a true art — and has to be separated from the more obvious critical duty of making or breaking reputations. I did some of that, but chose for my main task a series of weekly editorial essays, brief but packed, whose purpose was a commentary on the ups and downs, the ins and outs, of the life of books, interpreting, summarizing in the light of history, prophesying when I dared to do so, and defining as well as estimating values wherever I could distinguish them. Nor did I hesitate to turn from books to the phenomena of human nature; or to nature itself, which with me has always been a passion, whenever I felt that the cockneys were getting too far away from mother earth. These editorials were 'assays,' as the essay was originally called; that is, experiments in the search for values, leaving the working-out of what was suggested to others or to later and more extensive work of my own. I wrote scores of them in the trains when I was commuting weekly from New Haven or elsewhere, and found the easy rhythm of the cars good for the style. Naturally I had an idea captured and pocketed before I got aboard. They served their purpose, I think, in recording the flow of the times and in pulling together the loose bundle of facts and opinions out of which a magazine devoted to liberal leadership had to be made. Many — probably too many — of them were reprinted in four separate volumes.

But there was more than just liberalism to a program that the dogmatic fellows on the Little Magazines often called wobbling, and which was to be quite incomprehensible to the cat-and-dog fighters that were soon to begin to spit and snarl over conflicting theories as to how to make a brave new Marxian or Fascist world. The Chinese have a description, and doubtless a word, for what I was trying to do. I believed, as did some of their philosophers, that one must know *how* and *what* to read before taking sides. And also that some values at least had been determined once for all, so that the first duty of a critic was to search them out. Systems, sources, futures, honesty, and perception come next on the agenda for the instruction of that general audience which Whitman had felt was essential to the success of good literature.

And so *The Literary Review* began to slide weekly from the presses. I took opinions as to merits and demerits wherever I could get them, including the publishers whose advertising support meant new opportunities for expansion. They supported us, but were by no means enthusiastic. I had thrown my nets widely for contributions, and most widely in the academic pools, which I knew best. The trade thought the magazine was unnecessarily erudite. And indeed it soon became more authoritative in its reviews of serious books than any other general reviewing medium in America, though still inferior in this respect, but not in others, to the London *Times Literary Supplement,* which my academic friends constantly urged upon me as a paragon of scholarly virtues. It was — but some of my colleagues' respect was due to the anonymity of the reviews, which were often written by brilliant but untried young men whose words carried an easy authority not justified by their careers. I could well understand that many publishers and booksellers thought at the beginning that *The Review* was just another hurdle for a difficult trade. One eminent publisher, now dead, told me in one year that *The Review* was worth a million dollars to his business and in the next accused me of costing him that amount. Both superlatives were determined by the book he happened to be backing. Reputations were easily gained in those lively days by books which were said to be authoritative and novels which were said to be great. The trade felt that we were putting tank blocks on the road to quick success. We did, and also, thanks to the number of learned professors on our list of reviewers, helped to destroy many a harmless and unpretentious volume that flattened under scholarly criticism like a tin can under a roller. Yet even though the publishers did not love us, they were far more aware than the intellectuals that our chief desire was to create a wider public for better books. They gave us moral support with a reasonable amount of advertising, and hoped we would grow mellower and find our audience before we went bankrupt.

The inevitable day came at last when the *Evening Post,* staggering under its debts, was swallowed in one expensive gulp by the Curtis family organization, then at the height of its influence. Henceforth, until a later transfer of the property, our *Evening Post* became a New York edition of a Philadelphia newspaper. I came back, unaware, from a brief Southern vacation to find a brisk managerial person in charge, who was unimpressed by our practical idealism (for our section of the paper had made money) and our national circulation and influence. We seemed to him a string quartet proposing to play in a corner of his two-ring circus. And soon I was writing what I knew to be a farewell editorial, summarizing what we had tried to do. I entitled it 'And Twitched His Mantle Blue,' feeling sure that the new proprietors would not recognize the quotation from Milton or know that the next line in *Lycidas* reads: 'Tomorrow to fresh woods, and pastures new.'

The Literary Review became first a hodge-podge, then a heading with a few reviews beneath it. But our friends would not let us die. Mr. Lamont wished to save at least this much of his *Evening Post* and offered his support. Britton Hadden and Harry Luce, two of the founders of *Time,* had been closely associated with me when they were undergraduates at Yale and later used to bring their experiments with the new magazine, written out in long-hand on yellow paper, for my inexpert advice. They wished to co-operate. And so we migrated — editors, columnists, poets, reviewers — carrying a baggage of morale, enough money for a new start, and a draft of our subscription list which we personally had built with great care.

We left Vesey Street for the noisy second floor of an East Side factory where *Time* had its headquarters, and there launched *The Saturday Review of Literature,* which was *The Literary Review* come of age, more humorous, wiser, more literary, better printed, but with the same will to further the cause of good thinking, good feeling, good writing, and good books.

This was in 1924. New York and American literature were growing fast. The real end of the nineteenth century was close at hand. We were fortunate in our nearly four years of existence to have learned the hard way by economy and by experiment what could and could not be done before the new age brought new conflicts and new kinds of literature. It would be more modest, and more truthful, to say that we had begun to learn. I had shaken off some pedantic ideas and no longer yearned to publish articles that only scholars could understand, and which no one, not even scholars, read. Much more important, our team of editorial scouts had scurried through attics, studios, newspaper desks, Connecticut hilltops, Greenwich Village hideouts, and college studies, and also had recruited choice minds from England, Ireland, France, and Germany. We had brought back good writing sometimes from places where no good writing had been done before. In circulation we were still only a little whirl in the great cycle of intellectual weather. But we seemed to have found the right appeal; and men and manuscripts followed us to our new office, where the floors reverberated to the machinery below in a new rhythm of a new age.

Most important for us who had worked together, we had lived intensely in what I have called a brief golden age of American writing, before the great boom and the great bust and the preliminaries of a new war. We had become part of that literary scene which I still think was the first classical pausing moment of perfected art, especially the novel, since the great days of the eighteen-fifties. And we had experienced what never can happen twice with the same excitement, an initiation into the literary and journalistic life which swirls around a young and active magazine. Of that I have more to say, and if I overlap *The Literary Review* and its brain-child, *The Saturday Review of Literature,* history will not be falsified even if the chronology is sometimes confused.

4

The Passion for Print

THERE IS NO BETTER PLACE for observing the habits of writers than the editorship of a critical magazine; I mean every kind of writer with literary aspirations — hacks, parasites, the frustrated, immature geniuses, little great people and great little people, the famous, the outmoded, and the decayed. An editor of a mass-circulation weekly or of a monthly of ancient literary prestige may meet more celebrities (and pay for the opportunity), but his affairs are conducted at opulent luncheons designed to induce the right mood for a profitable contract. We dealt, after all, chiefly in reviewing, one of the most meanly rewarded of all professions, yet irresistibly attractive to the writing kind. And the writers who made reviewing a trade, or wished to make it a profession, came to see us without invitation.

Every writer longs to have a say about his colleagues, and is more tempted by the opportunity than by cash. And many a writer who cannot sell his creative work counts on reviewing to earn his daily bread. No celebrities waited in our anterooms, though sometimes they called on us there. If we wished to cajole them into reviewing, we wrote careful letters in which each word was personally guided toward indefensible areas of their minds. But since everyone but celebrities wanted to review books, or were sure they could write better reviews than the critics of their own books, or needed a new hat or a hot dinner, we could see most of scribbling New York without going out into the rain.

The founding of a new literary magazine is like setting up a feeding-table for winter birds trying to survive until spring. They arrive by flocks from all the neighboring thickets and soon are squabbling for crumbs. So it is with literary aspirants who want reviewing. In New York, from tenements and lofts, from shared apartments and from the best uptown addresses, from Syracuse, Bangor, and Spartansburg (just arrived), they hurried by foot or taxi to our library reception room, each with his or her good reason why a book (almost any book) should be given for review. Most of this swarm were not prospective or even potential critics. They were the belletristic fringe of the multitude that wished to write. Would-be journalists went to the newspapers. The girls and boys (many of them were only that) who came to us were writing novels, short stories, or plays, and hoped to earn a few dollars and get their names in print while they waited for an acceptance or a try-out. Many of them were very able, but usually not in our direction. Most of them had only two qualifications for reviewing: they liked to read and could write a passable English. Ninety-nine out of a hundred among the young had a fixed (and fallacious) belief: if you could not get your own books published, you could at least tell what was wrong with the books other authors had written.

I was sympathetic with the slightest budding creative talent. Yet I soon found that overstimulating a feeble critical talent was like manuring the soil of a New York back yard. Fearful things came up — and mercifully withered. Nevertheless, yielding to fresh young faces (charming girls in particular), I dealt out lesser novels for experimental reviewing. The results were devastating. If the review was favorable, it was pointless; if it was pointed, it was savage. I did not realize then how much easier it is to damn than to praise with any effectiveness. I was not then aware of the primitive cruelty of the young intellectual's mind, nor how the hidden self-distrusts of an unformed personality could be soothed by aggressiveness or impudence. After a year or so of this service to the youth movement, we had accumulated a vast stock of unpublishable reviews, and with those we published had earned the undying hate of numerous mediocre writers whose books had been slaughtered when they deserved only oblivion or reproof.

Criticism and reviewing are, of course, two quite different arts. Criticism values and sets in perspective a seasoned work of art which is ready to be placed in its relation to literary history. Reviewing need do no more than describe and define a current book, with an opinion as to its merits. Criticism requires an erudition and a trained judgment no youth is likely to possess. Yet reviewing books puts as strong tests to the intelligence, since the reader of an unpublished book must rely on his own reactions. Unlike the scholar at work upon the past, he has no absolute knowledge as to whether he is reading a failure or a success. His book as yet has no history. But such problems never troubled our aspirants. They were all Davids asking for a sling and a Goliath to pop at.

I had not been long in New York before I discovered that Grub Street was still a reality. Today it is lined with expensive apartment houses inhabited by ghost writers and the more successful anthologists; but in the early twenties it was more like its ancient hack-infested predecessor in London. In New York's symbolic Grub Street lived a race of professional reviewers. Those who worked for us were elderly and must have long since gone to an endless rest for tired eyes and bruised typewriter fingers. For they worked hard. Reviewing should be an avocation or a by-product of the study of literature, but these honest hacks made a job of it which was poorly paid by cash and saleable books. One I remember particularly who introduced mass production into the business. Well educated, with an encyclopedic mind that never lifted above the level of competence, he had too little personality to teach, too little originality for research, and too much real love of books to go elsewhere for a living. But he had to live and support his family, so he set up a factory of reviewing, feeding to his intelligent wife and daughters armfuls of books, some from us, more from the Sunday supplements. He was foreman, reviser, and reviewer of the more difficult volumes. This was most useful to us in the days when we tried to review everything, but I doubt whether the whole establishment earned as much as seventy-five dollars a week.

It was seldom dull in our reception room. We could count upon at least one paranoiac a week. I do not mean paranoiacs in the strict medical sense, though a few of them were definitely crazy. Our would-be reviewers of this kind were obsessed creatures of one idea, which they tried to sell us. There is something about writing, perhaps the chance for self-expression, that attracts such brains, and something about criticism that has an especial appeal. Criticism gives to the obsessed mind a long-sought opportunity to avenge his fancied wrongs upon a society to which he has never been able to adjust himself. Nor is this neurotic desire to be found only in the unbalanced. Pope with his twisted body made it into an art of abuse.

I learned to recognize these neurotics by a furtiveness of gesture and a side gleaming of the eye. Usually they were as harmless as a neat little man who was one of my frequent visitors. He was a moth dazzled by the flame of the Shakespeare-Bacon controversy which has attracted so many uncertain intellects, although it was the Earl of Oxford, not Bacon, that concerned him. He came to me one day actually trembling. Lord Robert Cecil, whom I had known in London, was being sent over on some diplomatic mission, but my friend was sure that this was camouflage. The Cecils had been offended by some slurs of his upon their famous Elizabethan ancestor. Lord Robert was coming for *him*. I never saw him again.

Some of these able but erratic men were dangerous. I was nearly strangled by an expert in early American history because I had given the book he wanted to a rival historian, escaping only by dodging into the crowded traffic of Forty-Fifth Street. Others were pathetic, such as the old and rummy composer of excellent sonnets who would sit for hours muttering to himself in an anteroom while I worked behind a locked door and the stenographers were afraid to pass him in order to go home. Sometimes it was not paranoia at all, but the calculated malice of the spokesman in *Job* who wished that his adversary had written a book. A critic of rising reputation once got from my innocent hands the new novel of an established writer. When he finished the review there was little left of the book but the dust-cover, and we, at the time fanatic upholders of free speech, published it as written. Later I was told that the reviewer had recently been kicked downstairs by the author in a Greenwich Village brawl.

Never paranoiac, but too often intolerably dull, were the scholars, the masters of those who know, whom we were determined to draft for the education of our reading public. Most of the scholars in the humanities of my generation (it was not true earlier) had been trained to set aside earnestly any attempt to be interesting except to fellow specialists. Or if the advisability of interesting others occurred to them, the result seldom showed in what they wrote. Many of the academics then were good lecturers, but when they reviewed, they reviewed for each other and the public be damned. A great authority would write ten words on the value of the book he was reviewing, and a thousand on minor errors and misprints. Or, still more frequently, he would devote his space to telling how he would have written the book. That this was chargeable to the overspecialization of the modern university was probably true. But how to account for the sheer bad writing of so many of my scholarly contemporaries, who never seemed to get beyond correct grammar and syntax? I do not know, unless it was because the discipline of the great classics had relaxed and faded.

In politics, economics, and history we did better, for these were the years of controversy over the causes of the first World War and the imperatives of reconstruction. The scholars in government, economics, and the sociology of change were aware of the absolute necessity of influencing public opinion. They learned to write effectively if they were not already skillful, and if they failed in their great cause it was not because of a halting rhetoric. Indeed, the curious may find in the files of our two magazines for the twenties, and in many another periodical of the times, a convincing analysis of what was bound to happen in a world weary of war, but still bogged down in nationalism. There were, of course, plenty of bad guesses, yet there were enough facts and good counsels available in the twenties to have prevented World War II. Unfortunately the tide of self-destruction was rising, not falling.

What one remembers is how few books and how few competent reviewers there were on military or naval tactics and strategy, or on the broader questions of how democracy might win World War II, if it came. Yet the fault was not in the direction but in the tempo of our thinking. We were not rid of war, yet insisted upon concentrating on the problems of peace. We were busy tearing up the road blocks while mines were still under the pavement. We said good-bye to force while forgetting original sin. All this the books of that time make clear now, but it was not so then. Yet there was nothing wrong with the postwar desire to escape from its military problems. We shall have to go back some day to the mood and the will and the ideals of the twenties or we are all lost. It is to be hoped, however, that we shall have proceeded with more wisdom and fewer brave words. Even a believer that books are bullets in wartime and electric charges in peace knows that words sometimes darken counsel. Readers and writers always tend to think that what is proved in print to be right is more likely to happen than what is proved to be wrong. Human events do not move that way.

Science, both pure and applied, and the fellow travelers of science, psychology and sociology, were also intensely productive in the twenties. We were not concerned with technology, but sociology and psychology and biology, and physics in its relation to philosophical thinking, belonged in our responsibility. In psychology and sociology particularly our reviewers were often as inarticulate as the books they reviewed, and, like them, were so involved in specialists' jargon that they seldom worked through into clarity. As editors responsible for a reasonable intelligibility, we floundered about, gradually discovering who could tell and would, and who knew well enough but could not tell what he knew. And, as it happened, in the field of scientific scholarship we scored one success that had the elements of the sensational. This was in the early days of *The Saturday Review*.

I had met in England while doing some work for the Society for Pure English, a C. K. Ogden, whose career since has been extraordinary. He has already published somewhere his account of the following incident. A psychologist, a physicist, a philologist, and I do not know what else, he lived in the twenties on the lower floors of a London house crammed with gadgets such as machines for running records backward so that the hearers could analyze the rhythms, and astonishing electrical devices. It was not to see those that I called upon him, but to discuss the now famous Basic English, for which I. A. Richards, the critic, and he were responsible.

The range of his knowledge of new thought and investigation was unequaled in my experience — it was truly incredible.
And so I thought of him as a reviewer when, in 1926, an in-
terim (the thirteenth) edition of the *Encylopaedia Britannica*
was brought out in three volumes to be added to the prewar
complete edition of 1911. The idea was to bring us up-to-date
in all important knowledge of what had happened in the world
since 1911. Mr. Ogden was fortunately in New York, and
agreed to undertake a review from which a university faculty
might have shrunk. He asked only a free hand and sufficient
space; and got both.

I remember his light figure as he hurried into the office almost at the deadline, with an armful of manuscript. A few pages
were enough to show that it was a massacre. The editors of the
edition, unwilling to delay, had shoved wads of new material
into an old reference book with an insufficient consideration of
new fields of developing knowledge and new men. The resulting omissions were startling. Ogden's review was a survey of
the new thoughts, new procedures, and new talents which had
been overlooked. It listed names of which I then had never
heard, but which were clearly of primary importance, and discoveries and discoverers that I knew to be indispensable for a
reference book, yet were not even recorded in the index of the
three volumes. As the proofs came up, we began to throw out
reviews, articles, poems, then whole departments from the number in order to get space, until finally the week's issue was
chiefly Ogden — a brilliant, devastating criticism of a reference
work about as useful in some of its important sections as a 1911
telephone book.

A few weeks later, the vice-president of the American branch
of the *Britannica* (it has changed ownership since) came to my
office. He was sorry to make trouble, but he feared that they
would have to sue *The Saturday Review* and its editor for libel-
ous statement. They had suffered heavy financial damage from
that review. 'But you know,' I said, 'that the courts have ruled
that a review, no matter how hurtful to a book's reputation, is
not actionable unless it contains malicious misstatement.
Otherwise there could be no criticism.' 'Yes, of course,' he replied, 'but we shall sue you for maliciously choosing an incom-

petent man to review a great work. That is cause for an action.'
Many times I have been challenged for this or that and thought
of the right answer only hours later, and too late. This time I
was ready. 'If Mr. Ogden is incompetent, why did your editor
choose him to write the article on psychology for this edition?'
We were not sued!

The modernist critics invaded our office frequently (the verb
is exact) with lightning in their eyes and grenades in either
hand. Change was under way, a rapid change in underlying
values most easily detected in experimental literature when
written by perceptive and talented men. We knew that as well
as they did, but were far less sure which was talent and which
merely experimental. They wished to upset all the old categories and set up new ones, and they wished us to help them
do this before the end of the month. The war had disturbed old
values, though in the earliest twenties it had not produced, at
least in the United States, a recognizably new literature. Yet
readers of T. S. Eliot's *The Waste Land* in 1922 were aware
that something definitely new (in talent as well as in values)
had come into English. It was difficult to tell from what they
wrote just what our modernists wanted, since they were more
eager to attack other modernists than to blast accepted books.
Yet one thing was clear, like Walt Whitman in 1855, they felt
that the diction of current art was inadequate to express new
sets of experience. So far they had little to say in any of the
new modes, though much to feel, and there were no T. S. Eliots
among them. The sayers in this country were the E. A. Robinsons, the Robert Frosts, the Willa Cathers, whose roots were in
our Age of Confidence, and who were summing up magnificently the results for our day of the Great American Experiment.

The great controversy of the ideologists, which was not to
reach its peak until the nineteen-thirties, nor translate itself
into action until the preliminaries of the second World War,
was already beginning. But my modernist callers did not want
to live their lives differently; they wished to find new ways of
describing how people they did not like lived their lives. They
differed from a Sinclair Lewis chiefly in experimenting with new
techniques. One of their passwords was 'non-representative

art,' which meant essentially to work with what I suppose Santayana would call essences, letting form and story be deduced by the mind, if comprehended at all. Some of them were wild men (I had met their confrères in the London world) whose restlessness was more significant than anything they wrote about it. Others, like Paul Rosenfeld, Malcolm Cowley, and Kenneth Burke, were to build distinguished careers on intuitive recognitions of new trends in the art of literature forecasting new tastes.

I myself was deeply sympathetic but puzzled and skeptical. Change was coming, but it did not seem wise or right for a magazine like ours to shift the emphasis from the fine products of a summary period in order to proclaim a new age which clearly had not arrived. Also I thought that new ways of estimating the imaginations of men were reflections of profound changes in our attitude toward God, Fate, and our fellow man. The new semi-science of psychology was already indicating that such a turn in man's long road was ahead of us. But were these restless prophets, who were not themselves creative artists like T. S. Eliot, able to see beyond their own dogmatisms? I was dubious because of my own past experience when, in company with many another literary historian, I had trotted after Brunetière and his philosophy of literary evolution only to land in a swamp of bad criticism based on ill-comprehended science. I had my choice, to be labeled conservative or radical, and chose to be called conservative; an interesting experience, for in New Haven I had always been regarded as radical. But conservative in this sense only, that I decided our chief function was intelligent teaching, and that we would let the vigorous Little Magazine of the day conduct the reconnaissance, since what was said there could be written for professionals who alone at that stage would find much of it intelligible. We kept the emphasis of *The Review* upon books of high artistic value (fortunately there were many of them) which were not only successful in their art, but were being read by the intelligent public. Modernist prophecy we in no way suppressed, but set it in the back of the magazine, and published much prose and verse from abroad as well as at home which in our opinion gave samples of the future. And we offered a column

now and then even to the wild men. Ezra Pound, who was going wild by this time, offered to do some prophesying, but characteristically sent in comments on a local and not important
art show instead — and was abusive when not paid twice our
rates. Our readers were sufficiently warned of rough water
ahead, and told of new types of genius appearing. As I look
back, I think our compromise was right. In these early twenties Americans were writing books that no change of taste is
likely to exclude from our permanent literature. What the
Frosts and the Glasgows were publishing was finished art representing a great period of American life at its peak, even if,
perhaps, nearing its end. By the nineteen-thirties the story
would be different. A critic's (or a reviewer's) first job is to
estimate, not to prophesy.

There were other contributors, less erudite but equally eccentric, who could usually be found in our anterooms. Not a
week passed without a visit from at least one indignant and
usually hungry poet. We were still in what is called the Renaissance period of American poetry. Poetry was being more widely published and more widely read than since the mid-nine-
teenth century, with the natural result that more young men
and women than usual decided that they were predestined to
greatness in verse. I can, unfortunately, record no genius
picked up in our reception room, and only one considerable
reputation. The good poetry, and we published much that has
since gone into the anthologies, came by other routes. Our visitors were usually youngish men who had been born too late to
speak with the fire of discovery of new poetry in America, and
too soon to be pioneers of the new age coming. This, however,
is a generous statement. Usually they were only mediocre writers who could put on a better show with verse than with prose.
If they proved anything, it was that the garret-and-starve tradition had outlived its validity. No writer had to starve any
more, at least in New York, nor to ask that his weak efforts
should be published in order that he might have time to learn
his technique and thus grow great. My own proffered advice
(brutal because I am not a poet but at least objective) was that
no creative artist can write more than three hours a day, which
left time enough in a society like ours to earn a modest liveli-

hood, all a poet has the right to ask. Bad advice, I think, for a Shelley or a Keats, but not for a Shakespeare or a Milton. But then no Keats or Shelley or their palest similitude ever appeared in our office. Yet by way of insurance, and because we respected even the resolve to make literature, we set up a little fund, and many a youngster just come to New York was helped to a meal or so and given at least sympathy when he needed it most. It was usually much better for the magazine to feed him than to publish his poetry.

I learned more from the mail about the practice of poetry — or rather verse — in the United States than from our reception room. I discovered that verse-writing in materialistic America could only be described as a passion. Other editors must have long been familiar with this fact, but I do not remember seeing it discussed except as a comic trait of the 'booberie.' It is much more than that. No sooner did our *Review* begin to get around the country, with its poetry well displayed on the front page, than trickles, then a flood, began to seep into our mail bags from a vast, subterranean, muddy sea.

I cannot be sure, of course, but I believe that more so-called poetry is written in the United States than anywhere else in the world. The long envelopes poured in by every mail from all over the United States, Alaska, and our insular possessions. Evidently there was a nation-wide chorus of singers, welcoming every new opportunity to be heard. Some of this verse, of course, was written by crack-pots, or by the utterly naïve, the kind that gets printed in very rural newspapers and the *Congressional Record*. A tiny portion was professional. But in general this poetry was quite unconscious of rhythm, and so differed from folk poetry, and was built out of platitudes and *clichés* on a rhyming scheme. Rhyme was its only distinction from bad prose. I still remember a couplet from a poem descriptive of life in Iowa, more rhythmic than most, and funnier —

> *The pigs were resting in the shade,*
> *Sleeping sound while pork was made.*

But no matter how commonplace were these streams of verse rippling down from our emotional watershed, I still call them very significant. Most of them run underground, I suppose, and never see the daylight of print. In every American community there must be at least ten times as many hearts whose secret vice is poetry as the inhabitants suspect. It is a secret passion for self-expression, but it is much more, for no matter how commonplace the poems, they at least indicate idealism, aspirations, and cravings for beauty and emotional truth. Perhaps — I should say probably — they are unconscious reactions of the somewhat sensitive mind to the standardized life of Main Street. But this generalizes too far. The America most of these verses celebrate is not what we know as Main Street, but the country, or the shaded rows of by-street houses, and a life a little dull, but as contented as the freshly mown grass plots. Life on such a low plane is too easy for anything but descriptive poetry, and that is what we usually got, with enough vague desire for something livelier to uncover a not too palpitating heart. They knew what they wanted, these versifiers, even if they had not learned to feel it deeply or to say it with any beauty or power.

ᘓᗑ 5 ᘓᗑ

The Literary Zoo

CRITICISM has been called, by writers who have suffered from it, a parasite on literature. This is not true, for criticism itself is, or should be, creative. But I agree that its relation to books is somewhat like the doctor's to the human body. If life and books were not always struggling to be born and to survive, there would be no doctors and no critics. Critical magazines are by-products of literature, and literary editors should be (but seldom are) more concerned with authors of the books they review than with their staff of reviewers. Either extreme is bad, for in literature the book is nearly always more important than its writer; and a review is usually to be praised for what it does, and not for what it is as a piece of self-expression. Nevertheless, the great experience for me in New York was to see in person as well as in print the literary and literary-journalistic fraternity of authors — if so warm a term as fraternity can be applied to so jealous a profession. On the whole, I think it can.

When I settled into New York in the twenties, I found the social organization of the writing community there very different from the grouping by coteries with which I was familiar in London. Both societies had their non-resident and resident members. The more distinguished the novelist or poet, the more likely that his hardest work was done in Connecticut or the Middle West, in Dorset or in Wales. For such people New York and London were market towns and social and intellectual clearing-houses. But London for the English writer was much more important than New York for the American. London for him was a social directory as well as a *Who's Who*. There a slowly dissolving class system was still solid enough for circles which seemed to my American eye primarily social. Osbert Sitwell and H. M. Tomlinson might be writing some of the best prose of the decade, but you would not expect to meet them at the same address. Lady Colfax's parties (food, wine, and talk all excellent) were evidently intended to bring together a new aristocracy of art, successful both in finance and social esteem, and an earlier aristocracy of birth or of money. Rustic or proletarian talent was not to be seen there, unless from the stage or the pictures. Nor earnest minds whose work was better than their clothes or their manners. Nor the unpublicized but greatly gifted, who cared more for their art than for readers. They had their own coteries, where it was the talk that satisfied the appetite.

Touching and impressive was the last of the Victorian salons as I knew it in 1918. Over it presided Mrs. W. K. Clifford, widow of a famous Victorian philosopher, author of a one-time daring best-seller called *The Love Letters of an Englishwoman*, protégée of Browning, close friend of the young Kipling and of Henry James. She was at home every Sunday afternoon in her dingy but decorous brick house near Paddington Station, and there one met black-draped or black-suited figures (or so I remember them) who had been associates of Tennyson or the pre-Raphaelites, or literary hostesses in Meredith's or Arnold's day who had written memoirs of their times. And also authors of books long forgotten except by a teacher of English. They still talked brilliantly of names and incidents heard by me with thrills of recognition. The women knew how to be both daring and ladylike, an impossible achievement today, and some of the men, that great legal authority, Sir Frederick Pollock in particular, were truculent to the point of excessive rudeness in a way familiar to me from Victorian novels. No social radicals nor writers about sex or the proletariat in that company, who, however diverse in their heyday, now seemed to have all lived and written together on some staid and respectable London square.

It was different in New York, where the classification seemed to be by skills, temperaments, and degrees or kinds of success, with little reference either to social or financial background. How could there be, since nearly everyone had come to New York from somewhere else and was trying to find a place in what was rapidly becoming the least stratified city in the world.

I spent the summer of 1920 in the bachelor quarters of Franklin P. Adams (F. P. A.), then writing his column 'The Conning Tower' in the New York *World,* which everyone who wished to be regarded as intelligent was reading, especially for its departments and Frank I. Cobb's admirable editorials. My first introduction, therefore, was to the upper level of smart personal journalism. The characters of the scene were well-paid short-story writers, editors of highly personal columns, clever artists, popular musicians, semi-professional conversationalists, and dramatists of the new satiric school. Some proved to be far less important than they were supposed to be then; a few (a very few) more important. I could give a score of names — Edna Ferber, Deems Taylor, Fannie Hurst, Marc Connelly, Henry Sydnor Harrison — but that would be pointless. Their historical existence for many New Yorkers was not so much in their work or themselves as in the columns that recorded sayings and doings. There, and especially in 'The Conning Tower,' they were made to live as a sophisticated society of week-enders, poker-players, light-verse adepts, wisecrackers, sardonic philosophers, and critics skeptical of the current 'normalcy.' The people were real, but that society was invented as much as any satiric novel. It was contrived for the lonely New Yorker, usually new-come to the great city, and yearning for companionship. For him, the wit and intimacy of this lively circle had the heart-warming interest of a society column in a small town. F. P. A. especially offered him a vicarious experience of living on the sophisticated end of a metropolitan Main Street. And these folk, most of whom I came to know, became creatures of the imagination, their society more symbolic than real. Don Marquis of the *New York Sun* dealt in obviously symbolic characters, but the effect was much the same. He was a man as lovable as a Shakespearean clown, with the naïve, romantic idealist's heart, and the same realistic eye. He too was representing in his own ironic fashion a new way of life and feeling spreading outward from New York. His best creations were archy the cockroach, that frustrated but indomitable experimenter in modernism, and mehitabel the office cat, a perfect symbol of the New York cockney, tough, intelligent, and *toujours gai.*

Of course I had come to know more or less well some American writers of distinction when they visited Yale, where I, as assistant editor of *The Yale Review*, had become a greeter in a small way, and shared the opportunities and embarrassments of those who take care of the private life of the great or the near-great on tour. Thus I was responsible for the digestion as well as for the intellectual entertainment of one of the greatest, and certainly the most literary, of American philologists, Horace Howard Furness, Senior, who launched the Variorum Edition of Shakespeare. It was he whose editorial note on a lumbering comment by a German scholar was only a six-word quotation from Sterne,' "My God!" said my Uncle Toby!' A withered little man, nearly eighty, in tight black clothes, with a beaming smile and innumerable anecdotes, he traveled always with his valet, whose duty it was to put him together in the morning and take him apart at night. I first encountered in those years, though I was among the earliest to select for publication some of her poems, Edna St. Vincent Millay. Wrapped in a gown of heavy brocade, she recited before enraptured undergraduates and was, for them, poetry itself as it should be taught.

Vachel Lindsay came to Yale at my suggestion. His reputation seems in eclipse now, but I prophesy endurance for his best poetry beyond much that has been written here since. He made the folk imagination both articulate and symbolic. He was the folk imagination incarnate, and never seemed quite real as an individual person, so that his suicide when he had outlived his time and his talent seemed out of character, as if some legendary creature had discovered that he was only a human and suffering man. I took him to our little Elizabethan Club where Yeats a little while before had intoned his high and mystical poetry. When the audience arrived, Vachel sat down, stretched his wrinkled pants like the legs of an Illinois chicken, dropped his sand-colored eyelids over his pale blue eyes, and began to chant in the nasal voice of a Mid-Western revivalist. The nice boys from the ivory towers of the best schools and the Gothic dormitories of Yale tittered at first. But as he began to swing the persuasive rhythms of *General William Booth Enters into Heaven* and *The Congo*, and as the rich imagery lifted the homely language into poetry, they warmed, and soon were chanting with him. Yet to them it was only a show — America, a rather vulgar America speaking, but not literature as they had been taught to regard literature. Vachel himself came to feel that way about his performance. Like Peter, he denied the spirit that was his true Lord. Years later he confided to me that his true greatness (he was a vain man) was as an art critic! This was nonsense. There is nothing in any modern literature more original, more inspired with a *genius loci* than his best poetry.

Celebrities are too often like circus animals on parade. To know them one has to see them outside the exhibition and in their natural environment of living and working. This I was soon able to do in New York, for in the New York of the twenties there were always more of them visible than elsewhere in the country, and behaving like writers and artists, not as prima donnas or specimens to be seen and heard at a price. That talking, scribbling New York into which I was introduced soon lost its romantic strangeness, and, as it became familiar, divided into categories, like any small town. As an editor, I met sooner or later with all the groups, and as my acquaintance and friends increased in number, I found the best parallel for these interlocking circles of the literary and journalistic in a great New York institution, the Bronx Zoo.

The *haut monde* of the journalistic world, where I was first introduced, the clever people who had made writing a trade and a profitable one — the witty society the columnists wrote about — these had their symbol in the great flying cage of the Zoo, where birds of every size, color, dignity, and indignity flew, squawked, scratched, screamed, and sang. The men and women of this useful society were, like these birds, well fed and profusely articulate. They enjoyed showing off, and had much to show. The successful women who wrote short stories and serials for the mass magazines reminded me of the macaws, decorative if not always beautiful, incredibly intelligent, eager for flattery, disdainful (except in their writing) of the merely human, with always a gleam in their observant eyes which said — some day I may bite you, in print. With them were the flocks of merry little journalists twittering the news of the town. And over the floor stalked the dignified feature writers, the herons, the ibises, the storks, their long beaks ready to impale any idea that looked like food for an article. And one big parrot with a beaked nose, watching the confusion and waiting for a moment's silence to make just the right remark, was F. P. A. himself.

The most talkative, though not the noisiest and dressiest society, was in Greenwich Village. That was the monkey cage of New York, and I mean nothing derogatory, for if monkeys are often imitative and sometimes dirty, they are highly intelligent, quite immune to dull respectability, and always reaching for something new.

Greenwich Village is too expensive now for experimental writers and adventurous intellectuals, who usually have more promise than cash. Its cafés have become tourist resorts and have been cleaned up and restored to at least an appearance of the pre-Civil-War decorum of the days when the Village was built. Only toward the river can you find the old Italian slums, with blonde heads of poetesses glimmering from upper windows. In the earliest twenties we lived in its heart for three years, having found a beautiful house of the eighteen-thirties, with young radical writers on the third floor, and noise and dirt outside our shuttered windows. It was a Tammany-ruled New York then, with bad smells and winter streets blocked with dirty snow or heaps of muddy refuse. In the hard winter of 1920 a dead horse lay for two weeks on a drift in Macdougal Street.

The gathering places for the intelligentsia in those days were not in the speak-easies, which were numerous but expensive, but in garret studios crowded with people, mostly sitting on the floor, blue with smoke, and smelling of bad gin. It was a challenge for a professor come from the respectability of New Haven to join these gatherings, where someone was always talking well if you could hear him, where young people were ridding themselves of inhibitions, and the evil of conformity to mass opinion was the one theme on which everyone agreed. My memory is of a babble of talk in corners and circles in which the word Russia popped like a cracker every few minutes. Yet this was not the Russia of Marxism so often as the Russia of the experimental theater. Most of these young people were not economically radical. Many of them had a small allowance

from home, more a small but sufficient job, and their objection
to capitalism was that in some way, not sharply defined but
having some relation to best-selling novels, Broadway plays,
and million-circulation magazines, it was suppressing art — or
at least their art. Their radicalism was for Joyce and Proust
and Eugene O'Neill against Booth Tarkington, Edith Wharton, and the serial writers in general. I heard of many of them
later on the staffs of *Time* or *Vanity Fair,* or in the best advertising agencies.

Yet it would be a foolish critic who estimated a monkey cage
by its most restless chatterers.   Not one of these gatherings
lacked some daring and sometimes profound spirit who tolerated the confusion because it was, after all, over art and thinking. I remember Dreiser, with heavy forehead and bluish lips,
settled in his convictions with the dignity of an old-man gorilla.
And Eugene O'Neill, sad and sensitive, to be compared to one
of those delicate simians with great eyes who seem to know so
much more than they say. And Hendrik Van Loon who had
married into a Village restaurant, rolling a body as big and
pink as Walt Whitman's and banging down every argument
that was going against him with his great, if rather inaccurate,
erudition. And Malcolm Cowley, pensive and analytical. And
Ernest Boyd, his clothes always matching his red-brown beard,
fleering and flying at whatever was being talked about at the
moment. He did a good demolition job on fake reputations,
but broke his shins once in print over Milton, who was everything disagreeable that Boyd said of him, but also (what he
never mentioned) a great poet.

In spite of much posturing and some insincerity, I liked the
Village assemblies because at them the present, no matter how
distasteful to the talkers, was made alive. At some of the clubs
or at sedate dinner parties I met another and older breed, that
also found the present distasteful, but only because it was unlike the past. These were the elephants of criticism, old or
looking old and unperturbed by novelty. The less creative
among them controlled the space for criticism in the Sunday
supplements and the general magazines, and they were good
writers, even if the current literature they chose to praise had
hung a little too long and was beginning to smell of a passing

age. Novelty for them was a paper bag, absurdly blown up, to be stepped upon by the elephant and burst with a sound pleasing to all conservative ears.

Of a like age with these fading Titans of criticism were the remnants of the novelists' hierarchy of the last generation, who grumbled and growled at the new men and especially the new themes. William Dean Howells belonged with them, but his mind had stayed perceptive into old age in all but a few directions. I saw him at close quarters once and knew that, though easily shocked, he neither grumbled nor growled. Another old man, however, and a radical realist in his youth, I knew quite well, and often talked with him. Hamlin Garland sought me out as having an editor's power to accept or reject, and urged me to take a stand against the new fiction. His abuse was general, but what he had in mind particularly were the social studies of Sinclair Lewis with their belittling of the descendants of the old frontier, and especially anyone and everyone who, like Sherwood Anderson, dealt frankly with sex. I think myself that the tabu on sex in the nineteenth-century novel was much less harmful than the apostles of a new freedom supposed. Sexual excitement, so opinion held then, was either private and so not a fit subject for public art, or it was against the current moral code and so should be kept out of print, although unhappy results could be used for a climax. The limitations imposed by such a tabu are obvious; yet few then questioned the wisdom of reticence. It was a rule, and in literature, when a rule is accepted, there is plenty to write about without breaking it. I doubt whether reticence in matters of this kind troubled such writers as Poe, Hawthorne, or Mark Twain, or whether their works suffered from it. Later, H. H. Boyeson complained of the iron madonna (the iron virgin would have been an even more appropriate term) for whom American literature must be censored. Howells was aware of her. Whitman, of course, broke through the tabu. Yet the anger, the personal grievance displayed by a once independent mind like Hamlin Garland's made me wonder whether my analysis did not stop short of the whole truth. I began to see that far more was involved than I had supposed. A fundamental change in the relations of men and women had been under way for half a century, and those who fought for the old tabus were really fighting against a tide that seemed to be swirling them from old moorings. Their violence was personal. More of this later, for the impact of these changes became more dramatic in the later nineteen-twenties.

6

Who Was Who

WHEN I BEGIN TO THINK of individuals among these writers, my parallel with the Zoo loses much of its value. As Thoreau said, everything is essentially the work of one man, yet Thoreau was too anti-social to admit the other half of the truth, that all works of art, with the rarest exceptions, spring from coteries or groups of the like-minded, and are strongly influenced by their audiences. Thoreau himself had few intellectual friends, but the intimate group which contained Emerson, Alcott, Channing, and Hawthorne, if too universe-minded to be limited by the word 'coterie,' was one of the most dynamic and productive groups in America. In any case, whoever was around and about in the nineteen-twenties with a lively interest in the shapes of the imagination must remember better than the coteries the chosen creatures of the literary epoch. I mean the strongly creative writers who came to full power a little before this time and to full influence in the twenties. I know that it is artificial to separate them from the European ideas to which they often responded, and which they influenced in turn; and impossible to place them in literary history without analyzing the last confident phase of the nineteenth century from which they sprang. But this book is a memoir, not a critique, and at this point at least I am more interested in the memory of personalities than in critical analysis. And I shall limit my portraits to the Americans I knew who seem to me now to have been in the midstream of the course of American literature.

These men and women were the final product to date of our literary art. They were not necessarily the best known of our writers, not the most 'advanced,' but they were the most mature and, in my opinion, the best in art. I choose among them for this memoir those I knew well enough to retain strong impressions of mind and personality drawn from life as well as from books. To resume the comparison with the Zoo, they were the stately herbivores, or the great cats agile and powerful, who seemed to have come to the end of an evolutionary curve that reached its height for them in these years. Such writers were no longer a becoming as so many American writers since the classic pre-Civil-War period have been, and as the Hemingways, the Fitzgeralds, the Dos Passoses, and, in a different category, the Wilders and the Benéts were in the earlier twenties. They were such a fulfillment as often comes at the end of an age, before new and usually calamitous events shake society and a new philosophy of living begins to take over.

Of those I knew well, the most provocative was that strange genius Clarence Day. Ironic, an unsparing realist with a kind heart (how American is this Hegelian antithesis!), he was admired by a few in his lifetime for his satire sharp as an unsuspected razor blade, and known by millions after his death as the creator of the affectionate high comedy, *Life With Father.* He came closest, I think, to Montaigne of any American of our day.

Clarence had been in Yale just before my time, and had graduated into his father's business of finance. Here he learned, if it was not congenital with him, the excitement of speculation. I think he was a gambler by instinct, the appeal being, not profit as such, though he liked money, but the opportunity of studying human nature, particularly his own, in the tensity of expectation. He was shrewd, but as incurably optimistic in business as he was realistic in his judgment of character and temperament. The world for him was a chance for dangerous play, in which men and women differed from the various animals they resembled chiefly in being unaware of their limitations. He liked his world.

Toward middle age a chronic arthritis got the better of him at last and set him on his back for life. Already he had indicated literary power in an extraordinary class-book edited by him, which told without malice the truth about his classmates — something unprecedented in collegiate experience. By the

time I came to know him he had published *This Simian World*
(1920), one of the least known of first-rate American books, and
was beginning the series of sketches called *Life with Father* and
God and My Father, which he intended to be foundations of a
play. Some of these I published in our *Review.*

When I first began to visit Clarence, usually at such incon-
venient hours as six to eight P.M. or between midnight and two
in the morning, he was a spectacle as well as a delight. By this
time he was almost rigid except at the neck and waist, and
slept, worked, ate on a long high bed-table on which he was
stretched like a mummy. He would be dressed in a kimono of
some austere brown material; his head was bald, what hair he
had and his beard, when he wore one, bright red. His eyes
were bright blue, and their flashes and his ready smile and frequent rages were like fire in the stiffened mass of a volcano.
There was frequently someone waiting to see him in the anteroom; often a woman who had come out of turn. He was mag-
netic to women and always offered a North to their South. If
they brought him flowers, he would toss them out of the window beside him. He hated outdoors and the country.

Yet the secret of his power over a multitude of friends was
not his helplessness nor his eccentricity. He had the gift of
making his visitors talk with complete honesty about themselves, and not from conceit. Something he said to each caused
a self-discovery which led to confessions of impulses, desires,
and ideas, which, in his presence, always seemed to come out
straight and clear. The craft of writing and the profession of
publishing fascinated him. Writing as an art bored him unless
it said something and said it strongly. He respected journalism more than literature because someone was always ready to
pay for it, which showed that it was wanted. Yet when he began to write himself he wasted no time on hack work, but did
what he wanted, guessing that sooner or later this would be
more profitable, as it was. Literature, according to him, was
only a secret vice unless it reached the general public. He
raged at editors (myself included) and publishers who would
not get for him an immediate success. We were asleep, he said,
and preferred a small public for what we thought was literary
to the large public which takes trash and tripe only because it

cannot get what it wants and needs. His sketches (both in line and in words — the former often savage) he dropped as a wandering hen drops her eggs, anywhere they could be published, best pleased when they reached the most readers. When the publisher of his books insisted that his work was caviar for the sophisticated, he thumbed his nose at him and got a contract with the New York *Sunday American,* which no intellectual ever read. He knew that his studies of an American family which lacked self-knowledge and was therefore fit for irony, had the stuff out of which popularity was made, but only his wife believed him; and it was she who carried his work after his death to the kind of success he would have thoroughly approved.

Among the novelists who reached their height of achievement in the twenties was Willa Cather. She had already shown what Americans could do with the rich experience of pioneer life. A personable woman, of finely cut features, with a delicate flush which deepened when ideas warmed her imagination, she was definitely an intellectual aristocrat. She had a way of summoning you to a tea or a conference which proved not the less stimulating because commanded. Actually, as one soon found out, she was guarding her working hours and working energy. She had a fierce devotion to her art which was not vanity, but came from a clearer view than that of most of her contemporaries of the difficulty of achieving even a relative perfection. You can read about it, written of others but applicable to herself, in a book of her essays called *Not Under Forty*.

Willa Cather's mind had the precision of a scholar's, the penetration of a critic's, and the warm intellectuality of a creative artist. She had led an active editorial life on the staff of the old *McClure's,* which had put the vitality of new European minds and the audacity of the American muckrakers into a cheap and readable magazine just when the genteel periodicals were going stale. It could be tough; it was sensational; respectable editors regarded it as a portent of vulgarity — which only shows that the vulgarity of one generation may prove to be the respectable realism of another. She had done her job in the literary, not the muckraking department, and had wholeheartedly retired into the art of fiction.

As we sat talking, she would ask me the news of that old
editorial world; what had happened as a result of this or that,
or where were the old fighters now and what were they doing.
I could only reply that I lived in an ivory tower in those days
and did not know the answers. But this was an introduction to
our real talk. Miss Cather was one of the few writers I have
known who passionately desired to talk of the craft of good
writing with only the most indirect reference to her own work.
In this she had what I should call a Gallic mind. The subject
matter of her most important books was taken from what was
most vital in American pioneer experience, yet the tradition of
her craftsmanship was certainly French. The name of Flaubert
was often on her lips. She had the not uncommon passion for
perfection — but what she liked to analyze as we talked was
what constituted perfection for a given situation or a theme.
This is French rather than English or American, and when
pursued in writing by an Englishman or an American often
leads to artificiality. Not so with her. She wished to know how
the great ones achieved, not to imitate them. Her idea was
that the consummate artist in fiction gave himself entirely to
the situation he chose for his story, following its *nuances,* not
shaping it to preconceived effects. That was what she wanted
to talk about; what she did herself in *O Pioneers!* and *Death
Comes for the Archbishop.*

Not long ago I sat with Miss Cather at a meeting of the National Institute of Art and Letters, at which she was to be given
the gold medal in fiction, their highest honor. She had been
ill, her face was drawn, her pace a little unsteady. That day a
special award for lifetime service was given to Samuel McClure,
then well into his eighties. When he was helped to the platform, the color came back to her cheeks, and, with the warm
impulsiveness one finds always in her best heroines, she ran
forward and kissed and embraced him. I do not suppose that
Willa Cather was the greatest American novelist of the nineteen-tens and twenties, bigness was not her *métier* — that she
left to the Upton Sinclairs, who had less art. Certainly she was
the most skillful, and one of the best.

My first meeting with Ellen Glasgow was uncomfortable. It

was some time in the twenties, when she already had a long list
of titles under her name. Her face was like a camellia, one of
those tight-petaled camellias of old Southern gardens, that risk
and often defy the February frosts, and retain a virginal fresh-
ness even when age has touched them. Ellen Glasgow was very
deaf, and this in a day when corrective instruments were in the
experimental stage. Hers was a sound contrivance on a long
cord, which she would move from place to place on the table
where the conversation looked promising. When it plopped
down before me, I talked alternately to the disk and to her,
with not very satisfactory results. The truth was that I was
then unfamiliar with her earlier books, though I had just read
her starkly realistic *Barren Ground.* Nor was I aware that she
was a major historian of our times who had, almost single-
handed, rescued Southern fiction from the glamorous senti-
mentality of the Lost Cause. Somehow I stumbled in my ignorance, and the box was lifted in the middle of a sentence
and planted elsewhere. But it came back again later, and our
friendship dated from that day.

We visited her often in her old stone house in Richmond,
the most comfortable house I have ever stayed in, with good
food, good talk, and good drinks inside and a cardinal and
mocking-bird in the garden. But always my best communica-
tions with her seemed through her books. Always I came home
to pull down one of her volumes to carry on the discussion in
my own way. For, like Willa Cather, she talked constantly of
the technique of writing, but always it was her own, except for
brilliant sallies at successful contemporaries whom she regarded
as incompetent writers or able charlatans. There was some
vanity here, and vanity, of course, is the occupational disease
of writers. It is the vanity of the parent for the child. But there
was a much deeper reason for her egocentricity. Her endeavor
to get the time values of the life she knew best into literature
— a half-century's task — is not easily matched in our American story for steady, coherent purpose. It was not really vanity
that made her talk so much in that meticulous voice of the deaf
with its slight crackle. It was the desire that her total purpose
should not be overlooked in the success of some of her most
popular volumes. There has been no greater theme for our

fiction than the wreck of a way of life in the South after the great war. Her strong, clear imagination preserved that story for us, and both the romantic and the sordid values of the one great defeat and reversal suffered by Americans in three centuries of history.

She came to live near us one summer in a Connecticut farmhouse, bringing with her the household which was her background, a companion friend and Negro servants. Her *entourage* was not at home in New England. They found snakes in the well, an unfamiliar language in the stores, dangerous adventures in their car on the thank-you-marms of dirt roads in the hills. Ellen was unperturbed. She read the austere scenery as if it were a book about the people it had shaped. She felt that New England, if it had been her theme, would have been as much within her competence as the South. Yet it never warmed her. The stories from the local folklore which I told did not much interest her. For her they were not significant.

The chief figure in the American phase of the literature of the early nineteen-twenties was, I believe, Sinclair Lewis. He was one of those hot personalities who would have been at the bawling center of controversy in any age. I think he was violently misunderstood then by the public at large and has never yet had a final and satisfactory estimate. For he was too deep in social history to be valued rightly by the critics of belles-lettres, and too powerful an artist to be read objectively, as, for example, Upton Sinclair, by the uncritical. Walt Whitman, in his 'Democratic Vistas' of 1871, had called for a 'literatus,' a prophet-poet who should come out of the people, and preferably from the West. He should be an image-maker who would show us how and why we were being shaped by democracy. Walt was thinking of a mystic orator like himself, a spokesman for spiritual expansion and beauty of life for the common man. What we got — and from the democratic West — was Sinclair Lewis, a young man who thought (as indeed Whitman did also) that democracy was not functioning for the individual; a man with a sharp eye and a raucous voice, who instead of orating idealism exposed the vulgarities, the materialism, and the spiritual emptiness of the sons of the pioneers. He was an image-maker — we shall not forget George F. Babbitt — but his images were designed to irritate, not uplift, the public, and most emphatically did so. Apparently he felt that democracy, especially in the Middle West, needed a whipping before it was told to be good and glorious. But to number Sinclair Lewis among the debunkers would be a stupid mistake.

I have known him well, though never intimately since our paths seldom cross, for forty years. I knew him first as a Yale undergraduate, a nonconformist, getting what he could — and he got a great deal — from that stronghold of intelligent conformity where radicals, once they are accepted as Yale men, can say or do what they please. (It is said that Gibbs, greatest of mathematical physicists, was saved for his university by some elder statesman who remarked that he might be incomprehensible, but he was a good Yale man.) Sinclair Lewis would often drop in for an evening in the room in 'dirty Durfee' where I was living with Chauncey Brewster Tinker. This would have been in 1906. Tinker, a conservative in literature but never a reactionary, was a brilliant lecturer who could make tradition glow with life. The young man and the older were temperamentally alike, though worlds apart in their ideas of how to live. Both had ignitable minds which would explode at a hint of the cheap or the false, but as to what were true and what were false values, they could seldom agree. For Sinclair derived his emotional consents from nature as interpreted by the scientists, and Tinker from Doctor Johnson and the Word of God as validated by the Anglican Church. Thus it came about, as often with a child of nature, that Lewis worshiped Tinker's impeccable taste while distrusting his philosophy; and Tinker was increasingly annoyed by a writer whose idea was to lash sensual man into finding his own way to salvation. Santayana would have enjoyed their conversations, then and later, and been supercilious to both.

Of course, in those college days we saw in Lewis only an insuppressible energy, and I did not hear much of him again until *Main Street* in 1920 and *Babbitt* in 1922 made him famous. If *Main Street* is reread now, what is most striking is Lewis's naïve belief in 'culture' and 'the intellectual,' popular terms in his day at Yale. Carol Kennicott fails entirely in her attempt to make life beautiful for Gopher Prairie, and it is clear that Sinclair's own idea of reform at that time went little farther than awakening his duck-shooting, back-slapping friends from a mental lethargy. Education was what they needed, in which he followed H. G. Wells, who was his Doctor Johnson. It was not his philosophy but his incomparable powers of observation that made him a great novelist. When he came to *Babbitt* he had begun to digest his own education, saw that George was a tragic figure, and with complete fidelity to every mood and gesture brought him to life, letting him buzz down man's long road over concrete and under green lights until he discovers that his experience has been all mileage without a destination.

Too many easy judgments were formed of Lewis in his percussion-powder days. He had a face of boiler plate, but his mental skin was as sensitive as a baby's. If he drank, it was, as with Poe, to quiet his nerves, usually with contrary results. There was a noble independence about the man, to be respected even when he used it to sneer at the genteel age, which was his enemy. I have seen him rise from a dull dinner party, say 'I'm tired,' go through the nearest door, pop into the most available bed — and emerge two hours later in excellent humor. Once he chose an ambassador's room, which made difficulties with protocol.

But Lewis was always and essentially a realistic idealist, a true, if surprising, product of the liberal late nineteenth century in which he had his roots. He was always, you will note, on the side of the angels. But his eye and ear were too honest to please the respectable, who prefer *genre* paintings to candid photographs. The trouble was not his choice of characters — the country was full of Babbitts and Elmer Gantrys. It was the overpowering and often unpleasant reality he gave to them. Only in moments of intense perception do we see both type and individual in a person we like or hate. We are blind to the type, or do not recognize the individual. Sinclair's gift was for realizing, and always with a satiric point. Dialogue was his best medium. Some of his most brilliant dialogues were never written down. Once at my house he rode high on an imaginary conversation between Shakespeare and Ben Jonson. Jonson was the patronizing high-brow; Shakespeare was the popular writer, humble in a dangerous way before Art and Learning. He could give the people what they wanted, since he was not writing for posterity like his learned friend. To this day I see Lewis's quizzical Will and pompous Ben more vividly than in any historian's portrait. It is the art that Shakespeare himself practices in Polonius and Falstaff, and excellently adapted to letting society recognize its own warped or frightened soul behind an inescapable verisimilitude.

The best phrase for Lewis was written by Horace when he spoke of the writing world as a *genus irritabile*. He was a fighter, as little restrained by good taste as an angry cat. Yet when he was not irritated he was generous and fair. I have heard him defend and praise at a public dinner, a fellow writer (equally irritable) who had but recently attacked his intellectual integrity.

Among the poets of the day my circulation was less extensive than among the novelists — and this was true also of the playwrights. I not only saw less of them (except William Rose and Stephen Benét), I wrote less about their work. My brother-in-law, Lee Wilson Dodd, with whom from our undergraduate years in Yale to his death in 1933 I was intimately associated, was both playwright and poet. Perhaps this is why I have been more conscious of my limitations as a critic of poetry and of the theater than elsewhere. I doubt whether a critic without an instinct for expression in recurrent rhythms or a first-hand knowledge of the requirements for stage presentation can go further than general philosophical and literary criticism in these arts. Certainly I never could, and I have always breathed most freely among story-tellers, critics, scholars, essayists, and biographers. Yet the major figures of an epoch are many-sided. Among the poets of the early nineteen-twenties I knew some well, and I cannot leave this chapter unenriched by their names.

The beginning of the American poetical renaissance for me was Robert Frost's *North of Boston*, which I read in 1914, a memorable experience. His rhythms, lifted from the colloquial speech of New England into a style exactly suited to his subjects, pleased me unutterably, since this was what the new American realists in fiction were just beginning to do in prose. He did not at first attract the college-trained, who would have expected Whitman's 'literatus,' when he appeared, to write like Tennyson. I heard a young English instructor reading aloud to another 'The Death of the Hired Man' from *The New Republic,* where it first appeared. 'Some rural boob trying to make the unpoetical poetic,' was the comment. When, later, Frost came in person to our Elizabethan Club, it was a different story. His domed head, his drawled questions to himself, so hard to answer — the man at least was a born teacher, his audience said, and a New Englander, not some East Side foreigner or radical.

Frost is not to be associated with New York, and yet, although I have tramped with him on Vermont mountains and sat with him in his Vermont dooryard and been with him at many an evening session from Cambridge southward, I see him best in the early twenties perched on the edge of a bed in the Yale Club in New York, where we talked until early morning. His well-known face — early Roman done by a Greek artist — is immobile except when he reads or talks. As for his poetry, it is proverbial wisdom against a native background so accurate in its projection of virile New England beauty that only Thoreau and his kind are worthy to praise it. And the wisdom speaks through character. There is more character in Frost's brief narratives than in any of our contemporary novelists, although, when it comes to personality, the best exceed him.

We seldom talked of his poetry, but met more easily on a different ground, where I was a speculative professional and he an amateur of genius. I mean teaching, which, being an art, is often misused by the professionally trained and needs correction from self-taught talent, as painting needs a fresh eye. Frost, like so many of our great New Englanders, with whom I number him, although he was born in California, was a congenital Yankee educator. His poems are ways of seeing and saying the truth. In his talk he annotated their themes, rambling, like a Platonic philosopher, round and round the point, never crudely stating it lest it cease to be the point and become a dogmatism.

I think Frost must have talked much to himself (as I have heard him do in company) before he began to write poetry.

Certainly in talk he became more and more articulate, the nearer he got to the colloquial speech of such wise and weather-bitten farmers as speak in his poems. As he spoke they (and not we) seemed to be answering him in his imagination. I make no difference in my memory between his talk and the best of his poems, except that in them the imagination had ceased experimenting, having found the images it needed and the rhythms required. Perhaps the Chinese are doing the same thing now that they are making a literature out of their own colloquial tongue.

I wish I could add Edwin Arlington Robinson to this gallery, but I knew him only as a lank, quiet man, shy except in talk of public affairs. The fault, of course, was mine. His early poetry had touched my intellect rather than my emotions, and in the pleasure of finding so approachable a personality in a writer of such cerebral power, I enjoyed the human and forgot the poet. But another of that constellation, Elinor Wylie, I did know well. Many have written about her, and my only excuse for adding the one word more which so tempts the memoirist is that she interested me both as a human being and as a superb lyric poet.

Elinor, when I first knew her, which was shortly after 1920, belonged very definitely among my animal parallels. She was a bird-of-paradise, but not like the silly show-off creatures of the natural history books. I have watched them alive in their cages at the Bronx Zoo, noting their streamlined bodies, their brilliant eyes, absorbed and withdrawn. Then suddenly comes some impact of emotion from another cage, or perhaps only a beam of spring sun. The body of the bird is held rigid in a posture of oblation while feather by feather the plumes rise and then fall in a shower of vibrating color. But the oblation is not to the spectator; rather to some invisible power beyond sight. That was Elinor sometimes, not when she read her poetry, but when some thought of her own, or challenge from another, had roused her imagination; or when she was angry, which was not seldom. Then her eyes flashed topaz, her color flushed, and the swanlike neck which was her distinguishing feature seemed poised to strike. Such encounters, and I had several, always reminded me of a fencing bout I had once with an Irish swan, with only a cane to protect me from his fierce bill.

My defense in bouts with this creature (I mean Elinor, not the swan) was my unqualified admiration of her best poetry. This she knew; but knew also that I was critical of her sometimes ruthless sacrifices of anything to literature. I was a Quaker and she was a poet, so naturally we clashed. Yet so long as my spirit praised, she, like any artist, took no real offense from my words.

Elinor Wylie as a writer was of no time — and least of all of the present. Even her delicate, fragile prose romances, such as *The Venetian Glass Nephew*, in which history becomes as symbolic as a Hindu carving, refuse to be set into the frame of her period. I know few novels that so depend upon the overtones of their style, and that is their weakness. But in her poetry there was no weakness. She was a perfect lyricist, by which I mean that content and poetic form were inseparable. And the content of thought for each of her best poems was a hymn to intellectual beauty. In this, and in little else, she resembled Shelley, who was confessedly her master. She did not share his revolutionary ardors, being too self-centered. Indeed, she was one of those poets not uncommon in literary history, who escape the sociological critic in search of their ideology as does the lark when you try to clutch him on his nest in the grass.

One personal weakness she had which may explain the narrow limits of her genius. She came of a talented family which, since President McKinley's day, had been leaders in the social life of Washington. Her escape from that conservative society, with its traits of a small Southern town, had been dramatic — a runaway and two divorces, for which she had been cruelly punished by local opinion. Unjustly punished, for no one who knew her well could doubt that whatever pain she inflicted, hers had been greater. And whenever her name came into print, the same lengthening story would be dragged out from the newspaper morgues. When I knew her, she had a morbid sensitiveness to gossip. Fearless in literature, she was afraid of the respectable and the 'unco guid.' I have known her to refuse to give a reading because she had heard that a lady notorious for her aggressive conventionality was to be in the audience. She would have faced Sappho, Shakespeare, or Doctor Johnson — but not the possibility of a snub. I think it was this sharp reaction to the genteel society in which she was born that alienated her from her own American times. In pure poetry, not disembodied but deracinated, she felt safe and at home.

The central figure of the poetic life of the twenties, though not of its literature in general, was Amy Lowell. Yet not so much as a poet as a dynamo, sending impulses of energy wherever interest and excitement were needed. A good poet, an erudite and sometimes insolent critic, a rich and aggressive personality, she would have been a renowned bluestocking in any age. On the lecture platform, or in her vast home in a park at Brookline, or in her suite at the Hotel Belmont in New York, where she held court for a few weeks each year, she made poetry exciting (as of course it ought to be) and stimulated the adrenal glands of her listeners. Large of body, though not tall, wealthy, a patrician, she was snobbish to those who claimed social equality on any other basis than their talents. In her walled square at Brookline she let fierce dogs roam at night, for since her talking hours were eight to midnight and her working hours midnight to morning, she did not wish to be disturbed by the uninvited. Her house guests she visited at breakfast-time to say good-bye. One frequently impoverished and somewhat impudent poet who came the wrong night was chased up a tree by the dogs, leaving most of his overcoat behind. Miss Lowell, shrewd daughter of the canny Lowell line, argued replacement values for an hour, then began on poetry.

This aristocrat, with a magnificently intolerant mind, had a fierce belief in the nobility of genius, but never concealed her conviction that the Lowells were a superior breed. She imposed her will upon popular audiences — ordered them to read poetry, and read they did. Contradiction she would not, I think could not, endure. Invalid in body, often moving with difficulty, I have seen her sitting at home like a chained eagle, lunging at what she called the pedantries of Harvard, of which her brother was president, or crushing with one claw some reviewer who lacked scholarship and a gentleman's education. A great human being, somewhat childish in her likes and dislikes, but immensely vital, she stirred all of us into activity, poets and critics alike.

I may seem to have drifted from my portrait of a literary magazine in being. And indeed this *Who Was Who* might burst the limits of my book if I should continue with many other literary friends or acquaintances of mine. There were the Colums, Padraic and Mary, a happy pair who could drive criticism and poetic creation in a sound harness. I think of them as Irish in personality, European in mind, in spite of their long residence here and their invaluable contributions to the books of our time. There was Edgar Lee Masters, the man of one great book, written before the twenties; and Leonard Bacon, poet, satirist, scholar, who would have been at home in any full-blooded age of the intellect, but was still little known in the early twenties; and dozens more of whom it would be a pleasure to write. Yet I have not really got away from my theme. In any period like this one literature gives images for the imagination, and some of these are abstract like ideas and ideals, and some are in art, and some in living personalities. As an editor, I was an evaluator, to use a new cant term of the nineteen-forties, and my job was to be familiar with all three modes of image-making, and to clarify communication between them and the intelligent American reader.

↺ 7 ↻

The March of the Ideologies

YES, they began to march in the earliest nineteen-twenties, even here in America. The Russian Revolution was shaking off its blood drops and trying to settle down to a way of life. In 1922 Mussolini had marched upon Rome, as ill-omened and perhaps as disastrous as any invasion of that ancient capital. In New York, literary liberals were angered but not much alarmed. The fetid romanticism of Mussolini's speeches and the decadent romantics of his poet laureate, D'Annunzio, disgusted us. The style was enough to damn these braggarts, we thought. We were still too isolated from the unpleasant truths of Europe to recognize destroying worms erecting foul and poisonous lengths from the flabby body of post-war Europe.

Our literary ideologists among the journalists, novelists, poets, and playwrights were Communists and Fascists. They were few in number but steel in their convictions, and their writings sounded like super-intellectualists demonstrating on Union Square. Most of the Communists were young, highly intelligent, and sincere. I suppose they were what later came to be called Trotzkyites, since they all seemed in favor of an international movement run by a party, and had evidently not considered what a national movement controlled by a dictatorship might be like.

Their concerns, like mine, were with literature, for in its pure and naïve stage, any revolution based on ideas makes its first attacks in literature. Revolutions try to persuade until the slaughter begins, and they seek a voice. In the old *Literary Review* office we never saw the leftists. Owned by a banker and supplementary to a conservative newspaper, our editorial headquarters must have seemed to them a den of capitalistic lions and subservient snakes. Indeed they said so. But when *The*

Saturday Review began its career, obviously like them poor and intellectual, and also (quite unlike them) tolerant, they began to come round to see us, and of course I met them in the Village and elsewhere.

There were two varieties. First were young boys and girls just out of college, well dressed, well educated, and passionate over a first conversion. Actually, they were just a new generation of the old American fighters against plutocracy, and their spiritual ancestors were not Lenin and Marx, but Thoreau, Whitman, Bellamy, Dreiser, and Frank Norris. What they had discovered in Marxism was what youth always craves, a formula that could be made to work without the delay of experience and the trouble of thinking. Marx gave them the formula, which, having little knowledge of the problems of a national economy, they applied to what they did know, or thought they knew — literature. We needed a new literature — that was quite obvious to any creative youth. Base it on Marxism, and presto, old short stories retold themselves in new ways; stale poetic themes got a new point; and originality, and presumably success, could be attained almost overnight. A literary magazine worth its paper would tell the world about it, and about them.

Our visitors, however, were more frequently of another variety. These were the bohemians, the tramps of literature, who had adopted radicalism as a new means of extorting a hand-out. Most of them were satiric poets, or writers of passionately malicious attacks upon whatever or whoever was of good report among the respectable. Communism for them was just another brick to throw. All had grievances, most had lived a tough life, the best were indifferent to truth, the worst (and most frequent visitors) had to be handled with gloves. I mean that at every opportunity they bit the hand that fed them.

It did not yet occur to me that the new faith in violence which was encouraged by all these short cuts to a more perfect state was more dangerous than attacks on existing institutions, many of which needed to be attacked. I believed, and still believe, that the American soil will never be ready for pure Marxism, which is out of date already, and that if we go radical it will be in our own way. But not until 1933, when in Central Europe I first encountered in personal experience a militant

Fascism, did I realize that a resort to violence was the disease of these new ideologies and that a departure from law was more dangerous in a society like ours than the ideologies themselves. For true Communism I have always had not liking, but respect, tempered by hatred of the bloody violence by which it was sought in Russia. In America, where a simple form of Communism was tried in many promising communities before the Civil War, it was destroyed by prosperity. I have lived long enough to see its original aims in Russia thwarted by a dictatorship. But at least even Russian Communism proposed, if it did not actually seek, good life for all men. Those who have read the minute analysis of the Russian system in the Webbs' bulky volume know that the political means were, and presumably still are on paper, although pitifully subject to the will-to-power and the ruthless dogmatism of the governing clique. But Fascism I detested as soon as I realized what it meant, because of its rejection of every ideal for a future society except the efficient tyranny of the few over the many. Our rather distressing plutocracy has been by comparison a mild and limited monarchy. For me, the wave of the future is democracy, often fouled and broken among the rocks, but still rolling on over a long shore. There are, however, in democracy no easy ways to gain the beach.

As the great boom of the nineteen-twenties swelled toward bursting, the young intellectuals became more vociferous and the bohemians screamed out their complexes. They all wanted a new criticism and got it, but the results were disappointing. They bombed successfully the last pillars of the genteel age, yet there was too much rhetoric and invective, and too little analysis of anything but the Marxian formula, which had a way of looking like a foreign uniform whenever it was pulled on a native American. Michael Gold, one of the fiercest of the young Communists, accused Thornton Wilder of being a prophet of the Genteel Christ. This seemed to miss its point, and Wilder went on about his business of finding a new medium for American art, which, in its way, was as radical as Michael Gold's ideas.

What was wrong came out very clearly when this new school turned from criticism to imaginative creation. Then what these agitators called Proletarian Literature was born. It was based on the assumption that our novelists and playwrights had ignored the proletariat as Marx defined it, and which theoretically must, and so did, exist in America. The slavery of the masses to the plutocrat, so they said, had not been described in terms of the proletarian imagination. Here, ready at hand, was the making of a new literature. They made it, but something was wrong. There were one or two good novels, *Union Square,* by Albert Halper, I particularly remember. On the stage, where the play had to be human and dramatic if it was to be presented at all, Clifford Odet's inspiration came from the movement. Yet in general, one has only to look over the selections edited by Granville Hicks in 1935 as *Proletarian Literature in the United States* to see how little he could find worthy even of the short-term life of an anthology. In general and in particular, the more Marxian the book, the less excellent as literature. The difficulty, of course, was that the formula did not fit, and the characters, when they were characters and not synthetic types, had to spend most of their time explaining why they acted as they did.

I was enough interested in these samples of the United States of America according to the formula of a nineteenth-century German Jew, to do some investigating on my own. I was particularly interested to know how those who represented the proletariat, so-called, and who presumably had belonged to the masses themselves, reacted to the picture of their society. I was interested in an audience which ought to be a good judge of the books about it. So we sent out from *The Saturday Review* a questionnaire to labor leaders and spokesmen of the underprivileged who had once been underprivileged themselves. We asked them how many of the proletarian novels they had read, and, in general, what they read in fiction. The answers were about as useful as the answers to most polls and questionnaires, but at least we got one significant fact. Intelligent labor leaders not only did not read proletarian novels, but, with two exceptions in our many replies, had never heard of them. When our correspondents read at all, they read precisely what most bourgeois business men read, except for an occasional tract on radical economics. They had no interest in the writers who

wrote about them, and for good reasons. As Mr. Joseph Free-
man said in the preface to Mr. Hicks's anthology, these novelists and short-story writers may have voted with the so-called
proletariat, may have thought with the Communist Party, but
they lived with the bourgeoisie, which was the real 'mass' of
Americans. And their novels were not even truly representative of this mass. They were steam-heated plants grown in an
intellectual's apartment, and they were definitely not the new
literature, which was already on its way.

I have never set up as a profound critic, but have trusted to
what erudition I possess plus intuition and judgment carefully
and steadily exercised. And it does not require much erudition
in order to know how often in the long history of human imagination a formula, such as Pope's identification of nature with
Homer, or Brunetière's theory of the evolution of literary
types, or Doctor Johnson's application of a strictly Anglican
morality, or the research scientist's belief that art is to be
judged by what science calls a fact — how often such pedantries
have made jackasses out of good critical minds and able practitioners of the art of literature. Among the counts I hold against
that windbag Thomas Carlyle is the harm his vaporous sermon-
izing on society did to one of the great books of our literature,
Moby Dick. Melville, who knew men and events better than
philosophy, was impressed by Carlyle's rhetoric, and swashed
paint by the bucketfuls on his magnificent story, which should
have been as stark and meaty as a late Shakespearean tragedy.

Because these winds of new ideologies blew to me through
literature, and because the defeat of a new international order
for which we had fought had made us for the time intellectual
isolationists, I did not at first see that we in America were feeling a side blast of a world conflict far wider than art. I did not
see that these dogmatisms, which seemed irrelevant both to the
ills and to the ways of American life, were bound to threaten
all free and creative literature, including our own. Fortunately, we had our little interval between wars in which to consider
what was coming up from the roots of the great American experiment, and to become excited about art and truth before all
intellectual energy was devoted to politics and war. We thought
we had been educated by violence in the last war. We were to
learn that it had been only a preparatory-school course.

8

Death of the Iron Virgin

THERE IS ALWAYS a new literature just published, or at least someone thinks so and writes to the editor about it. In these early and mid-twenties, we were as eager as the rest to discover the shape of things to come, but more concerned than the Little Magazines with the good or bad shape of books as they were. Nevertheless, much of my private reading was in experimental or pioneer books, and when I got abroad, as I did three times in the twenties and three times in the thirties, my first question was always, Who or what is new? For years I had been international in my reading, getting translations when I could not manage the originals, which was usually the case except in French. I had been fortunate before I came to New York in a long series of summers in remote (and then quite motorless) Connecticut, where the only excitement was the postman, and an earnest reader could sink before an open fire into books of all the ages for whole afternoons and evenings. Hickory, apple, and ash fires are best for reading; chestnut is too noisy and oak too likely to go out. I stored my fat of good reading then, and have drawn upon it for thirty-odd years, until it grows lean in spots and in others is only a broken-down residuum of pleasant memories.

By the twenties I had enough erudition to stop for a while the storing process and begin to look at current literature in more than one dimension, and especially American books. The aroused nationalism I had brought back with me from the first World War was still strong and unsatisfied. I wanted to know our roots and what had grown from them. It was the time when *The Dial* (the third magazine of the name in America) was printing each month novelties from abroad. It was the time when Marcel Proust and James Joyce became widely known here. I drank in Proust as a great stylist and technician, but there was no subject matter equivalent to his in our American civilization. I had been fascinated by the analytical monologues of Joyce's *Ulysses,* which lifted hidden areas of consciousness into light and escaped entirely from the moral conventions laid out like highroads for the American imagination. Yet *Ulysses* was Catholic in a sense that few Americans, even Catholic-Irish Americans, could absorb intellectually, and it was also defeatist, a word not yet familiar in our vocabulary. I felt, and rightly, to judge from the results, that its influence would be upon technique rather than upon the subject matter of our writers.

It was therefore in no narrow spirit of chauvinism that I began to read widest and hardest in American books, and most hoped for a new literature on our soil, even though all but the best of our contemporary writing was thinner, more ephemeral, and more superficial than its opposites in foreign masterpieces. Yet the apple tells from what tree it rolls. I was interested in the tree as much as in the apple.

Of course, there had to be a new literature after the first World War, but the new men whose background had been a world in confusion had to grow up and become articulate first. There was plenty of novelty in the early twenties, a novelty, however, in appraisal of our past and immediate present rather than a shift of values between one generation and the next. Sherwood Anderson was an example. I knew him, though never well, a handsome, breezy fellow, fond of Village parties and women, whose talk and appearance never so much as suggested (at least to me) the mystical, brooding soul underneath. I 'stuck my neck out,' as the saying went then, in a review of his *Many Marriages* (1922), in which I compared it to *Pilgrim's Progress,* not in excellence, but in its purpose, which was to show a worldly (in this case a mechanized) man who stripped himself of wife, children, and finally of his clothes in the attempt to free his spirit, which in Anderson's hero meant his pinched and starved emotions. It was not a good book, and an Ohio business man stalking naked before his family was definitely absurd. Yet, though I was howled down by rival critics, I stuck to my point, which was that Anderson, though better elsewhere than in his novels, was making us feel the sterilizing effects of industrialism and the dehydration of a culture built on money and standardized for that kind of success. He seemed, and seems to me now, a new voice in the long American conflict between the artist and the plutocracy. The Titans of commercialism in Dreiser's earlier novels, the big, bad wolves of Frank Norris's stories of monopoly, began to seem old-fashioned. Now it was a system that was the villain of the piece, and the heroes were little people, who were to be saved somehow by a release of their inner nature. The Marxist formula was no answer for Anderson. Only in his short stories could he really say his say. Before his death he sent me a message of thanks for my defense of him many years earlier. It pleased me, though if I were to do it again I should take a less chaste and pious book than *The Pilgrim's Progress* for the comparison.

What we were getting in these early nineteen-twenties was really a mopping-up process, in which great talents formed in the Zion of our confidence were revealed in their maturity, and the last hampering conventions of the previous age cleared away for the benefit of all. The most troublesome of these conventions, let us state it formally, was the limitation in British and American literature upon the depiction and expression of sexual desire. It was in these years that the final rounds of a battle almost a century old were fought. This is what Boyesen had meant by the iron madonna. This was the tabu that could not be broken except in the literary equivalent of a speak-easy. This was the suppression that became intolerable for many, though by no means all, good writers when realism triumphed over romance in the early twentieth century. It is probably more than a coincidence that the climax of the battle came in the years when the United States went publicly dry and privately wet, and law was defeated by custom.

There was a real battle — at least in my office and my correspondence. The new frank and free books drew heavy artillery fire from the philosophers, bazooka shots from the flippant, and stink bombs (I use the figure purposely) from the foul-minded seeking notoriety. I do not mean to be flippant myself, for this was one of the most important revolutions in taste since the common people began to read in the nineteenth century. Yet when I remember the humorless books on how to be successful sexually which came to our reviewing shelves every week or so, and the equally humorless denials in other books that sex life in America had any importance except for the birth rate (and to mention that was indecent), it is hard to keep to the point.

The battle for frankness did not begin, of course, in the nineteen-twenties. It was in 1855 that Whitman demanded freedom for soul *and* body, showing what he meant in *Leaves of Grass*. Also the somewhat synthetic bohemians of the eighteen-nineties, such as Edgar E. Saltus, had made quasi-historical characters say and do what the authors did not dare pin upon their contemporaries. Dreiser, too, had broken the tabu, and been suppressed. Yet in these early twenties a new and much extended audience of readers of serious books began to use their common sense, and protest that women, youth, and the home no longer needed protection from the facts of life.

For a while it was the good writers who needed protection against their fellow writers, and still do. The first effect of the cracking of the tabu might well have frightened an editor not well read in pre-Victorian literature. Soon every week brought a new novel to our shelves which was serious, dull, and filthy. No need to mention titles; these books are all dead now. What had been released along with the exploring imagination of the gifted writers were the twisted mentalities who were determined that everything sexual should be revealed, even if they went to jail for it. This is very different from pornography, which is a trade, not a mission, and is always functioning underground.

Such writers did not go to jail, for no one read them except editors and the morbidly curious. The 'unco guid' were after more distinguished scalps, and their instinct was right, even if their tactics were wrong. It was the artists, the real writers with a deserved public, whose books were powerful and persuasive, and these were the ones who suffered. The societies for the Suppression of Vice largely ignored the dull sexual realists, the pornographers, and slickly smutty magazines, and tried to suppress real talent before it could shape the public imagination.

Their great defeat came in the famous decision of Judge John M. Woolsey on the question as to whether the United States Customs should be allowed to forbid the importation of James Joyce's *Ulysses*. Judge Woolsey admitted the indecency, defended its place in a major work of art where sensual man was the subject, and asserted the right of Americans to publish and read books composed in this respect for adult consumption. I was an *amicus curiae,* as they call it, in that action. In my report I insisted that Chaucer's *Wife of Bath's Prologue,* that glory of medieval humor, would have to be thrown to the puritan wolves if *Ulysses* was given to them to tear to pieces. Of course, it was the direction of the attack upon books important because of their originality in the history of literature, that made the situation intolerable. And victory was won, except in Massachusetts. There bad laws and an unnatural alliance between puritanical Catholic Irish and the remnants of Boston's genteel age have kept up the persecution. With the rather lamentable result that, for example, *Strange Fruit,* a controversial novel about the relations of Whites and Negroes in the South, was condemned in Massachusetts and characterized as a sex book because of its use in a passage, where realism justified it, of a four-letter word; while accepted, important controversy and all, in the South where the scene was laid. The old Puritans, of course, were concerned with heresy in religion or politics, not with sexual frankness, which they practiced extensively themselves. But the habit of censorship is persistent, and dangerous because it is so difficult to get agreement upon what shall be censored. After a very few years of the new freedom in the twenties, the sexual novel, whose only excuse was information about the hidden ways of sex, ran its course.

Yet if we had no fanatic for sexual sincerity with the power of style of D. H. Lawrence, in irony we had at least one masterpiece, about which the battle raged. The Virginian, James Branch Cabell, was, in the early twenties and before, an idol for young stylists, and his novel *Jurgen* (1919), belongs, I think, among the enduring contributions to American literature of this period. Cabell was a typical product of an aristocratic society (his own) grown smug and conventional. He was too much of a gentleman to write a book dirty in words and overt acts. I think the new realists of sex must have bored him as much as they did me. Yet the stale and hypocritical moral code of his native state enraged a man who had been nourished by the great romantic literatures. He was no fanatical puritan in reverse like D. H. Lawrence, for whom the full expression of sexual desire was a moral passion. Lawrence's lean, ascetic face, with its sparse red beard, his burning eyes, his dogmatism, gave me a vision of what Savonarola may have been like. I spent an afternoon with him once, coming away with an impression of a will stronger than a reluctant body. He could write like an angel, but it was a rebel angel determined to put sex into heaven. Cabell was no such puritan. His passions of all kinds were, I should say, cool, and it is evident that he shared the conviction of most writers whose youth was passed in the eighteen-nineties, that saying it beautifully (or wittily) was rather more important than what was said. If he could score a hit on the ideals of 'pure Southern womanhood,' then current, or upon the stale religion and stiff moral conventions of his native society, he was content. A little cynical, like most realists, he was more interested in the demolition than the results. Allusion and symbolism were his weapons — both shrewdly contrived to mean much while saying little. Not until the prudes attacked him when *Jurgen* was published did he become elaborately indecent under a veil of words, so that he might safely laugh at his more stupid critics. It was not good for his art, which reached its peak in *Jurgen,* an extraordinary feat of the imagination, even though the new generation does not like the brilliant artificiality of its style. This novel brought about legal action from which he emerged with a grievance as well as a notable victory for free speech. I published a protesting letter from him once, which, on rereading in print, said only too plainly to the shocked editor, See if you can catch me this time. No one did, or, like myself, kept discreetly silent.

Sherwood Anderson and Sinclair Lewis were often charged with obscenity by enemies more angry than discriminating. What their critics really meant was frankness in statement and description, a very different matter. Neither man, so far as I can remember, was ever lewd in his books, as Cabell (like the great satirists of earlier ages) most certainly was, if your mind was sensual enough to translate into gross terms the play of his intellect over passion and prudery. Sexuality, like avarice, greed, jealousy, ambition, and fear, has now taken its rightful place on the artist's palette, to be used or misused according to his honesty, his intellectual health, and his skill. The new American literature of the Hemingways, the Dos Passoses, and the rest, was to benefit by this gain in permissible frankness when frankness is requisite to art, and the art is worthy.

No thorough study of the relations between creative literature and the sexual passions has ever been made, at least for English. We know of English literature that reticence in the affairs of sex did not become a social custom when men and women talked together or read the same books until the decades just before and just after 1800, sometime between Lawrence Sterne and Jane Austen. The Shandy household talked with a freedom which would have shocked a New York dinner table in the twenties, though probably not in the forties. Whereas, among Jane's witty and intelligent females, the merest suggestion of what she called 'indelicacy' was a fault which differed only in degree from adultery. By the eighteen-thirties and forties, restraint on these topics had been frozen into habit, and not only in the fashionable writers of sentiment.

What thawed the ice of linguistic chastity, and made literature again as articulate in sexual passion as it had always been in love? Surely no sudden warming of the amorous imagination. We have testimony that deacons in rigorous New England of the last century were noted for their repertoire of dirty stories, and sociologists believe that the quantity, if not the quality, of sexual relationships outside as well as inside marriage is fairly constant throughout Christian ages. It seems very probable that the revolt against Anglo-Saxon prudishness began with the rise of feminism in the nineteenth century. To put it abstractly, it was an inevitable, if belated, aspect of democratic progress. This was bound to happen when woman began to be regarded as a companion rather than as helpmate of man, with equal rights and privileges. In 1855, Walt Whitman was calling for athletic women, sunburned, vigorous, ripe for love, equal in vital force to men. And after the contemporary

female of the classes who set the fashions had given up in-
validism and the glamour of frailty, which was her first resort
when industrialism and a lowered birth rate had made her job
at home a relative sinecure, such women came in abundance.
They were not likely to be content with books which left a
quarter or a half of their emotional life untold. Any strong-
living woman of the latter nineteenth century knew far more
about the motives of the female characters of the novels she
read than the male authors were allowed to tell. The tabu was
bound to be broken.

Whitman's experience in breaking it was not encouraging.
The hullabaloo set up by the guardians of literary morality
over his alleged indecencies obscured his real greatness and his
full purpose for half a century. My impression gained from a
study of the literary Gestapo that hounded him is that it was
the men, not the women, who felt themselves responsible for
reticence. The men were prudish (though not with each other)
because they seem to have been afraid that the subservient,
loving, and utterly pure women they had created out of their
romantic imaginations would, if encouraged by reading, become human beings with senses like the men's, and get off the
leash of domesticity. Surely this is why Doctor Johnson approved of that snobbish and somewhat stuffy novel *Evelina,*
which Fanny Burney wrote in defense of innocence and 'deli-
cacy.'

Of course, once the 'new woman' (that favorite nineteenth-
century term) began to appear in society in three dimensions,
one of which was sexual, the 'pure woman' who must be protected from even a knowledge of the facts of life began to seem
a little absurd. Honest writers (both men and women) demanded the right to describe a woman with the same freedom
used for a man. Soon they used more freedom. For one cause,
I should say, of the breaking of the tabu was the ancient rancor against the sexual tyranny of wife or mistress which men
had been forced to leave unexpressed in print since the late
seventeen-hundreds. Indeed, it may be said that this moral
grievance had not been allowed to blow off freely since the
Middle Ages, when unromantic monks, frustrated by asceti-
cism, had told the succubus just what she was made of, and de-

scribed woman in general as man's pit of misery and concealer
of weapons never sanctioned by law. The desire to make
woman human in books, now that she had made herself entirely human in social life, was no stronger than the pent-up desire
of men to show that the 'purity' of Victorian literature was the
least characteristic of feminine attributes.

The better-balanced writers of this transitional period broke
the tabu, not because they were more courageous or more vindictive than their Victorian predecessors, but because they were
more truly interested in women as human beings only different
in provocative ways from themselves. The shrinking female
needing protection from the ardent facts of life, the young girl
upon whose chaste imagination no sexual truth must breathe,
did not protest because they no longer existed, if indeed they
had ever existed. Old-fashioned editors in the second decade
of the twentieth century still believed in them. Indeed, Robert
Underwood Johnson of *The Century* is said to have rejected a
frankish story with horror because, as he said, his circulation
list contained 'expectant mothers.' But with feminism realized,
the iron virgin, who had never been more than a symbol, lost
control of the reading lists, and died, except in the imagination
of the most fearful. To be a little cynical myself, men could
now write what they pleased within reason, because, in vast
majority, it was the women now who bought the books.

And then Freud came to general knowledge, absorbed as
foreign philosophies always are absorbed by our native intellectuals, not in his whole, but only in such parts as would
nourish emotional ideas already familiar and troubling the
imagination. Freud said to the American creative writer (at
least that is all that was understood of him), Sex is important
without reference to the birth rate; sexual intercourse is a
vitamin; without it your being may warp. Frigidity and repression cause many of the complexes which you, as a writer,
have found so difficult to explain in your characters. The more
advanced in our literary world accepted this thankfully —
truth (a great deal of it), half-truth, and Viennese specialties —
as their grandfathers had swallowed evolution without really
digesting it. One result was many a short-lived reputation
gained by distributing to the public in interesting form some

of the facts of life hitherto undisclosed in popular literature. The valuable product, however, could in no sense be called Freudianism, or any other -ism, but a background — which naturally included the sexual — for many a typical story which had been at most three quarters told. For new plots are seldom invented. It is only the motivations, the interpretations, and the conditioning of the characters which are new.

$\mathcal{O}$ 9 $\mathcal{O}$
Literary Gymnastics

I AM GETTING to the period of the latter nineteen-twenties — the age of inflation, expansion, and Boom. It will be given some day an adjective as inappropriate as 'gay' for the eighteen-nineties, which will indicate that a good time was had by all. This is sadly untrue. We know now that a large part of our population had no share whatsoever in that gilded prosperity. What is not so well known, or perhaps forgotten, is how many Americans well above the marginal line of bodily comfort were acutely uncomfortable spiritually in the Boom days, and perhaps more dissatisfied with their country than in the Great Depression that followed.

New York in the latter twenties seemed to me and to many to be suffering from an hysterical fever with very unpleasant symptoms. The foolish, the wasters, and the dumb were the types of success. They made money faster and easier than anyone else. Every wise man knew that the bubble would burst, but the economically ignorant, who spent their days in brokers' offices or collecting tips on street corners, kept buying for a rise, which always came, and sold only to put their profits into expensive living and another speculation, which always succeeded. Conversation to a sensible man became intolerable, since it began to have the slightly intoxicated tone of a party always having one more round. It was not the money-making which was annoying but the moral relaxation which comes with easy gains. This sounds, and perhaps is, priggish, but only because the deeper reason for the distress of many a mind is hard to phrase. One felt that the values we lived by were being upset. If a moron could make ten thousand dollars in a week, he could spend half of it in a month, and this unsettled both him and society. Perhaps this new phase of industrialism,

330

some thought, might mean the triumph of a sharp but low grade of intellect, too unimaginative to be afraid of failure, and therefore successful in an economy where gambling seemed to be more profitable than hard work. Yet even this does not make articulate the *malaise* which so many of us felt in a gross materialism triumphantly successful. I felt far more out of adjustment with the society I knew then than in the suffering, stoical days of the Depression.

The masses of the people — and the speculators were masses, even the office boys out for lunch took fliers — were not so dumb as they seemed to be to more level heads who neither made money by gambling nor lost it. These had, as the people often do, a sound and instinctive belief in the future of a country which was only approaching its peak of productivity. They knew that the price of stocks had no relation to their dividends, but they believed that our great industries could produce and sell far more, and 1941-45 proved that they were right. All that was wrong in their calculations (if you could call them that) was the time element; and the failure, which was soon to be manifest, of banks and corporations to realize that wealth and productivity were synonymous terms. When stocks and living both became too dear, and the factories shut down in order to save that intangible called money, productivity and with it purchasing power declined, and we spiraled into the Great Depression. I should add a contributing factor to the Boom that caused the Bust — anyone but a literary man, a scholar, or a scientist could borrow easy money at the bank!

This excursion into amateur economics is not irrelevant to literature. I have always believed in Spengler's theory that every manifestation in any given age has some true resemblance to every other manifestation of the same age. There was in these latter twenties inflation, expansion, speculation in the art of literature as well as in the stock market and industry. We missed the easy money which never seems to get all the way to the men who sell words for a living, but shared the other symptoms.

While some were cracking the tabu on sex, other writers, less socially inclined and more speculative, were feeling the expansive energy of the times and beginning again the cyclical battle against the conventions of form and language which first stiffen, then clog, and finally choke free and true expression. A style of writing when it reaches maturity becomes fluent and easy for the second-rate mind to handle. But the first-rate writer, in emotional contact with the underlying realities of his time, soon finds that his vocabulary has become half *cliché,* and his rhetoric has hardened into a stereotype. The new rhythms of life about him will not become articulate in stale verbiage. He needs new figures, new sentence structures, even more than new words. This happened — or so he said — to Whitman, who shook off meter and end-rhymes from his poetry, and let the vocabulary of everyday prose flow through his verse. Now imitators of his loose rhythms and rough words begin to seem old-fashioned. I think the eighteen-nineties took more pains in the choice of words familiar in literature than did the nineteen-twenties. What the new writers were experimenting with, while we were seeing *The Saturday Review* through its early years, was a fresh use of these words and others drawn from colloquial speech, and still more, new techniques of literary structure.

Gertrude Stein was one of the most daring of the experimenters. Since she was an expatriate, living in an artistic and literary coterie in Paris, I never chanced to meet her until she came home, and then found her a sensible, intelligent woman, in appearance one of the executive type of highly civilized Jewish women so familiar in philanthropic and art-management circles in New York. Her real strength, however, was not in her sense, but in what seemed to be her nonsense. The pages of disintegrated grammar and repetitive diction which she wrote and called fiction, used to upset me like a bad dream. I could not read them without getting madder and madder, the more so since, if they were patiently translated into standard English, the content, like the content of E. E. Cummings's capital-less poetry, seldom said very much.

It was some years before I understood what she was trying to do and why brilliant writers like Ernest Hemingway, Archibald MacLeish, and Thornton Wilder, who had a great deal to say, acknowledged their debt without seeming to write in any way like her. Hers was a one-woman revolt against the dominance of rhythms over the word itself, which had lost its suggestive quality by being fitted into a standardized syntax or a required grammatical form. This rebellion she conducted with great shrewdness and considerable literary skill. Her nonsense, composed so as to strike the ear and emphasize the connotations of words, was sure-fire publicity, at least with those concerned with writing. If it meant nothing significant, it seemed to mean what others had inadequately expressed. It would be unjust to say that she sought publicity for its own sake. Perhaps she felt what was the truth, that too many writers were writing competently in English which was not better than competent. The crudities in all but the best books of the nineteenth century had disappeared, and even a college boy could write a professional diction. In novels, in editorials, in books of non-fiction, the rhythms of a civilized style swung along so easily that a reader could shut his eyes and guess what was coming next. Open *Harper's Magazine* or *The Atlantic Monthly* of, say, 1914, or any book of essays published before the twenties and try it for yourself.

She broke the sentence to smithereens. She picked the English words with color and significant sound, regardless of meaning, and not the long art words but short and familiar ones. And by repeating them, twisting the parts of speech from their natural order, starting, stopping, backing like a mad automobile, she forced the attention away from plain sense, if any, to the peculiar feeling and suggestions of the words themselves. One could get the same effect by emphasizing color instead of form for the body; painting, let us say, effective colors at random on the naked skin, and walking down Fifth Avenue. But thanks to weather and anatomy, the experiment would not be useful. Here is what she did, the theme being the value of repetition:

> Repeating then comes slowly then to be to one who has it to have loving repeating as natural being comes to be a full sound telling all the being in each one such a one is ever knowing. (*The Making of Americans.*)

The effect of this upon a writer whose youth had been spent trying to learn the smooth-flowing rhythms of the eighteen-nineties and nineteen-tens, and the choice of nice and effective

words like 'delectable,' was devastating. It was not a question
whether Robert Louis Stevenson, a stylistic god for those days,
wrote better than Gertrude Stein. He wrote a hundred times
better. It was a question of writing unlike R. L. S., since he
and his age were dead, and a new hurly-burly world was in the
making. Hence Gertrude Stein's admirers, if they were real
writers, took nothing from her but a fresh view of words. They
imitated her repetitions — see, for example, Hemingway and
Thomas Wolfe — but kept English syntax. She encouraged in
them the staccato rhythms which were characteristic of our
native speech and much of our writing, but they made no attempt to substitute the sound of a word and its vague suggestions for necessary sense. They did make their books read more
like men talking well in the nineteen-twenties and less like
something called literature. In short, she pulled more than
her own weight. Even the young editors of *Time* devised an
emphasizing variant of English diction in order, so they said,
to differentiate the new magazine from the declining *Literary
Digest* which represented the taste of earlier decades. I have
little doubt that they were subtly and unconsciously influenced
by the experimenting going on in the early nineteen-twenties,
and perhaps directly by Gertrude Stein's twists of sentence
order. Yet I still cannot read her without losing my temper.

Other signs of a new and restless age coming were the experiments and novelties in technique and specifically in the composition of literary works. Some of this originated abroad, of
course — such English writers as Virginia Woolf, for example,
and the Russian stage were influential. But there was plenty of
home-made invention. I felt the urge myself, not, however, in
my writing, but in the make-up of *The Saturday Review,* where
I experimented with double-page spreads for leading essays,
which were costly, and which in a less expansive decade I would
not have been allowed to try. Really important, however, were
the oncoming novelties on stage and screen, and I do not refer
to experiments which have been forgotten, but to achievements
which have not. The most moving and impressive stage show
I have ever seen was *The Green Pastures* by Marc Connelly
(1930), based on Roark Bradford's Negro folk-tales. I saw the
second performance, and my eyes were wet with enthusiastic

emotion through most of the performance. It was perhaps the only great religious play of our American times, great because the subject matter was the poetry of the Old Testament revised and transmitted through fresh and primitive minds. Yet also because of a new dramatic technique which gave a marching epic form, with full use of chorus and stage pictures, and transferred to the stage some of the potentialities uncovered by the moving pictures, but with more sincerity and the immediacy of flesh and blood.

Playgoers of that epoch will remember, too, the expressionistic *The Adding Machine* (1923) of Elmer Rice, and the stirring robot play of Karel Capek, *R. U. R.* (1923). And of course the modern tragedies of Eugene O'Neill — with the technical novelty of *Emperor Jones* (1921) and the psychiatric projections of *Strange Interlude* (1927) and *Mourning Becomes Electra* (1931).

But I remember with a personal as well as an artistic interest the work of a then young man whose work critics and literary historians have disagreed violently in placing. Thornton Wilder had been a student of mine at Yale in creative writing, whose chief distinction was beautifully written beginnings which seldom got to a middle and never to an end. When I picked him up later in a volume of short stories called *The Cabala* (1925), he still seemed a gifted amateur writing for his own pleasure. Then came his widely successful novel, *The Bridge of San Luis Rey* (1927). It was celebrated for its excellent style, and I used to see mothers tucking it into the pockets of their boys on their way to preparatory school, hoping it would do something for their marks in English. What was not so well recognized was that here was an American writer deeply concerned with form, not new forms only, but the right form for anything he chose to write about. This was quite as much a fresh view of one of the essentials of good literature as Gertrude Stein's word-conscious prose. It should have been no surprise that later, in *Heaven's My Destination* (1935), a book with utterly different subject matter, he found an easy, jocular style for an almost painfully American type, or that in *Our Town* (1938) he wrote a drama of equally familiar Americans which was broken down to dramatic essentials, and then put

together only far enough to let the imagination of the audience, stifled with overfeeding by Broadway producers, once
again do its work.

And there was in sheer size of imagination as well as body,
the biggest of them all, Thomas Wolfe. His first book, *Look
Homeward, Angel* (1929), I confess seemed to me a mighty
eructation of rather disagreeable home and college life. I
changed my mind radically when *Of Time and the River*
(1935) was published, yet was still blind enough to his whole
purpose to spend an evening arguing with him about the benefits of a classic sense of measure, which (so I said) might have
saved him several worn-out typewriters, and his publishers and
reviewers nervous exhaustion. He knew as much about classic
measure as I did, and had read voluminously, though not, he
admitted, nearly so much as he claimed for himself in *Of Time
and the River*. Classic measure, however, was impossible and
probably undesirable for him. An awkward man, shy, and always falling over furniture even when cold sober, he was a bull
in anyone's china shop, yet clearly one of those vast personalities that emerge in dynamic times like the sixteen-hundreds or
the nineteen-twenties. What is reading time or conciseness to
men like these? He treated me always with great respect, as an
older man who admired his talents, also a much smaller man
who might break, like the furniture, if he got excited. One
result was that in our occasional meetings I heard more of self-
criticism and self-confession than of the belly-discharging vitu-
perations that others reported.

He was either a man too big for his job, or it was too big for
him, I am not sure which. I mean that his immense physical
vigor overstimulated a native expressionism encouraged by the
expansiveness of the times. He could not stop writing once he
began. Or, if interrupted, he seems to have begun again some
miles or years ahead, and filled in the gaps by later additions to
another part of a continuous story. It was quite unimportant
to him how his scenes, episodes, whole sections were arranged
— as I discovered when, after his death, I tried to get disen-
tangled from his unpublished writing a complete novel of manageable length with beginning, middle, and end. It was there,
but he had detached and reattached it until no one would take
the responsibility of giving it separate birth.

The engine in his brain worked too fast. Perhaps this is why the finest of his narratives deal with movement, like the justly famous train ride from South to North. But I suspect that the brain tumor which killed him followed earlier lesions. His intellect was never clouded for an instant, yet some control was weak. Tom Wolfe knew what he meant and what he wanted to do, but too many words rushed to the call of his mind.

What he proposed to do can be readily deduced. He had gone back to the freedom of the eighteenth-century novel, when a Fielding or a Richardson could let himself go for volume after volume, omitting nothing that he saw, felt, or believed, in the interest of mere narrative. Richardson had a philosophy of virtue to control him; Fielding, a philosophy of human character; Balzac, to skip to the nineteenth century, characterized life by its passions chiefly, and by analysis endeavored to interpret the bourgeoisie. For Tom Wolfe, society itself, its flow and impacts, was the subject. How one man, himself, saw it, what it did to one mind, was his theme. His work is autobiography raised to fiction, just as Thackeray, Dickens, Trollope, raised biography to fiction. His subject was the confused society of the nineteen-twenties — confused by unexpected results of industrialism, nerve-shaken by the first World War. The fine discriminations of a Stendhal were premature for such a society. One had to describe it first. There were many other expressionists, as they called themselves, especially in Europe, at this time, who felt as he did, but he was the most powerful. And I am sure that for him expressionism was a means, not an end. He proposed to go on until the ego which was the hero of his books came to some sort of balance, and his voluminous evidence resolved itself into — what? I am not sure; certainly not a philosophy, perhaps into a faith or a hope. There are a few paragraphs toward the end of one of his last novels which show that the crystallization was beginning:

I think the true discovery of America is before us. I think the true fulfillment of our spirit, of our people, of our mighty and immortal land, is yet to come. I think the true discovery of our own democracy is still before us. (*You Can't Go Home Again,* page 741.)

I believe that had he lived, these paragraphs would have been the themes for whole books.

And this is what I mean by saying that Tom Wolfe's job was perhaps too big for even his great capacity, as (physically at least) Balzac's was also. What he wanted to write — and never finished — was one great novel, a fictitious autobiography of a mind of the age, exposed to everything it was able to see, feel, and take part in. No isolated experience, no line, no trend was enough. This novel would have to be written through — in how many millions of words? — and then, only then, finally organized. For until it was finished he himself would not know what was its climax, not even what was its plot. We have the bits and sections, a half-done picture-puzzle. It would have been the longest, possibly the greatest, novel of our times.

Henry L. Mencken has said that the American language is as creative in the twentieth century as was the English in the sixteenth and seventeenth. American literature, as these few instances for which I had a personal concern indicate, was very creative in the structures of expression throughout the twenties and early thirties. The pace began to slacken in the mid-thirties, and has been slower still in the forties. Even the Little Magazines, which are the laboratories of experiment, show few adventures in form. But that may be because novelists whose values have differed more sharply than did Tom Wolfe's from the ideas of the last generation, have taken what they need from the experimenters. Tom Wolfe belongs definitely with these new men, but he is big enough to sprawl over two chapters of this memoir.

10

The Really New Literature

I REMEMBER THE DISMAY with which I read Ernest Hemingway's first powerful book, *The Sun Also Rises* (1926). What troubled me was nothing moral in the current sense of the word, and I thoroughly enjoyed the fresh style, seemingly careless, colloquial, and profane, actually skillfully and (I think) painfully wrought line by line. It seemed to catch new rhythms of talk. The novel reflected the life of psychological derelicts floating in alcohol and tormented by oversensitive nerves. Yet these derelicts, expatriates in Paris, were evidently symbolic of a change in values, more easily seen in these neurotics than in better-balanced youngsters of the new generation at home. I was disturbed because I knew, slightly at least, some of the originals of the characters of the book. They had seemed to my still confident mind to be people astray in life for no good reason except their own weakness or willfulness. But Hemingway had drained them even of will. In his story they were broken souls trying to keep going by a constant intoxication, which was as often intellectual and sexual as alcoholic. Yet the novel was not cynical. There was some deep concern in the author, although his characters did not seem worth it. That concern was to clarify and strengthen itself later.

It would have helped me if I could have read then Edwin Seaver's shrewd remarks to be made twenty years later in a preface to the new writing of the nineteen-forties. The authors brought up in the years of the first World War and the Long Armistice, so he said, were more interested in man himself than in his character. Men of good will — successful or unsuccessful, strong or weak — had been the heroes of the nineteenth-century tradition. But in *The Sun Also Rises* the actors lacked not only good will by any definition, but will of any kind — which was still true of the work of Mr. Seaver's selected authors of 1945.

While we on *The Review* had been assessing and publiciz-
ing the brilliant work of the writers of the nineteen-twenties
whose formative years had been spent in pre-war days, a natural but portentous change had come in the literary scene. A
new generation had arrived, still unformed, but quite certain
as to what they wanted to do. I do not mean the so-called 'lost
generation.' That was a literary term applied to writers and
the characters they wrote about. It was intended to describe a
neuroticism which the war and the Depression may have encouraged, but which was congenital rather than acquired. The
new writers liked to write about such types, and to find neuroticism where no one had looked for it. But to call these
writers themselves 'lost' is nonsense. Such men as Tom Wolfe,
John Dos Passos, Ernest Hemingway, Thornton Wilder, or
even Scott Fitzgerald, and later John Steinbeck, may, some of
them, have been psychologically upset, or philosophically shak-
en into an anarchy of values, but no writer who succeeds in saying his say is lost artistically. nor was neuroticism more characteristic of this generation than of any other, except on its sensitive fringes.

What was happening was less dramatic, but devastating. Such
a writer as Hemingway evidently has had the props and securi-
ties of American confidence knocked from under him. 'Good
will,' in his experience, had not worked. Emotionally hurt himself in youth (as his short stories indicate), all talk about virile
Christianity, and a progressive America going on from ideal to
ideal, gave him a pain. Just as the new economists had discovered that orthodox economics was merely a description of prosperous England at the peak of her industrialism, so he and
many others seem to have decided that American confidence
and idealism were deductions from the success of the American nineteenth century. This discovery did not necessarily
make them sound philosophers or historians. But it did set
them free to look closely at Americans of all kinds of will or its
lack — neurotic, plain bad, unmoral — with unprejudiced eyes.
So seeing, they saw at least freshly, and, being artists, found language and form for what they found. Among them, I think
Hemingway was the most successful.

These writers were definitely not debunkers. Those gentry

belonged to a different species of older men who had been soured by what Brooks Adams called the degradations of democracy. They were reformers, not iconoclasts. I knew quite well William Woodward, whose novel *Bunk* (1923) I read in manuscript. In that novel he invented the word 'debunk.' His purpose was to take the starch out of big business, and *Bunk* was followed by numerous books, some of which he wrote, deflating our national heroes from Washington down to the most recently publicized financiers and industrialists. But this was very different from the work of a Hemingway or Dos Passos, who were not interested in, it might be truer to say were indifferent to, the American values which the debunkers thought had been corrupted or glamorized.

Hemingway is certainly no debunker. He likes the kind of tough, conscienceless, erotic, and often neurotic, individual that had been a villain in genteel novels and a minor character in the stories of Willa Cather or Ellen Glasgow. He likes anyone with life in him and does not care how he uses it. Maybe that is just right for an unflinching realist, maybe it is right for a philosopher, since it would be hard to prove that the men of good will have been particularly successful with our world in the last quarter-century. But in spite of his close observation, Hemingway is no realist at heart, and certainly not a philosopher. His personality, his moods, and his temperament color everything he writes. Morally he is quite irresponsible. It is sensual, not moral, man that interests him, and every book is in terms of himself, precisely as were Tom Wolfe's novels. That gives them their emotional drive, and he is too much of an artist usually to let subjectivity destroy the illusion of an intensely real world outside of himself. His fondness for bloodshed and violence may be described as a premonition of what was to be fatally characteristic of the new world ahead. It can be described with equal truth as the weakness of an oversensitive man frightened (morally I mean) and inclined to bluster.

I believe that Hemingway has come to doubt his theory of life without principle. The significant aspect of *For Whom the Bell Tolls* is not its frequent tenderness. Hemingway had been tender before when he found a cause for tenderness. It is the moral conflicts of its hero, who may be himself. Through that long, desperate attempt to blow up the Spanish bridge, he tortures himself with the question, Why is he, a scholar and an American, risking his life with this gang of likeable ruffians? And he finds the answer at last in something in his own moral nature of which Marcus Aurelius and Saint Augustine would both have approved.

I have never met Ernest Hemingway. Some years ago I was on the way to Key West with my long-time friend Hervey Allen, author of *Anthony Adverse,* one of the best of modern novels in the romantic vein. We were on our way to see Robert Frost, who had been ill, but Hervey told me that if we stopped at the right bar we should probably run into Hemingway. 'I warn you,' he said, 'that if he is in a certain mood he may be difficult. 'What does he do?' I asked. 'Beat up the biggest man in sight.' As Hervey was at least twice my size, I felt safe. If Hemingway beats up anyone, I am sure it is from inner necessity. The roughness and coarseness of his vocabulary are deceptive as to his real nature and purpose. He needed a language for the turbulent, half-foreign America, where violence is often a sign of a new vigor and certainly of a new society forcing its way up. And he has had the courage and the patience to go to the sources for it, and then get rhythms which make it articulate. No wonder he has been influential.

In this respect, at least, he might well have been considered in the last chapter, although his reorganizing of English style for the purpose of coming closer to American life came a little later than the literary gymnastics described there. So did the take-over of the methods of American journalism and the American movies by John Dos Passos in *Manhattan Transfer* (1925). I think Hemingway's stylistic change was more fundamental. He developed a new articulateness for seeing and hearing the Americans who interested him. Dos Passos invented a kind of literary television, calculated to put the new background of noise, movement, and confusion against which Americans were living, into a novel like a moving picture but without its plot. He made a sensation in Europe, for this was the way America looked to them in photographs and sounded in American newspapers. But I doubt whether his books have enduring quality. There is too much of the 'stunt' in them; too much of the

visual and auditory; too little depth and wisdom. Reading
them is like a conducted tour by subway to Coney Island. I
should call them 'Life in a Crowd.'

These men, Hemingway, Wolfe, and Dos Passos especially,
were evidently writing for their exact contemporaries, and the
new generation responded, not only here but all over Europe,
and as far away as Australia. We who were older read, marked,
learned, and were either violently opposed or, as in my own
case, sure of their vigor and their skill but skeptical of their
estimate of underlying American values. I was content myself,
as a critic, to repel the common charge that Hemingway was
crude, a menace to the English language; and that Tom Wolfe
was a lax writer who used a shotgun instead of a rifle.

I was skeptical of the moral irresponsibilities of Hemingway's characters and the anarchic confusion of John Dos Passos's
American society. I doubted whether either was truly typical,
though I did not doubt their truth. These highly original
writers seemed to me prospectors rather than miners equipped
to follow shows of gold down to the vein itself. I believed with
Whitman, whom I was beginning to read intensively, that our
American writers of the past had left unexplored vast areas of
our remarkable social history, and that our popular novelists
had specialized only in the respectable or the romantically ir-
regular. I believed with Thoreau that the resistance to standardization was as common in America as anywhere else, and
more vigorous because there was more to resist and a stronger
tradition of freedom. I understood, therefore, that this dragging into the sunlight of print of these miscellaneous repro-
bates, neurotics, amateur prostitutes, lost souls, and many people quite worthless from either a Puritan or a Quaker point of
view, was a reaction from omissions or varnishings-over in the
literature of our democracy. Whitman had tried to do it romantically nearly a century before; now it was to be done with
at least a strong appearance of realism, and with no responsibility for good will, or moral influence, or the welfare of the
United States, or for anything except art.

Yet, while this is historically true, it is only part of the truth.
The ideas of what was right, what was wrong, what was worthy,
what was subversive, which underlay such diverse books as

those of Willa Cather and Sinclair Lewis, and even of Dreiser, and of most earlier American writing, were altered, or at least challenged, in this new literature. The values had changed. Part of this change, I felt sure, was in response to a slow change in what the sociologists would call American mores — a change easier to state than to analyze. But part, and especially in Hemingway, was a reflection of a decadence in the great European society from which we Americans come. In Paris, in Berlin, in Vienna, in Rome, to a less extent in London, there was a disintegration which in these mid-twenties was observable in the smart sets and international gambling society and in politics — but most articulate among writers. This moral anarchy is obvious now, looking back from the nineteen-forties, but its extent and seriousness were not obvious then. One felt in the writing of young Americans under strong foreign influence both a response to new sets of values in America and a prophecy of greater and more dangerous changes in which our society might follow the downward curve of European culture.

My old friend Archibald MacLeish — always a spokesman for youth — burst out some years later when we were on the eve of war, with much that had been on my mind in the mid-twenties. The irresponsibles, he called these new skeptics of nineteenth-century ideals — from T. S. Eliot down. He accused them of sapping the morale of a whole generation of intellectual youngsters by infecting and enfeebling the deep, if unconscious, roots of their American tradition — by paralyzing their confidence and destroying their will. Soon that pugnacious critic Bernard De Voto joined in the attack. MacLeish was right in general, I think, for I could see the effect he described on whole college generations at Yale and at Harvard, where I had opportunities to observe. But he was wrong in the personal nature of his assault. The best of these iconoclasts were honest thinkers and artists who were bound to represent a tendency of their times — sure also to reflect an international decline in morale to which, as writers close to other writers abroad, they were particularly sensitive. As well condemn Shakespeare for his monarchism! Yet it is clear now that such American novelists as Hemingway and Wolfe were much more neurotic than the America they described. A Hemingway world, a Wolfeian world, would be intolerable, not only to the Deity, but to the people who lived in it. What they reported was true enough, but there was a great deal they did not report because it did not interest them, or they could not understand it. This is no reflection on their art or their value to literature. Yet, as one rereads this defeatist literature — let us say *The Sun Also Rises* — recognizing its prophetic quality, the historical fault seems to be that it did not then occur to Hemingway (or to Dos Passos) that in America as it was, something could be done about it. They may have been right in long terms, although in short terms the response of American youth to the ordeal of war proves that they were wrong. But there was at least a resemblance between this negation of old values and the tragic decision of the German leaders to smash civilization as we knew it in order to make a society which they could control for their own bad ends.

When the 'troubles,' as they say in Ireland, came upon us, there was surprise among the critics of society that our young people of both sexes and on both home and fighting fronts demonstrated every quality that lack of will, lack of purpose, lack of loyalty, are supposed to deteriorate. Of all these lacks they had been accused. Allowing for good fortune in powerful leadership from the older generation, nevertheless it is probably true that the work and fighting of the young people was better than the show put on by the generations of from forty to sixty who, all through the thirties, had been criticizing their morale, their ideas, and their education. Their education especially, which scores of debunkers had been attacking, seems to have been an adequate preparation for a long bitter struggle involving as much of science as of fighting, and more individual action than had ever been asked of soldiers before. I had myself been one of the critics (not the debunkers) of American education, especially at the high-school level. Yet when I was asked a score of times in Australia in 1945, Why were the American common soldiers more intelligent than the Australian troops? I had to answer that they certainly were not more intelligent, but more of them had been through a high-school or college education.

Not every important writer of the twenties thought that the United States had worn out its old values and would have to get a new set from Paris, or Russia, or Greenwich Village, or from the pessimistic philosophers. When I say old values, I do not necessarily mean the best values, but whatever it was that kept us top-side up through all the materialisms, injustices, and plain greediness of the nineteenth century — the values that make American social history the story of an unconquerable minority fighting another minority of land-grabbers, monopolists, dirty politicians, and fat-souled money-makers, while the people at large kept on working and breeding.

The typical fighter in print of these twenties and thirties for American tradition good and not so good, the chief opponent of the debunkers, the café and dead-end boys, and the pessimists of genius, was another old friend of mine, once my student at Yale, Stephen Vincent Benét.

Steve, when I first knew him, was a chunky, bespectacled Yale undergraduate who could do anything with his typewriter, although he by no means limited his activities to words. He was so fluent a writer in either prose or poetry that I prophesied for him a career in journalism rather than literature. It seemed that he would broaden rather than deepen, and that the journalistic magazines which were being read by all America too impatient to read a book, would be his habitat for life. His father, his grandfather, and a great-grandfather had all been officers in our army. His first ancestor here was a Catalonian settling in Florida, and his proper name was Benet not Benét. Some ignorant pedant at West Point had persuaded one of the family that the name should be accented as if it were French.

Steve was a dogged arguer. There was a light in him, like the key flames in a gas stove, that burst into a blaze when his imagination was stirred or his principles attacked. He was a liberal, but not of the genteel variety. Scratch his liberalism and he would fight back with everything available. He was obstinate too, but in a good cause, not out of personal prejudice. I have seen him in his later years spring at the throat of one of our learned judges who had been playing intellectually with anti-democratic ideas, and hang on until his opponent gave up.

He, too, had his year or so in Paris. He, too, suffered from the uncertainties of the young in the Long Armistice. He could be, and usually was, as anti-sentimental as those who called themselves the lost generation. Romance for him was a form of art, not a wash to cover the grossness of American experience. What he wrote specifically of his own country was not so much truer than Hemingway's picture as utterly different. Hemingway took the Hawthorne, Melville, Mark Twain line of underlying pessimism and extended it brilliantly into our own times. Benét followed the Emerson, Whitman curve. He had less intellectuality, less spirituality than Emerson, less power, though a better sense of humor, than Whitman, but he played on their side.

I lost track of Steve for a while, but picked him up again with intense interest when *John Brown's Body,* which he had been writing in Paris on a Guggenheim Fellowship, came into my hands. He was still fluent and mellifluous, but a new strength backed his fluency, and he could be harsh, vigorous, and epigrammatic as well as melodious.

I do not know just when it happened, but I think I know what had happened. This son of a migratory army family had lived all over the country, and had taken into his impressionable mind significant qualities. If he did not know people — at least some kinds of people — as well as Hemingway, he knew their imaginations, the American imagination, far better. He got to know much more specifically than did Whitman the constant influence of expansion in a continent, even upon the insensitive. American neuroticisms he left to Wolfe and Hemingway, not denying or shrinking from the facts. The clay feet, if any, of the heroes — John Brown or Lincoln — he left to the debunkers. Economic thwartings and injustices he left to the sociological novelists, not denying (as Whitman was often inclined to do) their existence. His job was with the peculiar imaginative effect upon great and small of life in expanding America — and who can deny its peculiarity in world experience! To put it into a sentence, this poet sucked life-blood from American history, making literary tissue out of it. And while what he took was only part of our national experience, it was a vital part in great danger of being sterilized or scrapped

by the intellectuals of the twenties and thirties. They, naturally, could not look forward a decade and a half to see that the
energy, the responsibility, and the faith that were shown in
their books as disintegrating were still basic in the American
temperament. Therefore, I still regard *John Brown's Body* as
the most prophetic American poem of the nineteen-twenties.
As for its merits, it lacks the packed power of T. S. Eliot, but,
unlike his erudite and deeply intuitive work, it is written in
easily assimilable language, and has therefore become that essential literary achievement in any generation, a poem for the people. Especially when read with the parallel and later poem
Western Star, more mature in verse yet of the same inspiration,
this poetry of Benét's is better than Longfellow's narratives.
Nor is this mild praise. Personally, I think that a few Longfellows in the past twenty years, to carry poetry where metaphysical obscurity would never reach, would have been a godsend
to American literature. I remember a remark of President
Wilson's that the Democratic Party always weakened when it
drifted too far from the essential needs of the common people.
There is a parallel with American literature, although I certainly would not have all American poets Longfellows or
Benéts. In Australia they have a cocktail called 'one and two.'
The one is vitality — gin being the symbol in this instance. The
two are vermouths — one bitter and one sweet. This is how I
felt about Hemingway and his confrères and Stephen Vincent
Benét. We needed both kinds of philosophy in the twenties
and thirties, and needed them strong.

My comparison between Longfellow and Benét is misleading,
since it conceals the fact that *John Brown's Body* and *Western
Star* as much as *The Sun Also Rises*, belonged to a new type of
American literature. They represent the flowering of new
kinds of interest in Americans and the American scene which
grew more and more intense and broadened steadily through
these decades. I do not think that 'nationalism' is the right
word for this urge, since it was not very political, not aggressive,
and certainly not 'patriotic' in the old flag-waving, 'we-are-the-
people' way. In fact, scores of books were devoted to unearth-
ing elements of our past which may have been picturesque or
important, but were certainly not likely to make us proud.

Now everything American comes into print: the life of our highways and rivers, the great adventures of railway-building, the politics that elected Jefferson, and the economics that made Jackson a new kind of leader; the American small town which proved to be a fresh experience for the race; the psychology (often morbid) of religious cults; and a series of biographies of great or near-great Americans who only now began to be studied candidly and without the bias of romance or the limitations of mere realism.

Naturally the creative literature which sucked all this new knowledge into the imagination was itself new. It is shrewder and sounder than the work of the genteel age, and has been freed from inhibitions by the tough boys of the twenties. In this contrast I am willing to include the great poet of the American common man, Walt Whitman. If that great dreamer, great orator in print, had known at first hand (as Benét did, for example) more American social history, he would have less often tiptoed precariously toward the empyrean, as Max Beerbohm depicts him in his famous cartoon.

The Diamond Age of Lecturing

I HAVE NEVER BEEN a professional club and forum lecturer, although for some years I made brief but very extensive tours throughout the country under the sponsorship of a lecture agency. The interest of these tours was not primarily financial. I think I should have netted more dollars if I had stuck to writing, with an occasional trip near-by at lower fees than my publicity-making agent charged for me. But I was a congenital Easterner editing a paper that went all over the United States. I had never lived (nor my ancestors before me) far from the smell of Atlantic tidewater, and it did me good to get West and South — to listen to the talk on club cars, to wander the streets of Mid-Western cities, to read local newspapers, and talk to home-staying characters. I omit from these benefits the inevitable entertaining, which is the lecturer's most fatiguing chore, because the kind of people who give and go to entertainments for more or less celebrities are much the same in type from coast to coast. Some of this hospitality, however, was very rewarding and led on to friendships. And I was never one of those neurotic lecturers who refuse food and drink and even talk until they have put their show on the stage. Only twice have I undertaken large adventures with the spoken word: once in 1923 in a University of California Summer School, in a new environment with subtly different ideas current; once in 1945 on a government wartime mission to Australia and New Zealand. In both instances, and particularly the latter, I got at least as much as I gave, and the financial considerations were negligible.

Therefore I speak impartially when I say that literary lecturing in America has never had its due in histories of literature and education. I do not mean, of course, university lecturing

to students, which is part of an educational system, and obligatory whether it is brilliant and meaty or meaty and dull. Nor
professional entertaining such as Mark Twain was master of,
and also that generous and enthusiastic personality 'Billy'
Phelps, my old teacher and friend, in his mellow, loose-shod
later days. I mean lecturing on literature, art, music, drama,
foreign affairs, or what have you, which is definitely intended
as adult education for those characteristically American group-
ings who wish to be knowledgeable without taking too much
trouble about it. A whole literature of satire in pictures or in
print has been directed against these organizations. Let the fun
go on. I could add items of my own, as of the chairman of the
literary committee of a vast woman's club in Ohio, who said to
me as I arrived, 'You was here before, wasn't you?' To which I
was happily inspired to reply, 'Yes, I were.' I shared the stage
that day with a dancer, who (quite rightly) gave more pleasure
than my heavy-going lecture on criticism.

Yet the writer of a memoir who takes American culture seriously, must counter this satire with questions that are also serious. After all, these audiences voluntarily assembled (which
have no parallel elsewhere unless, and under very different conditions, in Russia), are often much more significant than the
lecturer who addresses them. They want the latest word on art
or the most durable wisdom in public affairs; cravings so important in a democracy like ours that it is unwise to make fun
of their superficiality. I felt often that my audiences came to
hear about new books so that they would not have to read
them — and have again and again been confronted by the evidence of aroused interest floating back like bread on the waters
after many days or years. And I should like to say a word for
the lecturer himself. If all writers of informational books
wrote as well as the best 'popular' lecturers have to talk, and if
all teachers took as much pains to be clear and interesting as
the club and platform lecturer has to be, there would be more
education in the schools and colleges, more profitable reading
of serious books, and less profit for the lecture bureaus.
The radio has now restored the eminence of the spoken word,
but has not yet equaled the achievements in popular adult
education of the itinerant lecturer speaking in person. The

very size of the radio audience makes it a vast corpse attracting
the buzzards of commercialism from the four winds. Its un-
paid-for educational programs are too often dull and impossibly
placed. Its 'talent' is urged to be cheap in tone, following a
principle which also guides the proprietors of the moving pictures, and which I believe to be a fallacy: that the public pre-
fers the bad to the good. It is true, of course, that audiences
and readers prefer sprightly trash to dull excellence. Yet at
present the radio is better at news than at education.

But I am writing of the nineteen-twenties and thirties, not
the forties. Those years, for writers and critics and editors,
were certainly the Diamond Age of lecturing. Even the academic hierarchies were celebrity-hunting like the intellectual
proletariat. The chief difference between the two markets was
that the universities sought great rather than notorious names,
and would accept from the erudite 'ers' and 'uhs,' word-chok-
ings, and repetitions of things already in print, with a dumb
patience of which no woman's club or Rotary luncheon would
have been capable. It was not in a university, but, I think, in
Carnegie Hall that Maeterlinck, then in the bright sunset of
his fame, read an address translated into a phonetic English in
which he had been coached on his trip over. As he pronounced
his script, it sounded like no possible language. 'For God's
sake!' shouted someone in the gallery, 'say it in French!'

We had been measurably (in millimeters, not inches) inter-
nationalized in the first World War, and there was a coast-to-
coast demand in the twenties for foreign lecturers, particularly
English men of letters, and Irish and Scotch whose dialect was
sometimes easier to understand. The fees paid were enormous
and caused wounding jealousy among the native talent. The
English especially had exported their literary men during the
war as a shrewd and successful form of propaganda. After the
war, although the propaganda ceased, the publicity continued
on its own momentum to the great advantage of many a British author whose best market was in the United States.

I remember John Drinkwater, a good poet who made his
American reputation with a play about Lincoln. He was an excellent showman as well as a playwright, and earned his fee (of
seven hundred and fifty dollars a lecture, so it was reported) by

looking every inch a handsome poet in a fervor. He draped
his graceful body over the lecture stand and read from his own
poems — it was easy money. And there was Lord Dunsany
from Ireland, the mystic romanticist of the Irish Renaissance,
equally famous for his one-act plays and his eccentricities. In
no other period would a shy, awkward man, scarcely articulate
in speech, have been dragged from his Irish seclusion to earn
stage money as a celebrity. I remember a painful evening in
New Haven. Dunsany hee-ed and hawed unintelligibly to a
large audience, then came across the street to a reception prepared for him at our little Elizabethan Club. It was full of
gaping undergraduates who stiffened into silence when Billy
Phelps led in the distinguished visitor. For once Billy could
think of nothing to say, and it was Lord Dunsany who got in
the first word. 'I say, this is a little silly! I think I shall go
home.' And he did, leaving supper, party, and guests to amuse
themselves.

The men from overseas made the most money, but if, as
notable writers they deserved it, as lecturers most of them emphatically did not. The British celebrity as a rule made no attempt to interest his audience. He gave good material, usually
in a very bad package, and the hearer could unwrap it himself
or go home. Such a brilliant talker in private circles as H. G.
Wells could only be described as inept on the stage. Sir Walter
Raleigh, that great Oxford scholar, once in my hearing read
galley proofs of a book, on the platform, to be sure, but apparently speaking only to himself — and the book had been published! Such admirable writers as Harold Nicolson and V. Sack-
ville-West were helpless before an audience. Little lecturers
should be seen but not heard was the principle they acted upon.
I think that the idea that large groups of unintellectual people
really wanted to hear what they had to say never occurred to
these speakers. Such groups certainly would not in England,
so why here? The Americans paid money to look at celebrities,
precisely as Oxford undergraduates went to unendurable lectures in order to get a degree. That was what they believed.
And if they were famous enough they got away with it — once.
Of course there were many notable exceptions among foreign
visitors, the Abbé Dimnet, for example, and Julian Huxley.

The reception of our local talent was much more significant than this exploiting of famous names. Books and criticism had become news in the twenties, perhaps for the first time in the United States since the tiny but underpaid Lyceum audiences to which Emerson lectured.

Some of us have forgotten that first great age of American lecturing which took up where the great sermonizers of a previous age left off. Emerson was only one of a legion, but the greatest. Beginning at home, in and near Concord, he extended his tours out through the raw Middle West, where he drove frozen miles by buggy across the prairies, and taught the expatriated New Englanders transcendentalism, and what was more important, the ideals which were to save the United States from becoming an empire of materialism. That he ate apple pie for breakfast was his passport to democracy. Thoreau, staying closer to home, labored with a poor delivery. As he said, he cleaned up so well behind him that he was seldom asked to come back for another lecture. When published, his not too successful addresses on walking and wild apples went round the world in essay form, as did Emerson's.

By 1920, a new national literature in poetry, fiction, and drama had come into being, and had aroused that intellectual curiosity which is quite different from interest in notoriety or success. From Texas to Maine American writers could count upon audiences who wanted to be told why Sinclair Lewis did not like his Middle West, why sex had entered (they meant re-entered) literature, why Americans no longer wrote like Englishmen, why poets now dealt with what had been called the unpoetical, and what had happened to the standards taught to them in school by which one judged good literature. It was impossible to lecture without a question period afterward, which was often more interesting, both to the lecturer and audience, than the lecture itself. For the first time in their experience many of these audiences learned that good books, especially American books, were not merely amusement and self-improvement, but more exciting than life itself, since they revealed and interpreted the hidden currents of emotion and half-conscious trends of thought that flowed through their own communities and themselves. What the good lecturer did was to create awareness — he did not really educate, he did not have to. He led the horse to water, and left him there. Fortunately in those days the water was good.

And the American lecturers were good also. I would cite Billy Phelps, and Will Durant especially in the twenties, and John Mason Brown and Edward Weeks of *The Atlantic Monthly* in later decades. They were what I should call penetrative lecturers. By this I mean that they were not necessarily or usually erudite or profound, but had that skill of communication which sent the hearer home with an idea, or a fact, or an enthusiasm firmly and usefully planted. It was not a gift so much as a craft, often an art. I remember a vast dinner of some association. I was sitting next to Will Durant, who was warned a few minutes in advance that he would be called upon for some informal remarks. They were informal, but also coherent, pointed, and packed with sense. No wonder, since in those few minutes allowed him he had penciled on the tablecloth between us an elaborate outline of heads and subheads. He never glanced at the outline while he spoke, but it had organized his ideas before he began.

So great was the success of literary lecturing until the ominous approaches of war diverted the public mind from the arts, that the publishers thought they had found a new form of advertising. Every author of a new book was urged to speak at every book fair, women's club, or men's luncheon that would listen to him. I doubt whether he sold many of his books as a result, although if he was inspiring he undoubtedly sold books of other writers. Seeing and meeting an author often seems to end all curiosity as to what he may have said in his writings! So it was usually the authors' imagination not their pocketbooks that profited. They stepped out of their Greenwich Villages, Connecticut farms, editorial chairs, or university libraries and were for brief but inspiring moments face to face, emotion to emotion, with the populace for whom they wrote. Only those who understand how important the sense of an audience is to a writer, can appreciate what it means to see your ideas, your verses if you are a poet, stick visibly like arrows in the minds of actual people whose faces betray the results. The vigor, the confidence of the literature of American writing in the twenties and early thirties, must be partly ascribed to a more concrete sense of communication between writer and reader than hitherto since the great decades of the early nineteenth century. Scores of writers never took to the stage, and in many cases that was most fortunate, for they could write better — far better — than they could speak. But the best of these independent spirits were talked about even if they did not talk. Walt Whitman's line, though still unrealized except in beginnings, became intelligible to many an American writer:

'To have great poets, there must be great audiences, too.'

12

Better Books and More of Them

LECTURING, TEACHING, AND STUDY all tend to become institutionalized and stereotyped, especially in mass education. There never are enough born lecturers, born teachers, and born students to make general education work without some kind of standardization. But this is not true of good reading, for good reading is a highly personal experience, whose quality depends upon the taste, the intellect, the imagination, and the sensitivity of the individual reader. Still, he has to get the books. I find too little in histories of literature and criticism of how books get to the reader. It is easy to forget that until the nineteenth century the general reader, who is quite as important in the history of civilization as the scholar or creative writer, had little or no access to libraries, and that as late as the early decades of that century the price of books was measured in guineas not shillings.

As I look back on my own reading history, I see that I grew up in what, if a literary name is to be given to it, must be called the age of the magazine. From towards the end of the nineteenth century onward, the price of new books, which had been heavily reduced, went up steadily until the cost more than doubled. From about this same period the price of magazines went down. And it was not until the first administration of Franklin D. Roosevelt that in this country the cost of mailing a book was brought into reasonable proportion with the expense of getting magazines by post. As late as the nineteen-twenties, there were thousands of sizeable communities in the United States where the only books that could be purchased were light romances or detective stories at the local drug store. It is the magazine that for half a century or more has made the United States by comparison with Great Britain or France a

357

country of widely distributed reading. But the good reader must have his books — fiction or non-fiction. In general only books can present an extensive beginning, a middle, and an end, and enough tissue, fat, and vitamins to nourish the imagination and the mind.

I used to feel very strongly, when we were getting *The Literary Review* going and trying to distribute *The Saturday Review* throughout the country, that there was too much shadow-boxing in our job. Most of our clientèle wanted to see books, to be told about them, before they purchased; and that was very difficult outside the big cities. I used to relieve my mind by writing editorials about the price of books, but they never told how to make books more accessible because I was neither a manufacturer nor a distributor, and did not know. I even spent a year or so looking for some young industrialist with a million dollars who might enter the conservative and custom-bound publishing trade and show how the thing could be done, even if he spent his million before it began to pay. I did not find him. And indeed it was not until more efficient manufacturing processes, and a great war in which millions of soldiers wanted books to take their minds off tedium and danger, that the problem of cheap books (though not cheap new books) was solved. The question of how to make good new books accessible was tackled much earlier, and I was lucky enough to be one of the agents, if in no sense the inventor, of the solution.

It was in 1926, when *The Saturday Review* was well launched, that I was asked by Robert Haas, later a member of the firm of Random House, publishers, to be chairman of the board of judges of a new enterprise to be called the Book-of-the-Month Club. The prime director of the enterprise, Mr. Harry Scherman, had come from a long American experience in distributing classics in cheap form, and had seen that his mail-order technique could be used for new books on a far broader basis than the timid German experiments. The Book-of-the-Month Club was small and experimental at first. I do not believe that we went beyond 40,000 subscribers in our first year, and when we judges chose for our first book, the very literary and specialized *Lolly Willowes* by Sylvia Townsend Warner, I am sure that the proprietors thought they would lose their subscribers and their collective shirts. They did not — and to the judges the chance to use what judgment they possessed, and what standards they lived by, in the actual distribution as well as in the criticism of books, became a challenge as well as an opportunity. As for me, as an editor I had been leading horses to water, and now I could help to see that they had something to drink. We thought that we might be able to create a new kind of audience for good reading, and we did.

William Lyon Phelps was asked to join our committee but refused for a good and characteristic reason. He had a one-man's audience already and preferred to be his own committee. So we began with myself; the wise and kindly William Allen White, who knew his Middle West as well as the books he advised us to send them; the generous and salty-minded Dorothy Canfield Fisher, a novelist herself, and a warm and utterly honest critic; lumbering Heywood Broun, with his wide experience in variegated journalism and a personality of unusual influence; and the ample Christopher Morley, well-read and a source of enthusiasms.

In all my experience as a teacher, a writer, a critic, and an editor, I have never had so satisfactory a sense of accomplishment in what our ancestors would have called the furtherance of good literature as in my more than twenty years on The Book-of-the-Month Club. I could have got more academic prestige, perhaps more intellectual prestige, if I had given all my time to a professorship or to the editing of a literary journal obviously not run to make money; but the conviction of superior long-term usefulness on the Book-of-the-Month Club remains. We judges were on salary, and had no ownership in the business as such, and from the beginning were never subjected to an ounce of pressure from the management in making our decisions, so that our devotion to our work was no more sullied by commercialism than a professor's in a good university. We benefited as a professor benefits when endowment and fees increase, so much and no more. And fortunately in my own case, the work of reading and judging fitted in like the teeth of a wheel with my other activities. Intensive reading such as we had to do was an ideal job for a writer or an editor, since the reading could be fitted into any time or place, from trains to backwoods cabins, leaving the time for routine executive work or creative writing free of interruption. It is true that the flow of an endless river of print through the mind might, so I felt at the beginning, debilitate the intellectual faculties. But I soon grew humbler and wiser. My reading supplied data for criticism, and was helpful in enlarging the background necessary for the writing of biographies, on which I was soon to embark. I ate my peck of dirt weekly or daily, and found more vitamins than clay in it. However, reading in earlier and foreign literatures, which had been a passion with me, became a luxury for which I too seldom had time. Whoever thinks that reading new books under pressure is a brief and easy way to earn a living, must think again. In a fine book every sentence becomes a responsibility. In a just-maybe book, an intensity of concentration is necessary unless one is to waste hours of time or judge erroneously. In an indifferent book, especially a novel, equal concentration is required, for at any moment it may turn upward. Poor books, like bad eggs, take care of themselves. I was not supposed to get them but often did, and could take a holiday after the first few chapters. I apologize for these personal reactions which, however, have some relevance to the obscure history of the habits and the technique of reading.

We learned some very important facts about the reading taste and reading capacity of this country in our twenty-odd years with the Book-of-the-Month Club. In all that time there have been only seven judges — the places of the two members who have died, Heywood Broun and William Allen White, having been filled by John P. Marquand and Clifton Fadiman. So there has been abundant opportunity to pool experiences and conclusions. The teacher of literature seldom knows how effective (or ineffective) his teaching has been until years have matured his students and settled their patterns of life. We could test our success and failures in a few months. Not, let me hasten to add, by the sales figures of the books we sent out. These were instructive but might often mean only that we had hit upon some unexpected quirk of public taste, good for that time only, or had failed in describing the book to induce our readers to take it. *Gone with the Wind* did not sell well for us when we sent it out. Many subscribers, as they had a right to do, chose another book. It was one of the most confident choices of the board, yet our first conclusion was that, as several times before, we had been too confident of a popular choice. Now it has gone into more than ten millions. What counted for success in our eyes was the impression made upon critics and readers, the impact of the book, which was easy enough to register. A strong impact meant, usually, long-continued sales. It meant, in certain instances, the deep satisfaction of a successful venture. This happened when we chose a type of book hitherto not widely successful with the American public, such as Pearl Buck's *The Good Earth,* or Clarence Day's *Life With Father,* or George Santayana's only novel, *The Last Puritan,* and saw it spread through the best readers in the country.

It took us a long while, too long, to learn a very simple truth. We could not choose a book on the basis of what we thought the public liked and wanted. We did not know. The publishers did not know, as was proved by their frequent (and expensive) attempts to make best-sellers by advertising, and their surprise when some Cinderella on their list was married to the prince of popularity. I should make some qualifications. There is a standardized type of light romance that the people will always take as they will take breakfast-food or sugar. Occasionally a masterpiece or near-masterpiece conforms to this type — a *Treasure Island,* for example — and will sell as well as a synthetic product intended to appeal to the simpler emotions (including the sexual). When minor masterpieces came our way, we welcomed them; but the standardized type did not appeal to us and so did not tempt us to play down to what we knew to be a popular taste. Yet sometimes in the earlier years we would take, in a lean month, a just pretty good book, fiction or non-fiction, because we all agreed that this was what the general reader, if not our superior selves, wanted. Such choices often failed, and never succeeded with any emphasis whatever. And we began to see that there was only one safe procedure, which was to choose what we ourselves liked. If we liked a book well enough, the public, whose taste was perhaps less discriminating but at least as sound and healthy as ours, seemed to like it also. The only qualification was common sense. There were books upon which we, as highly experienced readers, might agree which were obviously too erudite, too esoteric, too specialized, or, as in much modern poetry, too difficult for the intelligent general reader. Yet it proved to be less dangerous to err in this direction than in a choice of the commonplace.

In order to free the interplay of like and dislike among five very different personalities, we quickly gave up voting, which always favored everyone's second choice, and adopted the Quaker principle of concurrence. The old Quakers in their business meetings never voted. If the majority could not persuade the minority to concur, the proposal was dropped. The proponents bared their hearts. The opponents searched theirs. With us, very frequently, the length and vitality of the discussion would itself prove that the book had more vitality than was suspected even by those who favored it. The minority, however, were not asked to subscribe to the high estimate of the majority; they were asked to concur in the decision to send out the book. If they would not, we dropped it, and its subsequent history usually showed that we were right to do so. Of course it worked the other way too, but I remember only one instance of a member obstinately standing out for a book in a minority of one, and unable to make the majority concur with his desires. I have been so often wrong in my predilection in our discussions that I am proud to say that the recalcitrant member was myself and the book John Steinbeck's *Grapes of Wrath*.

We learned that the general intelligent public, about whom writers and publishers were always talking, wanted leadership even more than advice in their reading. If we gave them a skillful machine-made article from the production line, they were vaguely disappointed, for they wished to read books they liked, but better books, and, to some extent, different books from those they had been reading. Why ask to have books chosen for them which they obviously might have picked for themselves? If they were told a book was good and why, and the report was honest, and the book when it came was not out of their range of interest, why then they gave it just that extra ounce of interest, that fillip of expectation, which, as everyone knows, makes the difference between indifferent and satisfactory reading. And furthermore carries the reader over and through the difficulties of a packed, an elusive, or a subtle book. Many an excellent volume, I am convinced, has failed to circulate as widely as it deserved because of the reader's sluggishness rather than from any fault of the author.

As our catalogue of books chosen grew in length, we could look back with pride to an increasing number of titles that had been successful with the public, but successful also when viewed as contributions to literature. My own list of our most fortunate choices would include: *Show Boat,* by Edna Ferber; *The Time of Man,* by Elizabeth Madox Roberts; *The Romantic Comedians,* by Ellen Glasgow; *Elmer Gantry,* by Sinclair Lewis; *The Seven Pillars of Wisdom,* by T. E. Lawrence; *Giants in the Earth,* by O. E. Rolvaag; *Abraham Lincoln,* by Carl Sandburg; *Bambi,* by Felix Salten; *John Brown's Body,* by Stephen Vincent Benét; *Kristin Lavransdatter,* by Sigrid Undset; *All Quiet on the Western Front,* by Erich Maria Remarque; *The Good Companions,* by J. B. Priestley; *The Good Earth,* by Pearl S. Buck; *Shadows on the Rock,* by Willa Cather; *Mutiny on the Bounty,* by Nordhoff and Hall; *Anthony Adverse,* by Hervey Allen; *Seven Gothic Tales,* by Isak Dinesen; *The Forty Days of Musa Dagh,* by Franz Werfel; *Heaven's My Destination,* by Thornton Wilder; *Claudius the God,* by Robert Graves; *Life with Father,* by Clarence Day; *Gone with the Wind,* by Margaret Mitchell; *Of Mice and Men,* by John Steinbeck; *The Yearling,* by Marjorie Kinnan Rawlings; *Benjamin Franklin,* by Carl Van Doren; *New England: Indian Summer,* by Van Wyck Brooks; *For Whom the Bell Tolls,* by Ernest Hemingway; *H. M. Pulham Esq.,* by John Marquand; *Darkness at Noon,* by Arthur Koestler; *Independent People,* by Halldór Laxness.

If my list is overbalanced by fiction, this is merely because many of our best non-fiction books were topical and informative, and have naturally not outlived their time.

And so we discovered, what any observers with like advantages would have found out, that the intelligent interest of the American public had been grossly underestimated by publishers and advertisers. It was a public better educated and less provincial in its interests than either educators or booksellers

had been willing to believe. It read by hundreds of thousands
books we chose and sent out that the publishers had hoped to
dispose of as caviare for the thousands. Non-fiction which,
except for some religious books and well-written histories, had
been published for prestige as much as for profit, now reached
the best-seller list and stayed there.

A new method of distribution was partly responsible for this,
but would have failed if there had not been throughout the
country an unaroused and unsatisfied demand. The statistical
picture of published books listed by categories and numbers
sold, changed in a decade. Non-fiction improved its percentage
greatly. The best-selling fiction became of much higher quality than the typical best-selling novel of the early nineteen-hundreds. I made a careful study of all this at one time and I am
sure I am right. It was a change in our national culture that at bottom was responsible. To say that America in the years just before, and after, the first World War had come of age would be
to say too much. Judging by the immense, the incredible success of the comic strip in the last decades, it might seem truer
to say that America had become adolescent. I should qualify
this by stating that in my opinion some comic strips are more
adult than many best-selling novels, particularly the kind that
was successful around the turn of the century, and is being
boomed again by certain publishers for the audience that has
been educated upon the synthetic romance of the moving pictures. But it is not too much to say that millions, instead of
hundreds of thousands, of American readers did come of age in
the two decades before we began our Book-of-the-Month Club
experiment. The proportion of college graduates, who had at
least done sound reading, increased; the proportion of high-
school graduates, who had at least been introduced to sound
and adult reading, increased enormously — the numbers, indeed, of high-school graduates doubled every ten years. Nor is
it to be forgotten that, after the end of the open frontier, economics and sociology became a problem for every intelligent
person, even if they did not know what the words meant; and
after our entrance into the first World War, history came to life
even for the most provincial? We, of course, did not create the
demand for non-fiction and for sounder fiction, but it pleased

us to think that by trial, error, and adventure, backed by original and adroit business methods, we had found one way of releasing it.

We learned also from sad experience that it was useless to choose a book because we thought it would do our readers good. The principle of the old-fashioned Sunday School library simply did not work with us. Temptation, especially when we got toward the war years, was very great. But experience soon taught us that the American reader wanted first of all a fine, an interesting, a memorable book. Advice, no matter how wise, information, no matter how important, he resented if that was all he got. He did not want to be sermonized, at least by our agency. This may seem to have been merely a symptom of that age of indifference to great issues through which we so dangerously passed in the nineteen-twenties, and which invited irreparable disaster. This is not true. We had the same experience long before the war clouds began to gather, and after they broke. Apparently the successful book with the intelligent American reader must be more than propaganda, whether for morals, economics, or politics. It must be first of all interesting, which means that it must touch the imagination. The Bible is propaganda from cover to cover — and is also a great work of uplifted imagination. Even so, my generation were made to read the Bible — for which I personally am deeply grateful.

The last important lesson we learned was not to be afraid of racial, religious, or political prejudice, provided that we had a good book. Again and again we expected a deluge of attacks because a novel, let us say, seemed to us strongly pro- or anti-Catholic or Jew or Protestant, dealt frankly with the Negro problem, or went far beyond the New Deal in its hopes and prophecies for the common man. We expected a deluge, and got a few raindrops. The assumption that racial, religious, and political groups in the United States differed more than they resembled each other was unwarranted. Actually they shared a common experience of American living, and when some aspect of that experience was honestly and imaginatively presented, would read of it with tolerance and sympathy, even if they did not agree with either interpretation or solution.

One exception must be made, but not, I think, a real exception. Three times we have sent out books that described the
despotism and the ruthless cruelties which have been used to
create and then to buttress the modern totalitarian state. The
first was the autobiography of Jan Valtin, whose career of dou-
ble-dealing with both Nazis and Communists gave some cause
for doubt as to his credibility. Whether he told the exact truth
or not, there is nothing in his revelations that has not been
duplicated and verified in later history. Violent and well-
organized attacks were made upon this book by the intellectual
leaders of the small American Communist Party. The second
was an apparently innocent novel called *The Fifth Seal,* by a
White Russian long an exile living in France, Marc Landau,
whose pen name is Aldanov. The hero of this novel was a vic-
tim of totalitarian cruelty, whether by Nazis or the Russian
Government was not entirely clear. To our surprise, violent
protests began to appear even before the book was published,
signed often by liberal men and women who were certainly
neither Nazis nor Communists. To our still greater surprise,
it became clear on investigation that these critics had not even
read the novel, and that all the hullabaloo had resulted from a
chain letter sent out by a tiny group of Leftists — who also had
not read the book! But the best description of the police methods instituted by the Soviets was one of the finest novels of
modern times — Arthur Koestler's *Darkness at Noon.* Against
this novel I remember no protests of the least importance. It
was too clearly not propaganda but truth for the sake of truth,
by an artist whose theme was human nature. Yet in many ways
it was the most damning indictment of what modern man has
learned to do to the souls of his fellow creatures.

We made many mistakes, both of omission and commission,
and learned how to correct them as far as our own fallibility
permitted, for we were a good-natured and conciliatory group,
taking each of us defeats without rancor, and backing our enthusiasms or our dislikes without fear of ridicule or sensitiveness to prestige. And we grew better friends, and our minds
worked together better and better as the years went on. All of
us knew that our responsibility was as great as our opportunities.

If there had been no other satisfactions in what we were able to learn and to do than the last to be recorded, I should still feel my association with the Book-of-the-Month Club fortunate. Time and again we were able to lift the talented but unrecognized writer from the ruck of best-sellers and publicized reputations and set him free on his way — free from the necessity of hack work or the pressure of relative poverty, and assured that not only his first book of importance, but also his next one, would have an audience ready which we had helped to make wide. Among American authors, Hervey Allen, Clarence Day, Stephen Vincent Benét, Stuart Chase, Walter Lippmann, Pearl S. Buck, Marjorie Kinnan Rawlings, Margaret Mitchell, John Steinbeck, Richard Wright, can be listed from the names now eminent, where our choice and our system were as effective on their behalf as the best-directed patronage of the classic eras of literature. For neither poverty nor obscurity is valuable for talent or genius once the first fruits are ripe and ready for the picking. And new names and new ideas in writing have a tough time of it anyway, even when given a hearing. The Greeks may have been always seeking a new thing, but that is certainly not true of our reading public. The new thing (and the good thing) has to be brought to them. Our success in doing so would seem to indicate that selling tripe to the people may be easier, but is not necessarily more profitable, than giving them good meat.

CO 13 CO

Good Talk

THE NEW VALUES in life and literature, the new techniques in fiction, drama, poetry, and on the screen, naturally set minds working and tongues wagging among the interested. And as I have said before, the interested in this lively era were numerous — and most active and vocal in New York.

New York, when I first came to know it better in the nine-teen-twenties, was still observably stratified in the social sense, though not, of course, as sharply as London. There was no 'Society,' no 'Four Hundred,' as there had been in the generation described in Edith Wharton's novels, yet many families still definitely 'belonged,' not because of wealth or prominence in this or that, but just because they had 'belonged' for at least a couple of generations. However, these families and their more numerous associates were only a part of a vague stellar structure of society made up of a dozen planetary systems. There were Societies rather than a Society, and this I found was true of London also, except for Court Society and its fringes, which was still loosely held together by rank and place at the top.

Social New York in the nineteen-twenties was coming more and more to resemble London. Now, I believe, the reverse is true. And, as in London of that time, a literary (or artistic, theatrical, or musical) celebrity, even a very minor one, soon found himself attached to a planetary system which revolved around several domiciles where ideas and the arts were staples of conversation instead of scandal or the stock market. It was no age of salons. Nevertheless, there were pleasant survivals of earlier modes of intellectual hospitality, houses where one could count on meeting not only distinguished talents but also women of wide social experience, while partaking of good food and drink, to which the arts and the intellect have always been partial. For a married artist or writer, the opportunity was real but limited. It was seldom that his wife and he could offer reciprocal hospitality, especially in New York where space to entertain against a suitable background was more expensive than anywhere else in the world. Nor did the wives enjoy playing second fiddle with the feeling that it would be their duty later to feed the whole orchestra. A bachelor, however, of decent manners with a liking for good talk and enough reputation to lift him above anonymity, could dine well in good company five nights a week, and choose among country estates to visit in the summer.

I was a bachelor perforce through many months of one winter, while my wife and my mother were abroad with my young sons who were at school in Switzerland. In that year my loneliness was tempered by a society of widows, a society which, for definite reasons, was most likely to be found in America and especially in New York. I was the bachelor diner-out this year in one of the more intellectual (and intelligent) planetary groups. I belonged with the indispensable extra men that could be called to the social aid of a household where there was no adult male. It was an agreeable experience, though bad for the waistband, and many of my hostesses have remained true friends ever since.

In the electric atmosphere of the United States, and especially in the days of the making of great fortunes, the women frequently outlived their husbands by several decades. For the husbands, it was the price of achievement, and although scientists now give good biological reasons why women past the age of child-bearing should outlive their men, I am sure that the fierce pressure of American economic competition upon the leaders of finance and industry in the heyday of *laissez-faire,* was the selective lethal agent in the families I am describing. It was a country-wide phenomenon, but if the end-products did not live in New York, they came there. You can see them now, the plushy coteries of opulent women, endowed for life as a result of the heart disease or stomach ulcers of their men, spending away their boredom in hotels, restaurants, and theaters. I am speaking, however, of women born to wealth or position and the civilized use of money.

The husbands of the women in the little solar system of which I write had all been men of large affairs, political or economic, and they were of the second or third generation at least of the successful. And the women, who had lived in the great world which is so much smaller numerically than the little one, knew music, had taste in art and literature, enjoyed the exchange of ideas, and, most of all, free and flowing talk. Being widows (or most of them), they had one great advantage in planning an interesting evening. They could and did ruthlessly cut out a man or woman from a married pair on the plea that they were lone souls and that the other he or she was not particularly interested in the subject that was to be talked about. It did not always work — in fact, if the system promoted conversation abroad it also increased domestic discord in many a home. Yet I admit that I have seldom attended more vigorous and entertaining parties, where nothing was blue except the ladies' stockings.

Let me say quickly that I regard good talk as a stimulant, not as a way of getting things done. And let me add, speaking as a writer and critic, that nothing is more stimulating than talk which is neither shop talk nor mere argument. I should make a distinction here in the usefulness of good talk between culture which in its narrow sense should be professional if it is not to be dilettantish, and culture regarded as a diffusion of good ways to live. For these good ways in art and ideas, there should be an interplay, as the eighteenth century knew so well, between creator, critic, or thinker, and companionship with others of receptive minds. This is the area where good talk functions. And the more intelligent the circle and the more experienced in worldly contacts, the more surely does the creative spirit get a sense of interest and support. His ultimate audience must be reached by print, paint, or musical notes, but nothing warms the inventive imagination like talk with friends and critics who do not have to be guessed at because they are present in flesh and blood and have brought their personalities with them. Plato knew this, and the artists and writers of Renaissance Italy, and the frequenters of the Mermaid Tavern, and the English governing class, and Goethe and Mozart and the Transcendentalists of Concord.

The most brilliant talk I have ever heard was in Georgian England of the nineteen-twenties and early thirties, and in Dublin in 1918. In England this talk moved in and out of literature and art in general, for my concern there was with the men and women who were writing books. In Ireland, it was the slowly dimming figures of the Irish literary renaissance who enthralled me. Since I was there on what might be called a diplomatic mission, politics was the chief theme, but I could never quite make out where literature left off and politics and economics began. They circled around and above each other like cars on a switch-back in a pleasure resort. In both countries good talk was the nebular matter in which one could see ideas like tiny stars twinkling as they took form, or exploding with a dismal pop.

Every other year at this time I spent a month or more in London, my duty being to recruit new writers and new ideas for *The Saturday Review*. These London literary circles seemed to be more civilized and certainly were more sophisticated than New York. Talk there ranged more widely, was more articulate, and more aware of complexities. It was also more brittle, and more supercilious, with the spun-glass quality of an aristocracy reduced to the perfect defining of its own chosen way of life. I felt more painfully an outsider with those Georgians than in 1918, when I had been a resident. You must, apparently, work, not merely talk, with the inhabitants of another nation if you are to break through the tough if almost invisible cellophane which separates nationalities. And I was more at home with my surviving friends of the last war period — H. M. Tomlinson, whose prose was the most lucid of his day, or Walter de la Mare, that strong, faery spirit, or H. G. Wells — than with my new acquaintances among the Sitwells, Logan Pearsall Smith, the expatriate Quaker essayist, Virginia Woolf, and others of less fame.

As for Ireland, in 1918 I spent a month there in what could fairly be described as the four winds of talk, all blowing at once. The literary Renaissance was still flourishing, and I encountered A. E., Doctor Gogarty, Ernest Boyd, James Stephens, and the playwrights of the Abbey Theater in many a pleasant battle of the tongues. But it was also Ireland's greatest moment of political stress. The fugitives from the Easter Rebellion were still in hiding, and I was taken to see some of them, down dark lanes to secret houses. Conscription was threatened by the British government, which seemed to the judicious in Ireland, and to me, an incitement to rebellion and anarchy, since most of the best fighters in Ireland were already serving in the armies abroad. Hence much of the talk was hot politics. As I was one of the few American civilians permitted by the British government to enter southern Ireland at this time, I was supposed to be entrusted with some secret mission; whereas my function was simply to get for various authorities at home (and my own satisfaction) a better understanding of a most complex situation. Hence I was talked to everywhere, in private and public, and when a sprained ankle kept me in bed, the talk flowed into my room and swept into topics in which I had little knowledge, and not much interest. But always, whether of labor problems, or of economics to Sir Horace Plunkett, with whom I worked as a voluntary secretary at the climax of the Irish Convention, or of literature, the war, and history, it always came back to Ireland and the Irish soul.

One result was that I carried back messages and letters of some importance to high individuals in the British government, and to those who had the ear of the Administration at home. But it was that brilliant talk, hovering on one subject, then shooting with the speed of sound to another, like a hummingbird between flowers, that I remember best. I saw the Irish mind tense and explosive at an emotional height. And I recognized its peculiar quality, which is to refer all discussion of practical action or current theory to beliefs which are not so much Catholic as personal to one of the oldest cultures in Europe, a culture that for a millennium has never been able to make a way of life in accord with its inner needs. And as this longed-for way of life had as many definitions as there were speakers, with, as a unifying principle, only opposition to what other groups and nations accepted as the necessity of the moment, provocation was constant, and wit and paradox flew like sparks from a generator. I was never convinced by the arguments, but strongly moved by the genius of the place, which was most interesting when least translatable into obvious common sense.

My Irish experience made me more objective when I came back in later years to England. If there was more consciousness of the outside world, especially in art, in the mobile, glancing talk of the Georgians in London, there was less emotion, a shallower relationship to the slowly disintegrating Europe of the Long Armistice. The Irish for a thousand years had opposed, when they could agree upon anything, what they felt was a spiritual decadence. The evils of the present seemed less important to them than the errors of the past. The Georgians were iridescent bubbles on the stream of disintegration itself. A breakdown of old controls had set them free to experiment with techniques of penetration into the modern consciousness. Neither the subtle corruption of power in Europe nor the cruder forces already visible in the United States, concerned them vitally. It was characteristic that the Irishman Joyce, when he came to experiment with the same penetrations in *Ulysses,* should have struck far below the level of sophisticated intellectuals, and have chosen for his theme an ordinary, sensual man. Talent was a dime a dozen in that England. Genius was scarce, although Housman, who was still writing, had it; and Virginia Woolf also, though far less than our Henry James, who had marked a way, though not their way, for these introverts of literature.   So also did that strange poet, Robert Bridges, who beat up obscurity into impressive epics. I stayed with him once on Boar's Hill near the sad-eyed Masefield's residence. I found him one morning on his back in a sun pocket in his garden, writhing his long legs while he composed a letter in French on a pad on his midriff. There is the same individuality, the same effort in his poetry.

But I missed something which was hard to explain then in these English intellectuals, especially in the group about the talented Sitwells, where the talk was best and literary production the most abundant. Their roots did not go beyond the cultivated soil of selected brains. There was a half-conscious refusal to be aware of the coarse, the crudely emotional, of what Whitman called the common earth. For that one had to go to the universities, where the Workmen's Educational Association was drawing blood from old culture for the nascent Labor Party. Chamberlain, the Prime Minister of appeasement, is said never to have read *Mein Kampf* before he set out to prove to Hitler that aggression was bad for business. There was common earth in that book, foul with sewage. Even the idle drinkers and fornicators in Ernest Hemingway's *The Sun Also Rises* were more aware of their maladjustment to life as it was being lived, than these more civilized British writers, who seemed content to adjust to each other.

But from Ireland and England alike I came home with a stronger conviction that good talk as a tonic for the imagination and as a stimulus for thought, had been too much neglected in formal histories. It has always been both the lubricant and the fuel for the creative mind. Here in the United States there has seldom been opportunity, or time to spare, for the kind of talk I mean, except in bright intervals at Monticello, in Concord, or in coteries at Charleston, Boston, New York, Philadelphia, Chicago, and San Francisco. Many of the rough corners and lacks of frames of reference in the powerful American writing from, say 1920, until today, are due, in my opinion, to just this failure in personal communication. For it is surprising how often a writer does not know precisely what he has captured in his imagination until, in a congenial but not too sympathetic atmosphere, he has heard himself speak it out in the tentatives of conversation. I learned this first in New York.

∽ 14 ∽

Literature by Remote Control

T HE NEW GENERATION (and many historians) have forgotten
the origin of the term 'The Depression,' the name by
which we call that true cataclysm of the nineteen-twenties and
thirties which pushed Europe into ruin, and for the first time
since the eighteen-fifties and eighteen-sixties daunted the su-
preme self-confidence of the United States. This is an interesting example of semantics, since the word was first used as a
whitewash by our professional economic advisers, who wished
to persuade us that the calamity of 1929-32 was only an unfortunate episode. Hard times — a collapse of the economic system — oh no! — we were merely depressed after too headlong a
prosperity. The thing to do was to buy sound stocks and forget about them. Many did!

The Depression nearly wrecked *The Saturday Review,*
which had gone into the black for the first time in that cul-
mination of speculative folly which we recall as 1929. It was
saved by two items of good fortune. For varying reasons the
book market is usually the last to suffer from sharp economic
declines, one of the reasons being that any wide-reaching catas-
trophe produces quantities of saleable books about its cause
and cure. Our other salvage was the loyalty of the then owner
of *The Review,* Thomas W. Lamont, who proposed to see us
through, and did. We trimmed sail, threw some luxuries over-
board, and tacked through the blasts, although it was to be a
decade before we got back again to stability.

My own emotional reaction to the crash and clutter of disintegrating fortunes, and the patient suffering of millions of
workers, was followed by an intellectual readjustment, as if I
had gone through a psychiatric analysis. Something died in
me which was probably ready to die, but whose passing I felt

with regret. I mean the sense of literature as a noble play in words. Or to put it in less dilettantish language, I lost my youthful conception of writing as an escape from the commonplace into a life of the fancy, with Truth and Beauty (both capitalized) as its aims. Such writing is dependent upon a belief that there are areas of sensation or pure thought into which the fine mind can lift itself and escape circumstance. I still believe in the theory. But from the Depression years until the confused present it has been impossible to put it confidently into practice. 'The world is too much with us,' and for much more urgent reasons than Wordsworth described in his famous sonnet, written in an earlier and easier crisis.

I felt this, as many must have done, especially in editorial and essay writing. What had seemed to be a *jeu d'esprit*, or an affectionate description, now began to tinkle faintly of insincerity, as if it were a game intended to take one's mind off reality. Humorists who had pleased me no longer seemed funny. We needed humor, and the younger men, like E. B. White and James Thurber, were soon to give it to us with more novelty than I could find in the twenties, and also (Clarence Day excepted) with a sharper edge of irony and more ominous implications. But humor in general did not flourish in the New Deal atmosphere, where the politicians and the economists always had, or said they had, the last word.

I myself, though not unconversant with public affairs, had no burning message to give to the public. I was confused as well as distressed. My interest in literary criticism slackened, like a hunter's zest for game when there is a forest fire in the woods. Not knowing the primary answers (and who did?), I looked back to where I could see clearly. Evening after evening I walked on the strip of turf before our cottage in the hills of Cornwall in Connecticut, or lay meditating in the morning sun before my working cabin of squared logs, through which the breeze, and sometimes a bird, blew out over the deep valley below. And I resolved that for my part, while the confusion lasted, I would study and interpret the American tradition, which is best preserved in our literature. For I felt, as Thoreau had said a century earlier, that our heritage of freedom was nearly spent; by which he meant, and I meant, that our sense of a peculiar strength from the nature of our history had sunk too deep into the subconsciousness to be a lively emotion. And I meant also that this sustenance from the past was spread too thin over a vast population, some fat with prosperity, others miserable in discontent, or too recently come here to understand the kind of past they, with us, were inheriting.

I found it increasingly difficult to do my thinking and writing in New York. Town born, I had come to live more and more, when I could, in the country. And in these years I settled into a pattern, physically difficult but spiritually satisfactory. I took no regular vacations, but spent the longer part of each week from early summer to early autumn in the hills. It was a doubtful plan of life for an editor, and my executive work suffered. But it seemed the only possible plan for a writing editor who expressed as well as directed the policies of his magazine. Perhaps an editor should not write himself. Of two of the best I have known in my time, Thomas B. Wells of *Harper's* did not write at all, and Ellery Sedgwick of *The Atlantic Monthly* but seldom.

It was not ordinary country in which, as Samuel Butler would have said, I tried to straighten my mind. Cornwall was a remote New England town, all rural, in the folds of the southern Berkshires. Lovelier hills, more beautiful lights, more excellent vistas, charming but never grand, I have seen nowhere. And it is a town with a history. As so often in New England, it has never been rich, never important within itself, but has been responsive to world currents sweeping far beyond its valleys. The Christianizing of the Pacific islands got one of its strongest impulses from these hills, and the first organized attempt to educate natives from our Indian tribes, as well as from the islands and the East, to become Christian leaders of their people, began in a Cornwall valley. Outlanders have always been attracted to Cornwall, and if after twenty-five years of residence they remain outlanders, nevertheless they get spiritual nourishment as well as recreation from the tough and stony soil.

About the time of which I write, the rather harsh Puritanism, which had been Cornwall's chief export, had been softened by winds of literature blowing in from the southward. In the elm shades of North Cornwall, near the ornate belfry of an old church, Carl Van Doren was beginning his career as a historian, with playful researches into Cornwall's eccentric past. He was literary editor of *The Nation,* and soon to be head of the Literary Guild. Later also, I could see from my hilltop, the orchard and green backward slope of Irita Van Doren's farm. She was in charge of the *Herald Tribune Books,* in which Stuart P. Sherman was publishing his brilliant weekly essays on literature. Beyond her hilltop house, Lewis Gannett, reviewer for the daily *Herald Tribune* had settled. In a mountain meadow below Cornwall Center lived Joseph Wood Krutch, literary critic and later dramatic reviewer for *The Nation.* In Cornwall Hollow, far below my cabin, were the poets, Chard Powers Smith, and Mark Van Doren who was also a scholar and a critic of fine perceptions. On our own Yelping Hill, I was working for *The Saturday Review* and the Book-of-the-Month Club. Lee Wilson Dodd, the playwright, lived and worked here also until his death in 1933, and later Townsend Scudder, the biographer and social historian. It is not too much to say that for some years at least the fate of a new book of importance was more dependent upon the hills of Cornwall than upon anything else except its own merits. And all of these editors and writers came as I did, and as many after us, not so much to rest as to tune our minds to a better balance after the turmoil of New York. We liked New York. We lived by its vivid interests. Yet one had to get away from the accent on financial success, from the pressure of massed population, from bigness, often without meaning. One had to get away for a while or be useless in the appraising of values in that essence of human experience which we call literature.

My brain, whatever can be said against it, is a sensitive instrument, and my intuitions, especially of disaster, prove too often correct for my peace of mind. In the Depression years and on up to the outbreak of war, I sublimated my growing uneasiness by my study of the American tradition. The first fruits were collected in a book called *Seven Years Harvest* (1936), the only satisfactory collection of critical essays I was ever able to bring together, because throughout the book there is to be felt, at least by me, this concern for our national heritage. And also in a much more ambitious and earlier volume called *Classic Americans* (1931), which was a close critical study of nine great American writers from Irving to Whitman. The lengthy critical essays in this volume were praised at least up to their deserving and some of the estimates have become standard in our literary history. But the book was a rhetorical tragedy, and I set down its story as a warning to younger authors. I had planned a complete history, which proved to be premature, and had begun with a long and rather perfunctory introduction on our colonial period, which cost me so much work that against my better judgment I let it remain in the final editing when the ash-can should have been its destination. Years before I had learned a guiding principle from my editorial experience. Always say in your preface what you hope your reviewers will say in their criticisms, and three times out of four they will do so. But this time I apologized for my failure to write a history, apologized for my introduction, and, in effect, wrote the first deprecatory paragraph for every important review of the book! I could make a thoroughly satisfactory book of *Classic Americans* in five minutes with a blue pencil. But an author seldom gets that kind of opportunity.

I suppose that on many a Cornwall summer night, in the translucent starry dark of those hills, all of us literary folk on our mountain meadows may have been strolling with eager minds, hoping for the birth of an idea. Ideas in literature, and I assume elsewhere, are conceived in the body of knowledge and experience, and born quite unexpectedly when gestation is complete and the moment is right. No one thinks out an idea. No one gets an idea unless there have been long and often quite unconscious, and still oftener seemingly irrelevant preliminaries. No great masterpieces, though many good books in prose and poetry, ever came off our Cream and Yelping Hills, and from that graceful Cornwall Hollow down which a French army once marched on its way to Yorktown. But much honest and some rich thinking was done there, and I am sure there was ripening of judgment and of wisdom.

I found the nights most stimulating when mid-August brought down early fall from the northern mountains, to which our hills led in long and ever lifting ranges. Then the slow curve of the wooded summits above our cottage would prickle against bright stars, and there would be pale flashes of aurora from the north. It was on such a night that the memories of the old ancestral town in which I grew up expanded into significance. Here in New England and a generation away from Delaware and the Brandywine of my youth, the quality of that American life in the nineties, so incredibly different from the present, so differently accented from a New England past, came to be felt, as a novelist feels the little world he creates from his imagination to represent reality. So after false beginnings, I wrote my *Age of Confidence*, which is the first section of this book. Ten years later, on the same hilltop, a line from Thoreau, of whom I had already written in *Classic Americans*, aroused my sudden and passionate curiosity. A great writer had been born in another small New England town, and made it his cosmos. I knew his books, but what was he like, and why, and conditioned by what subtle experience? Much of my biography of Thoreau I wrote in Cornwall woods, less dense but as secluded as Walden Pond.

If I were a Californian, I would take at due seasons to the meadows of the High Sierras. If I were a Carolinian, I would seek the ancient river plantations, now gone back to nature, or the beaches of the barrier islands, with palmetto jungles behind them. If I were still a Delawarian, I would spend part of my life on the upper Brandywine. Being what I am, a satellite of New York, I join many thousands of my kind in tribute of gratitude to the rocky hayfields, the rough ridges, the cedars, sweet bay, and laurel of Connecticut. And praise its small but varied beauty, and the tough independence of a country sterile in crops but productive of men.

∽ 15 ∽

Depression Blues

IN THE LATTER NINETEEN-TWENTIES I had gone three times for long stays in London and on the Continent. England was struggling with mass unemployment and the dole, but otherwise seemed not much changed from the country I had known since 1899. I remember making the trite remark to Sidney Webb one day on the terrace of Parliament, that the dole was arousing widespread criticism in the United States. 'Wait till you have such unemployment as ours,' he said. 'You will find that the one thing you cannot do is to let the people starve.' That was what our government did not learn fast enough after 1929. The age of *laissez-faire* was over.

Except for marching bands of beggars — singing or playing instruments as in Elizabethan times — London, at least, seemed normal. I had gone over in that year of 1927 to take part in a conference under the auspices of the Society for Pure English on standards for the language now spread throughout the world. Before I left, I talked with 'Hen' Root, our old gardener in Cornwall, a seventh-generation Yankee, and told him that I proposed to discuss our English with Britishers abroad. 'Ye be, be ye! Wall, I thought they spuk jest the same as we do.'

Lord Balfour, aging after his strenuous services in the war, was our chairman, and I told him this story. From America went Louise Pound, the authority on language history, Leonard Bacon, essayist and poet and one of our most dependable writers for *The Saturday Review,* and John Livingston Lowes, a distinguished Harvard scholar and author of that brilliant combination of literary criticism and scholarship, *The Road to Xanadu.* H. L. Mencken, of course, was invited, but could not come. For Great Britain there was Bernard Shaw; the Scottish dictionary-maker Sir William A. Craigie, later editor of the great historical dictionary of American speech; the head of the British Museum; Sir Henry Newbolt; and many other scholars and writers. We did not settle anything important in the choice and use of words; but our unanimous agreement on one point was enough to justify the conference, for it marked the end of one era and the beginning of another in the history of authority in our common language. Without a dissenting voice we agreed that there was no longer a single ideal standard for the English language except excellence. That the best written and spoken usage of New York or San Francisco were as authoritative as those of London or Oxford if their influences were felt upon the strengthening and broadening of the tongue. I do not believe that there was one of the many present at those discussions who did not uphold this doctrine later in controversies against pedants, and the makers of dictionaries and textbooks who tried to force standards of the past upon a growing world language. What we accepted in theory, H. L. Mencken was to continue to document in his admirable books.

There was, however, one bilious editorial writer on a famous English weekly, who turned a machine gun on us before we had time to get out of range. He was disgusted by the idea that authority could subsist in the crude English of America. He thought that the Scots still knew too little English to make rules for it — an obvious blast at Craigie. No one, he concluded, could speak intelligently of pure English but an Englishman, and, on further consideration, an Englishman living on or south of the Thames. Some Cambridge scholars answered him. Being a mildish crew without our Mencken, we Americans said 'wait and see,' and kept out of the battle.

Paris and France seemed to be recovering when we traveled widely there in 1927 and again in 1929. Even Austria, which I had never known in her brilliant prewar days, was struggling upward. When I hurried back in September of 1929 to the bedside of my wife who was desperately ill, leaving my two young boys to find their way home, it was the United States that seemed abnormal. The great boom had become feverish and sick. Then came the Depression, whose literary effects I have discussed in the last chapter. I had my own Depression too, a minor breakdown, the result of many combining tensions. For the first time I had forced upon me that mood of somber realism in which one contemplates the possible end of all activity. As I sat from time to time resting by order in the year of 1930, my too speedy mind slowed down to reflections which always ended in a sense of futility. Not personal futility so much as the seeming waste of the energy that had gone into restoring or reconstructing a culture which before the first great war had seemed so rich and good in spite of its unequal distribution, and so full of promise of new and brave things in our brief golden age of the twenties. This was the source of my confusion when I walked at night in our Cornwall hills. For I tried to deny my prophetic mind, which had been made oversensitive by undercurrents in my recent European experience too little noted at the time. I denied that the tight and soulless formula of Marxism, the revival of the philosophy of violence, the omens of irrepressible conflict, were true patterns of the immediate future. I denied, but the sense of futility remained. Perhaps much of what I and other Americans were proposing to do with American vitality and American tradition, was only a by-product of nostalgia?

I wrote *The Age of Confidence* in a mood of nostalgia. But nostalgia, if it is honest and not sentimental or merely romantic, provides reliable evidence for history. It gives first-hand testimony, though of course colored by one man's personality. The futility did not lie there. It was not really futility so much as frustration. All this energetic research in the background of our history, a history which even in the nineteen-thirties was still so little known and remembered that discoveries of new areas of intimate life were appearing in books every few weeks — all this was certainly not futile. Nor did I myself, when I turned from personal memories to close studies of the historical environment of our great figures in literature, and began to write biography, believe that my work was futile. Yet in the let-down of weary moments, when the mind dropped out of the past into the difficult present, some baggage of confidence always got left behind. There was a psychological block between Thoreau and Walt Whitman on whose lives I was working, and the next American era — some unfinished business of the immediate present hard as yet to define.

I understood the cause of my perplexity better after my first contact with Hitler's Europe in 1933. More of that later. But its nature for me personally was not clear until the end of the last war. All through this part of my memoirs I have used *The Saturday Review*, not so much as a subject as a thread on which to string reflection and experience. Recently I spent some time over the 1930 volume, which was nearly the last in which all of us wrote freely of change and tradition as if there were rapids but no plunging waterfall ahead. I found a ripeness and a wisdom in the literary comment of that volume which I miss to-day. There was a width of interest, which began and ended in the humanities with all the fields of speculation and knowledge in between. Public affairs — including the threats of war and social dislocations — were given their just place in the sweep of history, but only as the instruments of civilization. We did not, as now, feel dependent upon the course of events for sur-vival. The fat was still in the frying pan, not in the fire. Nor was there any cold disdain of the unfactual. Nor any defeatist unclasping of fingers that in worse times than these had grasped tightly the fabric of our Graeco-Christian civilization.

But for such a magazine the times were clearly going out of joint. The skies were changing and the writers with them. I could see that the passionate faith I shared with others in tried verities and values was to be no preventive of war and revolu-tion, though it might (I believe it will) be some day a cure. I understood a remark of Thoreau's, then on his deathbed, to the companion of many of his Concord walks, William Ellery Chan-ning, who was distressed by the approaching close of their friendship. 'It is better some things should end,' Thoreau mur-mured. A harsh remark until one considers that his meaning was that good things have to end with what has made them good. Otherwise there is no rebirth for them in a different world.

The Review of those days, which I use only as a symbol, had to die figuratively in order to change. In spite of its plenitude of thinkers writing of this danger and that, it was already de-fending a present in terms of a cherished past. Obscure bac-teria were poisoning the civilization it described. They could not infect the indestructible, but it would be the job of another generation to find out just what that was and how to use it. The fabric as it had been woven they would probably destroy. In the meantime, and in these thirties, the scientists were being diverted to technologies which would make the next war terrible. And statesmen, philosophers, priests, and scholars were either futile or frustrated, while fanatics and materialists of power yelled them down.

16

A Taste of Blood in the Mouth

MY OWN PERSONAL TRAGEDY as a result of the Depression was the death in 1933 of my brother-in-law, Lee Wilson Dodd, poet, playwright, and novelist. When his creative talent had run with the current of his times, his plays had been very successful. Yet I think it is for the best of his poetry that he will be remembered. Graceful, incisive, beautiful, it is a perfect transition between the romanticism of the age of his youth and the foreboding realism which began in his maturity. One long satiric poem, 'The Great Enlightenment,' has kept its cult of admirers, and may be better known twenty years from now than when it was published in 1928. A wit who delighted in his own mind without a trace of egotism, his perfect humor had a curious underblend of pessimism that was not so much cynical as oversensitive. This very fine poem spoke with two voices, one idealistic, the other doubting. The modern world was in truth always too much for his virile but delicate spirit. It frightened him before it began to frighten us, yet he could not resist its sophistications and its comic crudities. He sucked at its flowers like a hummingbird, jabbing at the fat and ugly ones, and then flew away.

What happened to him was symptomatic of the bearing-down of the new age of steel upon connoisseurs of life and prophets of eternal values. Such men are always in danger of rough handling, for their own times are usually ahead of or behind their theories of how to live. Writing, for Lee, was a spiritual necessity. Financially it supplemented an income from his inheritance. When his investments shriveled in the Depression, he could with difficulty afford the pleasant and exciting speculation of playwriting, where his returns had been greatest but his failures, as is usually the case, numerous. The curtain rang down when Henry Miller, the then famous actor, collapsed from influenza on the first night of a very promising play written for him, and died. No manager would touch the unlucky production, and the tide of Lee's literary fortunes rapidly ebbed. With a considerable establishment to support, and only the remains of an income, he turned to what might be called free-lance teaching in various colleges, and was to succeed George P. Baker in his playwriting course at Yale. That spring he died of a weakened heart. I, at least, knew that part of the trouble was actually a corrosive disease of the heart — not the physical organ, but the creative, emotional core of being to which we give the name. The delicate cutting-edge of his mind had to be kept sharp or his fastidious spirit could not use it. His kind of imagination would not function amid the distractions of teaching. He could be useful, and was, but not the self he wanted to be. A more earthly spirit would have been content with a different success. He willed to do so, but his subconscious defeated him. He died like a forest shrub transplanted to a lawn.

All of us had bitter vicarious suffering like this to carry in our daily minds through those years of 1932 and 1933. We had suffered losses more irreparable than fortunes; yet there was an alleviation in the reviving strength and courage of the country. Listening to the first inaugural address of Franklin D. Roosevelt, on the radio in my son's room at Harvard, I realized with a surge of emotion that however dark the international picture, something could be done and would be done about our breakdown at home. Right or wrong — how could I know? nor at the moment did it seem to matter fundamentally. *Laissez-faire* was dead and we had a leader who knew it. Confidence and a new line of trial by error was what we needed. I thought so then. I think so now. The New Deal was only the wobbling course of a curve still undetermined. But it moved. Franklin Delano Roosevelt became for me that extra ounce of personalized power which guides the vast impersonal forces of an age to the infinitesimal but vital degree in which they can be guided. When broadcasting at the time of his death throughout Australia where I happened to be, I used Whitman's line 'O powerful, fallen, Western Star.' No one questioned the transference from one great dead American to another.

There was a break in the clouds over the home front in 1933. I felt it strongly, and living in the eastward-fronting island of New York let the mind turn abroad. A temporary relief of a local ache lets the invalid realize the full extent of his sickness. That was the way many of us felt in New York, and far beyond New York, as could be told from the flow of letters and print over my desk. Writers, sensitive as they have to be to spiritual change, looked up from their own worries to see dusk falling over Europe, and the never dying beasts of the night crawling out of their holes — violence, fanaticism, hate, and greed. And guessed that Hitler, the new leader, whom so many refused to take seriously, had, like Milton's Satan, attained a bad eminence.

It happened that I had been president of the American Center of the International P.E.N. Clubs, an organization sponsored by John Galsworthy after the last war, with assemblages of writers in every country in Europe except Russia (which had refused to join), and elsewhere throughout the world. I had been a delegate to their annual Congresses in Vienna and in Antwerp, and knew that a vast majority of their members was committed to freedom of speech and a better understanding among nations as a foundation for peace. They were only scattered individuals in a confused world, but through newspapers, magazines, and the best books of the period, they were close to public opinion, and often its shapers. They were highly articulate, and proposed to remain so. Nor were they in general bound by vested financial interests or place and position to appeasement. Nor ignorant, like so many of their fellow nationals, of the significance of these private armies springing up in Europe, or the true nature of the Caesars and Napoleons who were going to make their followers great. Some were professional propagandists, but more were creative artists; and all but a few guessed that they were faced with the possible destruction of the culture that had made their work possible. This year of 1933, the Congress was to meet in Yugoslavia, a storm center of Europe. I was asked to go as delegate, and with a not too creditable relief at escaping for a while from the frustrations at home, took ship with my wife and set out for the heart of the gathering hurricane.

We sailed away for the Mediterranean on a typical cruise ship with a passenger list that gave the pleasant illusion of such leisurely sight-seeing trips as we used to enjoy before the first war. There was the usual American who had been shocked in the past by the gambling in European casinos and was going abroad to see them again, playing bingo, which he did not regard as gambling, en route, and wirelessing daily to the broker in charge of his speculative account. There was the usual couple going abroad for the twentieth time, and the couple going abroad for the first time. And the tall, dark Englishman who proved to be the brother of a duke and was on his way to an ambassadorship. But one striking exception made me realize that this was 1933, not 1913 or even 1923. Signor Dino Grandi, Mussolini's financial envoy to the United States, came aboard at Boston, with his suite, and for him the long arm of the Duce held up our ship for half a day.

It was all very pleasant and restful, but for me a baleful light hung over both horizons, and the sense of the end of a bright age was emphasized by our disrupted schedule. Thanks to Signor Grandi's belated arrival, we crept furtively at dusk instead of dawn into each of our scheduled ports, and saw the flowery streets of the Azores and the monumental squares of Lisbon by dusk, or evening lights. And Italy itself, as we crossed it by electric train, had lost its amiable quality. Blackshirts with revolvers searched our compartment and asked for our papers; and there was nothing gay in Venice except the white flames of carved stone lapping above Saint Mark's over the almost empty Piazza. So we came by way of the lovely Dalmatian coast to wall-encircled Dubrovnik, once Ragusa, an eagle's nest on the sea. That little republic had kept intact for nearly a millenium by carrying appeasement in one hand and courage in the other against Venice and the Turk. The democracies, I reflected, were trying the same policy, but, so far, without courage.

There was to be no appeasement at Dubrovnik, but, unfortunately, it was to be six years before the Western governments followed the example set by authors and journalists, and then it was too late. While our business was the general welfare of literature, the Congress, as everyone knew, had one chief objective, which was to assert a reasonable freedom of speech among all the nationalities concerned, and back this assertion by strong pledges from the leading writers of America and Europe. We had good representation for a meeting in a spot so distant from the centers of authorship and publication. Some four hundred delegates and members were present.

Hitler and the Nazis had come to power in Germany. The books had been burned, including volumes by some of those present at Dubrovnik or members of one or another of the P.E.N. Clubs. As writers, we were determined to make our own position clear in what was becoming in Europe another life-and-death struggle for freedom of thought and the imagination. And we were equally determined to make each national delegation take its stand for or against the ideals of the profession, and if against, to withdraw from an organization pledged to uphold them. Either before or after this Congress, Marinetti, the Italian modernist, had put the case for Italy with specious eloquence. No one in Italy wanted to write anything of which the Duce would not approve, he said — which of course was nonsense. But Italian practice, except in journalism, was on the border line. The great liberal critic Croce had not been molested. We held back a decision.

Germany was a kettle of very different fish. Our German Center had been eminent, with such members as the Manns, Feuchtwanger, Remarque, Zweig. Its writers, with only a few exceptions, like the dramatist Hauptmann, were on the side of the angels — battered angels they proved to be, who could not guard their own. With the overthrow of the German Republic, a fury of repression had been let loose upon the arts, and especially literature. We were deeply concerned as to what the German delegation would have to say.

The German P.E.N. Club had been strangled. When the Germans finally arrived, they were, with one exception, unknown to us all, and also to international and even to German literature. The exception was a mild little fellow who had functioned before as secretary, and now looked for orders before he opened his mouth. Their leader was a tall, lean lawyer, Edgar von Schmidt-Pauli by name, who had written, as we learned by underground, a campaign life of Hitler. He was

Hitler's own appointment, and the rest of the delegation were his agents. The German P.E.N. Club, as we had known it, was dissolved, dead.

Schmidt-Pauli, as was rapidly made clear, had been sent by Hitler to Dubrovnik with a definite commission. The Congress had invited Ernst Toller, then an exile from his native Germany, to address them on freedom of thought. Schmidt-Pauli had been ordered by Hitler to see that his mouth was shut. Also no discussion of the repression of German writers in the past few months was to be allowed to get on the record. Toller, a Jew, a radical, and one of the best playwrights of Germany, had been for a brief moment the rather ineffective leader of the Munich revolution at the end of the first World War. He had been a Communist, but was so no longer. His attacks upon the pussyfooting of the Social Democratic Republic had been so annoying that he had been imprisoned for several years, in which time he had written his best plays, known all over Europe and in America. He was a small, dark man, with cavernous glowing eyes, an artist and an intellectual, not a fanatic. I liked him though he was not an easy companion. Some fire in him seemed always about to break out. His history, his personality, and his eloquence, all made him dangerous for a dictator. Since his imprisonment, and now in his exile, his ardor had shifted from politics to freedom of the mind. The conflict in Germany had become for him a premonition of a world turned servile. He was as good a symbol as one could find for the resistance of Western culture to the new tyrannies. Hitler wanted him muzzled. I believe that this was the first open reach of Hitler's steel hand beyond the German borders. Schmidt-Pauli, at first suave and conciliatory, was the glove on the gauntlet.

Outside the stuffy little opera house of Dubrovnik where we held our meetings, we enjoyed the usual recreations of a conference, more pleasant than usual because of the friendly Ragusans and the charm of that city of old ivory backed against violet mountains. The town was heavy with tradition, yet its hospitality was like that of a Mid-Western conference at home. There was, for example, a supper in an ancient banqueting room on the high walls above the sea, to which every Ragusan lady brought a cake of her own baking. And there was an excursion through the Dalmatian islands to see the burial vault of a wealthy family, which had been sculptured by Mestrovic. Also eager literary discussions in the gardens of the twin monasteries of the town, or on the pavemented Main Street of Dubrovnik, which is a seafarers' walk walled by palaces converted to shops. In the opera house the tension increased until on the second day the agenda brought us to Ernst Toller's speech.

That meeting was one of those dramas in actual life which, without art in their making, are more climactic than the best theater. We were crowded into the dusty plush seats of the orchestra and filled the boxes which, in European fashion, ran round the auditorium to the corners of the stage. Schmidt-Pauli's speech surprised me, for I did not yet understand the Nazi technique of the fifth column — which was to breed termites and let them eat out the hearts of the enemy. Toller, he said, represented no one but his fanatical self. He was a bad choice as speaker on issues which concerned us all. The decision was left to our common sense. In the buzz of conversation that followed, someone moved the next business, which was Toller's address. He sat in front of me, a manuscript which he never used in his hand. I could see his tensity, but no great reason for it, since it was clear how the vote would go. Then a heavy-set Belgian asked for the stage, known to me as a journalist, but better known later as a leader of the Belgian Nazis, one of those who opened the gates of the frontier. He looked us over contemptuously, and spoke like a man taking time off for children. What we needed was unity and conciliation, and the strength, wisdom, and (with emphasis) the magnanimity of the Reich. Germany would lead us to a new world where the right literature would have its right place, and dilettantish art be swept out with the rest of decadent liberalism. I got the sneer and the threat, though not all of his French. So did the rest, and the opera house was quiet with that absence of sound which is more silent than silence itself. I felt rather than saw a chill spreading. The words meant more than they said. Groups visibly sat closer together or edged apart.

Then in a burst of melodrama, the very beautiful Dutch novelist, Jo van Ammers-Küller, sprang to the stage. She was one of the most popular writers of Holland, and I had known her before and had liked both her novels and her good looks. Now her color was high, her eyes hysterical, and her voice, low at first, rose almost to a shriek. 'You cannot do this,' she said; then screamed, 'You cannot do this to Germany! Germany is stronger than all of you put together. The future is Germany's. You must yield. You are babies. You know nothing. It will be the end of us all.' Someone led her into the wings. H. G. Wells insisted that Toller, though expelled from the German P.E.N. Club, should be allowed to speak. The motion was carried in a tumult of yeses and noes. Then the Germans rose and walked out to applause, cheers, and hisses, while hysterical delegates from bordering countries shouted from steps and railings. Some followed the Germans, but returned.

Toller spoke, passionately and with great eloquence. His speech I had to read afterward, for I was too deeply stirred by this sudden crack in our complacency to pay attention. I had, seen visible fear rising like cold fire. And I realized with a shock that what was a row over principle for English and Americans, and an affirmation of faith, was for these Europeans, imaginative men and women all of them, a quick vision of armies in their cities and bombs on their homes. They could guess the invisible wires that stretched back to Berlin, and I have no doubt Schmidt-Pauli smiled inwardly as he saw the reaction to his finger on the switch. For most aggressions begin with the mind and are rehearsed in the imaginations of the most vulnerable.

After the turmoil and the speech, I presented the resolution I had brought from our P.E.N. Club, which reaffirmed the principles upon which the P.E.N. was founded, and called upon the Centers of the P.E.N. to resist the attempt to use literature as propaganda in defense of persecution inflicted in the name of chauvinism, racial prejudice, and political ill-will.

It was passed, as I remember, unanimously, the deserters having withdrawn, and got itself into our minutes as the Seidel-Canby resolution, a name which my correspondence from Europe has borne ever since. Its publication, with violent attacks in the German and some Austrian papers, gave me some uneasy moments later that summer when I had to cross a neck of Germany in our car on the way home. Officials, studying my papers, kept consulting a list of names on which I was sure Seidel-Canby appeared. For I guessed, and I am sure rightly, that when Hitler read the resolution, as he certainly did, he had gritted his teeth, not over the ideas, which would have been meaningless to him, but over my seeming South-German middle name. It is probably not German, but a transliteration of Swedish made in Pennsylvania in the eighteenth century. But there would have been no chance to explain that.

The Germans refused to resign and asked for a hearing. It was given them in London the next winter with H. G. Wells presiding over an international committee. There they refused to subscribe to our resolution, and were expelled. But Schmidt-Pauli, sharp lawyer and clever journalist, got to the telephone first, so that newspapers in Germany, and all the neighboring states which got their earliest news service from that source, announced that the German delegation had resigned because the P.E.N. Clubs had gone Communist.

That whole Dubrovnik show seemed at first a good story to tell. And when the little ex-secretary of the old German P.E.N. Club, who was left behind as a spy, on one of our excursions stampeded over the shoulders of women in a bus which seemed about to plunge into a Montenegrin abyss, I felt contemptuous of the whole gang of them, and proud that we writers had proved tougher and more far-seeing than the politicians. More far-seeing perhaps, but not strong enough to stand against the hurricane that later drove so many of our P.E.N. Club members into death or exile. The wrecks of the European P.E.N. Clubs survived only as refugees in London or New York, and are but now beginning to be reconstituted.

It was, of course, far more than a story. On the trip through Serbia which sixty of us took afterward, young people from the universities mobbed our train and carried Toller on their shoulders. The opera in Belgrade had to stop when he appeared; a session in the university where five of us who were delegates spoke, broke up at the end in a wild tumult calling for Toller. And this in a dictatorship only less absolute than Tito's today! I believe that meeting to have been a significant, if tiny, episode in world history. Personally directed by Hitler himself, as we learned afterward, it was Schmidt-Pauli's mission to intimidate the journalists and the writers — some of them the great writers, some of them the most important journalists — of other nations. With a few he succeeded. He shook the confidence of all.

❦ 17 ❦

Ancestral Voices Prophesying War

A T BARCELONA, in 1935, I was a delegate to another P.E.N. Club Congress. We sailed to Gibraltar on the *Rex,* spending a week in Spanish Morocco, where, in Xauen, that Moorish city founded by refugees from Granada, I saw for the first time the Moslem Orient. Except for a Spanish garrison outside the walls, Xauen was untouched by the West. So little visited is this gray and lilac town built against the cliffs and waterfalls of the gray Riff Mountains, that even the Columbia Encyclopedia does not include its name. As we traveled there by bus over a military road, we saw Moorish soldiers training in the fields, the next year to become mercenaries for the reconquest of Spain; but in 1935 Franco was not even a name to us. We spent a month in Spain, acquiring more than a tourist's information as to the politics of the Republic from our ambassador, Claude Bowers, who took care of us in Madrid. I was struck by the intense separatism of the country. The talk was all of Catalonia oppressed by Castile, and the unrest in the Basque North. Communism was little spoken of; Falangism still less. I was depressed by the fearful dirt and poverty of the villages, and the stagnation of the cities, except Barcelona. I was shocked in run-down but beautiful Seville by the innumerable plump clerics waddling through the beggars, and astonished by the incredible gold treasures of the cathedral, and the reports of the wealth of the church in land. We traveled for hours through vast estates where the peasants earned only a peso a day. Spain needed everything — except civil war and a dictatorship of the old familiar pattern of South America in its bad days.

In Barcelona I made friends with many literary men and women and members of the university faculty. They were risk-

ing their liberty then by opposing the stupid bureaucratic cen-
tralization of the government in Madrid. Next year they were
to fight for the Republic, and now they are, or most of them,
dead or in exile. I was able to tell my friends at home when the
civil war broke out, that these leaders certainly were about as
radical as the members of the Yale and Harvard faculties who
had voted for Roosevelt.

H. G. Wells led the Congress in his cockney French, which
the English and Americans understood very well but no continental European, including the delegates from France. When
translated, his speech chilled the hot spirits who wished the literary world to take action against every violence and injustice
to a writer or journalist in totalitarian Europe. Wells' common
sense depressed them. As politicians and diplomats we writers,
he said, were too weak and inexperienced to do more than pass
resolutions. Our job was to write; our opportunity was to make
clear the underlying issues which Western culture had to face.
One book of high imagination could accomplish more, perhaps
now, certainly later, than a score of committees. He was right.

The P.E.N. Clubs had one more meeting before the curtain
went down. It was in 1939, on the eve of the war, at the World's
Fair in New York, and was attended by distinguished representatives of nations (including India and China) still free,
and by many eminent men and women already refugees. Some
of these delegates never went back, and those that did were
many of them soon in concentration camps. Yet the Congress
was a splendid gesture, the last chance for the independent
European imagination to speak freely before it was proved to
be too late. But only the Americans, or some of them, were
still confident that something could be done to avert war.

Later in the week a few of us took all the delegates to Washington, where we lunched on the White House terrace with
Mrs. Roosevelt, and visited the President in his office. Her
graciousness, and the beautiful simplicity of that little palace,
made a profound impression upon these Europeans, whose
minds went back so easily to pomp and ostentation, and who
had already seen the brutal and the predatory beginning to
divide the spoils of Western culture. They liked the way in
which Mrs. Roosevelt herself acted as guide and historian of

the White House. They liked the President's easy smile and warm handclasp, and his flashing recognition of a name known to him in books. It was the last that many of them were to see for a decade at least of a scene that suggested stability. Simplicity, tradition — these were the words they used oftenest on the trip back. It still seemed curious to me that Europeans should find tradition manifested here, when I, in my youth, had so often sought it abroad.

I was not one of the confident Americans. In 1933 and 1935 I had spent many hours in talk in Austria with a great European, a woman who made me understand what that term could mean, which was something quite different from a great American. She was the Gräfin Margit Czapary, of an ancient Silesian family, the widow of a Hungarian nobleman who shared her deep interest in history. Together they had reconstructed a thirteenth-century castle around an ancient keep on an eagle's shelf above the river Mur south of Salzburg. By my day her fortune had been wrecked in the first World War, and Burg Finstergrün had become a guest-castle to which one was introduced by friends. It was a walled structure of vast rooms heated by great porcelain stoves fed by domestics from the corridors outside, and from every window there were views of the Austrian Alps. In place of archdukes and chancellors the Gräfin now entertained each summer English and American visitors, pleasantly blended with her Austrian and Hungarian relatives, and always a musician to play for us after the stately dinner at which every guest was seated each night in a different companionship. There were tea and talk also on a turfy knoll from which one looked down a thousand feet to the rapids of the Mur and the tiny village of Ramingstein. A visitor who did not like so many ideas mixed with the talk of tennis and trout fishing, soon left for a more conventional environment. But if he were like-minded, he knew within twenty-four hours that he had found a spiritual home, and came back as often and for as long as he could. Alas, Burg Finstergrün is now an institution, its treasures of medieval art all scattered, and the Gräfin dead, having only by miracle escaped a concentration camp.

She was a liberal and a modern in her knowledge and sympathies; but also an ardent Catholic (religious, not political), and a survival of a type which the Middle Ages at their superb height must have often produced. She was a great feudal proprietor still, owning villages and forests, and the guardian of the rights and welfare of her peasants, of which she was the sympathetic and intelligent advisor in every difficulty. At the starvation period after the first World War, she had saved them by teaching the uses of our Indian corn, which she was able to get in quantity. Ownership for her was a trust. I doubt whether this principle was common in the Middle Ages, but it was commoner than now.

When we heard her great hoarse voice, or the tap of her staff, for she was slightly lame, and saw her heavy figure approaching in its dress like a uniform of black and white, it was a Presence which needed no title to distinguish it. She regarded me as typically American (I hope rightly) and would appeal to me over the heads of assembled English, Scotch, Poles, Austrians, not for my judgment, but as to one psychologically outside the tight European complex. 'Isn't it? Isn't it?' I can hear her say, a quaint unidiomatic interjection in her fluent English, which was sometimes a question but more often a statement. She named appeasement before the word was current for what was going on in the international conflict, and prophesied unhesitatingly its results. Her knowledge of European history was profound, and intuitive and emotional as well as informed. She knew intimately the Austrian heads of state, and was familiar with both men and events in her native Germany. She knew Goering, who had spent summers in his youth in her neighborhood — knew too much about him, and too much about Hitler to accept the current estimates. For we have forgotten that in those years nearly everyone here, and a dangerous many abroad, thought that Hitler was only a rashly blaring demagogue. The Gräfin did not underestimate his powers. She smelt evil, and understood his dangerous blend of shrewdness and fanaticism. Every ounce yielded by France and England gets him a pound, she said — and he will use it. Europe will be conquered if he is not stopped soon. 'Isn't it?'

It was a shock to come back in the late summer of 1935 to a complacent United States, disturbed by the plight of the European Jews, but seemingly indifferent to any political and military implications for us in the general European situation. No, not indifferent, for there was a dangerous undercurrent throughout the world that we all felt. We were cultivating wishful thinking in order to down uneasiness. Hitler was a tool of the industrialists, Germany would never risk war, keep your nose out of other people's business — everyone remembers how the talk went.

I did not prophesy our entrance into the war. My Quaker training made me shrink from that idea. In 1933, I argued with the Gräfin against the certainty of a European war. In 1935, she convinced me. By the time I came home I feared, but still did not believe, that we would be drawn in. But only a few historians and correspondents among my friends would listen to me. So I wrote two long editorials for *The Saturday Review,* of which I am more proud than of most of my writing, although they are too dated now ever to justify reprinting. One was an urgent appeal to take Hitler seriously. I said that he should be compared to Mohammed, not to a mere demagogue like Mussolini, or to a tool of the vested interests seeking wealth. He had Mohammed's blind if elemental fanaticism with a ruthless will to power and the ability to get it. He had both the shrewdness and the single-mindedness of the God- or devil-touched man. But Coleridge who wrote of Mohammed —

Choosing good from iniquity rather than evil from goodness,

would have had to reverse his terms for Hitler.

And I wrote another editorial essay on the lost youth of continental Europe, already lost although they did not know it, for their minds were corrupted, or their bodies were doomed by an ideological war. No one, so far as I can remember, paid any attention to either editorial. Now, as I reread them, they have the underemphasis of truth become a platitude.

⌒) 18 (⌒

From Books to Men

THE YEARS leading up to the second World War, the war itself, and the present battle for peace, are such a time as
Wordsworth had in mind when he defined poetry as emotion
recollected in tranquillity. We have lived through increasing
intensity and its decline into fatigue, but the tranquillity, or at
least the objectivity, is to come later, I fear much later. I myself felt strongly that the literature of those years — particularly
the thirties and forties — was in a state of becoming, and was
involved in a future of highly uncertain change. The Gargan-
tuan work of Thomas Wolfe is an obvious example. Even the
earlier work of James Joyce could not in its nature be otherwise explained. I met Joyce in Paris in 1937 while he was, I
think, still at work on *Anna Livia Plurabelle,* that experiment
in language as radical and as difficult as Gertrude Stein at her
toughest, though far more beautiful and more significant in
content. I remember him as a cadaverous man, unhealthy of
countenance, looking like a clerk until you saw the depth of his
eyes and heard his shy, pleasant voice. But with both Wolfe
and Joyce it seemed impossible to form a clear view of their
work. One turned from it to wonder what actually were to be
enduring values in the changing societies being described. And
here and elsewhere a literary editor such as myself, found himself constantly trying to think like a historian, a sociologist, or
an economist, for which he was inadequately trained. There
was unfinished business of politics and war before confident
literary estimates could begin again.

Young editors, like my friends of *Time,* responded as I could
not. They sent their mechanized divisions out through the
nation gathering in masses of new readers whose interest had
been aroused by the emergency into a demand for more and

more intelligent news with plenty of facts and no nonsense about philosophy. Realism, so-called, captured journalism. This is what is happening, the editors said. Our research staff says so, and our writers know how to make you read it in a few minutes' time. If we have made an error or two in our statements, we will tell you so next week. Western civilization and the machine age may be slipping, but we are not. We give you the news; there is no time to argue its ultimate significance. And within these limitations they did a good job. It took more than journalism to do a better one.

You cannot handle literature (or make it) that way. Probably all of us felt that it was too late to apply the prophetic truth of poetry, or the lessons of philosophy, or the fervors of religion, to the approaching crisis. They had been given a chance in the age just ending and had been ineffective when it came to the test. This was defeatism, of course, and rather cheap cynicism, but there was some truth as to the time element involved. When one age passes into another there is often a briefish period of crisis when the top is lifted from the routine world and even the common man can see the great anonymous forces of change working in the depths, seemingly quite independent of man's will. Then the old culture is felt to be out of joint with what is going on. Its truths may be still true, but they have to be reoriented and reapplied, and that takes too much time for an emergency. On how many occasions have men given up the New Testament and Plato, and repudiated the current books of literature and philosophy with their obsolete references to conditions already passed away! It is this which caused what Julien Benda called, in the famous prewar book of that name, 'trahison des clerics,' when men of creative imagination left their tasks to shout and argue with the ideologists.

The Review was in financial difficulties again. It needed to be set on a new course, but this was a risk (for all change is risk for a magazine) unless there was a new helmsman more at home than I among the reefs of controversial public affairs. It needed a mind seeking conflicts rather than trying to reconcile them; a younger mind with no compelling memories of an age of confidence, or of the brief golden age of the nineteen-twenties, which now could be seen as only a bright interval; perhaps a Puritan-positive mind rather than a Quaker spirit like mine. And so in 1936 I decided to resign, not from *The Review*, from which I hope my interest will never be divorced, but from my editorship, held for fifteen years, which is enough for one purpose and one policy.

We selected as my successor that fiery individualist Bernard De Voto, on his way to becoming a distinguished social historian. He fenced magnificently from his much-expanded editorial page, cutting down hydra heads as fast as they grew, and sometimes inventing them. But I felt that the rest of the paper was an incumbrance for his lively spirit, and he came to feel so too. His successor, George Stevens, was an admirable managing editor, of such modesty and self-knowledge that he took the job under protest and kept it only long enough to find his place as the book publisher he had always wanted to be.

The end seemed near. I remember well the evening in 1938, I think it was, when all the associates of *The Review* met for dinner in the Union League Club at the invitation of Mr. Lamont. It was to be a mortuary dinner, of that I had no doubt. But as the evening lengthened, we talked with such rich memories, with so much affection for our past, with such pride in *The Review*, that I felt this burial at least was to be worthy of the spirit of our hopes. As I put together in my mind some words for a fitting obituary, Mr. Lamont asked for silence, said he did not wish *The Review*, which had become an institution, to go under without one more attempt to find somehow, somewhere, those who would guarantee its continuance, and offered twenty thousand dollars to carry on while we made a last effort. It was a magnanimous gesture — I feared that it would prove only that — but we pledged our energies.

It was later, almost too late, that in a casual meeting in Central Park with my friend Molly Colum, I learned that an old acquaintance of mine, Harrison Smith, was forming a group of magazines. He took over *The Review*, effected economies in production, and found on his own staff that first requisite, a new editor, a modest young fellow, historian and educator by training, who at first would not allow himself to be called editor-in-chief. Norman Cousins had precisely the right outlook, the capacity, and the creative skill for the new times. For a while the ship leaked and scraped bottom, but with the aid of J. R. Cominsky as business manager, a man of like creative power in his own field, the new course was set and *The Review* was off again, with less capital but far more prestige than at the beginning, and soon with a rapidly increasing circulation to extend its influence.

I was busy enough with the added responsibilities of the Book-of-the-Month Club, as the subscribers to that organization began to go up into the hundreds of thousands. Nevertheless, I had already profited by the relief from editorial detail when I resigned my editorship of *The Review,* and now, with a mind cleared by its re-establishment, I was able to throw my creative energies into the personal task I had been working toward for years. Yielding to the changing needs, as I saw them, of the times, and my own desire, I had determined to swing from books to men, and specifically to the great American figures in my own field of literature who seemed to need new description and interpretation for a new generation. I wished to write biography. No sense of futility troubled me there. A nation either lives by its usable past, or is in danger of becoming only a distributing and defensive machine. The strength of the Communist is his certainty of the transcendent importance of the State. His fervor can be opposed only by a like certainty of the importance of the individual as developed in a democracy like ours. But only felt history can keep blood flowing through the confidence of the American in the kind of democracy which has been created here. Biography, since it deals with the individual, who is the unit of human history, tells the story direct. I was but one of many who felt this urge, which came, I suppose, from the obvious fact that industrialized, poly-racial America had been committed to world responsibility before our own sources of power and dominant traits were well understood even by the educated. Indeed, I came late, but not too late to find writers in our past whose significance for the world as well as for us had not been studied for the new times because historians had until recently grossly underestimated the world importance of the history of this country and its greatest men. I chose Henry D. Thoreau, and after him Walt Whitman, and spent the best working hours of three years on each biography.

I chose Thoreau, who had traveled widely only in Concord, because I was sympathetic with the most characteristic, though perhaps not the most important, essence of his temperament. Like him I had been, if in an amateurish way, deeply sensitive to every aspect of nature. As a child I, too, hurried toward fields and forests, knew birds and trees by name, and more minerals than Thoreau learned to identify, though far fewer plants and flowers. What his fellow townsmen thought was his wasteful idleness made sense to me. I could feel, as he did, the dulling of the spirit which drained life and color out of visible nature, and the sudden revival when winter wheat in the earliest spring, or a plot of blood-root lilies on a slope of the Brandywine, thrilled the nerves of sight until consciousness responded. It was not much by way of approach, yet it was an open door to a great imagination, and I felt that once inside I might have some advantage in interpreting the man.

For while it was Thoreau the naturalist that I understood instinctively, it was Thoreau the champion of values in living that made me curious. What prophetic genius made this determined eccentric of the rough land and the decorous village see that the next great human struggle was to be between the individual and the state? Whence did he draw his courage and his obstinacy? How did he come to rest always upon essentials, and put them in words like 'simplify' or 'civil disobedience' that named them for his successors? My ancestors, the Quakers, had tried to make friends of all the world and had conspicuously failed, even among themselves. Here was their opposite, though as mystical as they were, who rejoiced in minorities, and was willing to be a minority of one. I wanted to know how much sound thinking and significant experience lay behind his vigorous and beautiful prose.

It was an immense satisfaction to get down for hours and sometimes for days to quiet and patient investigation of text and fact, after years of dispersive work with telephone calls for punctuation marks and an idea to be delivered in haste like a child born on a journey. I had been as critical as anyone in my time of the scholarly research in the humanities of American

universities, which got out the facts and then left them piled
like unburnt coal at a mine mouth. Yet I had often felt like
my friend John Livingston Lowes of Harvard, who said that his
idea of happiness was endless research with no necessity of doing anything with the results. Of course it was precisely because he did do something with his results that he became outstanding among American scholars. And in my own case, while
I thoroughly enjoyed my concentrated labor, I most emphatically wished to make the results count for Thoreau's reputation with the modern age. It gave me a deep pleasure to be
told shortly after the publication of my biography and a previous Selections from his works, that Thoreau, who had been
passing out of currency except in anthologies, was the most
often mentioned and quoted in newspapers and magazines
among all the classic American authors. The credit was by
no means all mine, but my books had helped to restore and
renew a great name.

As for Walt Whitman, I do not remember hearing him mentioned when I was in school only twenty-odd miles from his
house on Mickle Street in Camden, New Jersey; nor as an undergraduate at Yale; nor, except unfavorably, in the graduate
school. This 'dirty old man,' as they had liked to call one of the
few of his American generation who took a bath every day, this
'sloppy,' 'slovenly,' 'incoherent' poet — what was the truth
about him personally, what was the secret of his power? I was
right to be curious, since I had in my own lifetime seen his
reputation change from failure, and not even magnificent failure, to the name of the greatest and most original poet of the
American nineteenth century, and our chief contribution to
international literary history.

I had read intensively in Walt Whitman in the nineteen-
twenties. Now my purpose was to go deeper, and also further.
From what draughts of experience, what qualities of environment did the *Leaves of Grass* get its unique qualities? For I
could not believe with a group of his earlier admirers that you
could write it all off to inspiration. This job of biography
proved to be far more elusive than the history of Thoreau.
Walt's important life, with a few exceptions, was his inner life.
This he recorded with unexampled fullness in the *Leaves,* but,

except for fragments of journals and scattered notes, left it un-recorded in his letters and his talk. When I had possessed my-self of all available facts about his career, I was able to relate his experience and his environment to his poems, but still had only those poems as source for what the man really *was*. Biog-raphy became not so much narration as interpretation. I was able, I trust, to free the record of his external life from confu-sion, suspicion, and the exaggerations of hero-worship; and to meet the vindictive attacks of men whose hatred of Walt sprang from their own weakness or prejudice, or was only the reaction to original genius of little and time-bound minds. But it soon became clear to me that the true subject of every biography of Whitman must be not the young editor whom everyone in Brooklyn knew, or the old man of Mickle Street, but the 'Walt' that Whitman dramatized in the *Leaves of Grass*. That Walt was not only the symbol of his inner life, but the secret of his power in modern literature. My book was hard to write, but exciting, since it became essentially a study of an American ex-perience sublimated into poetry. I suspect that few new facts of importance about Whitman will be discovered. A little re-mains unpublished about his unfortunate family, of which I knew enough, though the discoveries were not mine, to com-plete the picture. One possible fact I have discovered since I completed the book. He had, it seems highly probable, an illegitimate son, named Whitman for him, with a striking re-semblance to his father and a rather extraordinary career. I have hoped to verify this, if only to substitute a loving re-lationship for the unbased stories of licentiousness in his youth when in New Orleans, and the charges that he was impotent. This last is as unsupported by evidence as the statements that he was an active homosexual, whereas all we know is that his emotions were more easily aroused by men than by women and his craving for paternity intense. But I fear I shall not be able to get before it is too late the complete evidence of this care-fully guarded secret, and prove or disprove the existence of his son. That is why I mention it here. And at the most, such facts and all external facts, will never be the essence of a Whitman biography.

But another purpose became clearer to me as I worked on

my book. Here was, of course, the great poet of democracy.
Here indeed was the only major poet of the nineteenth century who knew at first hand the democratic process and was a
democrat himself in actions, desires, and ways of life. Was he
a romanticist of democracy, for, of course, like most writers
of his time, he was a romantic in spirit? Was he a prophet of
a democratic future, or merely an idealizing historian of democracy's aspects of poetry? I found abundant evidence, some
of it not used before, that Whitman knew at first hand the practical workings of the democratic system in politics better than
any other major author of the century; almost as well as Lincoln himself. I assembled the evidence of his bitter pessimisms,
as strong, if not as lasting, as his hopes. And I concluded, as
any close reader must, that the great democratic poems of his
later life are not based upon romance but upon a long-term
idealism, realistic in its hopes, and to be invalidated only by
man's refusal to fight for his own individuality, for his soul,
personality, freedom for full self-development, in a modern industrialized state.

And thus, after so many frustrations, I was able in the years
1939 to 1943, when democracy was on trial as never before —
from its basic philosophy to its power to endure — to bring my
own work in line with the necessities of the times, and to write
a book that was as much a study of a great democratic imagination as literary criticism or the events of a life. I am not sorry
for this push by the time spirit, nor did the book suffer. A
biography especially should bear the impress of the circumstances in which it is composed. It should answer the question,
'What does this man mean to our generation, and probably to
the next?' Hence no really great man ever gets a definitive
biography. For he himself is not entirely defined by his own
age, or by any other. Time, as Thoreau said, is the best publisher.

We All Become Realists

A N EDITOR *emeritus* does not have to resign from the literary and journalistic circles of New York, but he escapes
from the endless cycles of publicity and publication. What I
lost by not keeping up with the celebrities, near-celebrities, and
synthetic celebrities, I made up in objectivity. I got rid at last
of the horrid necessity of looking for a book or an article in
every acquaintance, and deciding what to do about it. And
instead of reading every new book with a pen pointed for criticism, I was able to think of myself as a searcher for values.

As the war approached, the somewhat brittle hardness which
had for some time been characteristic of scribbling and editing
New York became a dominant trait. It was most noticeable in
the bright young men of the news and editorial magazines,
who changed their jobs, it seemed, every few months, but never
their minds. And in the competent young women, well dressed
and witty, who had taken over the contact work of the publishing houses. They were all realists, these young people, according to their own definition of realism. Romance, the standard-
bearer of literature in the nineteenth and early twentieth centuries, had become a commodity, produced by what my friend
Molly Colum called the tradesmen of writing. The most successful of these tradesmen, the serial writers for popular magazines, were exceedingly skillful, and knew how to make their
books sound like realism while feeling like romance. Less admirable was the *Forever Amber* school, where the success was
due to a clever saucing of bawdiness in a synthetic historical
story. Whatever the writers intended, the trade saw in
this rather naïve eroticism only a saleable commodity and ad-
vertised it as such. They were realists, and so were the young
men and women who scouted and criticized for them. And

much of their profits were spent in backing the new hard realism which was the literary, if not the popular, fashion of the times. For a million copies sold no longer made a literary reputation — indeed it was quite possible to sell a million copies of a sentimental romance without getting any reputation at all among the critical and the discriminating.

All this changed the metabolism of the New York community. The causes went deep, and were related to the new and more sophisticated audience for books of which I have written earlier, and still more to the ominous undercurrents of the times. Not uninfluential were the bitter or despairing books which were coming from Europe about disintegration, moral and physical, abroad. And yet it would be a mistake to say that the advance of the growing fringe of literature from romance through realism to its extreme in what the erudite call naturalism, was only a symptom of disillusion and distrust of the future. The most successful romances of ancient history, the so-called Greek romances, written in the Eastern countries of the Roman Empire, were the current fashion in precisely those decades and countries when that empire, even in the East, was often in chaos, with anarchy on the sea, barbarians in the land, and the whole Roman world aware that a great age was coming to an end.

What happened in New York was a shift in emphasis. Publishers and historians are equally aware that the market for good, indifferent, and inferior romance is perennial. With their left hands, the editorial departments were supplying the public with whatever newly flavored romance they could get, at a time when the best writers, with only a few exceptions, were busy with everyday life and all its smells and drabness, and typical people with all their lust, vanity, stupidity, and suffering. With their right hands, these same editors were promoting this new realism. Needless to say, the sales force distributed their energies quite differently! Yet realism for the time being was what one called literature. Dreiser had come to full recognition, James Farrell's unattractive Chicago Irish won him praise for his honesty, Hemingway (only in part a realist) was a model for young writers. And from every small town in America came books whose accuracy to the last bar- and bedroom scene was unimpeachable, even though only the frankness kept them from boring the reader. With a few exceptions, like *Anthony Adverse* and *John Brown's Body*, and such realistic idealism as Marjorie Kinnan Rawling's *The Yearling*, or the romantic symbolism of Thornton Wilder, the important novels for two decades had been on the side of realism. The same was true of drama and poetry. An author, instead of a beneficent gentleman with a beard, was now supposed to be hard-faced, satiric, with an unhappy past and a wide knowledge of scabrous circumstance. And what all the (superficially) hard young publishers' assistants were keen about was the book of prose or poetry that described behavior and let the reader deduce what he pleased from it. The word 'imagination' temporarily went out of use. Imagination was something that trifled with the reality of an all too real world.

In New York the symbol of this slow change from imaginative to scientific truth, was the breakdown of the old literary dinner into an infinity of cocktail parties. I had attended some of the last of the literary dinners in the late nineteen-tens, and had read of them in their prime. Publishers paid the bill then as now, I suppose, but the commercial purpose was carefully concealed. The chairman was some literary Olympian of sorts, like Robert Underwood Johnson of the flourishing *Century* magazine, and the other speakers, equally bearded, were gentry whose faces might be expected to adorn the walls of schoolrooms and the sanctums of the better publishing houses. The author honored by all this ceremony was a 'man of letters' who had contributed not only to the pleasure, but also to the morale, the orthodoxy, and the decorum of his country. Needless to say, Walt Whitman, in spite of his beard, was never invited to this kind of literary dinner, and Mark Twain's most notable appearance ended in scandal when he invented drunken stories about the great of that day. There was always something mortuary in the atmosphere of these dinners, and the best that could be said of them was that the guests were usually housebroken. This is not a necessity for authorship; too much gentility is often a handicap in the pursuit of truth. Yet there was something to be said for entertainments in the genteel age by comparison with one of the first of a new type of publication

party I attended in the nineteen-twenties. Although many
notable writers and critics were present, the speaking was
drowned in uproar, and the dinner ended perforce when a well
known critic slid with a running jump the length of the table,
which avalanched food and drink in our laps.

The literary cocktail party, having been invented to fit the
new age, got off to a good start in the Prohibition era, when
thirsty authors and critics would go anywhere for a drink. By
the late thirties, it was beautifully adjusted to the new conditions. Desirable guests could be categorized according to their
interests, segregated, and entertained accordingly.

For a party to celebrate a potential best-seller — synthetic,
honestly romantic, informative, or sentimental — the invited
were the more easy-going reviewers, and the noise makers of
radio and press. Also a few movie scouts to listen to the conversation, for the proprietors of the moving pictures seldom
trusted their own judgment, and liked to get a prehearing of
what the public might be expected to say of the book being
considered for purchase.

For the serious book, whether fiction or non-fiction, one
asked the intellectuals, with representatives of the book clubs,
and the more esoteric critics. For the guest of honor whose
book was hard-boiled realism somewhat indecent, or a solemn
study of share-croppers or factory workers oppressed by the economic system, there would have to be a sprinkling of social
workers, and of spokesmen for the left, who invariably retired
to corners where they called each other Trotskyite or Stalinist.
For the 'vanity book,' published to satisfy someone's desire to
get a name in literature, and paid for in one way or another by
the author, the publisher would manage to collect a few individuals whose names were more familiar in the society columns than in the critical reviews, and with them the author's
family connection, and a few reviewers whose good nature was
notorious. I frequented enough of these entertainments, which
were much more sprightly than conventional tea parties, to
meet the new people and pick up the gossip of the trade from
old friends who were habitués. The great advantage of the
cocktail party as compared with the literary dinner, was that
you could leave whenever you wished.

I seem to be describing a trivial and materialistic atmosphere as the literary climate of the late thirties and early forties. That would be grossly unfair. Technical competence was never better recognized. Indeed, the tradesmen of letters frequently wrote better than those who had something important to say. The search for new talent was eager. If the stage weakened and poetry swung between an imperfectly articulate intellectualism and a too articulate imitation of the past, fiction was still full of energy. But it was in such irony as John Marquand at this time began to develop, that excellence and popular appeal were most often blended. This was no longer the enthusiastic twenties. Combative idealism, and what I should call constructive imagination, seemed both to have slackened. The hardish, competent literary world of these years estimated very shrewdly the values of what it got. For it, books were something to be intelligent about, not a passion, as in my beginning time. Like the literature the writers read or criticized, they were less expansive, less in deadly moral earnest than the Wolfes, the Andersons, the Robinsons, and the Frosts.

Serious readers swung between the detective story and the kind of book that gave them the largest amount of fact colored by wishful thinking. Uncompromising realism had its greatest opportunity, and perhaps its greatest prestige since the fictionized sociology of Zola. Yet many of us felt that a swing toward a more imaginative, more emotional literature was not far ahead, nor has the interlude of war and the disillusion of peace changed my own belief that this is true. The pursuit of realism in the United States has given us some of our best American literature and raised the standards of honesty in writing by many degrees. It has been successful in spite of attacks by the genteel, in spite of neglect by a wishful-thinking public, and in spite of the difficulty of making the common man seem as important and as interesting as, of course, he is. Nevertheless, out-and-out realism, while it contains invaluable elements for a literary diet, seems to be short of vitamins for the nourishing of the imagination. For example, it is evident that in this confused age leadership is the crying, the shouting need. And it should be equally evident to the historically minded that the vitamins of idealism have been part of the diet of every great leader whose career shows good will toward men. And the vitamins of idealistic romance have been important in the expansive, the hopeful view of life. This was what Walt Whitman meant when he said in effect that the duty of literature was to present to the imagination new and better types of humanity which might serve as examples for inspiration and imitation. Realism is the best corrective of fanatical idealism and too emotional romance. But it is not good soil for the kind of imagination which can give a disillusioned society a push out of a bad present, and the courage to try to make a better future.

There is a barometer which often records in a curious way the end of a fashion or a whole literary movement at least as accurately as critical opinion. I mean the study and teaching of literature in the universities. New literary schools, pioneer authors, and fresh moods and methods of writing, begin to be taken seriously by the scholars, edited, lectured upon, and used as examples of the literary wave of the future, just as their vogue is ending, their novelty exhausted, and they are ready either to be forgotten, or to take their place in literary history with eras that still shine but have ceased to give out heat. When the universities begin to take what they call modernism seriously, it is a danger signal for critics. It may mean only that radicalism or sex in literature has become respectable, but usually there is a better reason. Hemingway, for example, became academic material when it was recognized that he had made articulate idiosyncracies of the last two decades which have to be admitted as material for literature because they now are seen to have been obviously there. Yet recognition by teacher and scholar seems usually to come just as a Hemingway, or a Proust, or an Eliot has finished his job of pioneering, and, if he is still alive, is preparing to go somewhere else, or lapse into repetition. I remember that I myself helped to edit Robert Louis Stevenson for freshman classes at a time when it was daring to use any contemporary text for college instruction. But this was at the very moment when that brilliant stylist, so influential upon my generation in its youth, was being outmoded in the literary world by new styles and new points of view. The fault was not in teaching Stevenson, of course, but in describing him as a modernist when his virtues were already those of a classic of a period definitely ended. I remember in my earliest teaching years talking of Rudyard Kipling with the agreeable feeling that I was introducing my classes to the literature of the future.

Therefore, when the scholars in our universities praise realism as the long-fought-for goal of American literature, I become skeptical. One might suppose from recent statements that all literary creation had painfully moved toward the depiction of American man as his most disillusioned neighbors see him! It was a good job, but only one job out of many. When the half-god realism has a shrine built for him by historians and critics, and every ambitious scholar is rushing up his little chapel or monument near the altar, and candidates for the Ph.D. begin to work upon Dreiser instead of Melville and Hawthorne, then perhaps the time has come to walk to the next hilltop and look ahead.

20

Values in the Great Transition

THROUGHOUT THE SECOND WORLD WAR I was involved, like most American writers too old for military service, in bond drives, and also in work for the Writers' War Board and other organizations, concocting articles for translation into many languages, which one never saw in print. At last by a fortunate chance I was drawn into the margins of the war itself. I was sent by the Office of War Information in the early spring of 1945 to Australia and New Zealand on an invitation originating from the University of Melbourne, but much extended. My mission was to explain the cultural history of the United States as made articulate in its literature to nations with a democratic experience like our own. They had been bombarded with military, naval, political, and economic propaganda, but knew little of the United States in the more personal fields of social and literary history. There an American could explain without trying to coerce or persuade. I flew out in converted and excessively uncomfortable bombers, flew up and down the Australian rim and to Tasmania, flew the length of the New Zealand islands, and then back home again, crashing and nearly burning to death on the way. It was four months at a high pitch; literally, since all of my journeyings were in the sky, and figuratively, since my interest in what I saw and my concern for what I had to tell were equally intense.

The story does not belong in this book except for one unexpected experience which, when I got home, stirred me into writing, not about Australia, but more confidently about my own estimates of American ways of life as I had seen them in the more than half-century recorded in this memoir. For in the Antipodes I found a community which, until the Japs had appeared on the horizon, was still in its age of confidence — content, as we had been, with a comfortable life, and calling its society the paradise of the common man; as indeed it still was, provided that no more than abundant food, shelter, and freedom were asked for in your paradise. What impressed me was how tenaciously the Australians and New Zealanders of all kinds clung to the values of their pleasant living — the wild interior regions open to the rugged; the spacious cities, excellently served (except for British cooking and lack of heat); short hours of labor, unlimited recreation on magnificent beaches or through flowery hills and pungent eucalyptus groves; horse-racing an obsession, and political experimentation a national triumph (or, if you were a conservative, a national disease). Here was at least a parallel to the United States before bigness, organization, and competition began to change our values, and the growing complications of a vast industrialized state weakened our easy confidence and pushed our intellectuals into psychological and social analysis.

The same shift toward introspection was beginning in the Antipodes, but there was still an honest naïveté like our own in the eighteen-nineties, and still confidence that they had created an enduring way of life. Bigness was still just a man's way of viewing his opportunities because the land was big. I had difficulty in explaining to my pastoralist friends in Australia that my farm in Connecticut was thirty-two, not thirty-two thousand acres! Values were still set in simple terms of the pleasure one got from just being alive — and I found that the easiest American book to explain to the Australians was Thoreau's *Walden*. In Tasmania, after a lecture, an elderly gentleman, who from his appearance was a grazier from some inland station, came up to me apologetically. 'I know little of your country,' he said, 'except that it is as big as Australia; not much even of its geography. I have heard, of course, of your Great Lakes, and the Mississippi, and' — his eyes twinkled — 'of Walden Pond!'

I am quite sure that if I could be shot back along the timeline to the Concord of Thoreau and Emerson, I should be most impressed by both the change and the persistence of American values since that day. And should find much to confirm, and probably something to disprove, my own theories of the history of American literature. For literature is not only the best index of values in a given age; it can also be said to consist of values on which imagination builds, and for whose expression techniques are invented. And the best defense of a literary memoir like this one — so I thought as I flew back at eight thousand feet above the puddled clouds and turquoise glimpses of the Pacific — was that if its theories were only deductions, its memories were the same source material as was used in the making of all good books.

That my generation in America (and of course elsewhere) has seen in its time one of the greatest — I think the greatest — transitions in recorded history, I have no doubt. It is not necessary to cite as proof automobiles, airplanes, and radios, or greater wars, bombings, and social unrest, which are all results, not causes. The great change has been psychological. My consciousness seems to me at least a century away in its content from my father's.

Sometimes transition has been from smallness to bigness, as ours has been; sometimes from bigness to smallness. I am glad I have lived in a dynamic, expansive era, even though the frightful hazards of an atomic age have been the result of our unbalanced growth. The opposite experience must have been soul crushing. You can see its evidence in the ruins of a Roman villa in England, where some Romanized Briton, though escaping personal violence, must have seen his markets slowly contract, his great house molder, his utensils wear out because there was no way of replacing them, his baths dry up, his heating vents clog, his tiles crack and fall, until the place became uninhabitable and he had to move to some wooden hut like the shacks of the barbarians. Our experience has been the reverse, which does not mean that our children may not see the tide go out as it did at the end of the fourth or fifth century.

In spite of two global wars our advance has been spectacular, and it is still possible to say that our decline in moral organization has been only change. Great changes we all have known. In my early youth, as it is recorded in this book, the struggle was to escape from small-town conventions. Not from the life — we liked the life — but from its limitations. We youngsters shared the confidence but not the content of that bourgeois culture, which was becoming stagnant. The tiny river of time in which I lived was splashed with little fish leaping toward freer waters. In my later youth I got into a larger pool, the happy college life of the turn of the century, in which thousands of young Americans played at being romantic and sometimes worked at getting educated. It took me years to wriggle out of that one, and when I did, it was into the shallows of a rather sterile scholarship. In my early middle age, the net of circumstances caught me out of those waters and I was thrown protesting into the big and brawling main stream. And in later middle age I swam with the rest of the world through rapids and toward what seemed cataracts ahead, and began to remember more often and more tolerantly the green pastures and still waters of my youth.

Certainly I learned what wisdom has always known, that in every present there is a past trying to stay alive, and that the society that forgets its past gives up much self-knowledge. When I came back to literature after the dislocations of the recent war, I felt no inclination, as did so many of my contemporaries, to separate the past from the present. I was more, not less, convinced that there would have been no such dislocations if more powerful people had been able to read and digest more powerful books, such as have been available since the Greeks and the Hebrews. I am well aware how and why the right lessons have not been learned and applied from these books. But I have seen no reason given in sociology, anthropology, or psychology why such a use cannot be made of them. In other words, I am a conditional optimist, which is much pleasanter than being a conditional pessimist, because you think just a little better of the possibilities of your fellow men.

And I am a conditional optimist, also, as to the position of the writer in our economy. Literary wars are being fought at the moment, in which producers (especially from Hollywood), publishers, agents, journalists, creative artists, and the tradesmen of literature are using symbolically every weapon devised by law and journalism, yet it is to be noted that the row is not, as so often in the past, over the results of scarcity — starving in garrets, poverty wages for hack work — but overabundance. So much money is being made from writing that there is a proper inquiry as to what is the writer's just share. Naturally, I am on the writer's side. But all this is irrelevant to literature, which, whether treated fairly or not, earns more, and more easily than in any earlier period, except in the case of a few of the Titans of the nineteenth century. To cite instances — Oliver Goldsmith in his way, Edgar Allan Poe in his, or Daniel Defoe with his talents, could not have failed to become rich in twentieth-century America. The modern writer may not get his share. If he can write well for the millions it is probable that the producers are still picking his pockets. But if he wants to make literature, and still keep off relief, he can do it. Probably ten times as many potential playwrights of talent and writers of superior fiction have been ruined by the gold of Hollywood in the last twenty years as by hunger, hardship, or economic frustration.

Perhaps Western society is decadent. I doubt it, because while I read about decadent people I meet very few of them in America, especially among the young. And a vast number of decadent people are required for a true decadence. I do not like all of the values of the oncoming generation, but I think they are more steadily held than we held ours, either in the nineteen-twenties and thirties or in my youth. The young are closer than we were to America's formative age of the Republic in its first half-century, and to the height of its morale in the eighteen-thirties to the eighteen-sixties. And they have seen the Germans take their values second-hand from a fanatic; and are watching the Russians try forcible feeding of a vast population that has never been taught to think for itself. They ought to learn something from the experience. Probably what they do about their own values will be as great a test for the United States of America as the atomic bomb or the disease of supernationalism now approaching its crisis.

If anyone under forty reads this book, I hope he will realize that it is essentially a study of values in a smaller and more observable world than his own — and has no other moral purpose. And if, since it is the memoir of a writer and teacher, it is limited in scope, I submit that this is not too narrow for usefulness. Actual life seldom tells a story for itself which is both true and intelligible. This is a writer's job, and a teacher's opportunity.

Index

Index

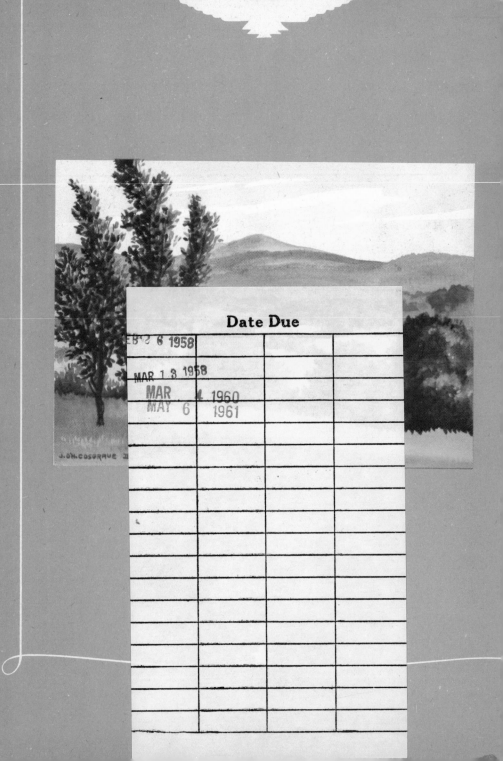

Date Due

FEB 2 6 1958			
MAR 1 3 1958			
MAR 4 1960			
MAY 6 1961			

J.OH.COSGRAVE